A SHORT HISTORY OF
AUSTRALIAN
LITERATURE

Paul Sharrad

Orient BlackSwan

All rights reserved. No part of this book may be modified, reproduced or utilised in any form, or by any means, electronic or mechanical, including photocopying, recording or by any information storage and retrieval system, in any form of binding or cover other than in which it is published, without permission in writing from the publisher.

A SHORT HISTORY OF AUSTRALIAN LITERATURE
ORIENT BLACKSWAN PRIVATE LIMITED

Registered office
3-6-752 Himayatnagar, Hyderabad 500 029, Telangana, India
E-mail: centraloffice@orientblackswan.com

Other offices
Bengaluru, Chennai, Guwahati, Hyderabad,
Kolkata, Mumbai, New Delhi, Noida, Patna

© Orient Blackswan Private Limited 2024
First published 2024

ISBN 978 93 5442 291 1

Typeset in Simoncini Garamond Std 10.5/13.4 by
LiteBook Prepress Services, Chennai 600 069

Printed at
Shree Maitrey Printech Private Limited, Noida 201 301

Published by
Orient Blackswan Private Limited
3-6-752 Himayatnagar, Hyderabad 500 029, Telangana, India
E-mail: info@orientblackswan.com

Contents

Preface	v
Map of Australia	vi
Map of New South Wales, the ACT and Victoria	vii
Introduction	ix
1. Convicts to Reform *1788–1850*	1
2. Boom and Bust to Federation *1850–1901*	16
3. Commonwealth to Collapse *1901–1930*	49
4. Susso to Soldiers *1930–1950*	76
5. Prosperity to Vietnam *1950–1965*	97
6. Dissent to Dismissal *1965–1975*	125
7. Multicultural to Bicentenary *1975–1988*	152
8. Deregulation to GFC *1988–2008*	195
9. GFC to Covid *2008–2020*	243
Glossary of Australian Terms	271
Useful Resources	277
Comparative Timeline for Australian Literature	286
Index	328

Preface

This book owes its existence to those who pioneered the teaching of Australian literature in India, mostly under the rubric of Commonwealth (later postcolonial) literary studies. It pays tribute to C.D. Narasimhaiah, R.K. Dhawan, K. Radha, C.T. Indra and Eugenie Pinto, Malathi Mathur, Santosh Sareen, Pradeep Trikha, Deb Narayan Bandyopadhyay and others who have not come immediately to mind.

My thanks to Padmaja Anant for adding this title to Orient Blackswan's 'Short History' series. I trust that it usefully fills a gap in study materials to support teaching of Australian works in India. Special thanks are due to my assiduous copy editor, James Kanjamala, whose careful checking has made this book a much better work. Needless to say, all remaining shortcomings are my own.

Paul Sharrad

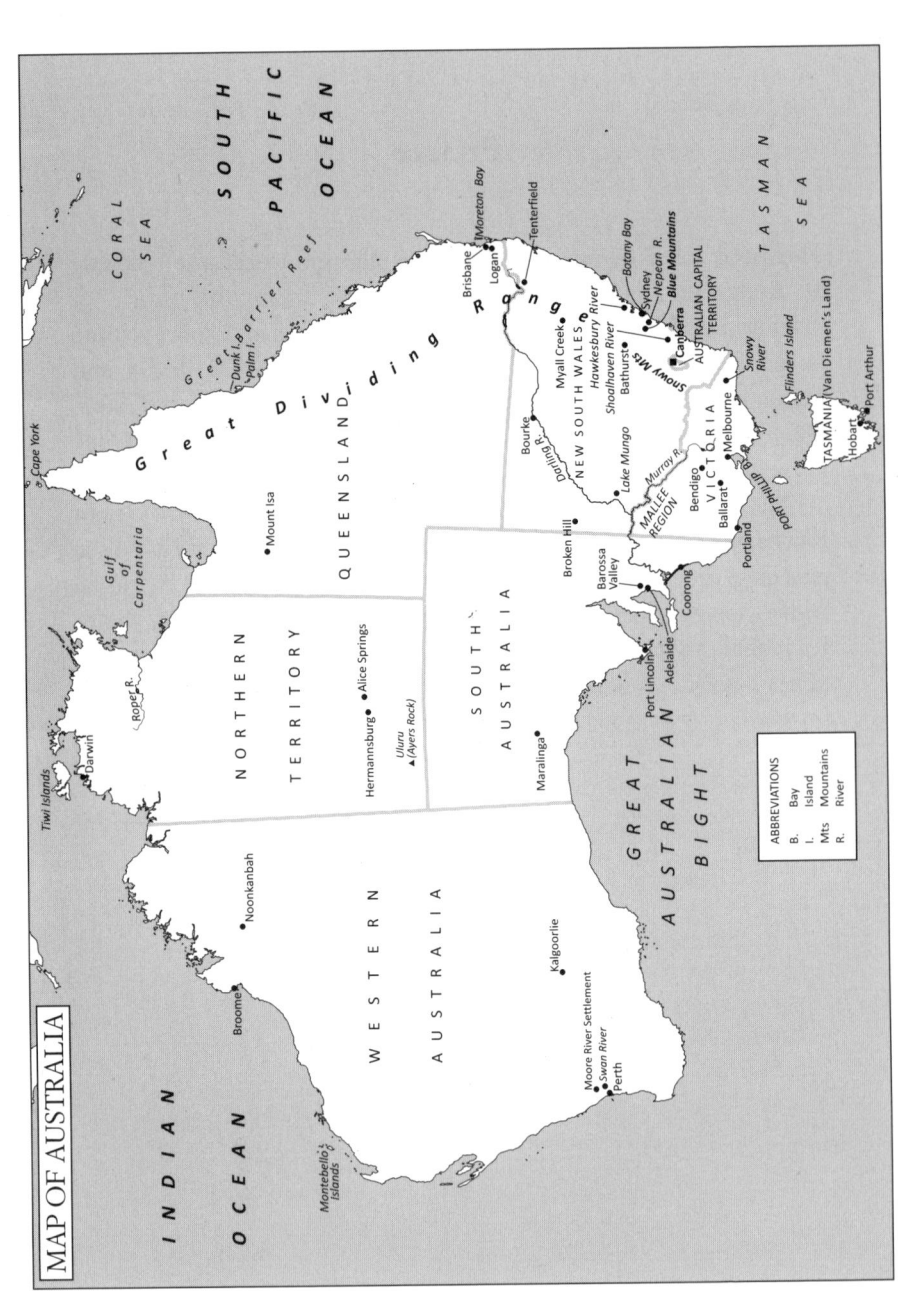

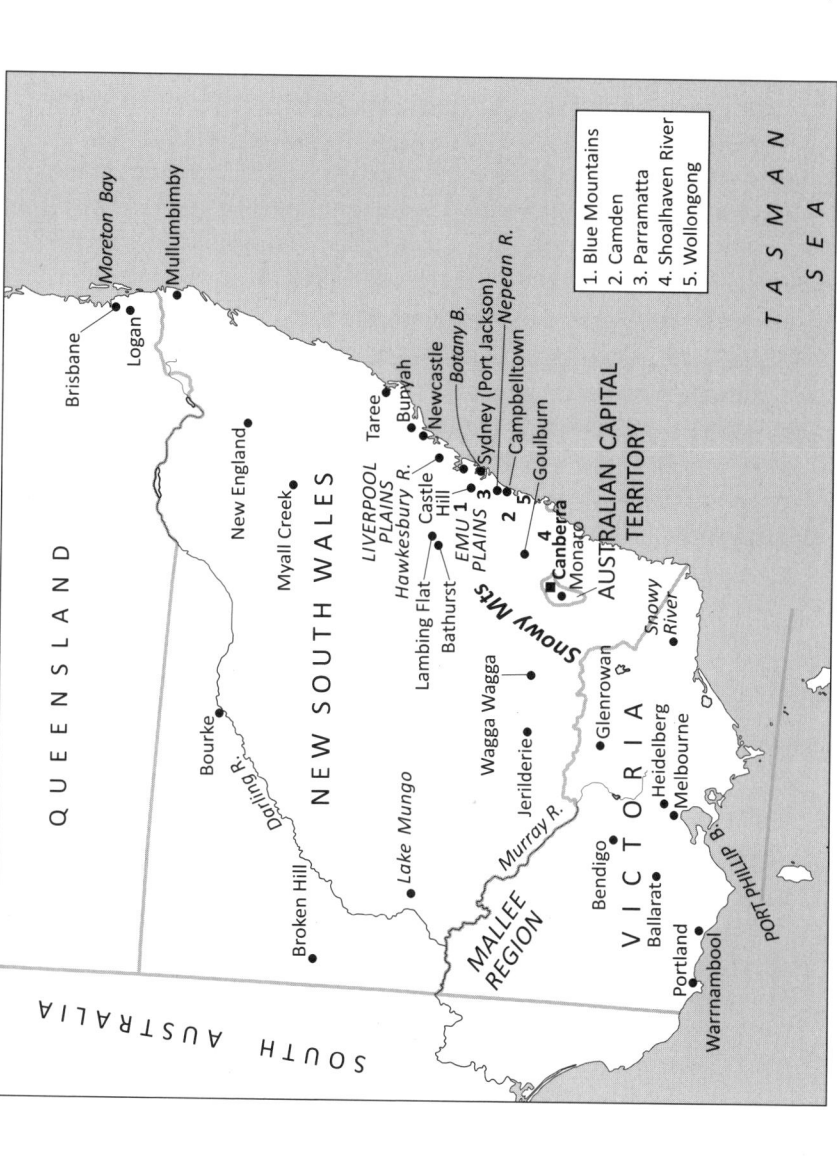

Introduction

The purpose of this book is to provide an introduction to Australian literature for Indian readers, providing some context within which to make sense of the writing being discussed. There are two factors that make such a book seem like a viable project. One is the historical links between two countries once governed by the British Empire. Much produce, many colonial officers, architectural styles, and even fragments of language migrated from India to the southern colonies, and today both nations share not just an interest in cricket, but also modes of administration arising from the imperial system. The other validating factor is the contemporary movement of South Asians southward, so that nowadays they collectively form the second-largest immigrant group in Australia, poised to become the largest. These connections have resulted in the inclusion of Australian texts in Indian university courses in English, and the emergence of groups across the subcontinent focused on Australian Studies. A perennial complaint of staff and students has been the lack of study materials, and this book is one attempt to address the problem.

The challenge for any literary history intended for foreign readership is to give as full a sense as possible of the literature without presenting a meaningless list of names and dates. This requires some socio-cultural contextualising whereby the reader might grasp what inspires particular works, and why they were and are valued in their home country. It also requires supplying outlines of selected works to show important themes and styles. Consequently, there are limits to how encyclopaedic the history can be.

There are real differences between India and Australia that have to be explained. One outstanding disparity is the ratio of people to space: Australia took a century to reach a population of two million in the sixth-largest country on earth. As well, though it shares with India an Anglo-imperial past, Australia's colonialism was quite distinct: India was a 'garrison' of a white minority ruling a large 'native' majority, while in Australia, the small Indigenous population was rapidly overrun by ever-increasing numbers of white settlers. The same imperialist attitudes toward 'colonials' applied to the inhabitants of both countries, but in Australia—apart from the Aboriginal minority—the peasants, farmers and artisans were nearly all British in origin, so a doubleness of sensibility arose among them more complicated than the 'black–white' binary of Indian colonialism. Racial filiation between Britain and Australia meant that limited parliamentary self-governance could be negotiated peacefully rather than requiring violent struggle for independence. Another difference centres on language and its relation to writing. We might posit a similarity between Australian literature and the 'binocular' vision of that section of Indian middle management and aristocracy that adopted English as a means of creative expression. However, people like Tagore had a written literature in a mother tongue behind whatever Western form of expression was used. Indian writing in whatever language also inhabited a natural and social landscape with which authors were intimately familiar. Australian writers were seen as having no language or literary tradition behind them other than those of the country against which they were trying to define themselves. Moreover, white folk were struggling to come to terms with a land that was seen as radically alien. The language they devised to express their world became a different kind of English from the 'Queen's English' to which they were culturally subordinate.

Some contrasts to other settler colonies might help clarify elements of Australian culture. As a dumping ground for political dissidents and penurious criminals, the Great South Land was never the envisioned utopia that the United States sometimes was; it was more a hell on earth to be endured, with truculent reliance on and active mistrust of authority. Although Christianity was the basis of social values, the alignment of clergy with the government and the long concentration on brute survival led to a generally anti-clerical and secular society. With the exception of several gold rushes, the prevailing attitude was not optimistic self-help; any pressure for social improvement was generally expressed through socialistic collective action. The convict system created a cultural caste hierarchy, so that families for a century or more would hide their ancestry out of shame. However, socially, anyone could rise or fall; some convicts became rich and respectable. (Now people research their genealogy, taking pride in finding a convict ancestor.) As in the American colonies and after, wealth became the only major determinant of class; otherwise, a demotic egalitarianism was the norm. The downside of this anti-elitism was a materialistic anti-intellectualism from which viewpoint all arts were a trivial hobby or a bourgeois affectation.

Australia defined itself in opposition to Europe in terms of its natural world. Seasons occurred at opposite times to those in Europe (and Aboriginal lore recognises more seasons than the official four); plants and animals abounded that were completely unknown in Europe. Philosophy books there had to be rewritten because a common syllogism in logic relied on the fact that all swans were white—Australia had black swans. Farmers introducing Western animals and crops were at a loss for many years about how best to manage them in an unfamiliar environment seen by many as monochrome, melancholy and outright hostile. Once the grass plains of Victoria and New South Wales, then Queensland, were encountered, there was a vision of promise for a pastoral industry but often explorers perished and droughts brought ruin. Nature was seen either as an empty space to be exploited or as a menacing wilderness. Although the Aboriginal population knew very well how to survive, they were commonly seen as having nothing of value to communicate to white society. As hunter-gatherers placed at the bottom of the Darwinian evolutionary ladder, they were regarded as little better than troublesome fauna, and were predicted to die out. European diseases and murderous 'dispersals' looked like making this a self-fulfilling prophecy. The nation is still coming to terms with this history, and with the conundrum of having to define itself in terms of two phenomena (the land and Aboriginal culture) that it for so long disregarded, feared, or actively despised and mistreated.

Indian readers will need to keep in mind the entrenched tendency in Australia to social uniformity. Because the population was for so long absolutely dominated by people of British and Irish origin, there was a fundamental homogeneity that later was institutionalised under policies of assimilation: everyone was expected to conform to Anglo-Celtic culture and to speak the English language. Apart from the many languages of Aboriginal tribes, which had little impact on the national mindset, there were no autonomous cultures such as Tamil or Bengali. There were minor differences among the colonies that carried over into state stereotypes (Melbourne was cultured, Sydney was brash, Adelaide had churches and no convicts, Queensland was tropical and redneck with closer ties to the Pacific, Western Australia was just a long way from anywhere). Nonetheless, there was always traffic to and fro across the continent and every settler was united in being European exiles isolated in an alien Asia.

Another factor distinguishing Australian attitudes has been what historian Geoffrey Blainey called 'the tyranny of distance'. If India has a long history of trading across land and sea as far as Rome and China, and if North America was a relatively short voyage from Europe, Australia (from the European settler's point of view) was the other side of the world. For several decades, mail and travellers could take six months to reach family, and even within Australia, your nearest neighbour or town could be two days away by horse. Still today, Australians can travel huge distances without encountering a roadside stall, a small village, or a single person (hence the national fixation on cars). Some commentators attribute the phenomenon of 'mateship' to such distances: you needed self-reliance, but you also needed company to stay sane and survive.

For Australia, the stresses of isolation were accompanied by terrors of proximity: Dutch explorers from the near north had made landfall several times before Botany Bay was established, and La Perouse's expedition landed only a couple of days too late to claim the land for France. Russia was feared to have designs on the country, and always there was an uneasy awareness of greater numbers of people in an Asia seen as crowded and looking to occupy Australia's 'empty' spaces. (This was racially labelled 'the yellow peril'.) New Zealand's distance from a European 'home' was even greater, but there distance was also seen as a protective insulation from world upheavals. Australia, by contrast, was both isolated and surrounded by alien neighbours. The willingness of states and the nation to go into 'lockdown' once a disease like Covid starts travelling, or when significant numbers of refugees start arriving, is a modern legacy of this 'island continent' anxiety.

With that preamble, we can move to some points of debate that have permeated histories of Australian literature. First, there is the historian's question, 'When was Australia?' Strictly speaking, there was no Australian literature as a national corpus until the separately governed colonies of the continent were politically federated into the Commonwealth of Australia in 1901. Until Matthew Flinders circumnavigated the land mass and put 'Australia' on his map (1802–1803), the continent was most often referred to metonymically as 'Botany Bay'—wrong in itself, because the first colonial settlement quickly shifted to Sydney Harbour—or collectively as 'New Holland' (thanks to early Dutch voyages). Otherwise it had been 'the Great South Land' or 'Terra Australis Incognita'.

Even when the geography and politics of the continent came into alignment, there remained the question of when an Australian literature came into its own. For many years, writers and critics kept coming up with new moments of 'arrival' when local literary print culture might be said to have achieved self-sustaining momentum, distinctiveness and a creative 'maturity'. For some, this problematic of historical development is still to be resolved, and part of that ongoing unsettlement is critical unease about a model of history as a singular narrative of development-as-progress. Small academic wars have been fought over how the history of Australian literature has been constructed, and the resulting revisions have shifted the record from single to plural, simple to complex. Rather than operate according to literary periods (the boundaries of which are usually as unreliable as a mirage in the desert), chapters here are structured according to generally discernible social-political changes that have had a role in shaping the nation's consciousness and cultural production.

The second focus of debate is the meaning of 'literature'. In the wider sense of any artistically shaped utterance, Australia has a literary history going back 65,000 years. Its texts take the form of songs, dances, sand drawings, carved stones, memorial poles, message sticks and cave paintings that tell of totemic creation figures, hunting parties, the arrival of ships, and graziers on horseback with guns. Australia has a much shorter literary history if confined to European definitions of literature as written text. For most people, Australian literature means the artistic writing that followed British incursion in 1788. A dearth of material in early times, and the broadening of definitions of print literature under pressure from cultural studies, feminism, and theories of text have resulted in the inclusion of letters, diaries, memoirs, et cetera, as objects of literary study. In addition, examples of the song epics of Aboriginal 'Dreaming' cycles are increasingly included in anthologies and have inspired modern adaptations. In this book, mainly for reasons of brevity, literature means poetry, fiction and drama, with mention of significant 'hybrid' works.

We have, then, to think of two, three, even four literary histories in and around 'Australia'. These coexist and increasingly intersect as the land becomes politically unified and separated from subservience to colonial authority. The main strands of Australian literary history have been Indigenous and 'settler' (Aboriginal and white). For the many Indigenous language groups spread across the land, the story has been one of maintaining culture, often by secrecy and performance of rites relating to specific locations. Negotiating the links in story from one region and language group to another later becomes a process of negotiating a sense of pan-Aboriginal identity in opposition to the steady construction of a pan-Australian white settler identity. Aboriginal literary history becomes twofold: the recording of pre-contact culture and the tactical adoption of white technologies by which to survive in modernity and convey Indigenous experience to the nation as a whole. For white settler society, literary history records a process of selecting and reshaping imported attitudes, languages and cultural forms to express local life and nature, often with one eye on being sold in a wider overseas market and one eye on creating a 'home' audience and giving it a sense of collective identity distinct from northern hemisphere origins. To a small extent, this has involved recognising and appropriating aspects of Aboriginal cultures; to a large extent, it has shared with those cultures a strong focus on the land as the ground of being, even though relationships with that land have been radically different.

Arguing over what counts as *Australian* literature has been an ongoing cultural sport and accounts for other strands in the historical narrative. Writing by Australian citizens resident in the country and representing the land, language and society of the nation is the common denominator in eligibility for prizes and inclusion in critical discussion. To this field, we add or exclude writing by non-resident Australians preferably about Australia but occasionally (acceptance depending on the fame of the writer) about the countries they reside in. Also sometimes considered is writing about Australia by visitors. These were often colonial officials spending years in the country before being posted elsewhere or retiring to Britain, or they could be famous literary figures like Anthony Trollope and Mark Twain, who made world tours and produced travelogues describing the mores and terrain of 'distant cousins'. Until very recently the common understanding behind all these categories has been that Australian literature means literature in English. Despite the longstanding Anglocentric hegemony that remained blind and deaf to an Aboriginal presence and actively kept other ethnicities out of the country, Australia has become one of the most polyglot countries in the world, and its literary field has gradually included writing by immigrants of non-Anglo backgrounds and, more recently, writing by them in languages other than English. This expansion has also begun including creative expression in and translation from Aboriginal languages.

If we accept the idea of literature as creative expression appearing in print in Australia, then we have to be aware that its history is a particularly limited and distorted one. It excludes the bulk of pre-1960s literary writing, which for reasons of colonial cultural politics and economic viability had to come from British presses. Reaction against the colonial control of creative production for a long time encouraged a resolutely nation-centred history. Only since the 1990s has there been significant attention to the global networks of literary influence and production (from and in the United States, for example, as well as the circulation of Australian texts in translation to all corners of the globe). Such networks infused writing in Australia from the very start of colonisation.

Another possible history of Australian literature arises once we distinguish small-L literature from capital-L literature (the capital-L meaning an officially approved body of 'high culture' creative writing). A history of what has been read as literature increasingly includes popular formula writing, some of which attained bestseller status. However, for many years what counted as literature was mostly determined by commentators looking for works of high aesthetic value. Whether judgement came from nationalist writer-critics in the 1930s or later academics, that value was largely received from departments of English in Britain and the United States.

Australian literary history thereby becomes a tale of competition between metropolitan Euro-American models of style and theme and 'provincial' championing of what Australians found appropriate to convey their environment and lived experience. Cultural nationalists favoured a self-conscious compendium of images and ideas about what it means to be Australian. Such an earnest project of expressing an emergent identity was, for a century or more, good reason for the international arbiters of 'universal' literary taste to dismiss Australian works as 'derivative', 'shrill' and 'sociological', forgetting that their own literatures deployed 'tradition' as a veil obscuring such qualities. The formation of 'Australian Literature' as a serious body of work worthy of scholarly study reached a watershed in the 1960s. University courses devoted to the nation's creative writing proliferated and the local publication of critical editions and studies of Australian authors increased. In this context, a history of Australian literature becomes a history of the critical reception of creative writing as dominated by academics, though that has changed as university teachers lost their hold over the media.

To hazard another generalisation among these many quick outlines, a history of Australia literature shows that the literature itself is heavily interested in history. This is to be expected from immigrants from Europe conscious of shaping a new society and being told by colonial rulers that they had no history. The effort to construct a national history 'out of nothing' is both intensified and problematised by a the long-suppressed awareness that there has always been an Indigenous population with a history longer than any other people's, but a history that from a Western point of view was dismissed as 'prehistoric'. (The current national anthem celebrates being 'young and free', a matter of dispute if you are an Aboriginal person.) Out of these elements, we find poems filling a historical void with legends of heroic explorers, rebellious convicts, romantic bushrangers, and rollicking shearers and drovers. In fiction there is an emergent tradition of historical panorama, from Henry Handel Richardson's *The Fortunes of Richard Mahony*, through Eleanor Dark's *The Timeless Land* trilogy (a title declaring the paradox of making a chronology out of timelessness), to Peter Carey's *Oscar and Lucinda*. Besides filling the void, there is the drive to correct what we know of the past and acknowledge the place within it of First Nations peoples, women, non-Anglo-Celtic people, and faceless workers in factories. Voicing the silences of a history of oppression, we find life stories such as Sally Morgan's *My Place*, fictionalised histories like Eric Willmot's *Pemulwuy, The Rainbow Warrior*, plays like those of Jack Davis, and novels attacking the very concept of history, such as Kim Scott's *Benang*. Alongside these Indigenous challenges to white history, we find a continued effort on the part of white writers to reimagine the past. Not infrequently this provokes public debate about who can tell whose past and whether novelists can validly supplement the work of the historian (as in the case of Kate Grenville's *The Secret River*).

Bearing in mind all these contending possibilities, what you can expect here is a rough charting of Australian literature as it emerged under official recognition, with attention to works and authors that won prizes and inspired scholarly analysis. Related to this is the history of what has lasted as a visible presence in society. This can be seen in school textbooks, books that remain in print (not necessarily measures of aesthetic merit, though an indicator of perceived social relevance), works that inspire stage or film adaptations, writers that consistently attract public attention. As the list implies, a literary history is also a tale of literary institutions: the health of the publishing industry, intellectual fashions in schools and universities, government funding of the arts, and so on. This particular literary history, framed as it is by the adjective 'short', will touch on all of the above, but will perforce be selective. There is an appendix of useful resources for further reading that will provide more context in which to make general sense of specific periods and works and point to other work not covered here.

CHAPTER 1

Convicts to Reform
1788–1850

SOCIAL AND POLITICAL CONTEXT

Britain had become weighted down with prisons full of poor folk driven to petty crime, workers arrested for agitating for their rights (Chartists), Irish political dissidents, debtors and outright criminals, all given harsh sentences by landowning or mill-owning magistrates. It had been exporting indentured labourers and convicts to its colonies in the United States but once America gained its independence, that 'market' dried up, and Australia was proposed as a distant and thinly populated land where, at worst, Georgian England could be rid of its unruly underclass, and at best, an Enlightenment regimen might encourage people to become reformed, self-supporting settlers.

The latter prospect seemed unlikely. A thousand people, none of whom wanted to be there, landed in 1788 on a totally unknown landmass on the other side of the world. Most of the 'First Fleet', as they were known, resented the rest of their fellows for keeping them in chains and obliging them to work long hours under the threat of crippling floggings. The land offered animals that seemed travesties of normal European creatures: birds that laughed, mammals that laid eggs, trees that shed bark instead of leaves. Then there were natives who could lurk undetected in the forest and seemed to follow no organised social system that white folk could relate to. Everyone's ambition was either to escape (China was rumoured to be walking distance northwards) or to serve out their allotted exile and return to Britain.

Immediate demands, however, were to hunt for and cultivate enough food to sustain settlement and to construct adequate shelter that would accord with the order of a military garrison and penal institution. To secure protection from Aboriginal attacks and discover local resources, some dealing with 'the natives' had to be negotiated and exploratory forays into the surrounding country carried out. Governor Arthur Phillip organised the capture of several Aboriginal people, Bennelong and Barangaroo leaving their names inscribed on Sydney's shores. They proved quick to acquire some English and white customs, but also indifferent to much of what Europeans assumed to be a self-evidently superior culture. Unused to Western diseases, the tribes rapidly succumbed to everything a lousy and scrofulous bunch of sailors and convicts carried, smallpox in particular decimating the local population. Misunderstandings, fear and hostility resulted in spearings of whites, and in 1790, Phillip sent out the first punitive expedition to capture killers or kill a sufficient number to deter future attacks. This would become a less restrained pattern as settlements extended into the countryside.

Within the white garrisons, the distinction between convict and free was the fundamental basis of society. Within that, there was the added division between English and Irish, prejudice against the latter leading to an unsuccessful rebellion in 1804. Britain, of course, did not want all of its human exports to return home, so inducements to an improved life were created for both sectors: from 1801, prisoners could be assigned to less onerous work and eventually earn their 'ticket of leave'; soldiers could take up allocations of land; civil administrators who could not be commanded to go to the frontiers of the empire were offered land and assigned labourers as well as a salary. None of this was done with the consent of Aboriginal peoples. After the first few years in which all of the occupying settlement starved for lack of regular supplies and ignorance of local climate and what to grow in it, land grants spread inland to the fertile river flats of Parramatta and south through country suited to grazing sheep and cattle. Military man John Macarthur and his wife Elizabeth became rich on their country estate, introducing Spanish merino sheep in 1796, and convict James Ruse used his freedom to create a farm growing European crops. They set in train the nation's prosperity based on supplies of wool and wheat to Europe. To speed the creation of a fully functional society, free immigrants were encouraged from 1805. Between 1801 and 1803, Matthew

Flinders and George Bass mapped the continental coast, allowing for the visual apprehension of a vast landmass with the island of Van Diemen's Land (now Tasmania) to the south.

Some of the free settlers and some freed convicts realised that they could make a good living by taking a herd of sheep or cattle and a few convict labourers and pushing beyond the limits of government control to establish a 'run' as unlicensed squatters. Eventually, this lawless occupation would become ratified in colonial records and squatters would become a colonial class of considerable influence. Many of the early generation of military men had not only taken up land but also bought into the colonial supply trade, in particular the unofficial currency, rum. The favourite tipple of soldiers and sailors, and less likely to spoil than beer, this item established the lasting reputation of Australians as hard drinkers. Increasingly, governors sent to control unruly development, impose taxes to pay for infrastructure, and regulate dealings with the Indigenous population, were faced with a lobby of merchants and squatters who wanted to maintain a monopoly of trade and develop their estates without restraints. The conflict led to the 'Rum Rebellion' in 1808 in which Macarthur and his ilk deposed Governor William Bligh and protested his 'tyranny' to the Colonial Office.

Governor Lachlan Macquarie took over management of the colony between 1810 and 1821 and set about creating civic infrastructure, liberating more convicts and encouraging more free settlers. Many of the sandstone buildings constructed during his term of office remain as elegant landmarks in Sydney. In his time, too, the wall of the Great Dividing Range was crossed by explorers and the inland city of Bathurst created a focus for new settlement. An increasing number of convicts were diverted from Sydney to Hobart (founded in 1803), and Van Diemen's Land—its 1830 penal settlement at Port Arthur in particular—became a byword for harsh treatment. In 1828, martial law was declared there against Aboriginal people and the myth of extermination of the island's Indigenous population promulgated. Convicts were also diverted to the west of the continent, with the founding of the Swan River colony in 1829. Meanwhile, settlers in Van Diemen's Land had been looking across Bass Strait at the 'unoccupied' southern mainland. In 1833, Edward Henty created a station at Portland, and two years later John Batman and John Pascoe Fawkner did a deal with Aboriginal tribes on Port Phillip Bay to start grazing around what is now Melbourne. This led to a rush of 'overlanders' droving stock south from Sydney to 'open up' country between the two settlements.

In 1831, the first shipment of free colonists whose passages were assisted by government arrived. This organised programme led to changes in society. Labour conditions had been regulated by the Masters and Servants Act of 1824, the imbalance between men and women in the colony started to diminish, and a civil police force and court system were created to supplement the 'troopers' who patrolled outside of the settled areas. Ordered settlement by free workers was part of a mildly utopian but fully capitalist plan devised by Edward Gibbon Wakefield in England. He founded a commercial company that would acquire lands in the central south of the continent and parcel them out to artisans and yeomen farmers for a fee. Large landholders could sponsor labourers who could then earn enough to set up for themselves. No Aboriginal person living within the spaces marked off by Wakefield was ever consulted, but in 1836 the colony of South Australia was founded as a social experiment free of any convicts.

This movement accorded with sentiments being voiced at other colonial sites. By now, squatters were rich and living like English squires, and were becoming tired of British folk deriding them as convict trash. Religious leaders and locals with political ambitions, if not touting republicanism, were pushing for a morally improved and self-determining state. Squatters benefitted economically from having assigned convict labour, but intransigence, runaways, rustlers and bandits (known as 'bushrangers') were a constant pest. Gradually several interests combined to persuade the Colonial Office to abolish convict transportation. This occurred for New South Wales in 1840. However, people had been sentenced to prison terms of seven or fourteen years or for life, so it took a generation for a convict servant class to merge into the free citizenry. In 1850, an Australian League formed to promote not only the end of transportation in all colonies, but also land reform and male suffrage. Meanwhile, a series of exploring expeditions tracked major rivers and crossed the continent (from Oxley in 1818 to Sturt in 1828, Mitchell in 1831, Eyre in 1841, Leichhardt in 1845, Stuart in 1860, and Giles, Warburton and Forrest in the 1870s) so that the various settlements were coming into an awareness of the full extent and potential of the continent.

Cultural Context

The first book published in Australia was a set of government regulations: *New South Wales General Standing Orders* (1802). Paper and printing presses were extremely limited in number and a penal society run along military lines—and including political prisoners and labour agitators among its literate convicts—needed to control what was circulating by way of news and opinion. In any case, most people were not literate and were too busy struggling to survive to spend time in literary pursuits. The first newspaper was the *Sydney Gazette*, appearing in 1803 as the voice of administration and merchants. A commercial newspaper did not appear until almost thirty years later: the *Sydney Herald*, surviving to this day as the *Sydney Morning Herald*.

Aboriginal cultures were highly developed but mostly manifest in song, dance and painting, and white society tended to dismiss all Indigenous art as 'primitive'. However, early contacts showed that the First Peoples could quickly learn literacy, and Bennelong was the first to pen a letter to someone he'd met in England. Much Aboriginal writing followed, most of it petitioning government representatives for better living conditions, freedom of movement and removal of intolerant 'protectors'. In an attempt to create a buffer between settler ferocity and Aboriginal life, George Augustus Robinson took Indigenous Tasmanians to an island settlement, where a newsletter, the *Flinders Island Chronicle*, was produced around 1836 by an Aboriginal editor, Thomas Brune.

As guards and prisoners began to settle and have families, many worried about the ways in which their children would grow up. Those with money could hire governesses or send their offspring to boarding school in Britain. (The Wentworth family, for example, sent their son to study law, and in 1823, he penned a poem at

Cambridge honouring Australia as 'a new Britannia in another world'.) Those with reduced means either engaged children in the unremitting work of home and farm or left them to run free and get a 'bush education'. Subsequent literary work would debate the enviable free-spirited outdoor life of young Australians versus the mindless ignorance of the youth raised with only materialist values. As in England, churches provided some schooling and 'dame schools' taught basics. Teachers gradually spread through towns and the Presbyterian John Dunmore Lang catered for better students by founding the Australian College, Sydney, in 1835. Sydney University was established in 1850, its architecture emulating the Victorian Gothic style of Cambridge colleges. Its Latin motto, 'Sidere mens eadem mutato', shows the Eurocentric focus of the colony ('The same learning under new stars'), and the inclusion of Australian animals on gargoyles indicated the challenge to colonial writers: how to relate distinctive present surroundings (frequently known only through Aboriginal words) to a linguistic and cultural heritage that defined the colonial world as barbaric. Popular culture was acknowledged with the opening of the Theatre Royal in Melbourne in 1841, and there was a colonial art exhibition in Hobart in 1845. For many years, however, the arts would be dominated by work and artists imported from England.

Non-fiction

The search for literary origins tracks back to writing that is part of nation building. That served a practical, often documentary purpose, but could encompass elegant style and set up images that would shape future ideas of self and place. One such text was William Dampier's *A Voyage to New Holland in the Year 1699* published in 1703. Tales of world voyaging were best-sellers for Europe's literate elite, and Dampier's encounter with the dry west coast of New Holland spread a view of the antipodes as desert, and of Aboriginal people as the most wretched of creatures. James Cook's journals, seventy years later, popularised a more Edenic vision of the Great South Land and represented the Aboriginal population in romantic light as the happiest of humanity for having as much as they needed for a pre-industrial accommodation with nature.

Subsequent journals and letters swung between these two poles of hostile wretchedness and innocent promise. They were directed at European readers curious about a new land and officials interested in the colony becoming economically sustainable. Watkin Tench was an officer in the marine corps sent out to keep order in the first fleet of convicts. He published an account of his first year at Sydney Cove, *A Narrative of the Expedition to Botany Bay* (1789) and followed up with *A Complete Account of the Settlement at Port Jackson* (1793). Tench's sanguine temperament is reflected in his opening words: 'To an active and contemplative mind, a new country is an inexhaustible source of curiosity and speculation.' He describes the all-encompassing struggle to survive as a levelling social force, setting in train the egalitarian and pragmatic ethos of Australian society: soldiers took up the same tasks as convicts and a wheelbarrow was valued more than flashy military display. Linked in hardship, isolated from supplies, officers and prisoners had the same rations and, unlike later accounts, Tench downplays any harsh treatment other than hard labour. He does note that Aboriginal (called 'Indian') attacks on workers arose from poor treatment and that theft of their belongings had to be prohibited. The capture of Arabanoo (called 'Manly' by the settlers) in order to learn something of the language and motivations of the natives is recorded in some detail, followed by accounts of the fatal impact of smallpox on the native population and the later capture of Colby and Bennelong. Sorties into the interior find the Hawkesbury and Nepean rivers, but little of promise to the Western eye other than 'the trackless immeasurable desert, in awful silence'. The extreme isolation of the colony is indicated in the fact that the next ship to arrive had taken almost a year to get there, and the desperate rush for letters from Britain revealed that the French Revolution had occurred. Tench provides extensive details of the growing number of small farming ventures, climate and soil types, and he closes with speculations about the viability of a whaling industry. He includes a naturalist's observations of the kangaroo and extensive ethnographic commentary on the Indigenous peoples, their technologies and their languages (including some wordlists).

He notes their intelligence, but faults their 'levity, their fickleness, their passionate extravagance of character'. Tench the Enlightenment amateur scientist is careful in his observation and admits when his knowledge reaches its limit. Of the convicts, Tench is optimistic. Though he notes thefts of food, he sees most behaving well and many deservedly earning their freedom. He also records their 'flash' argot, which shapes much of Australian English thereafter, suggesting that its replacement by 'proper' English will be an aid to reforming the criminal.

As pressure on the Sydney settlement increased, new penal outstations were created and farmland to support them was required. Farms and sheep runs began to spread along valleys and upland plains to the south, Camden and eventually Goulburn becoming centres of agriculture. Expeditions to map the country ensued and explorers' narratives were pored over for new antipodean curiosities, water sources, mineral wealth and productive land. Charles Sturt published *Two Expeditions into the Interior of Southern Australia* (1833) in which he records his team's voyage down the Murray River and the discovery of the Darling River, flowing from the north. His narrative supported a myth of rivers running west into an inland sea, and his tracking of the Murray's mouth led to the founding of the colony of South Australia. By contrast, his *Narrative of an Expedition into Central Australia* (1849) records sand and sun that almost sent him blind. The desert interior is marked with labels like 'Disappointment' and 'Despair' and lakes (in a drought year) were only vast salt pans. Sturt generated a popular image of Australia's interior as a 'Dead Heart', the 'Never Never' 'beyond the Black Stump' that was the ultimate wilderness limit to white ambition.

Thomas Mitchell was the government surveyor, and, following the reports of a convict who had lived among Aboriginal tribes for some years, he set off north and west in 1831 to chart the country. Settler attitudes to the land as they cut out clearings for farms are indicated in the place names he records: Hungry Flat, Devil's Backbone, No-Grass Valley. Extending the work of John Oxley and Charles Sturt, Mitchell describes rocks, trees and fish in some detail (fish being linked with his constant search for water), and gives a regular account of contact with Aboriginal groups, noting how they have been pushed out to remote locations under the impact of farming. He describes customs, the firing of grass, the making of fish traps, and the disastrous effects of smallpox. The limits to his explorations are set by both lack of water and large groups of hostile tribesmen. He lists his team: convicts with a range of skills hoping to gain freedom from their contribution to the colony's future. He records temperature and soil types, noting how, away from rivers, the dry shallow soils are fit only for cattle grazing, but discovers the fertile Liverpool plains during his tracking of the Namoi and Gwydir rivers in northern New South Wales. Mitchell's published accounts are *Three Expeditions into the Interior of Australia* (1838) and *Expeditions into the Interior of Tropical Australia* (1848), in which he sets forth a vision of 'Australia Felix'—open plains ripe for exploitation:

> Though Australia calls up no historical recollections, no classical associations of ideas, it has other, and not less valid titles to our attention. It is a new and vast country, over the largest portion of which a veil of mystery still hangs; many of its productions vary in a singular manner, from those in other parts of the world.

The explorers who exerted a direct imaginative pull on the literary imagination have been Edward John Eyre and Ludwig Leichhardt, both commemorated in poems by Francis Webb, and the latter in Patrick White's novel, *Voss*. Eyre crossed from Adelaide to the west coast of the continent in 1841, and Leichhardt went north to the Gulf of Carpentaria and disappeared while heading northwest towards what is now Darwin. Eyre's journey is taken as heroic struggle against heat, dust and drought, whereas Leichhardt embodied the mythic figure of self-sacrifice to a cause, heroic endurance and transcendent failure.

Novel

The first fiction from Australia had a double purpose of entertainment and education. It reported on the particular conditions of a penal colony and could be read as a deterrent to English readers in danger of romanticising a life of crime, or as protest against the harsh regime of convict labour, or sometimes as self-exoneration and a sign of civility aimed at securing favour from local authorities. The first literary work printed in Australia, *Michael Howe, the Last and Worst of the Bushrangers of Van Diemen's Land* (1818) by Thomas Wells, has an air of historical reportage, as does the first book-length novel published in the country, Henry Savery's *Quintus Servinton: A Tale Founded Upon Incidents of Real Occurrence* (1830–31). Servinton's life parallels Savery's: business success followed by collapse, forgery to cover debts, and transportation to Hobart. In the novel, Servinton's wife joins him in exile and engineers his freedom. Savery was able to write the book while a convict because he had been assigned to office duties. Like many subsequent writers, he went on to work on a newspaper before trying his hand at farming. Unlike his fictional counterpart, he again fell into debt, forged repayments and died in prison. *The Hermit in Van Diemen's Land*, variously attributed to Thomas Wells and Henry Savery, appeared in 1829 and established the long tradition of sketches of colonial society, both fictional and factual, often satiric in either mode.

Novels also described frontier excitements of encountering strange animals, an alien people, fire, flood, and the work of building a home and a prosperous farm. Some of this writing was simply intended as exotic colour for popular entertainment, but often it had the underlying agenda of encouraging British readers to emigrate as free labour. Anna Maria Bunn's *The Guardian: A Tale, by an Australian* (1838) has been recovered as the first novel by a woman and first novel published in Sydney. Bunn was Irish, the daughter of a soldier briefly posted to Australia. Charles Rowcroft's *Tales of the Colonies* (1843) reflects his four years in what is now Tasmania. His *The Bushranger of Van Diemen's Land* (1846) purports to be a cautionary tale to counter any romance of noble banditry, but is something of a sensation novel sprinkled with curiosities such as a character dancing with a kangaroo. Rowcroft's books were typical of a lot of 'Australian' literature: published in England for English readers by an Englishman who spent time in the colonies. Thomas McCombie varied the model by being Scottish and spending a good deal more time than most in Australia.

He edited the *Port Phillip Gazette* after a stint of squatting and served on the colony's Legislative Council, returning to Britain to publish *Arabin: or The Adventures of a Colonist in New South Wales* (1845). It established a trope of the ordinary hard-working emigrant making a comfortable life after hardship, whereas the lazy young aristocrat out to experience colonial life fails. It also depicts Aboriginal life and questions how white settlers should respond to it. Alexander Harris also spent many years in Australia, labouring as a timber cutter before taking on farm work. In among the usual romance and adventure, he provides realistic accounts of society in *Settlers and Convicts* (1847) and *The Emigrant Family* (1849).

As an example of how subsequent research rewrites literary history, *Ralph Rashleigh, or the Life of an Exile*, written 1844–45, was first published in edited form in London in 1929 as a historical memoir. Literary scholar Colin Roderick tracked its origins as a novel to convict James Tucker, writing under the pseudonym 'Giacomo di Rosenberg', and published the full text in 1952. Tucker wrote a picaresque tale of a young burglar transported to a chain gang at Emu Plains. He is assigned to a farm near Campbelltown, captured by bushrangers and pressed into working with them, tried and sent to another chain gang in Newcastle, attacked and then adopted by Aboriginal people after he escapes, following which he rescues two shipwrecked women and returns with them to Sydney, eventually gaining his freedom. Oscillating between cautionary tale and adventure romance, and showing the brutality of both gaolers and convicts, the book has attracted critical interest and moved from invisibility to canonical status.

For some time, there were few children in the colony. Indeed, there were few women until later shipments of convicts added to the population and more free settlers arrived with families. The pioneer Australian text for young readers is Charlotte Barton's *A Mother's Offering to Her Children by a Lady Long Resident in New South Wales* (1841). Barton came to Australia as governess to the Macarthur children, married into a farming business, then fled a second marriage to penurious life in Sydney, where she published her book. Set around the Shoalhaven River to Sydney's south, it comprises a mother's evening dialogues with her four children, retailing stories and poems about shipwrecks, geology, animals and plants, mining, life on pastoral 'stations' and Aboriginal lore. Everything is peppered with moral lessons. The mother declares sources for her tales, including explorer narratives.

POETRY

It is significant that the first poem published in Australia had the title 'The Vision of Melancholy'. All literate inhabitants of New Holland were exiles from Ireland or Britain and often lamented their separation from a familiar landscape and society in the language and conventions of Georgian and Victorian England. After all, for some decades the primary prospect of publication and readers lay 'back home' in Dublin, London or Edinburgh. There were, of course, other modes of verse circulating in the form of songs, some of which were eventually preserved in writing. These were in ballad form set to Irish and British tunes. Most of them lamented conviction for poaching or petty theft and transportation 'for seven long years' to Botany Bay, Van Diemen's Land, or, in the case of 'Moreton Bay', to the northern penal colony later to become Brisbane. Verses in the voice of convicts included rage at unjust imprisonment and cruel treatment and threatened retribution. 'Jim Jones at Botany Bay' records being subject to flogging and shackled in 'the iron gang' and ends:

> And some dark night when everything is silent in the town,
> I'll kill the tyrants one and all, and shoot the floggers down.
> I'll give the law a little shock, remember what I say.
> They'll yet regret they sent Jim Jones in chains to Botany Bay.

The main type of resistance to tyranny came from escapees who set up as bushrangers. The general attitude is summed up: 'I'd rather range these hills around like wolf or kangaroo / Than work one hour for the government, cried bold Jack Donahue'. One early and still popular song is 'The Wild Colonial Boy', celebrating Jack Doolan/John Dowling/Jack Duggan as a tearaway youth who plays Robin Hood and ends his short life in a shootout with mounted troopers. It serves as a model for all the later stories, poems and songs about bushrangers.

'Frank the Poet' (Francis MacNamara) was given a ticket of leave in 1847 after fifteen years' imprisonment. He is reputed to have written the folk song 'Moreton Bay' and is remembered for his satire in rhyming couplets, 'A Convict's Tour of Hell' (1839). An 'old lag' dies and wanders down to the Styx, where he is given free passage, knocks for entry to Purgatory, and is told it's reserved for the 'Priests and Popes' who invented it. At the gates of Hell, Satan gives him a viewing of all his tormenters in life: 'Hangmen, Gaolers and Flagellators / Commandants, Constables and Spies / Informers and Overseers likewise', including Captain Cook, whose discovery enabled the creation of the penal colony. Frank is welcomed in heaven for being sufficiently purged of sin in life but wakes to find it all a dream.

Written literature first emanated from the other end of the social spectrum: government officers like judge Barron Field, or government-sponsored writers like Governor Macquarie's poet laureate, Michael Massey Robinson, who was paid in cows and wrote odes commemorating official events for the *Sydney Gazette*. Field was a friend of Charles Lamb, and his *First Fruits of Australian Poetry* (1819) was supposedly appreciated by Wordsworth and Coleridge, though perhaps as a curiosity for being the first book of verse published in the colony. The only poem preserved for attention is Field's portrait of the most distinctive exotic species from Down Under, 'The Kangaroo', a syntactically rambling celebration of the 'anomalous' mixing of known animals that somehow manages to be 'not incongruous / repugnant or preposterous' but 'graceful or ethereal'. As with most colonial officials, Field moved on to other postings, but a new set of locally born writers was beginning to emerge. In 1826, Charles Tompson, the first Australian-born poet to be published, showed the 'binocular' nature of later writing when he declared both his local 'currency' credentials and his cultural debts to Europe: *Wild Notes from the Lyre of a Native Minstrel* ('native' meaning an Anglo-Celtic person born in Australia).

Poetry production was sporadic and very much a gentleman's hobby, as indicated in the title *Stolen Moments* (1842), a collection by New South Wales political figure Henry Parkes. Of course, writing poems was also a sign of the cultured lady. In fact, the biggest change in Australian literary history has come about through the discovery and revaluing of work by the relatively few educated women in the colony prior to the 1890s. Many, like their male counterparts, published in local newspapers. One example is the writing of Irish-born Eliza Hamilton Dunlop. Her husband was a police magistrate who also settled on a farm in the Hunter region, north of Sydney. His wife recorded the local Aboriginal language and wrote her most famous poem, 'The Aboriginal Mother' (1838), in protest at the massacre of Indigenous people at Myall Creek. It was the first case where whites were prosecuted for such atrocity. Apart from other poems reworking Aboriginal song and story, her writing is summed up by the title of a series of verses: 'Songs of an Exile'. Fidelia Hill's *Poems and Recollections of the Past* (1840) was the first book of verse by a woman published in Australia. Periodical publications from Mary Bailey and Caroline Leakey have been shown to include agitation for women's suffrage, reform to the convict system and sympathy for 'fallen' women.

The most significant voice from this early period of poetical production is that of Charles Harpur. He was not only Australian born, but also born of emancipated convicts, and educated entirely within New South Wales. Harpur was seriously attempting a literary career rather than just dashing off a ballad or a bit of satiric occasional verse (though he did that too: doubled strands of literary and popular writing become typical of many Australian poets). His poems reveal his wide reading, with specific reference to Petrarch, Shakespeare, Marvell, Milton, Dryden, Shelley, Coleridge, Wordsworth, Burns and Gray, but he uses these models to write about Australian experience ('Lost in the Bush', 'The Bushfire', 'A Flight of Wild Ducks'). Gradually he sheds the gloss of Englishness and 'poesy' to present a world that is appreciated on its own terms, and not as a repetition or perverse inversion of Europe. This is best exemplified in 'Midsummer Noon in an Australian Forest' (1851). The poet captures the heat and silence of his bush retreat, relishing its comfort and beauty:

> O 'tis easy here to lie
> Hidden from Noon's scorching eye,
> In this grassy cool recess
> Musing thus of Quietness.

Life was not always so idyllic, and, though clearly over-influenced by Milton, Harpur drew on the Gothic romance of the colonial frontier to create an epic of settler tragedy in 'The Creek of the Four Graves'. He also philosophised on beauty, morality and the prospects of a flourishing democratic nation. Harpur's ability to sustain a literary career (not without a good deal of poverty) was aided by a society able to provide small government jobs (postal clerk, goldfields registrar) and by the emergence of a small coterie of Sydney intelligentsia with whom he could debate aesthetics and social reform.

DRAMA

The first play performed in Australia (in 1789) was the 1706 Restoration comedy *The Recruiting Officer* by Irishman George Farquhar. Characters with allegorical names, either apt or ironic (Plume, Brazen, Balance, Wilful) engage in cross-class romances complicated by mismatched desires and cross-gender disguises. The play included the threat of hanging and its satiric depiction of military men and Irish origins would have appealed to many in the convict audience. Such British models of melodrama and farce became stock-in-trade for antipodean productions, as evident in titles such as E.H. Thomas's *The Bandit of the Rhine* (1835) and S.P. Hill's *Tarquin the Proud* (1843), or that of the first opera written and performed in Australia, *Don John of Austria* (1847). Bandits took on local colour in Henry Melville's *The Bushrangers* (1834), establishing a long-running tradition of bushranger dramas, sentimental romance plots being another favourite, pioneered by Edward Geoghegan in *The Currency Lass* (1844). Thomas McCombie's novel *Arabin: or The Adventures of a Colonist in New South Wales* (1845) was dramatised by J.M. McLachlan with added songs in 1849.

CHAPTER 2

Boom and Bust to Federation
1850–1901

SOCIAL AND POLITICAL CONTEXT

Three things changed the fabric of Australian society between 1850 and 1900: the discovery of gold in Victoria and New South Wales, the break-up of large pastoral land grants into smaller wheat and sheep and orchard farms, and the foundation of state parliaments with elected Australian members. All three were related. Gold brought huge numbers of people into the country and many sought to settle somewhere when they left off prospecting, so more land had to be made available. Cities grown from servicing gold rushes needed food other than cattle and sheep. As squatters held vast estates without any official title, governments from 1860 allowed settlers to select sections of these holdings and crown land for dairying and horticulture. This meant back-breaking labour and years of uncertain returns, prompting popular scorn for the 'cockatoo farmer' (supposedly surviving on boiled cockatoos, but often on wallaby stew). Nonetheless, larger numbers of free people, however they worked, created a citizenry requiring public services and a voice in politics in exchange for building the economy and paying taxes.

The colonial government had suppressed news of sporadic finds of gold so as to keep the convict system under control, but by 1851, large deposits around Bendigo and Ballarat could not be concealed. 'Marvellous Melbourne' grew instantly into an imposing civic and banking centre, and Victoria was proclaimed as separate colony from New South Wales. That state had its own gold rush centred on the inland city of Bathurst. Later goldfields were discovered in Queensland and Western Australia, encouraging a sense of continental unity as people followed 'the rush' from colony to colony.

The proliferation of economic and social changes could no longer be managed by one Colonial Office centred in London. Local administrations and pastoral interests depleted of manpower sought to offset costs by having miners pay a licence fee. On the goldfields, a colonial police force was enlisted to check licenses and, inspired by the fines they could levy, police earned the name 'traps' for appearing at a shaft when they knew men would be working below without their papers. Resentment at such persecution and discontent with the profiteering and lack of facilities in mining towns led to an armed insurrection by miners in 1854. Ballarat's Eureka Stockade battle against police and troops was a tactical failure, but a strategic victory in that it focused the political mind on labour conditions and got a few workers into parliament. The Southern Cross flag of the Eureka rebellion remains a sign of worker solidarity and anti-establishment nationalism.

Parliamentary reforms ensued across the country. In 1854, Henry Parkes, an artisan-merchant rather than a colonial functionary or squatter, was elected to the New South Wales Legislative Council, previously reserved for members nominated by the colonial governor. A year later, New South Wales and Victoria established bicameral parliaments, and in 1856, South Australia legislated male suffrage, it and Queensland pioneering 'free, compulsory and secular' state education soon after. Van Diemen's Land renamed itself Tasmania in 1856 and Queensland became a separate colony three years later. As the population became more enfranchised, working conditions were more regulated. 1856 saw Australia's first May Day march in Melbourne to celebrate the institution of the 'eight-hour day'—eight hours of work, eight of relaxation, eight of rest—with the addition of that other national institution, 'the weekend'. Labour unions were formed (the Hunter River Coal Miners' Mutual Protective Association being founded in 1860) and itinerant bush workers gathered into collectives. This movement was underpinned by socialist ideals. Miners put down their tools in 1888 to claim better pay and safer working conditions. A maritime strike for better working conditions was supported by mine and pastoral workers in 1890, but the Queensland shearers strikes of 1891 and 1894 were broken up by troops under the control of the pastoral lobby, which held power in parliament. Workers organised into a Labor Party (the spelling deliberately American as a sign of anti-Empire nationalism) and the first Labor government briefly ruled Queensland in 1899. Disillusionment at the military suppression of workers' rights during the Queensland shearers' strike prompted a group led by journalist-ideologue William Lane to found a utopian socialist New Australia commune in Paraguay in 1893. A year later, South Australian women gained the right to vote and stand for election.

The settler population took seventy years to reach one million but doubled in the next twenty-five years. Gold rushes started the complication of ethnicity in the nation, with Maori, Europeans, Americans and Chinese flocking in. Anglo-Celtic domination was faced with Asians capable of competing with it by sheer hard work. The Victorian government placed an entry tax on Chinese immigrants from 1855 and white miners persecuted their competition, leading to massacres such as the Lambing Flat 'riot' in 1861. With regulation of Pacific Islander 'indentured labour' (often amounting to slavery) on Queensland sugar plantations in 1868, white settler hegemony was secured. Despite often hysterical projections of fear of invasion by more numerous and less wealthy 'coolies', the percentage of Australia's population originating anywhere other than the British Isles and Ireland remained minuscule until after the Second World War. Some Chinese left the mines to make a living growing vegetables, and laid the foundation for later multicultural Australia, but the path was set leading to the 'White Australia Policy', formalised when the colonies joined to become one nation.

The prospects for federation were improved by the creation of trans-colonial infrastructure. John McDouall Stuart completed the age of great explorations by crossing the continent from south to north in 1862. This led to the Northern Territory being set up as a proto-state under the control of South Australia, which in 1870 began the construction of the Overland Telegraph to Darwin, connecting with a cable to Europe. Melbourne had its own telephone exchange in 1880 and a rail service between Melbourne and Sydney was completed in 1883. By 1870, all British troops had left Australia and all convict transportation had ceased (after a brief resumption in Western Australia, which gained self-government in 1890). The basis for Australian industrial development was created in 1883, when Broken Hill Proprietary mining company was founded. BHP went on to become a steel manufacturer and one of the nation's largest companies. Awareness of a national entity was increased when the colonies sent troops overseas to support Britain in its suppression of dissidents in the Sudan (1885) and South Africa (1899), the latter generating the legend of crack marksmen and tough but unruly fighters that would be locked in to the national imaginary during World War One. Australia entered into international networks by setting up a committee to organise Antarctic exploration and an Australian Association for the Advancement of Science in 1886. Three years later, all state premiers met, and Henry Parkes delivered his 'Tenterfield oration' calling for national unity.

Progress at the political level, like ideas of a distinctive Australian identity, remained heavily invested in the natural environment. Major droughts took hold from 1876 till 1886 and again from 1895 to 1902. These, combined with the collapse of fourteen banks (connected to economic crises in London), created a depression. People who had rapidly become rich were instantly poor, starting a pattern of boom and bust that has continued into modern times. At that time, it delayed the federation of the colonies for several years and kept in place inefficient systems such as different rail gauges in each state and varying tariffs on goods, requiring customs houses at all border crossings.

CULTURAL CONTEXT

Vance Palmer in 1954 published a cultural history titled *The Legend of the Nineties*. It signals the pre-eminent place in national literary history that the second half of the nineteenth century has occupied, associated with the 'glory days' of the *Bulletin* and the 'bush' image of Australia as a land of promise that could nonetheless bankrupt or kill you. It was the time when people began to feel that there was an Australian literature, even if it was a rough-edged popular collection of yarns in prose and verse depicting local behaviour, attitudes and speech.

The nineties up to the First World War was the era of the 'bush ballad', no longer about convicts, but depicting drovers, shearers and bullock drivers in tall stories and comic escapades. Agriculture had developed to an industrial scale, but only in size: it still depended on large numbers of manual workers in the service of a few merchants and pastoralists. Squatters may have come from labouring origins, but that did not stop them assuming the airs of British aristocracy and sending their children to boarding schools to get a 'proper' English education. Their pastoral 'empires', spreading across areas equivalent to that of some European countries, attempted to build a sense of dynastic and cultured tradition but were still unsettled. The whole country remained in flux. People moved from one gold rush to another, from Australia to New Zealand and back again, from cattle stations in Queensland to markets and ports in South Australia, from shearing shed to shearing shed across every colony. Soldiers retiring from service in India would arrive to take up land and those who made their fortunes in Australia would frequently move 'home' to England.

The fickle nature of prospecting for gold consolidated a culture of 'get rich quick' already existing among those who were fortunate enough to secure land and build large herds. The concept of luck has governed a lot of Australian thinking, its sporting ethos, and its addiction to gambling. Luck plus the idea of raw talent have weighted one end of a cultural seesaw, with education and hard work hanging precariously at the other end. In literature, the balance appears in the contrasts between miners and squatters on the one hand and city clerks and country 'cockies' (selectors) sweating in unprofitable confinement.

The appealing image of sudden riches underpinned an age of literary romance: both love affairs and colonial adventure romance. Critics declared that the colonial frontier and a levelling society lacked the European material of romances of chivalry. Australia's expanses of blue-grey gums and saltbush plains, with only a scattered 'Indian' population to offer battle, promised only monotony. However, the horse-riding 'knights' of this new colony could find adventure in battling nature: wild cattle, bushfires, floods, snakes, kangaroo hunts, storms, drought, and occasional attacks by wild natives (regarded as an integral part of the natural landscape). Social order was to be found in the squatter's homestead, a 'castle' at the centre of a feudal estate.

In the convict era, the good-versus-evil conflict between law and order and the unruly, sometimes downright villainous, actions of bushrangers was morally loaded in favour of the squatter, but once gold fever took hold on the public imagination, a levelling anti-authority sentiment grew, and the bushranger took on aspects of Robin Hood or the persecuted rebel. If anyone could get rich quick, then robbing the rich was simply another means to a socially accepted end. A popular gentleman bandit figure was Ben Hall, whose gang ranged New South Wales from 1863. Later, the Irish family of the Kellys in northern Victoria were targeted by police and their son Edward 'went bush' with his mates around 1878 and terrorised stations and country towns in Victoria and New South Wales until surrounded in a sensational shootout at Glenrowan. 'Ned' became a popular icon because of his homemade armour. The romance of the bushranger ended in 1880 when Kelly was hanged in Melbourne, but it persisted in legend and literature. The idea of mythic victory founded on actual defeat gained traction through the fatal outcome of the Burke and Wills expedition in 1860. This expedition from Melbourne to the Gulf of Carpentaria had enormous press coverage and the death of its leaders took on the romance of doomed heroism. For the Australian reader, there was the added reaction that proper Aussie bushmen would not have failed so dismally.

There are a number of inherent contradictions in the colonial adventure romance: the present encouragement of new settlers looking for excitement relies on a past stable base; the valuing of talent rather than breeding is at odds with an ideal of feudal civility; the admiration of the free-spirited colonial woman who can literally get her hands dirty on the frontier runs against the civilising influence of the pious 'princess' content to marry, raise children, garden, play the piano and manage servants. All these elements are to be found in the quintessential Australian colonial romance,

Henry Kingsley's *The Recollections of Geoffry Hamlyn* (1859). In a series of convenient coincidences, all the central characters from a small area of Devon end up as neighbours on pastoral properties around the Snowy Mountains in the time when 'overlanders' were pushing south from Sydney beyond the limits of government-controlled settlement. Each sheep and cattle 'station' is a little England and all of them serve as bases for adventure, love affairs, the pathos of lost children and death, and the making of fortunes ultimately directed at recovering family estates in England. Good breeding wins out over brute energy, and the underpinning values are those of Church of England 'muscular Christianity' and jolly male hunting and horsemanship. Kingsley did spend a solid length of time in Australia, lived on squatters' estates and knew of what he wrote, though much of it was exaggerated for dramatic flourish. The book is a page-turner with pleasing comic tones and some self-disparagement on the part of the narrator (who is not above comparing himself to Dickens!). It contains several set pieces that show a close observation and appreciation of the Australian bush. Partly because Australia is viewed as exotic and mostly because it subordinates everything colonial to values and outcomes that are jingoistically English, *Geoffry Hamlyn* became a representation of everything later nationalistic novelists abhorred.

Australia post-gold rush was on the colonial tour circuit. Anthony Trollope visited in 1871 and published *Australia and New Zealand* and a squatter romance *Harry Heathcote of Gangoil* (1873). Joseph Conrad made several landfalls, starting in 1879. Robert Louis Stevenson, Rudyard Kipling and Mark Twain visited between 1879 and 1895. Kipling had some influence on keeping the ballad alive in Australia, while Twain influenced dialogue in fiction. Awareness of being part of a global network of Anglophone literature, the solitary nature of settler farming, and the drive to self-education among workers produced a nation of avid readers. To cater for them, Edward Cole opened his Book Arcade, a legendary mix of education and entertainment, in Melbourne in 1883. George Robertson set up a bookshop in Melbourne that led eventually to a chain of Angus & Robertson bookstores and the influential publishing house, which began with A.B. Paterson's

The Man from Snowy River in 1895. A.C. Rowlandson founded the New South Wales Bookstall Company to issue cheap popular titles in 1898 and an Australian Literature Society was inaugurated in Melbourne a year later. Writers found local readers for their stories, poems and serialised novels in magazines and newspapers. The most influential outlet was the *Bulletin* (first issue 1880). Its leading editors, J.F. Archibald and A.G. Stephens, introduced major authors from overseas, provided critical feedback (and sometimes working space) for writers, and published collections of stories and poetry. Stephens added the literary review *Bookfellow* (1899 to 1925) to this 'factory' for Australian writing.

A literary support system of anthologies and criticism began to form. Frederick Sinnett published the critical essay 'The Fiction Fields of Australia' (1856–57) and G.B. Barton sent booklets (*Literature in New South Wales* and *The Poets and Prose Writers of New South Wales*) to the colony's display at the Paris Exhibition, 1866. By 1898, H.G. Turner and Alexander Sutherland were able to map *The Development of Australian Literature*. Optimism that a national culture was emerging was validated when Australian paintings by Melbourne's 'Heidelberg School' and members of the Sydney Society of Artists (classic works by Fred McCubbin, Tom Roberts and Arthur Streeton) were exhibited in London in 1898.

Sporting culture developed as leisure activities on squatters' estates and in towns. The first cricket team to visit England in 1868 comprised Aboriginal players from Western Victoria. Horse riding was sport as well as work, and organised racing produced the principal national event, the Melbourne Cup, beginning in 1861. 'Aussie rules' for many years took the place of soccer. It is a catch-and-kick form of football unique to the country, combining elements of an Aboriginal game and Irish football, and had its first formal matches in 1858. Its popularity centred on the southern and western states of the country; New South Wales and Queensland favoured rugby, split into union (for 'gentlemen') and league (for workers).

The fine distinctions in football codes reflected a socio-cultural divide that lasted into the 1960s. Although politics and the general social ethos were secular, there was considerable antipathy between

Catholics (mainly Irish) and Protestants (Scots, Welsh and English), with a class difference among the latter roughly defined by an elite identifying with the Church of England versus merchants, artisans and labourers belonging to 'dissenting' denominations of Christianity: Methodists, Baptists, Congregationals and Presbyterians. The religious divide was perpetuated by the arrival in 1868 of a teaching order of priests from Ireland, the Christian Brothers. They built a reputation for dogmatic instruction and muscular religiosity focused on rugby. Catholicism was a social underdog for many years but gained standing when Sydney's Archbishop Moran became a cardinal in 1885. The church often played a part in political reform. Presbyterian divine John Dunmore Lang promoted public education and penned essays such as *Freedom and Independence for the Golden Lands of Australia* (1892). The other work sketching a vision of an ideal Australia was William Lane's novel *The Working Man's Paradise*, which he published in 1892 to promulgate socialism and raise funds for striking workers in Queensland. Social reform also included agitation for gender equity. Women gained entry to university in Melbourne in 1880 and Sydney in 1881. Louisa Lawson founded *The Dawn: A Journal for Australian Women* in 1888.

Prose Fiction

Catherine Helen Spence arrived in Adelaide from Scotland at the age of fourteen when the colony of South Australia was but three years old. She put great store by education and worked as teacher, journalist and social reformer, eventually becoming the first woman to stand for election to federal parliament. Her writing explores the nature of true gentility as opposed to bloodline or wealth, presents proper marriage as founded on love between equals, and supports prosperity based on dutiful application of skill rather than the luck of inheritance or digging for gold. Spence's first novel, *Clara Morison* (1854), features an engaging mix of young people making their way in the regulated but still uncertain society of South Australia. The heroine is a poor relation to Scottish gentry, sent away to find employment as a governess, but forced into domestic servitude. This she bears calmly until finding congenial company among friends who turn out to be cousins. She falls in love with a sheep farmer of comfortable means who has to resolve his prior engagement to someone 'back home' before he and Clara can marry. By this time, Clara's acquisition of practical housekeeping skills has complemented her ladylike attributes to make her fully qualified to manage a rural 'station'. The novel provides a picture of Adelaide society, of differences between its free settlement and the neighbouring convict colony, and of the crisis when everyone rushes to dig for gold in Victoria. The author infuses her romance conventions with a strong tinge of realism: the poor and invalid whom Clara tends to are not necessarily grateful or easy to deal with.

Spence's other works include *Mr Hogarth's Will* (1865) and *Gathered In* (1881), the latter giving a good outline of squatter society in Victoria. It is also of interest in that, among assorted citations of poetry (the Brownings mostly), Australian Henry Kendall is quoted. Spence was, however, a lady of her time, and deplored antipodean slang. Her hero in *Gathered In* summed up her ideas when he said, 'There is nothing for which we should be so grateful to the old country as for its literature. I hope it may weld the English-speaking peoples together firmly by-and-by'. Written in 1879, her last work, *Handfasted*, was not published until its feminist recovery in 1984. It was deemed too scandalous to circulate, as it described an isolated Scots community that developed its own social order, a feature of which was 'handfasting'—an agreement to trial concubinage of a year and a day after which a couple could separate without fuss or marry.

One of the first novelists born in Australia to be published was John Lang. However, his *Legends of Australia* (1842) only came out as a small-press serial in Sydney, and *Lucy Cooper: An Australian Tale* (1846) was serialised in a minor periodical in England. He is better known for his journalism and his novel *The Wetherbys* (1854), produced after he migrated to Calcutta. Satirical depictions of colonial life in Bengal failed to get him notice as an Australian writer until later, despite works such as *The Forger's Wife* (1855), which creates a colonial detective dealing with Sydney's underworld, and a story collection, *Botany Bay* (1859).

Lang's interest in colonial women and convicts was matched by Caroline Leakey. She travelled to her sister in Van Diemen's Land, where she saw the dehumanising treatment of convict servants and prison labour. She put her chronic illness and her evangelical Christianity to work in creating a parson and a wrongly convicted woman sent to Hobart. The latter chafes at persecution by snobbish and unfeeling employers and by malevolent or crass fellow convicts. Eventually she falls ill and at the end of the book dies, just before the rake who caused all her suffering finds her and drops dead in grief and repentance. The parson keeps a protective eye on our heroine, and preaches fortitude and God's grace to all, providing a lengthy digression to describe Port Arthur penitentiary and the need for reform to a system based on vengeance rather than moral improvement. The book's title, *The Broad Arrow* (1859), refers to the convict garb that was a badge of shame, clothing being a motif throughout. One point of interest among the sentimental scenes and pious homilies is a view of the colonies as a crossroads where people keep running into each other and secrets will out; another, is disapproving mention of the hunting down of Aboriginal people.

Louisa Atkinson, sometimes writing as 'Louisa Calvert: An Australian Lady', was the first Australian-born woman to publish a novel in book form. In *Gertrude the Emigrant* (1857), Atkinson creates an insufferably virtuous sixteen-year-old girl who arrives in the colonies and is snapped up as a housekeeper by a woman running pastoral lands south of Sydney. Gertrude is the epitome of domestic order (unlike her lovable but slovenly Irish Catholic counterpart) and struggles to sort out her feelings in relation to a charmingly direct 'currency lad' (who turns to drink and rustling) and her mistress's sternly upright manager (who is civilised by the young woman and ultimately marries her). There is also a snobbish young blatherskite relative from England who casts aspersions on his aunt's convict origins while taking her money. The romance plot is cut through with set pieces of fire, flood and accident, and the whole thing is held together by Gertrude's constant injunctions to pray, read the scriptures and live a pure life. The book was eventually resuscitated owing to the author's reputation as a naturalist, and it contains sympathetic descriptions of Australian flora.

Three women—Ada Cambridge, Rosa Praed and Jessie Couvreur (writing as 'Tasma')—have become canonical among nineteenth-century Australian novelists. Like others, they inject popular romances with exotic colonial adventures. Most of them also raise serious questions about the proper nature of marriage and whether the more socially flexible life of the Australian girl is compatible with ladylike decorum as defined by English mores. They protest at and simultaneously admire the hard slog of domestic life for women on small farms in the bush.

Cambridge became the wife of an English Anglican parson and, after a few 'clerical' works published in England, spent thirty years supplementing his stipend by writing forty or so novels and three books of verse as he tended to parishes in Victoria. Many of her books appealed to Australian readers for their views of English society, but many also set those views in implicitly critical Australian settings. She wrote an autobiography, *Thirty Years in Australia* (1903), aimed at attracting readers in England, where much of her fiction was published in popular 'colonial' editions. Her first Australian book was *Up the Murray* (1875), followed by *Dinah* (1879–80) and *A Mere Chance* (1880). These were serialised in the *Australasian*, appearing in book form in both London and New York. Titles such as *A Girl's Ideal* (1882), *A Marriage Ceremony* (1884) and *A Little Minx* (1885) convey something of Cambridge's focus. Two well-regarded novels were *The Three Miss Kings* (1883) and *A Woman's Friendship* (1889). *Materfamilias* (1898) could really be set anywhere, but happens to be set in Melbourne, with visits to Sydney. It is a monologue memoir by a headstrong and highly-strung snobbish woman from England who ends up a grandmother in Australia. As a young married woman, she flirts with a sea captain with no sense of her inappropriate behaviour, and eventually marries this long-suffering man. Her social aspirations lead to a home next to bush, where she loses a child in a shooting accident. She almost loses another to his fall from a horse and despair that love for the family governess is thwarted by his mother. The son's fiancée is regarded as a social inferior but also with suspicion as a 'new woman' with a B.A. Sentimental set pieces are interposed among tales that show the more measured and practical lives of young Australians. The prose is hectic, in keeping with the personality of the narrator, and after some irritation, we begin to realise that the whole story is a Browning-like exercise in ironic dramatic monologue at the mother's expense.

Rosa Praed, though born on a squatter's station in Queensland, was paradoxically more of an English writer than Cambridge. She deployed the same set of colonial adventure tropes and wrote books of sketches (as in *Australian Life*, 1895), moving with her husband to London when she was twenty-five and circulating in literary society. *The Bond of Wedlock* (1887) pokes fun at artistic pretensions, reflecting her familiarity with bohemian life and people like Oscar Wilde. Praed examines the nature of true love, the social restraints on intelligent women, and the unjust strictures of a patriarchal legal system. Her polished literary style impresses, but the novel is set entirely in London, with a side trip to Paris. Recovery of her work for Australian study focuses on her depictions of station life, her feminist agenda, and her sympathetic attitude towards Aboriginal peoples. Married to someone elected to state parliament, she also conveys some of the political machinations in Queensland (in *Policy and Passion: A Novel of Australian Life*, 1881). Her books were published in London and usually subtitled to indicate their colonial content, as in *Fugitive Anne: A Romance of the Unexplored Bush* (1903). *An Australian Heroine* (1880), *The Head Station* (1885) and *The Romance of the Station* (1889) all declare their antipodean credentials, the last title tracking the life of a newly married woman from a genteel squatter estate as she braves the isolation, mosquitoes and rough conditions of her husband's new property on an island in tropical Queensland. The book abounds with descriptions of nature and details the social mix of colonial life: Chinese vegetable growers, tobacco-cadging Aboriginal people, recalcitrant housekeepers, lanky taciturn stockmen, the ex-squatter who is a wife beater and cattle thief, the man who 'marries up' on the strength of riches from gold mining and torments his more refined wife, and the hard slog of getting a bush house into order among the spiders, dogs, hens, goats, cows, storms, fires and general chaos of pioneering. The novel quotes Australian poems and refuses the romance ending of the unhappy wife regaining her true lover. Some of Praed's work incorporates elements of magic and the fantastic, reflecting her strong spiritualist beliefs.

The clash between church-going piety and agnostic free thinking becomes a regular trope of Australian nineteenth-century fiction, especially as it contrasts the 'bluestocking' independent woman with puritan evangelists or bourgeois convention. The sceptic advocating a higher morality is usually a younger woman of a more 'colonial' upbringing. Matching *Clara Morison* for its overlay of this trope onto the scorn of English gentry for those 'in trade' is work by 'Tasma' (Jessie Couvreur). Encouraged by the success of *Uncle Piper of Piper's Hill* (1889), she went on to write popular romances notable for their injections of philosophising and a host of literary references, accompanied by scattered French phrases. These traits were a show by someone with an informal education as a child in Hobart, and an indication of her Belgian origins and eventual place of residence. Also reflecting her own life, her books usually set up a woman faced with an inappropriate marriage, providing occasion for some debate about the morality of divorce or legally sanctioned torment.

Subtitled 'An Australian Novel', *Uncle Piper of Piper's Hill* is really 'Jane Austen does the colonies'. Its drama of class and colonial snobbery only happens to be set in a Melbourne that does not connect in any meaningful way with the family-centred plot. During the voyage of an emigrant ship, a clergyman falls for a beautiful but shallow young woman, overlooking her elder sister, who is a reader with practical skills and selfless concern for her fellows. The sisters are going to join their uncle, a merchant who has done well out of being a butcher. As a colonial visitor sees him, Uncle Piper is 'a man with a home like a West-End magnate and the intonation of a groom'. The girls' father is a ne'er-do-well English gentleman whose nobility has not kept him from falling into penury, and the uncle houses the family and hunts up a government position for the father. The minister's widowed mother had some years past emigrated and married the uncle, taking with her a daughter by her first marriage, and giving birth to another girl before dying. Uncle Piper is desperate to prevent a liaison between his horse-loving indulged son from a previous marriage and his free-thinking stepdaughter. How they all discover their connection, learn to adjust their personalities, prejudices and fortunes, and how the minister, sent to a country parish, finds the more appropriate elder sister as helpmeet are the key threads of the novel. Australia is present only as a space in which the social mores of England are thrown into confusion.

Another novel taking up the cause of women chafing under expectations of domestic servitude, marriage and ladylike restraint is *Kirkham's Find* (1897) by Mary Gaunt. The eldest daughter of an unhappily poor but genteel family becomes fed up with mockery of her plain features and poor marriage prospects. She escapes to a small farm near Warrnambool in Victoria, where she produces honey and becomes self-supporting by dint of hard work, rejecting snobbish attitudes. Her pretty sister marries money but is unhappy, the message being that if one must marry it should be for love between equals. The Kirkham of the title is initially besotted with the pretty sister, but poor. He leaves with his mate to prospect for gold in northern Australia, eventually returning to regular work near the elder sister's farm and, of course, realises that she is a more worthy companion. The book is a good guide to the struggles and rewards of farming a small holding. It provides lessons to the female reader in how to calculate costs and prices and make a living. The sections devoted to Kirkham allow for colonial adventure episodes (including an attack by wild 'blacks' and matter-of-fact reportage of violent reprisals) and depictions of the harsh conditions of outback mining.

Marcus Clarke had a quintessential colonial life. He was born and educated in London, but his lawyer father died leaving no money. Family who had held administrative positions in Western Australia and Victoria sent him off to seek his fortune in the antipodes. Clarke worked in a Melbourne bank, went up country to work on a sheep station, wrote for and edited magazines, and swung between fame and bankruptcy. He cultivated literary company in Melbourne, founding the Yorick Club, and wrote pieces for the popular theatre, finally gaining employment in Melbourne's Public Library. Clarke's first novel is *Long Odds* (1869). Set in England and turning on concealed marriages, dubious claims to the family estate, murder and rigged horse races, it reverses the trajectory of many colonial adventure plots by having the heroine rescued by a travelling squatter and carried off to a prosperous happy ending in Australia.

The *Age* newspaper sent Clarke to Tasmania to research the convict era, from which he assembled another tale of mismatched family fortunes and mapped them onto some of the more sensational elements of convict history. Serialised from 1870, *His Natural Life* appeared in book form in 1874, and in a revised edition as *For the Term of His Natural Life* in 1882. In it, Rufus Dawes (actually Richard Devine, illegitimate son of a lord) is shipped off to Van Diemen's Land as a murderer. He saves the transport vessel from a mutiny but is blamed as an instigator. Later, he escapes solitary confinement and leads a marooned group back to Hobart, but his tormentor and rival for the family fortune, Maurice Frere, claims credit and Dawes is sent to Port Arthur penal settlement. Sensational tales of rape, fatal floggings and cannibalism add to Dawes's misery, and a fellow convict escapes and returns to England to assume Dawes's real identity as Richard Devine. That man is exposed and turns out to be both the murderer of Dawes's father and Dawes's half-brother. He suffers a stroke as his punishment. Meanwhile, Dawes and a female companion escape on a ship but are drowned in a cyclone. This tragic denouement was unpalatable to many, and a second ending was produced in which the woman drowns but Dawes and her daughter survive, do well in the colony, and return to England. The novel has held its dramatic appeal for readers and has locked in the 'black legend' of harsh and often unjust treatment of convicts in Tasmania. An admirer of Balzac, Clarke also drew on Hugo's *Les Misérables* and firmed up a taste for documentary realism and naturalism in Australian fiction. Stage and film versions have kept the story in circulation, giving it similar influence as the pervasive Ned Kelly legend.

'Rolf Boldrewood' was the Walter Scott-inspired pen name of Thomas Alexander Browne, sometime squatter and then country magistrate in New South Wales. His days as a grazier were set out in *The Squatter's Dream*, published more descriptively as *Ups and Downs* in 1878. With the careers of Ned Kelly and other bushrangers concluded but still popular in legend, Boldrewood took up a friend's suggestion to write a bushranger romance. This he published as a serial in the *Sydney Mail* and then as a book in London in 1888. *Robbery Under Arms: A Story of Life and Adventure in the Bush and in the Goldfields of Australia* is the memoir of Dick Marston, written from prison. He records in colloquial Australian English how his free-spirited youth, love of a good horse, and discontent at the drudgery of farming led him to follow his father's bad example and start rustling beasts. His sweetheart and a school friend who becomes a shopkeeper keep trying to turn him to a steady, honest and Christian life, but minor misdemeanours become major crimes as Dick falls under the influence of Captain Starlight, charismatic gentleman bandit. Eventually a policeman is shot, and Dick is given a life sentence for highway robbery. He is released after twelve years, to be welcomed by his loyal friend and beloved. The text regularly laments the path Dick took and preaches virtue, but the lively language and the colourful adventures all exert a powerful pull on the reader. There are parallels with Ned Kelly's life plus some fanciful gothic effects, and we are reminded that the Kellys were high-spirited youths and the country still relished its freedom from Old World restraints. Starlight's Aboriginal sidekick, Warrigal, is an unruly sign of settler unease linked with the contradictory aspects of sublime nature. Boldrewood's other novels were *The Miner's Right* (1880) and *The Babes in the Bush* (1900).

Catherine Martin has not enjoyed the critical attention bestowed on Cambridge, Praed and Tasma, partly because much of her work remained in serial form, and partly owing to her writing about South Australia, which did not conform to the convicts and bushrangers mythos of the eastern states. Martin can be compared with Catherine Helen Spence in that they both emigrated at an early age from Scotland and earned a living writing for the papers and teaching. Martin spent time on sheep stations and at mines and, twenty years younger than Spence, has a less earnest approach to her material. She wrote poetry (including the 1874 long poem 'The Explorers', about Burke and Wills), stories and travel pieces, along with five novels. Her three best-known works are *An Australian Girl* (1890), *The Silent Sea* (1892) and a late book, *The Incredible Journey* (1923).

An Australian Girl falls into two parts. The first centres on a cultured young woman fighting free of marriage, especially resisting one devotee, the moneyed heir to sheep stations whose main interest in life is horses. There are many rhapsodic descriptions of Adelaide suburbs as bucolic idylls of orchards and gardens, of the silent expanse of mallee scrub and its tiny wildflowers, and of the northern plains and the civilising plantations around station homesteads. These scenes are accompanied by amusing repartee as our heroine fends off her lover. There is satire of the vulgar taste of the nouveau riche, and comic depictions of how the poor of Adelaide (usually cunning Irish) take advantage of the solemnly measured charity work of a Protestant ascendancy. The book is noteworthy for featuring the German population that settled north of Adelaide and for including a number of Aboriginal tales. Its second half is conventional romance plotting. Heroine Stella moves to Melbourne and visits family stations up country. Her suitor's sister, married to a wastrel English nobleman, desperately protects her position in colonial society, and misleads Stella about the half-German doctor she suddenly falls in love with, so that she capitulates to the brother's repeated entreaties to marry. The couple travel to Europe where (of course) Stella meets up with her true love and discovers the deception. She undergoes a nervous breakdown, is cured by attending church, and resolves to return home to found a number of small farms on which Adelaide's poor can work their way towards a better life. In the process we find a comic depiction of artistic attempts to mix Australian icons and classical motifs and an argument over the relative merits of naturalistic fiction and idealised romance, plus a number of claims for Australia being a nation rather than a colony.

Two novelists who achieved fame in London were Fergus Hume and Guy Boothby. Hume's *The Mystery of a Hansom Cab* (1886) pioneered the Anglophone detective novel genre (John Lang's earlier work being unknown for many years). It combines high society and the demi-monde of Melbourne in a melodrama of concealed identities and blackmail. The novel inspired a stage version successful in both Australia and London. Hume was in Australia for only three years, returning to London to write several lesser-known novels with Australian settings. Guy Boothby was born in Australia, but spent most of his life in England, becoming a celebrity on the basis of his fifty or so sensation novels, many featuring the magician and criminal mastermind Dr Nikola. Among those with Australian settings, his best-regarded work is *In Strange Company* (1894). Boothby also wrote an account of his travels: *On the Wallaby: or, Through the East and Across Australia* (1894).

If the late nineteenth century in Australian literature can be characterised by simple generalisations, its features were adventure romance novels, 'bush' ballads, and the short story, also mainly centred on rural work. That said, Australia was totally reliant on shipping, and ships increasingly island hopped across the Pacific to either land in North America or work around South America and up to Europe. One writer who represented this maritime world was Louis Becke. He worked as a 'supercargo' (storekeeper and accountant) on trading vessels plying the Pacific islands. Like Robert Louis Stevenson's island stories, Becke's became hugely popular, in particular his 1894 collection *By Reef and Palm*. He recounted tales of lonely plantation managers, unscrupulous 'recruiters' of island labour for Queensland's sugar industry, sharp deals and native cunning. His work was prized for its 'tough' depiction of reality delivered in matter-of-fact, if ironic, manner.

Francis Adams, by contrast, declared that the definitive figure of Australian life was the bushman. His journalism in Queensland supported socialist equality for workers and an Australian republic, and he published essays, poems, stories and a couple of novels. His collection *Australian Life* (1892) depicts both the green coastlands of eastern Australia and adventures in the dry outback. The other aspect of Australia's popular image was addressed by 'Price Warung' (William Astley) in *Tales of the Convict System* (also 1892). Like Adams, Astley was a left-leaning journalist who contributed to the *Bulletin*. Based on historical research, he drew on convict folklore (such as secret cabals among 'lags' that included lotteries to kill each other to escape endless torment), shaping it into short narratives with a view to inciting popular outrage against the colonial regime. Cold factual documentary gives way to the inflated language of official bureaucracy and epic literature. Set against what is being recorded (murders, floggings, hangings) this generates heavy irony, pointing to the heartless violence behind a 'System' theoretically designed to rehabilitate its subjects.

Across the nineteenth century, newspapers and magazines published many hundreds of short stories. Most of them were simple 'yarns' reflecting readers' experiences back to them by way of comedy or melodrama, and having done their work, they disappeared. Archival research has recovered bodies of work that provide an unusual slant on the times and/or show enough literary talent to warrant inclusion in the national canon.

One of these recovered authors is Mary Fortune. Under several noms de plume, mainly 'Waif Wander', Fortune provided a woman's view of goldfields Victoria and colonial life, wrote poetry, a serialised novel or two, and over 500 stories, mainly for the *Australian Journal,* and mostly to do with crime. A selection appeared in 1871 as *The Detective's Album,* in which Mark Sinclair reviews some of his cases. This work is credited with being the first police procedural by a woman anywhere in the world.

Ernest Favenc's collection indicates the popularity of the crime story in its title: *My Only Murder* (1899). Favenc, however, was more inclined to humour, as in 'The Parson's Blackboy' in which a zealous evangelist pushes into the interior, but when he expostulates against bushmen cohabiting with Aboriginal women, he is laughed at. Later he discovers that a squatter has supplied him with an Aboriginal guide who is a woman in disguise. This tale appears in *The Last of Six: Tales of the Austral Tropics* (1894). Something of an explorer himself, Favenc published a history of Australian exploration, as well as a children's fantasy adventure novel, *The Secret of the Australian Desert* (1890).

Of this period, two story writers stand out for the longevity of their influence: Henry Lawson and 'Steele Rudd', the one for his 'bush realism', the other for his comic tales of misadventure among a yokel family of small-holding farmers. 'Rudd' (Arthur Hoey Davis) began sending his stories to the *Bulletin* in 1895 and a collection, *On Our Selection,* was published in 1899. Central characters Dad and Dave gave their name to a later radio serial. Latterly, the tales were received as mocking uneducated country bumpkins, but originally any humour was a desperate cover for despair at the hopeless poverty of the selector. Regular failures of wheat crops, fires destroying fences, and relentless manual labour leave the family surviving on pumpkins and debt. Humour sometimes rests on their self-defeating attempts to break out of penury by rat cunning and bush lawyer tricks. The stories also prompted movie and stage versions.

By far the most important story writer, though, is Lawson. His work remains in print and has garnered much critical analysis, on the one hand for his realistic counter to the rollicking celebrations of rural living, and on the other for the carefully managed ironic structure and sardonic tone that holds sentimental pathos at bay, leaving stoic endurance and tragic defeat to resonate behind the stories. Lawson also has the appeal of the creative genius not justly appreciated until he had died penniless (though biographers since have reassessed him as a drunken wife beater).

Raised around the goldfields of western New South Wales and scrabbling together some schooling along the way, young Lawson accompanied his mother Louisa to Sydney when she separated from her husband. Appalled by the dreary conditions of urban workers and slum dwellers (who feature more in his poetry, save for some tearjerker stories featuring the hapless young Arvie Aspinall), he went 'walkabout' into the north of the state (around Bourke, a town proverbial as marking the beginning of the far outback), recording the drought and the wandering lives of men pushed into itinerant odd-jobbing and droving by the 1890s Depression. Claiming greater authenticity than the 'squatter romances', Lawson's demythologising realism became itself part of a national mythos centred on laconic men struggling against malignly indifferent nature.

Lawson continued to write until his death in 1922, and he included tales drawn from travel in New Zealand, but the bulk of his work centres on 1890s inland New South Wales. Apart from his many contributions to the *Bulletin*, his mother published his first collection, *Short Stories in Prose and Verse*, in 1894, after which his best-known title, *While the Billy Boils*, came out in 1896, followed by *On the Track and Over the Sliprails* in 1900, and

Joe Wilson and His Mates in 1901. Angus & Robertson published these three titles, the last also appearing with Blackwood and Sons in Edinburgh.

There is a popular image of Lawson as the celebrator of mateship and unionism, but his stories debunk the ideal, men taking advantage of each other and being largely indifferent to the fate of others except as material for a good yarn. This is evident in 'The Union Buries Its Dead' in which everyone expresses solidarity with the victim of a drowning accident on the grounds that he was 'a union man', but the narrator quietly shows that most are too interested in having a drink at the pub and no one takes the trouble to find out the identity of the dead man, who is rapidly forgotten. The story is typical of one strand of Lawson's fiction, which has a nameless narrator documenting a situation, setting up the possibility of an emotional response to it, and then stripping away any emotion in a deadpan terse comment suggesting a tired nihilism: 'it didn't matter much—nothing does'. 'Hungerford' is another example of Lawson's ironic technique. An action or statement is repeated, giving the impression of an accumulating tall story until that sense is undercut: 'At least I believe that's how it is, though the man who told me might have been a liar. Another man said he was a liar, but then *he* might have been a liar himself—a third person said he was one.' Anticlimax is the dominant quality in many tales.

The other forms Lawson uses are stories linked by their central characters: Mitchell, Steelman and Joe Wilson. Mitchell provides short monologues that usually call into question the authority with which he propounds his views on marriage, women, sex, and so on. Steelman is a wandering con artist who earns a crust by 'bludging' off others until his smooth talking is exposed. Joe Wilson narrates his life in a series of episodes, revealing his good intentions, weaknesses, scrabbling after economic success, and the ups and downs of his relationship with his constantly disappointed but loyal wife whose intelligence sustains the family. All of the stories demonstrate the uncertainty and hardship of bush life, in particular its draining effects on women, as in the famous story 'The Drover's Wife', much reworked by writers since.

Poetry

A picture of late nineteenth-century culture is found in Bertram Stevens's *The Golden Treasury of Australian Verse* (1909). It came out both with Angus & Robertson in Sydney and Macmillan in London. Eager to impress with the number of competent verses emanating from the colonies, Stevens included New Zealanders and a total of seventy-two authors. He notes their parentage (Irish, Scots, English, with one German and a Scandinavian), emphasises their mainly English education, and lists their professions (lots of periodical editors, teachers and journalists, plus a few lawyers). Emphasising a distinctive colonial flavour, Stevens includes much of the balladry and 'wattle blossom verse' that subsequent anthologies downplay. However, comparison with later anthologies shows that already a national canon is forming: Adam Lindsay Gordon, Henry Lawson and 'Banjo' Paterson as popular balladists; Charles Harpur, Henry Kendall, Mary Gilmore, Bernard O'Dowd, Christopher Brennan, John Shaw Neilson and Hugh McCrae as literary poets. Two pieces worthy of note are James Lister Cuthbertson's atmospheric evocation of nature 'At Cape Schanck', and George Essex Evans's ballad 'The Women of the West', honouring those who left the comforts of town for 'the everlasting sameness of the never-ending plains'.

Harpur had written much of his poetry by 1860 but followed up with *A Poet's Home* (1862) and a long philosophical/aesthetic discussion in verse, *The Tower of the Dream* (1865). A selected works came out in 1883. His reputation was preserved mainly within Australia, unlike his contemporary, Adam Lindsay Gordon. Not Australian-born, Gordon was widely admired for his manly verse about horse riding based on his own prowess as a mounted policeman and steeplechaser. He published *The Feud* (1864), *Sea Spray and Smoke Drift* (1867) and *Bush Ballads and Galloping Rhymes* (1870). His eventual attainment of a memorial in Poets' Corner of Westminster Abbey was taken as a marker of the 'arrival' of Australian poetry in the Anglosphere. However, there is very little that is Australian about his verses. Modelled on Walter Scott's ballads with a bit of Browning and Shelley added, most of Gordon's work is set in Britain or loaded with Greek and Latin references. In Australian literary history, he is important for two things: one, his much-anthologised poem 'The Sick Stockrider', which *does* capture the voice and life of the stoic bush worker, and two, the introduction to his verse by Marcus Clarke. In this, Clarke declares that there is a poetry in Australia different from other English verse, characterised by a note of 'weird melancholy' that he attributes to the 'grotesque or ghostly' natural phenomena in the antipodes: 'our trees without shade, our flowers without perfume, our birds who cannot fly, and our beasts who have not yet learned to walk on all fours'. Nonetheless, the Australian poet responds to a strange, sometimes minatory charm and becomes 'familiar with the beauty of loneliness'.

Like Harpur, Henry Kendall was born in Australia. He lived in the forested lands of the east coast. His *Poems and Songs* (1862), *Leaves from Australian Forests* (1870) and *Songs from the Mountains* (1880) carry a load of 'poetical' diction and some weight of European influence and religiosity, but attend closely to the details and sometimes the music of the bush. Though he was a competent horseman, he avoided the 'galloping rhymes' of the bush balladist, following Harpur's example of trying to be a 'serious' poet. Kendall mixed with the literati of Sydney, moved for a while to Melbourne where he knew Marcus Clarke and Adam Lindsay Gordon, and struggled to make a living that would allow him to write. His verse still mentions daffodils, but also unashamedly uses Aboriginal place names. Kendall dramatises the life of a wild dog ('The Warrigal'), refers to Australia's seasons ('The Austral Months' and in 'Mooni', 'yellow-haired September / ... / When the ridge is burnt to ember' and summer's winds that may 'hiss with heat'), and is perhaps the first poet to mention spinifex ('Christmas Creek'). There is a tendency to colour the bush in gothic hues, but also an assertion that Australian nature can be as attractive to the soul as any English dell or mount. His most remembered poem is 'Bell-Birds'. It falls under the influence of the Romantics but Kendall, in keeping with many writers' encounters with the 'empty' expanses of Australian nature, reveals an undercurrent of struggle between adherence to conventional Christianity, celebration of the natural world as a liberating vital 'bible', and dismay at the bleak existentialism implicit in the vastness of the land.

That land was a harsh one for many. The one poem of Barcroft Boake's that is regularly anthologised is 'Where the Dead Men Lie', from a collection with the same title (1897). It is a threnody for the solitary bushman succumbing to drought or accident 'out in the wastes of the Never-never', though it concludes with two stanzas (often expunged by editors) damning the absentee pastoralist boss who carelessly profits from the suffering of his stockmen. One thing that impresses the reader distanced from these poems in time is the strong sense of nostalgia and fatalism. Despite the gaiety of roaming about with one's mates and achieving daring feats of physical agility, poems regularly record disappointment in love, exile from 'home', and longing for the 'good old days'. There is a sense of age and death waiting just around the corner for men with no internal resources other than respect for a tough land. Will Ogilvie's *Fair Girls and Gray Horses* (1898) epitomises the bush ballad: alternating four and three-stressed iambic quatrains (horse-riding verses employing the 'galloping' anapaest) loaded with sentimentality or celebration of pastoral occupations. He writes of the lost droving mate, buried 'where the brumbies come to water at the setting of the sun' and laments the futile struggle against the odds of the small-scale grain farmer:

> I stand by your fenceless gardens
> And weep for the splintered staves;
> I watch by your empty ingles
> And mourn by your white-railed graves

Barcroft Boake, Gordon, and Francis Adams all committed suicide, contributing to the sense that pursuing a literary career in Australia was asking for trouble. Lawson advised young poets to either head for England or shoot themselves!

In so far as gloom is a dominant tone beneath the surfaces of the ballad, the works of Henry Lawson and 'Banjo' Paterson stand out. Lawson pushes into political rage; Paterson skilfully assembles more cheerful material. Lawson certainly celebrated the life of bush workers (as in the rollicking poem-song 'The Shearer's Dream' in which the shearing shed is full of girl shearers, or the more dignified tribute to the sheer toil of the bullock driver and his beasts in 'The Teams'), but more often concentrated on the hardship of walking through the drought-stricken countryside in search of work ('Out Back') or the emotional strain for families when husbands and sons leave to earn a living droving ('Andy's Gone with Cattle'). He satirises the urban poet who romanticises the bush. 'The City Bushman' was read as a dig at 'Banjo' Paterson, including lines such as: 'Droving songs are very pretty, but they merit little thanks / From the people of a country in possession of the banks'.

As the reference to the banks suggests, there was a political dimension to Lawson's verse. He penned 'A Song of the Republic', setting up a binary between 'The Old Dead Tree and the Young Tree Green' but found in the latter the seeds of corruption, especially when it came to city life. 'Faces in the Street' and 'Second Class Wait Here' describe the grinding poverty of and discrimination against the poor, and 'Women of the Town' dares to mention sympathetically the street prostitute. Whether in the bush or in the city, distinctions of class and wealth are subjected to revolutionary attack, much of it poetic bluster, but carrying a certain sharp frustration, as in 'Freedom on the Wallaby' ('Our fathers toiled for bitter bread / While idlers thrived beside them', so 'the tyrants ... // ... needn't say the fault is ours / If blood should stain the wattle'). Key poetry titles were *In the Days When the World Was Wide* (1896), *When I Was King* (1905), *The Skyline Riders* (1910) and *For Australia* (1914). Lawson stooped to some jingoistic poems during the First World War, and with only one or two exceptions, his best verse is among his earliest.

Lawson was more popular as a poet during his lifetime, and some can still sing his 'Andy's Gone with Cattle', but it is Paterson's poetry that will be quoted today, usually lines from 'Clancy of the Overflow' and occasionally all thirteen verses of 'The Man from Snowy River'. Paterson also had a role in creating 'Waltzing Matilda', the unofficial national anthem. The title is an idiom meaning wandering through the bush with a bedroll ('swag') on your back, and the song tells of a swagman who steals a sheep to eat, is confronted by mounted police, and defies them by drowning himself in a waterhole. It has been taken as typifying supposed national traits of mocking authority and sympathy for the underdog. Paterson's ballads accord with what Lawson titled *Short Stories in Prose and Verse*—they have a narrative core, usually centred on a small cast of characters and a situation giving rise to dramatic and sometimes comic climaxes, as when a bush child is to be baptised by a rarely seen priest, thinks it is some kind of punishment, runs off, and is 'blessed' with a spray of thrown whiskey ('A Bush Christening'). In another poem a 'bushie' comes to town and goes to the barber; the local youth play a joke on him by starting his shave with a heated razor. Thinking his throat is cut, the hulk of a man proceeds to flatten everyone before he dies, and the smart set never toy with a bushman again ('The Man from Ironbark'). 'Clancy of the Overflow' (the term referring to floodplains in southwest Queensland) cements a trope in the walls of Australian verse: the tired worker in a dingy city office dreaming of the wandering freedom of the drover: 'As the stock are slowly stringing, Clancy rides behind them singing, / ... / And he sees the vision splendid of the sunlit plains extended, / And at night the wond'rous glory of the everlasting stars.'

'The Man from Snowy River' is perhaps the only poem in the country to inspire a political dispute today. Feral herds of horses (brumbies) now cause environmental damage in the high country south of Canberra, but Paterson's drama of herding them keeps some folk stridently proclaiming national heritage and opposing 'greenies' who would cull the herds. Deploying Paterson's ability to mix strict metrical form with run-on lines, the poem creates a headlong rush of narrative in which a young man races to prevent a valuable thoroughbred colt from escaping to the mountains with a wild herd. We begin with a Homeric catalogue of heroes and their attributes and are plunged into the values of horsemanship that were central to Australian life and the economy. The poem also plugs into a national sympathy for the underdog and natural talent by having a wiry local lad succeed where older and more experienced squatters and drovers cannot.

Paterson had the advantage of being a horseman who grew up on country pastoral holdings, so he knew the realities of what he wrote about, even if he presented them in a generally positive glow. Though he did take up a city career in law and then editing, he also went on hunting trips to the Northern Territory and served as a war correspondent in three campaigns. His poetry spread from the instant hit of *The Man from Snowy River* in 1895 through to 1917 (*Saltbush Bill, J.P., and Other Verses*), and he also wrote stories, a couple of novels and a book for children, *The Animals that Noah Forgot* (1933). His folkloric collection *Old Bush Songs* (1905) perpetuated the increasingly retrospective outlook of bush ballad romance.

Like many Australians of poetical bent, Victor Daley supported his poetry writing by working as a journalist. He exercised some influence as a founding member of Melbourne's Dawn and Dusk club and his work was important for showing that not all Australian verse had to be about horse riding or gum trees. Daley's imagination stayed fixed on his Irish roots and a romantic colouring akin to the Pre-Raphaelites. Typical titles are 'Dreams' (his most anthologised poem), 'To My Soul', and 'Blanchelys'. As 'Creeve Roe', he produced lively social satire and his 'When London Calls' is a sharp critique of the British Empire's impact on the colonial writer:

> The garden of the earth is wide;
> Its rarest blooms she picks
> To deck her board, this haggard-eyed
> Imperatrix. ...
> And when the Poet's lays grow bland
> And urbanised and prim—
> She stretches forth a jewelled hand
> And strangles him.

His collections were *At Dawn and Dusk* (1898), *Poems* (1908) and a selected edition, *Wine and Roses* (1911). Despite inspiring a critical monograph by A.G. Stephens, Daley's work has not appealed to later readers.

Many other poets have also dropped out of anthologies as modern taste rejects the overblown poeticisms, sentimentalities and religiosities of Victorian times. James Brunton Stephens, for example, was highly regarded for comic bush verse and patriotic declamatory poems extolling Queensland and Australia. The former retail racist attitudes towards Chinese and Aboriginal peoples and the latter sound pompous today. His major collections are *Convict*

Once (1871/1885) and *An Australian National Anthem* (1889). Sydney clergyman, politician and social reformer John Dunmore Lang published *Poems, Sacred and Secular* in 1872, and George French Angas, a painter who spent time in South Australia, added to another genre in Australian and British verse, the shipwreck poem (*The Wreck of the Admella*, 1874). In *Songs of the Army of the Night* (1888), Francis Adams amplified the revolutionary rhetoric of Lawson's poems, and 'Ironbark' (G.H. Gibson) added to the horde of bush balladry with work like *Southerly Busters* (1878) and *Ironbark Chips and Stockwhip Cracks* (1893).

Two women whose work has survived into modern anthologies are Mary Hannay Foott and Ada Cambridge. Foott survives largely because of the title poem in her collection *Where the Pelican Builds* (1885). The phrase refers to the far outback and the poem is a restrained lament for men who head west with high hopes but never return. Foott gives the ballad form the softer atmospherics of wind, sunset and melancholy, though 'The Future of Australia' is an upbeat vision of a golden land of plenty and freedom. Her other work is devotional and historical (centred on Europe); though she celebrates emergent nations, she remains dutiful to Britannia. Cambridge's verse is overshadowed by her novels but works the same theme of women resisting the 'yoke of servitude' that marriage entails. As 'An Answer' has it, 'Thy love I am. Thy wife I cannot be' (*Unspoken Thoughts*, 1887).

John Le Gay Brereton and Christopher Brennan were Australian born and both taught at Sydney University. Together they took verse away from the pallid nature lyric or the bouncy ballad. Brereton published *The Song of Brotherhood* in 1896, and *Sweetheart Mine: Lyrics of Love and Friendship* a year later. The latter indicates his lighter side, but many lyrical poems extend from love to invocations of the muse and philosophising about life, occasionally showing a modern stance of wry self-deprecation. He wrote a number of tributes to the South African novelist Olive Schreiner, as well as a tribute to Australian flora, 'The Eucalyptides'. Both Brereton and Brennan continued writing into the next century. The latter's first collection, *XXI Poems*, came out in 1897, but his influence and major work connected more to the next century, so is outlined in the next chapter.

DRAMA

Theatre had to appeal to the general public to make enough money to survive, so melodramas given some exotic colour remained the staple. Charles Whitehead, for example, created *The Spanish Marriage* in 1859 and William Forster staged *The Weirwolf* in 1876. Charles Harpur followed the most common Australian topic for theatre when he converted a long poem into *The Bushrangers, a Play in Five Acts* in 1853. Set around Richmond and Windsor west of Sydney, it features types with names like Wealthiman Woolsack, Filch and Stalwart. They use words like 'Zounds!' and 'Gadsblood!' or are bumbling oafs spilling malapropisms everywhere. Lengthy 'Shakespearean' speeches are interspersed with a lot of rushing to and fro as police and bushrangers shoot at each other.

Richard Henry (or Hengist) Horne had established his reputation as a writer in London, earning the sobriquet 'Orion Horne' on the basis of his popular poem of 1843. He arrived in Australia in 1852 to seek his fortune on the goldfields. Failing to strike it rich, he occupied several government positions and wrote a verse drama *Prometheus: The Fire-Bringer* (1864). In 1866, Horne was commissioned to write a theatre piece for the opening of the Intercolonial Exhibition of Australasia in Melbourne. *The South Sea Sisters* extolled the wealth of New Zealand and the six Australian colonies and was a masque oratorio of 300 singers and instrumentalists, its major success being a 'Corroboree Chorus' emulating Aboriginal song and dance. Horne also wrote verse ('Australian Explorers', 'The Blue Mountain Exile'), a novel (*Rebel Convicts*, 1858), and a guide to would-be settlers, *Australian Facts and Prospects* (1859).

Born in Hobart to a soldier who built up a small publishing house, Garnet Walch studied in England and Germany and returned to Sydney and Melbourne, where he wrote pantomimes, melodramas and vaudeville shows, including the jaunty *Australia Felix, or Harlequin, Jackass and the Magic Bat* (1873). Many plays were adaptations of popular standards (*Sinbad the Sailor*, *Beauty and the Beast*) but he devised a successful stage version of *Robbery Under Arms* (1890), and wrote *The Miner's Right* (1891) and the popular *Marvellous Melbourne* (1886) in which a gormless English 'new chum' is given a tour of the city and its colourful types by a con man.

In 1874, American actor James Cassius Williamson arrived in Australia. This event was important not for the man's acting skills but his entrepreneurial ability. J.C. Williamson became the nation's major theatrical agency and producer for the next two centuries, bringing international shows to Australia and sponsoring the careers of Australian actors and playwrights, generally at the popular end of the theatrical spectrum.

Children's Literature

Given the small number of children in Australian colonies (and the fact that many had only a rudimentary schooling and were working on farms from an early age), any writing for younger readers had to emanate from Britain and usually took the form of the colonial adventure romance with juvenile protagonists instead of adults. Typical of this genre are works by two English sojourners in the colonies, William Howitt and Richard Rowe. Howitt spent two years around the goldfields and returned home to publish a string of books including a history of Australian exploration and a travelogue, *Land, Labour and Gold* (1855). His best-known book for children is *A Boy's Adventures in the Wilds of Australia* (1854). Rowe spent five years around Sydney and produced *The Boy in the Bush* (1869) in which a couple of youths deal with snakes, bushrangers and children lost in the bush. They mock the 'new chum' Englishman and record attitudes of the time to Chinese and Aboriginal peoples, admiring the latter for their skill with horses.

A radical twist to the colonial novel for children came from Ethel Turner. She emigrated with her mother to Sydney as a child. After editing a high school magazine with her sister Lilian, the two went on to edit a monthly magazine that ran for three years. Turner wrote one of the most lasting favourites of Australian children's novels, *Seven Little Australians*. The book appeared in London with children's fiction publisher Ward Lock in 1894, and with one eye on the British reader, it included exotic scenes of cattle herding on a squatter's station plus sentimental standards (tuberculosis and death among children). However, the book's centre is family life and it begins with a warning: there will be no perfect children and no token naughtiness to enable the pointing of a moral (one chapter is titled 'Virtue not always rewarded'). A lack of pious idealism is excused on the basis of realism and a claim that the outdoors and sunshine of Australia provide greater opportunity for youthful freedom of spirit. Turner's seven characters range from a teenager to a baby and show all the traits of knockabout enthusiasm, romantic notions, love of food, propensity to tell fibs, and so on. Their father is a military man and stern disciplinarian, but he has remarried. His new wife is only twenty and unable to handle his six offspring and her own infant. The house is called Misrule and each chapter is a comic adventure in which the father is usually obliged to give way to the accidents and ploys of his children. Despite the entertaining irregularities of the household, a tragic end is meted out to the most energetic and assertive girl.

If plucky scions of British stock braving the colonial frontier provided the stuff of one genre, the adventures of girls in English boarding schools was another staple of juvenile fiction. Louise Mack gave an antipodean slant to this with her novel *Teens: A Story of Girl Life in Australia* (1897), published in both London and Sydney. Partly autobiographical, the book centres on a city day school and the different family backgrounds of Lenny and Mabel. In sequels, Lenny heads off to England to study art, and Mack herself travelled to write adult romances and work in different countries as a journalist. Much of her work centres on the Australian girl as livelier and less bound by convention than her British counterparts.

In 1899, Ethel Pedley gave an Australian colouring to another convention of children's literature: the talking animal. Published in Sydney by Angus & Robertson, *Dot and the Kangaroo* begins with a prophetic dedication:

> To the children of Australia in the hope of enlisting their sympathies for the many beautiful, amiable, and frolicsome creatures of their fair land, whose extinction, through ruthless destruction, is being surely accomplished.

Extinction was likely then as it is today because of a settler value system of materialist utility. The adage characterising its application to the natural world was, 'If it moves, shoot it; if it doesn't, chop it down.' Native animals were regarded by many settlers as pests that competed with sheep and cattle for grass and ate grain crops and vegetables. Getting children to revalue them as cuddly and cute equivalents to Peter Rabbit or Pooh Bear was a serious attempt to change culture.

Pedley begins with a standard colonial trope: the child lost in the bush. Little Dot eats some berries and discovers that she can understand the talk of animals. A kangaroo provides her with an animal view of humans as poor creatures unsuited to the bush. Dot gets a ride to a waterhole in her pouch, is saved from a snake by a kookaburra, interviews a knowledgeable but irritable platypus who sings a song about dinosaurs, and peeps at a nighttime corroboree. When she says how fearsome the Aboriginal tribesmen look, the kangaroo says they are no different from white folk—all humans kill kangaroos. Dot and her friend escape hunters and their dogs, meet with a range of birds, and in the end, a willie wagtail directs them back to her family's farm, and her father promises not to shoot kangaroos ever again.

Less of an Alice-in-Wonderland fantasy, and more of an ethnographic salvage operation, K. Langloh Parker collected stories from the Aboriginal people working on her husband's cattle station in northern New South Wales. In the mode of Kipling's *Just So Stories*, she converts traditional lore into children's 'fairy tales' about how animals came to be what they are. Though *Australian Legendary Tales: Folk-Lore of the Noongahburrahs as Told to the Piccaninnies* (1896) promulgates the myth that the tribes would die out and uses some patronising colonial language ('piccaninnies' being a 'pidgin' word for Aboriginal children), the writer does show respect for the people and their culture and includes both an appendix with a story in its original language and an extensive glossary of Noongahburrah words.

CHAPTER 3

Commonwealth to Collapse
1901–1930

SOCIAL AND POLITICAL CONTEXT

By 1901, all colonies had agreed to federate as states with individual parliaments operating under a national court and parliament. Districts of roughly equal voting numbers elected representatives to a lower house relaying decisions to a Senate of elected members proportionate to the population of each state. The British monarch remained head of state, each state having a governor, and the nation, a governor-general. The federal parliament met initially in Melbourne and passed a constitution that gave votes to women but failed to recognise the Aboriginal population as citizens, keeping them under the 'protection' of white governments. The settler population (still mostly Anglo-Celtic) sought to keep out cheap labour, and an Immigration Restriction Act instituted what was commonly labelled the 'White Australia Policy'. Prime Minister Edmund Barton resigned in 1902, and Alfred Deakin became the prime minister leading Australia into nationhood.

In the first decade of federation, telegraph cables were laid to South Africa and Canada, Australia took over administering part of New Guinea from Britain, a basic wage was legislated for all workers, and the Murrumbidgee Irrigation Area was set up, using river water to develop farms in the dry lands between South Australia and the Great Dividing Range in the east. Frederick Drake-Brockman completed the age of exploration by moving through the Kimberley region, where he built a dynasty of pastoralists, members of which played a significant role in literature and art in Western Australia. Herbert Hoover, later US president, travelled to the goldfields of Western Australia and co-founded what became Conzinc Rio Tinto, a major Australian mining company. Among the many infrastructure projects, Western Australia completed its 1,116-mile-long rabbit-proof fence to exclude the introduced species that would become a major pest elsewhere in the nation. William Farrar produced a strain of wheat adapted to Australian soils and resistant to disease. Five years later, the Pacific Phosphate Company shipped guano deposits on Pacific islands to Australia. The superphosphate manufactured from this enabled expansion of grain farming in the depleted soils of Australia's ancient geology.

Scientific and technological advances were prized, including the exploration of Antarctica and the establishment of a research station on Macquarie Island by Douglas Mawson in 1911. Pedal-powered wireless radio enabled provision of news, schooling and medical aid to settlers in remote parts of the continent. The Commonwealth Bank was founded in 1912 and a national postal service replaced the separate colonial ones. Australia created its own navy and military training college.

In 1914, Britain declared war on Germany and, as a land still tied politically and culturally to 'the mother country', Australia found itself immediately involved. HMAS *Sydney* sank the German cruiser *Emden* and the Australian army took possession of German New Guinea. Answering propaganda about 'the Hun' slaughtering babies in Belgium and hankering after foreign travel and escape from the monotony of farming life, young men 'joined up' in droves. Australian and New Zealand troops were sent to Egypt to combat the Ottoman Empire, which had sided with Germany. The desert campaign around Beersheba won fame for the Australian Light Horse cavalry. England sent colonial troops to take Turkish territory at the straits of the Dardanelles. This was intended to keep shipping lanes open for Russia and the Allies. In a serious miscalculation, men were landed at Gallipoli on 25 April 1915. They were on a narrow beach facing steep cliffs on the top of which were Turks with machine guns. The series of battles to take ground ended in complete withdrawal but created a legend that lives on in Australian politics and culture today. The landing date is a public holiday called Anzac Day ('Australian and New Zealand Army Corps') when veterans from all wars march and memorial services are held. Gallipoli founded a myth of national heroism based on the 'moral victory' of stoic endurance in the line of duty into which was folded a reputation for irreverent pragmatism and mateship. Many claim that Australia discovered itself as a nation during this campaign: people from all the former colonies, including some Aboriginal troops, fought side by side under an Australian flag. When they were sent on to fight in the trenches of France, Australians again experienced the folly of an aristocratic British command and eventually got to fight with more success and less antagonism under their own leader, General John Monash.

The war had a number of effects on Australia. Loss of a massive proportion of the male population and the return of traumatised veterans created a kind of social trauma and public mourning. Soldier statues and memorials to the dead were erected in small towns across the land and a Returned and Services League set up RSL clubs across the country and operated as a conservative political force for many years. Wartime emergency regulations split the country into Empire jingoists and an assortment of opposing groups (workers who were persecuted for striking, women who wanted peace, Irish-Australians who saw the war as an English problem, German-Australians who were interned). Prime Minister 'Billy' Hughes twice failed to get public approval for conscription, a symptom of continuing mistrust of central government control and of refusal to be coerced into imperial ventures. Australia gained status when it participated in the Paris Peace Conference and signed up with the League of Nations as its own country rather than a colony of the Empire. Equality with Britain as a dominion state was confirmed by the Balfour Declaration of 1926.

National development of infrastructure spread to international networking. Early radio links with Britain were set up, Ross and Keith Smith made the first direct flight from England to Darwin, and the Queensland and Northern Territory Air Service started up in 1920 and eventually developed into the national air carrier Qantas. Links between the coast and the continental heartland were consolidated with the opening of a rail line to Alice Springs in

1929 and the earlier founding of the Royal Flying Doctor Service. The unification of the nation was signalled in the opening of Parliament House in Canberra in 1927. The war also prompted industrialisation, Broken Hill Proprietary opening a steelworks in Newcastle in 1915. The Commonwealth Oil Refineries opened in 1920. Mining was boosted with the opening of Queensland's Mount Isa mine in 1924. A year later, Victorian brown coal deposits were used to generate electricity. All this had an impact on the home: local production of refrigerators began and Vegemite, the iconic national salt-yeast sandwich spread, was invented. In 1926, the Council for Scientific and Industrial Research (CSIR, later CSIRO) was inaugurated. To make up the loss of workers and fill the emerging factories, the 1922 Empire Settlement Act assisted migration for 300,000 British citizens. Rural farming was expanded by land grants to returned soldiers, though these were not always large or fertile enough for them to succeed.

Post-war growth was not without its challenges. Australia lost more of its population during the global epidemic of 'Spanish' influenza, and the twenties were a time of heatwaves and drought. Ecological disasters owing to introduced species became apparent with an infestation of prickly pear across Queensland. Politically, the Russian Revolution and the growth of an industrial as well as rural proletariat led to the foundation of the Australian Communist Party in 1920. The Country Party representing squatter interests started in the same year, along with small groups of right-wing militia in cities. Strikes escalated and the Australian Council of Trade Unions (ACTU) was formed as a 'peak body' that could negotiate with government. In 1926, there was a massacre of Aboriginal people at Oombulgurri in northwest Australia, followed two years later by the Coniston massacre in Queensland. These events were frequently papered over in historical record, but increasingly the violence of 'frontier wars' came to public notice and David Unaipon and other Aboriginal Australians petitioned federal parliament for a separate Aboriginal state. As in many other countries, this internal restlessness was exacerbated by the 1929 New York Stock Exchange crash which began Australia's Great Depression.

CULTURAL CONTEXT

The novel in this period shifts ground from work about Australia by people who mainly came from and returned to England to work by people born in Australia who wrote about their birthplace. Generally, there was a shift from coming to terms with a new landscape to writing about how settlers toiled to make a living, how they interacted, and how they spoke. The Federation era is also marked by an increasing number of books published in Australia (the Lothian Publishing company was founded in 1905 and Melbourne University Press started up in 1922) and books were awarded prizes and reviewed within the country. In broad terms, we can think of this early national period as one of parodic romance and anti-romance realism.

Institutions of national cultural importance were founded post-Federation. Popular magazines such as *New Idea* (1902) catered for women, and the *Lone Hand* (1907) rivalled the ongoing influence of the *Bulletin*, the more satiric *Smith's Weekly* appearing in 1919. The newspaper cartoon strip 'Ginger Meggs' began in 1921, featuring a knockabout freckle-faced boy and his friends, who inhabited the back streets of a clearly recognisable Australian town and spoke in local slang. Australia's first public radio station opened in Sydney in 1923, and for a short time, the country led the world in making feature-length movies, *The Story of the Kelly Gang* screening in 1906, followed by *Robbery Under Arms* (1907) and *For the Term of His Natural Life* (1908). By 1926, however, Hoyts Theatres was building 'picture palaces' across the country to show films from Britain and the USA. At the same time, the outdoor culture of Australia was being consolidated. Surf life-saving—part public safety volunteer service and part sporting club, featuring bronzed young swimmers—was inaugurated at Bondi Beach in 1907. A year later, Australia had its first international wins at tennis (Davis Cup and Wimbledon) and Don Bradman scored 1,690 runs in the 1928–29 first-class season.

For those with more high-culture tastes, the Melbourne Symphony Orchestra was founded in 1906 and Sydney's Mitchell Library opened in 1910. The Commonwealth government established a Literature Fund in 1908 to provide small pensions for ageing writers. The sense of a burgeoning national literary culture was strengthened by Walter Murdoch's essay *The Enemies of Literature* (1907), Norman Lindsay's manifesto *Creative Effort* (1920) and Nettie Palmer's *Modern Australian Literature* (1924). C. Hartley Grattan published *Australian Literature* in 1929 to introduce this body of work to American readers. International attention also developed thanks to D.H. Lawrence's trip to Australia, which resulted in his novel *Kangaroo* (1923). For those who thought the former colonies lacked history or social conditions of interest, A.H. Adams published *The Australians* (1920) and Arthur Jose edited the *Australian Encyclopedia* (1925).

NON-FICTION

By Federation, most of the exploration of the physical features of the continent had been completed, but the human side of life in the centre and north was still unknown to most Australians. In 1904, W.B. Spencer and F.J. Gillen published an account of their travels and anthropological observations, *The Northern Tribes of Central Australia*, which, with its sequel, *The Arunta* (1927), generated considerable public interest in Aboriginal culture. In 1926, Jack McLaren's memoir, *My Crowded Solitude*, was published. McLaren had worked his way around the Pacific and Malaya as a miner, diver, plantation manager and beachcomber, and published thirty or so books of adventure fiction based on his experiences. His time developing a plantation on Cape York and his observations on Aboriginal life there made *My Crowded Solitude* a best-seller. It had Robinsonian appeal and has had lasting impact for its attention to ecological concerns. If the north of Australia was still a largely unfamiliar frontier, the far south was even more so. Douglas Mawson published his account of Antarctic exploration in 1915, *The Home of the Blizzard*. The book's appeal was boosted by Frank Hurley's dramatic photography.

A different memoir came from Paul Wenz. This is of interest because Wenz was French. He married an Australian and worked on pastoral stations, eventually buying his own. Most of his stories and novels are in French for French readers—as seen in his 1905 title, *À l'autre bout du monde* ('At the Other End of the World'). In English, he published *Diary of a New Chum* (1908). Much of his material is the same as other writers about station and bush life, but his non-Anglo perspective frees him from Empire attitudes and imparts a unique curiosity, irony and sympathy to his observations.

Born in Australia but educated in England, C.E.W. Bean returned to practise law, turned to journalism, and was given the job of reporting on New South Wales's wool industry. His travels and observations of people and farming along the Darling River were published as *On the Wool Track* (1910), which was much read as social history. Bean became Australia's official war correspondent during World War One and wrote a multi-volume history of the war later, but his book that was in every second home for generations was his edited compendium of poems, stories, journalism and artwork, *The Anzac Book* (1916).

Another popular book for many years was Mrs Aeneas Gunn's *We of the Never Never* (1908). The Never Never was a term for anywhere 'back of beyond', in this case an area on the Roper River in the Northern Territory where her husband was establishing a cattle station. Taken out of city gentility to join him in dust, heat and a house of logs and bark, Jeannie Gunn recounts her sometimes comic, sometimes despairing efforts to deal with solitude, a fractious Chinese cook, and a sizeable number of Aboriginal people camped by the homestead. It is an entertaining guide to the challenges of white settlement a long way from anywhere other than Aboriginal life to which the couple accommodate themselves while remaining alien from it.

Prose Fiction

The Federation period of fiction is conveniently marked off by Miles Franklin's *My Beautiful Career* (1901) and the complete edition of Henry Handel Richardson's trilogy, *The Fortunes of Richard Mahony* (1930). To these two classics of Australian literary history, we can add Joseph Furphy's *Such Is Life* (1903).

Franklin's debut work perhaps gained something from appearing when it did. Representing Australian life as both relaxedly civilised and coarsely labouring suited the mood of a newly formed nation, and sympathy for the intelligent woman of an artistic bent battling against both genteel convention and brute poverty was a trope well established thanks to Spence, Cambridge and Praed. The book opens with a letter to 'My dear fellow Australians': 'Just a few lines to tell you that this story is all about myself'. The writer admits to being egotistical and to finding 'my sphere in life ... not congenial': 'Better to be born a slave than a poet ... For a poet must be companionless—alone!' Sybylla Melvyn declares that there is no plot to her story because she has found no shape to people's lives and outrages her elders by voicing socialistic and atheistic views.

Sybylla's father was a 'swell' working on several squatters' properties. He married the daughter of one of his employers, 'a full-fledged aristocrat' from a genteelly rich family. The father decides to make his own fortune on a small holding near Goulburn, which the daughter finds 'flat, common and monotonous'. Family income dwindles and the father turns to drink. The embittered mother holds the family together but cannot tolerate her daughter's fretting after a better life with an outlet for her musical talent. Packed off to her grandmother's station, Sybylla fends off the attentions of suitors and plays games with the seemingly indifferent young owner of neighbouring estates. Her straightlaced Victorian grandmother will not condone her training as an actor and singer in Sydney and she is eventually obliged to repay her father's debt by serving as governess-housekeeper to a slatternly ignorant family whose only interest is making money. Eventually she escapes their squalor but refuses the offer of marriage from the young squatter who has in the interim lost his properties in the 1890s Depression, gone to the city, and made enough to buy them back. Though she feels that she loves him, she will not surrender her proud personality, berating herself for 'snarling and grumbling' but finding consolation in being 'a daughter of the Southern Cross, a child of the mighty bush ... a peasant, a part of the bone and muscle of my nation'.

There's a lot of windy rhetoric in this that at her best Sybylla is aware of. She does little work to build her nation other than write her self-absorbed lament. *My Brilliant Career* clearly sets up the question about Australia's future: squatter privilege or 'cocky' slaving at wheat and dairy farming (disregarding the alternative of city work). Fickle economic fortune is also contrasted to loss of wealth due to drink and weak character. From a later perspective, the hectic and sometimes hectoring tones of a sixteen-year-old egotist can become as irritating as they clearly are to Sybylla's unfortunate mother. However, refusal of the usual motifs of colonial fiction and a conventional romantic dénouement give the book a freshness. Sybylla's reading also shows that there is now a body of Australian literature being consumed alongside the British classics.

Appearing under the name of its narrating protagonist, Tom Collins, Joseph Furphy's *Such Is Life* follows the wanderings of bullock drivers, shearers and drovers around the Riverina district and north to Queensland. It owes a lot to the picaresque mode of Cervantes and its self-aware successor, Sterne's *Tristram Shandy*. Collins is a minor government functionary who prides himself on his wide reading and sage perceptions. He camps out with other itinerants, swapping yarns and philosophising about politics, human nature and whether mere chance or some kind of pattern governs us. The narrative progresses via digression. Declaring himself an honest 'chronicler' as opposed to an unreliable 'romancer', Collins despairs of the length and sometimes banality of a complete record of his travels, deciding instead to give us diary entries from the ninth day of each month (a promise broken in the final chapter). This structure seems to present a set of random events, though the network of itinerant labour, the narrator's self-delusions, and ironic fate produce a pattern of recurrences and reversals. Comic misadventures turn out to have tragic outcomes. Some of the tropes of colonial romance (the woman disguised to survive in a man's world, the child lost in the bush, rivalry between squatters and wandering bush workers) are retailed even as they are mocked and a host of texts from Europe are cited in order to present a democratic antipodean Christian stoicism. National ideals are critiqued (bush mateship consists of trying to outwit each other in sharp deals or backbiting gossip). Tongue-in-cheek irony is the governing attitude, evident in the opening phrase, 'Unemployed at last'. Collins's/Furphy's realism entails obscurely detailed transliterations of dialogue from Scots, Irish, Dutch, German and Chinese, reflecting an international fraternity of the bush that is riven with prejudice.

Henry Handel Richardson (Ethel Florence Lindesay Robertson) grew up in Victoria but went overseas to study music in Germany and then married an Englishman, living the rest of her life in Britain save for a visit home to research her major work. Her first novel, *Maurice Guest* (1908), depicts lovers' entanglements among English, Australian, German, Polish and American music students in Leipzig, linking debates about art with ideas about modern sexual relations and marriage. Also partly autobiographical, *The Getting of Wisdom* (1910) places a girl from a poor country family in an elite Melbourne boarding school. Laura's emotional and artistic temperament rubs against the dreary restraints of poor respectability, the cold rigour of a lady's schooling and the cruel gibes of her richer fellow students. Smarting under peer ridicule, she has to learn not to tell tall stories and not to form over-passionate friendships as ways of maintaining her self-esteem. Laura remains a free spirit, running into an undefined future when she leaves school.

The Fortunes of Richard Mahony is an epic saga based on Richardson's father's life. An Irish Protestant doctor of touchy rectitude and passive will finds himself ever more beset by misfortune as he tries storekeeping on the Victorian goldfields. His young wife learns to understand his personality and tries to control his capacity for falling prey to spongers and rogues. She organises him into medical practice in Ballarat, where a few squatters establish his reputation and investments provide sudden wealth. The family 'go home' to England and live among small-minded people envious of their wealth but disparaging of their colonial and Irish origins. Richard and Mary return to move in Melbourne society, the focus shifting to Mary's management of her extended circle of family and friends. She is not a feminist, accepting the need of ageing women for the security of marriage, but the book shows up male fecklessness, exploitation of daughters and wives, and undue dismissal of their intelligence. Finally, experiencing mental exhaustion and suffering financial ruin when stocks fall, Mahony ends up in an asylum, still supported by his long-suffering wife, who becomes a postmistress in a country town. There is an overall tragic pattern of interactions between Mahony's personality and a society that is permeated by flux. The latter part of the narrative gains some interest by being refracted through the eyes of Mary's child. *Mahony* appeared as a full epic volume in 1930, having been published in three books: *Australia Felix* (1917), *The Way Home* (1925) and *Ultima Thule* (1929). The work was well received in both England and North America, earned comparison to George Eliot's novels, and became a classic of Australian literature for its social panorama as well as its literary polish and psychological interest.

After the first flush of national blockbusters, the two most important writers of early Federation, continuing into the 1940s, were Vance Palmer and Katharine Susannah Prichard. Palmer and his wife Nettie were influential essayists, anthologisers, networkers and promoters of a national literary culture. Vance wrote for a living, turning out vast amounts of journalism, poetry, a few plays, and many stories and novels. His productivity relied on Nettie's income as a journalist, but his work was tied to the male-centred culture of the time, as indicated by his early books *The World of Men* (stories, 1915) and *The Man Hamilton* (a Queensland squatter novel, 1928). Palmer's best-known book from his early period is *The Passage* (1930). Set on the coast of Queensland, it depicts the life, physical and emotional, of Lew Calloway, who has a spiritual tie to the rhythms of wind and sea, earning his living as a fisherman. His father was killed by a shark and his mother wants better futures for her smarter children but is ready to leave the more stolid Lew to work for their well-being. She also disapproves of Lew's friendship with Clem, whose family have visited the Passage for years. Clem is flighty and citified and 'not for the likes of a Calloway'. The plot runs on how romance between Lew and Clem survives setback and interruption, but the book's strength is its lyrical evocation of the rhythms and colours of the sea and the harmony between fisherman and ocean. Palmer added a modern concern for the inner life to the realist depictions of labour while including attention to social issues such as tourist development threatening the peaceful life of the Passage.

Katharine Susannah Prichard was a Communist and her short stories and novels focus on the conditions of workers and the lot of women. She documented firsthand experience, adding in some romance and conflict to dramatise a situation and to integrate socialist polemic into the story. This model of politically engaged social realist fiction was taken up by others like Dymphna Cusack and Kylie Tennant. *The Pioneers* (1915) is set in the Gippsland district of Victoria where Prichard had worked as a governess. It utilises conventional romance elements such as escaped convicts and cattle stealing. By 1921, she had moved into more realistic depictions of rural labour, *Black Opal* dealing with the hardships of small-time miners and their attempts to resist the rise of mining companies. *Working Bullocks* (1926) shows Prichard's ability to dramatise the specific details of working life: here, the labour of tree felling and carting in the forests and sawmill towns of southwestern Australia. The by now traditional conflict between émigré English squatters and Aussie workers supplies a frame in which a Lawrentian romance between an inarticulate bullock driver and a 'daughter of nature' undergoes trials, including fatal accidents that lead to brief strike action by their family and friends. They are goaded on by disillusion with a compromised union and by the urging of an itinerant ideologue, who declares them no better than working bullocks if they don't engage in direct action. Realism sees the strike peter out for small gains, but amid the descriptions of work and character there are moments of lyrical evocation of the environment and a modernist moment of stream of consciousness collage of memories and emotions centring on a dog fight that serves as a symbol for brute human conflict.

Many of Prichard's books mention Aboriginal people in passing, and her interest became focused on their lives on northern Western Australian cattle stations. In 1928, the *Bulletin* started a prize for fiction, and it was won jointly by Prichard for *Coonardoo: The Well in the Shadow* and 'M. Barnard Eldershaw' for *A House Is Built*. *Coonardoo* was serialised in the *Bulletin* and published in London and New York but went out of circulation in Australia because of its scandalous exposé of sexual relations between white men and Indigenous women. Raised together as children on a northern cattle station, Hugh Watt and Coonardoo form an emotional attachment. He 'goes south' to be educated and returns to manage the station. When his mother dies, Coonardoo's care of Hugh leads to a love affair and she bears his child. The crude and predatory attitude towards Black women in Hugh's white male society and the horror of cross-racial relations on the part of white women protecting their fragile frontier hold on 'civilised values' leads Hugh to push his companion aside and take a white wife. More than Prichard's other novels, this one is a Zolaesque exercise in naturalism—nothing ends happily. The wife learns about Coonardoo and quits the station; Coonardoo is married off to an Aboriginal man but seduced by a bestial rival of Hugh's. Disgusted, Hugh sends her away to a life of degradation on the coast. Hugh loses his station to his rival and Coonardoo returns to her country to die. One element that is consistent with other work is the sense of the land as presence and the energies of nature as part of human existence.

Another of Prichard's well-regarded books is *Haxby's Circus* (1930). Australia has a tradition of touring shows, including circuses from Canada, the United States and Russia, and for many years the staples of Australian circuses were two family-run companies, Ashton's and Wirth's. Prichard went on the road with the latter to gather authentic details of this more exotic form of Australia's itinerant labour. The paterfamilias is a bluff entrepreneur who pushes his family into performance and hard labour to keep the show on the road. His best worker is daughter Gina, a bareback rider, and his most popular, an Italian dwarf who hides his educated background and resentments at public ridicule beneath the antics of a clown. Gina falls and breaks her back, and Rocco leaves, encouraging her to use her brain and strength of character to rebuild her life. Gina protects her youngest sibling and her exhausted mother against her father's tyranny. Eventually they reunite and rebuild the circus, Gina becoming the boss. The tale is told from the outside, enlivened by serial dramas (floods, storms, murders, accidents), lots of dialogue and the interest inherent in clashes of personalities and behind-the-scenes views of a world that is exotic for most readers.

Norman Lindsay has retained a visibility in the nation's culture largely on the basis of his illustrations for the *Bulletin*, some jingoistic posters for First World War recruiting, paintings featuring nudes given a gloss of eighteenth-century romps and classical bacchanalia, and a children's story (see end of this chapter). He also wrote a number of novels, starting with *A Curate in Bohemia* (1913). Lindsay was an eternal adolescent taking delight in scandalising the 'wowsers' of Australian society (puritan killjoys and self-righteous upholders of middle-class conventionality). He celebrated bohemian hedonism and his books tend to set up farcical situations in which caricatures fall over each other. His first novel has an innocent from the country meeting up with an old school friend in Melbourne while in transit to his first appointment as parson to a rural church. His friend is an artist moving in a circle of cadgers, showgirl models and boozers. There is some satire of the vapid debates over aesthetics among poets and painters, and the hapless curate is pulled into misadventures. *Redheap* (1930) is a satire of small-town life enlivened by Dickensian grotesques and dulled down by Lindsay's denunciations of religion and social snobbery. A rather tedious young man of poetic ambition associates with town larrikins—a gang of wastrels whose interests run to drinking, chasing girls and committing minor acts of public nuisance. Lindsay's idea of libertarianism was shocking for dealing openly with sex outside of marriage, unwanted pregnancy and abortion. It also rests upon a sexist ideal of lusty young women of few moral principles who are prepared to be exploited by men. Lindsay continued to write into the forties, key works being *The Cautious Amorist* (1932), *Saturdee* (1933), *Age of Consent* (1938) and *The Cousin from Fiji* (1945).

A tougher and more realistic image of the larrikin was provided in *Jonah* (1911) by Louis Stone, a Sydney teacher who documented the lives and conversation of the urban poor. His larrikins are small-time thugs who hang about on street corners, fight gang wars, con people, thieve and gamble. They too chase women but live in a community that enforces an unspoken code of propriety, despite its otherwise chaotic mix of squalor, debt, drunkenness and rivalry.

Jonah is a hunchback with a ruthless reputation as leader of 'the push'—gangs inhabiting inner-Sydney slums, markets and factories. He has an illegitimate son with the daughter of a washerwoman with a good soul and much cunning. When Jonah is suddenly struck with affection for his baby son, she inveigles him into marrying her daughter and funds the start of his career as a successful seller of shoes. His mate Chook is smitten with the girlfriend of Jonah's wife and sets up with her as a greengrocer. The book is full of low-class slang, amusing tales, detailed descriptions of city life, and the vagaries of fortune and human emotions. It marks a radical shift from bush writing, even if the struggle to survive against the odds remains a common theme.

A book that gets regular mention but which few have read is *Mr Moffatt* (1925) by Chester Cobb. Cobb was born in Sydney but migrated to England, where he gained critical attention for his experiment with stream of consciousness. Frederick Manning also moved as a teenager from Australia to Britain. After service in World War One, he wrote *The Middle Parts of Fortune* (1929), a naturalistic account of trench warfare in which exhausted soldiers move about like automata and in quiet moments discuss life as an existentialist ordeal. Stripped of much of the profane language of the common soldier, the book was reissued as *Her Privates We*. Another expatriate who garnered more attention in Australia was Martin Boyd. His early work included *Love Gods* (1925) and *The Montforts* (1928). The latter title fictionalises his mother's family up to the end of World War One, exploring the upper-class sense of tradition and genealogy and how movement to and fro between Australia and England both maintains colonial ties and highlights growing differences between cultures in the two countries.

'Capel Boake' (Doris Boake Kerr) was highly regarded by her fellow writers between the wars. Boake wrote stories and verse but is most remembered for her novels, from *Painted Clay* (1917) up to the historical novel *The Twig Is Bent* (1946). Her first novel is a romance set in Melbourne. Helen grows up with only a taciturn father and books for company. She discovers that her father had taken her away from her mother as punishment for having left him to become an actress. Helen finds work thanks to her worldly-wise neighbours and experiences the trials of attempting a career as an independent woman. Boake was valued for her depictions, uncommon at the time, of young women working in shops. Melbourne is shown as part of the bustle of modernisation and international trading, and Helen's interest in the theatre forms part of her tussle between lovers, allows pertinent comments on plays, American movies and the difference between romance and real life, and results in reconnection with her mother.

E.V. Timms was an engineer who flew for Australia in the First World War, tried farming on a soldier settlement block, then turned to writing. Along with radio plays, mysteries and romance, his historical fiction set in Europe proved popular and he wrote many books, from *The Hills of Hate* (1925) through to a series of 'Great South Land' Australian titles ending with *Forever to Remain* (1948) about the settlement of the Swan River colony. Another prolific novelist who built an international reputation across decades was Arthur Upfield. He migrated from England and worked in a variety of jobs in rural Australia, using his experiences to create crime mystery stories. His first title was *The House of Cain* (1928), but he is most remembered for his best-selling internationally popular series about a part-Aboriginal detective, Bony, starting with *The Barrakee Mystery* (1929).

Apart from Lawson's fiction, the most influential book of stories from the first two decades of federation is *Bush Studies* (1902) by Barbara Baynton. Baynton grew up on a station in Queensland before moving to Sydney, London and Melbourne. She read Dickens, Poe, Tolstoy, Dostoevsky and Turgenev before desertion by her first husband forced her to earn some money by writing. Her one novel, *Human Toll* (1907), has not stood the test of time, but her stories of the bush have haunted readers and attracted attention for their resolutely horrific visions. Her bush is a place of terror and madness, threat and death. A shepherd is left on his own when his boss takes his pregnant wife away to town. In silent isolation, the old man talks to himself and his dog. He has lost an axe and tomahawk and fears attack from 'blacks' and possible robbery from a one-handed swagman (a vagrant whose name supplies the story's title: 'Scrammy 'And'). In fact, this ex-convict intends to murder the old shepherd and steal his savings. The dog defends his master until daylight sends the marauder fleeing. Finally, the boss returns, discovering the wounded dog and a thousand flies that hint to us that the shepherd died before Scrammy's attack. Baynton's other most reprinted tales are 'Squeaker's Mate' and 'The Chosen Vessel'. These dramatise the violence and the fear of it facing women in the bush. Squeaker is a lazy man who lets his woman do all the work. When she is felled by a branch as she chops down a tree, he is more worried about the broken axe handle than her broken back. She is put to bed in a room at the back of the house and abused by Squeaker for being useless. He takes on a younger partner who bosses Squeaker but is abandoned by him from time to time. Her fear of the invalid in the back room provides a moment of victory for the latter over both her tormentors. In 'The Chosen Vessel', a young mother is left to manage house and livestock while her husband is away shearing. She is terrified of swagmen, and lies awake at night as one prowls around the house seeking a way in. Panicked, she flees with her baby to the creek, only to run into the swagman, who throttles her. A stockman checking lambs killed by dingoes finds her body and rescues the baby. Another horseman has been inspired by a vision of the Virgin and Child encountered at night but the priest he tells reacts with horror, realising that the man could have saved the fleeing woman. Anticipating modernist collage and the discontinuous narrative of later years, this exercise in 'bush gothic' has become a companion piece to Lawson's 'The Drover's Wife'. Baynton captures the drawl and vernacular of bush speech and a tone of deep loathing permeates the stories.

The short story continued to be a popular form of literary production, bolstered by the proliferation of newspapers and magazines looking for material of manageable size and moderate fee. Among the hundreds of writers of romance, suspense, mystery, horror and comic yarns, one of the most consistently published and anthologised was Edward Dyson. He featured colloquial storytelling narrators and departed from the usual bush material by focusing on miners (*The Gold Stealers*, 1901; *The Golden Shanty*, 1929) and urban workers (*Fac'try 'Ands*, 1906). Nathan Spielvogel also distinguished himself from the general scrum of story writers.

He was born in Ballarat and wrote stories about Jewish life there as well as a best-selling account of his visit to Europe, *A Gumsucker on the Tramp* (1905). He taught for some years in the dry Wimmera district of Western Victoria, and published a collection of stories about life there, *The Cocky Farmer* (1907). Spielvogel also wrote verse for school magazines and local history.

The interest in Australia's First Peoples sparked by anthropological expeditions was strengthened by works recording Indigenous myths. In 1929, David Unaipon came out with *Native Legends*, the first book published by an Aboriginal author. Unaipon was a Ngarrindjeri preacher, inventor and activist, and his work brought together tales from the lower Murray River areas of South Australia. Originally a local printing in Adelaide, the book (without Unaipon's permission) was passed on to William Ramsay Smith, who republished the stories in London under his own name as *Myths and Legends of the Australian Aborigines* (1930).

POETRY

Walter Murdoch produced *The Oxford Book of Australian Poetry* (1918). Jack Lindsay and Kenneth Slessor followed up with *Poetry in Australia* (1923). Murdoch reproduced much of what appeared in Bertram Stevens's collection but deleted nearly all the bush balladists. He allowed a lot more of Bernard O'Dowd than most anthologists, and included later work by John Shaw Neilson, R.D. FitzGerald, Vance Palmer and Louis Esson. Lindsay and Slessor featured their own work, that of Hugh McCrae, Christopher Brennan, Neilson and FitzGerald, and included the war poems of Leon Gellert and work by Helen Simpson. Both collections contained an unusual number of pieces by Dorothea Mackellar, now known only for her 1908 'My Country', the second stanza of which was learned by generations of schoolchildren ('I love a sunburnt country, / A land of sweeping plains, / ... / Of droughts and flooding rains').

Both Murdoch and Stevens before him included work by Louise Mack. She fades from view later until feminist reconstructions of the archive. Mack was better known as a novelist (an early writer for Mills and Boon) and as a journalist (including work as the first female war correspondent), but she published verse in Australian periodicals through the 1920s. *Dreams in Flower* (1901) pushes into unrhymed iambics, though most poems are conventional in form. Some focus on relationships; many celebrate the sun and harbour of Sydney:

> And all the curving little bays,
> The hot, dust-ridden, narrow streets,
> The languid turquoise of the sky,
> The gardens flowing to the wave

'I take my life into my hands' confesses to a self-protective reserve that a lover cannot penetrate. The poem neatly turns to consider that the lover too may have erected a screen around the soul and ends in a non-romantic truce: 'So let us keep our silences!'

One poet who tends to drop out of the archive in later years is 'Furnley Maurice' (Frank Wilmot). Some of his work is so truncated in its phrasing that it becomes obscure, but he deserves a place in historical record for being a poet of the city, and his *tour de force*, 'The Agricultural Show, Flemington, Victoria', not only depicts a distinctively Australian mix of circus and celebration of rural industry but does so in a persona that suggests T.S. Eliot's Prufrock and the refrains of *The Waste Land*. This blank verse poem creates a sense of modern anomie, depicting the routine of tram travel to and from the office and the cries of the ticket collector as a city passenger muses on the rich displays of agricultural produce and the glitter of sideshows at this annual extravaganza. Wilmot self-published *Some Verses* (1903) and *Some More Verses* (1904), later appearing in the *Bulletin*, London's *Spectator* and America's *Smart Set*. His own smart set included Bernard O'Dowd and Vance Palmer and Melbourne's Literary Club. Later collections were *Eyes of Vigilance* (1920), *Arrows of Longing* (1921) and *Melbourne Odes* (1934).

Bernard O'Dowd had considerable impact on the literary scene during his lifetime but is nowadays known primarily for one poem. 'Australia' is a sonnet that echoes the interrogation in the title of his first collection, *Dawnward?* (1903). The poem asks whether the new nation will be a new Eden, 'Delos of a coming Sun-God's race', or just 'A new demesne for Mammon to infest'. O'Dowd was inspired by Walt Whitman, and he advocated for politically engaged 'poetry militant', though he gilded his work with poetical diction and odd symbols. For example, he mounts an attack on 'the weeds of paltry aim / That choke the growth of love' and denounces 'Song for the sake of Song' but puts these objections in the voice of the Greek god of wine, an unlikely revolutionary who invokes Tolstoy, Savonarola, Celtic myth, and St Francis ('Bacchus'). This is hardly the socialist protest of Lawson's verse and is confusing in its mix of allusions. *The Silent Land* (1906) promulgated a personal gnostic vision of another world beyond our mundane one and *Dominions of the Boundary* (1907) re-examines the Greek gods. *The Bush* (1912) is a long poem depicting a future Australia as heir to Greece and Rome and *Alma Venus!* (1921) explores the nature of sex.

O'Dowd is but one instance of the white Australian looking for a way to integrate the realities of antipodean life with the cultural imaginary inherited from Europe. His heavy-handed attempt to concoct a poetic from republican socialism, vague mysticism and Western myth found a livelier echo in Hugh McCrae's poetical version of Norman Lindsay's art. This saw the warmth and rustic life of Australia and the supposed innocence of a young nation as an equivalent of the romanticised paganism of arcadian idyll, both being in opposition to the dark and tired world of industrial puritan Victorian England. McCrae published his first set of verse, *Satyrs and Sunlight*, in 1909. At best his lyrics are an energising fillip and symbolist shock to the balladry of the bush, but they rely on a fundamentally cosmetic imposition of northern artifice on southern reality, and their Dionysian 'vitalism' often sounds like forced egotism. One of his strongest pieces is 'Ambuscade', in which the *élan vital* of satyrs and centaurs is appropriately embodied in a troop of wild stallions.

Mary Gilmore was born near Goulburn in 1865 and grew up on farms around Wagga Wagga. She taught school in Broken Hill and advocated for workers' rights, joining William Lane's social experiment in Paraguay. On her return, she edited the women's page of the *Sydney Worker* and was a founding member of the Fellowship of Australian Writers. From 1879, Gilmore had written poems for periodicals and her sensibility is that of a pre-World War One poet, but she lived a long time and published collections of verse into the 1950s. Key titles are *Marri'd and Other Verses* (1910), *The Passionate Heart* (1918), *The Tilted Cart* (1925), *The Wild Swans* (1930), *Under the Wilgas* (1932), *Battlefields* (1939), *Disinherited* (1941) and *Fourteen Men* (1954). Gilmore also wrote a popular memoir, *Old Days, Old Ways* (1934) and many essays and reviews. Her work favours the short lyric, being strongest when deploying a tight line and crisp tone. Early work concentrates on family, and (to use one title) 'hope and love', but has an ironic edge of social critique, as in 'Marri'd':

> It's rollin' up your sleeves,
> An' whit'nin' up the hearth,
> An' scrubbin' out the floors,
> An' sweepin' down the path; ...
> An' everything because
> A man is comin' Home.

'Eve-Song' is another frequently anthologised poem: 'I span and Eve span / A thread to bind the heart of man; / But the heart of man was a wandering thing'. As time goes on, Gilmore turns to verse about birds and trees, and increasingly to childhood memories of Aboriginal lore. Another regularly anthologised piece is 'Old Botany Bay', which honours the convicts who built the country. The title poem of *Fourteen Men* is a childhood memory of seeing fourteen Chinese corpses hanging from trees at Lambing Flat. Elsewhere in the collection, 'Some Modernists' mocks brooding poets 'seeking to bring gold from a shadow, / ... / But only their own kind talk to them, / Or use their idiom.'

A different poet entirely from those mentioned was Christopher Brennan. Born in Sydney of Irish roots, he trained with the Jesuits and studied in Germany, eventually teaching French, German and the classics at Sydney University. He has only one poem that is at all recognisable as Australian ('Fire in the Heavens', which makes a summer world into a cosmic conflagration of time, concluding with the piercing shrill of cicadas) but was celebrated for injecting intellectual and metaphysical weight into the 'dawn and dusk' lyrics of Victorian-era poetry. Brennan still uses 'olde worlde' poetical diction in his early work but moves towards common language and his varied stanza forms and line lengths take on more relaxed modern tones of blank verse. He makes the 'universalist' line of Australian verse into a respectably solid venture, digesting his extensive learning into his own mythic vision and (like Yeats) working a set of symbolic images—crystal, waves, stars, wind, fire—into an imaginative system anchored on a quest narrative (as in the sequence 'Toward the Source'). Love poems are transformed into mystical yearnings of the soul and the psychodrama is given a backdrop of modernist images (city gas lamps, trams, the ennui of evening skies, humans existentially 'lost in the vast' of dark space). There is a post-Wordsworth sense of the self-examining sensibility creating its own being out of art while regretting separation from ordinary life. Brennan is notable for introducing to Australian poetry the *livre composé* and symbolist style of Mallarmé. His major achievement, a sequence in *Poems 1913* (1914), is 'The Wanderer', with echoes of old English verse and a modern sensibility of restlessness. It is a meditative monologue in tones of a prophet-seeker ('for until ye have had care of the wastes there shall be no truce / for them nor you') who arrives at a state of Buddhistic equanimity. Brennan's sensibility is centrally Catholic, but one poem cites the *Rig Veda*. Brennan continues writing into the 1920s, producing a collection touching on the First World War in 1918 (*A Chant of Doom*) but it is his 1914 collection that remains his principal legacy.

The First World War mostly transposed the action ballad from bush derring-do to battlefront heroism, occasionally including some satiric commentary on the stupidity of officers and the exploitation of workers by ruling elites. Mostly, poems are steeped in patriotism and tributes to the Australian 'digger' who makes light of his hardships. Two examples of work by soldiers are Leon Gellert's *Songs of a Campaign* (1917) and *The Road to Palestine* (1918) by 'Trooper Gerardy'.

A.H. Adams wrote some patriotic verse about the First World War for the *Bulletin* but also couched it in light criticism. In 'Anzac Day', 'this most sacred day of all our days', is a muted remembrance of soldiers whose deaths saved them from realising the futility of the Gallipoli campaign: 'Triumphantly the wild flowers raise their flags, / The only victors, they!' His 'The Australian, 1915' depicts a stolid farmer grudgingly enlisting as a bit of a laugh. He becomes a typical Anzac, throwing himself into the game of war, living by his wits rather than rules, becoming a hero to the amazement of European potentates: 'So, with a grin, quite casually / He slouches into History'. This could describe the 'digger' featured in C.J. Dennis's *The Moods of Ginger Mick* (1916). This long poem versified the voice and thoughts of a 'ratbag' soldier who resists authority and dies supporting his mates. Dennis had already established a reputation as a ventriloquist of urban larrikin slang in *Songs of a Sentimental Bloke* (1915) in which a young tough with a soft heart records his courting of Doreen. Their story includes a comic account of the uneducated couple attending a performance of *Romeo and Juliet*. This collection has remained popular and led to film, stage and musical versions.

Dennis's books of poetry began with *Backblock Ballads* (1913), reflecting his life in rural South Australia and Victoria. Another set of rustic tales appeared in 1921: *Around the Boree Log* by 'John O'Brien'. The author was actually Father Patrick Joseph Hartigan, who recorded characters and events among his Irish Catholic parishioners in the bush. His most famous poem is 'Said Hanrahan' in which a laconic farmer predicts ruin, no matter what the weather turns out to be.

Two quite different poets who have passed the test of time are John Shaw Neilson and Kenneth Slessor. Neilson's fame is in part owing to the contrast between his writing and his life. He had only a few years of schooling and slaved as a labourer with increasingly poor eyesight in the drought-ridden mallee scrub and swamps of South Australia and Victoria, but produced delicate lyrics colouring the natural world with a mystic glow. *Bulletin* editors Stephens and Archibald encouraged him and curated his output as *Heart of Spring* (1919), *Ballad and Lyrical Poems* (1923) and *New Poems* (1927). Later work appeared in *Collected Poems* (1934) and *Beauty Imposes* (1938). Initially thought of as a naïve accident of literary history, Neilson proved to have read widely, but his direct contact with and close attention to the natural world produced a clarity and simplicity that has had lasting appeal. There is no nationalist flourishing of the uniqueness of Australian nature and only a little bush ballad storytelling; quiet is the dominant tone. *Fin de siècle* 'dawn and dusk' artifice becomes a calm association of human feeling with the processes of nature:

> Shyly the silver-hatted mushrooms make
> Soft entrance through,
> And undelivered lovers, half-awake,
> Hear noises in the dew. ('May')

A girl detects a magical aura in the glow of an orange tree that assumes a metaphysical presence. She dismisses her companion's chatter that seeks to pin down the nature and origin of its appeal: 'Plague me no longer now, for I / Am listening like the Orange Tree.' Another verse captures the ritual dance of long-legged brolgas 'on the blue plains in wintry days' ('Native Companions Dancing'). Sentimentality is kept at bay by regular hints at underlying suffering: beauty might 'impose reverence in the Spring' but it 'wounds us as we sing' ('Beauty Imposes').

Unlike Neilson, Kenneth Slessor came from an educated family, lived mostly in Sydney, and worked as a journalist amid the ferment of artistic debate. His early work was linked with the energetic encrustations of the imagery of the French symbolists and Norman Lindsay's paintings. At its strongest it has a tangible sensory impact on readers, pulling us into theatrical scenes of European history (Dürer working at his etchings in 'Nuremberg', 'Rubens' Innocents', 'Heine in Paris'), classical myth ('Earth Visitors', 'Pan at Lane Cove') and Australian legend ('Captain Dobbin'). Gradually, Slessor drew back from decorative artifice, creating atmospheric evocations of Australian scenes (on a country train in 'The Night Ride') and moods (a forlorn ex-lover finding that the romance of a botanical garden has given way to cold scientific taxonomy in 'Elegy in a Botanic Gardens'). Slessor also experimented with a sequence of word paintings of pieces by composers from Beethoven to Stravinsky ('Music') and introduced a modern self-reflective voice that ironises what might otherwise remain colourist aestheticism: 'After all, you are my rather tedious hero; / It is impossible (damn it!) to avoid / Looking at you through keyholes' ('To Myself'). Slessor's early collections are *Thief of the Moon* (1924),

Earth Visitors (1926) and *Cuckooz Contrey* (1932). His later output is covered in the next chapter.

Drama

Musicals and melodramas continued to stir the emotions of Australia's theatregoers. Bert Bailey and Edmund Duggan wrote *The Squatter's Daughter* (1907) under the name of 'Albert Edmunds'. The play was so popular that they made a movie version in 1910. With Beaumont Smith they also reworked Steele Rudd's stories *On Our Selection* for the stage (1912).

A.H. Adams was a New Zealander who migrated to Sydney, where he worked on the *Bulletin* and the *Lone Hand*. He wrote several novels and many short stories, plus a plethora of poems, continuing into the 1930s. However, as his poetry and critical reviews show, his primary love was theatre. He worked for J.C. Williamson, created an opera centred on Maori life and wrote the usual pantomime-style musical plays. To these he added *Gallipoli Bill: A Comedy in Three Acts* (1926) having already published *Three Plays for the Australian Stage* (1914). These three are all short comedies, the action mostly twirling around confusions over who loves whom and how they get what they don't expect (as in *Galahad Jones*). However, *Mrs Pretty and the Premier* includes satire of a Labor state leader who hands out positions to friends and wants to nationalise the lands of squatters, and *The Wasters* turns on the role of women in society, money versus class, and the nature of love and marriage. Adams notes the dearth of Australian plays of any consequence and emphasises his Sydney settings, declaring that the city is just as Australian as the bush.

The domination of Australian stages by musical theatre and English repertory tours began to break down as writers like Adams sought to create recognisable characters and real-life situations. One dramatist whose work took time to make an impact but which marked a significant turning point was Louis Esson. He visited Britain in 1904 and was inspired to work towards a national drama by the examples of J.M. Synge and W.B. Yeats. By 1912, he published *The Time Is Not Yet Ripe* and *Three Short Plays*.

The former is a political satire with some good comic lines and a feisty young heroine (selected by the Women's Anti-Socialist League to stand for federal election in the seat of Wombat), but it pillories rich capitalists and shows her sympathetic to her rival, a squatter with radical socialist ideals. Its gibes threaten to alienate the audience most likely to pay for serious theatre. *Three Short Plays* contains *Dead Timber*, seen by some as Esson's best work. His shorter play *The Drovers* gained a performance in London in 1920 and Melbourne three years later, and he formed the Pioneer Players in Melbourne with Vance Palmer and Stewart Macky, staging *The Battler* (also titled *Digger's Rest, a Comedy in Three Acts*) in 1922. This involved romances in a country town hit by the boom and bust of gold fever. Unfortunately, folk theatre that was not also melodrama, farce or musical failed to appeal. After Esson's death, a collection of later drama was published as *The Southern Cross and Other Plays* (1946).

Katharine Susannah Prichard won a prize for her one lasting dramatic work in 1927. This was *Brumby Innes*, the titular protagonist being a larger-than-life boozing and wenching cattle station owner in northern Australia. He is admired for his macho pioneering vigour but exploits his Aboriginal workers and preys on Aboriginal women. The content was sufficiently scandalous for the play not to be published until 1941 and it only received its full due on the stage in the 1970s. Betty Roland's *The Touch of Silk* was staged in 1928, but like Prichard's play, not published until 1942. It shows tensions arising from a shell-shocked war veteran taking his French wife back to a prejudiced bush town and away from the luxuries of Europe. The beginnings of such character-based reflections of social issues are represented in Doris Fitton's founding the Independent Theatre Company in Sydney in 1930.

Children's Literature

As well as her best-selling adult memoir, Mrs Aeneas Gunn's *The Little Black Princess* (1905) was popular with young readers. It is a strange book, part memoir, part ethnographic study of Aboriginal lore (with photos), and part a cute tale about a loveable imp of an adopted Aboriginal child, Bett-Bett, and her pet dog. The modern reader takes some time to realise that the prolific use of 'nigger' carries no racist charge for the narrator, but her evident affection for 'station blacks' and appreciation of the logic behind their customs is contained within a patronising view of them as amusingly quaint.

In 1910, Mary Grant Bruce published her first novel, *A Little Bush Maid*, after it had appeared as a serial beginning in 1905. This was the first in a series that would become Australia's equivalent of best-selling series for girls such as *Pollyanna* and *Anne of Green Gables*. Her Billabong novels continued to appear into the 1940s. Young Nora has an adventurous life on a squatter's property, enjoying the freedoms of an honorary male. The series reflects historical changes but stays loyal to 'proper' British values.

May Gibbs's cute gumnut babies appeared in *Snugglepot and Cuddlepie* (1918) and have become national icons, though most readers remember the terrifying black-and-white illustrations of wicked Banksia men (anthropomorphised seed cores of the 'bottle-brush' flowers of the banksia tree) more than any details of the stories. Their creator is now a figurehead for Australian children's literature. Talking animals (a koala, a penguin, a droopy dog, a thieving wombat and a possum) also feature in Norman Lindsay's *The Magic Pudding* (1918), though they coexist with humans and are all dependent upon the grumpy inexhaustible pudding-on-legs of the book's title. Lindsay's book appeals to Australian readers through dialogues employing local slang and an irreverent approach to the behaviour of characters in children's stories.

Chapter 4

Susso to Soldiers
1930–1950

Social and Political Context

At 1920, Australia's population was still only around six million and was concentrated on the southern edges of the continent. The Great Depression was a major shock to a young nation that had fed on dreams of egalitarian mateship and general prosperity. Society split into salaried and unsalaried. The rugged individualists of pioneering tradition suddenly found themselves reliant on handouts from the state (the Sustenance Allowance or 'susso'). By 1932, thirty per cent of workers were unemployed. In cities, many were evicted from their homes to live in makeshift encampments. Some went 'on the wallaby'—walking through the countryside seeking odd jobs on farms. City businessmen and politicians feared communist revolt and used the police and vigilante groups to suppress protest marches.

However, despite the machinations of international finance, Australia was entering a modern, globalising era. A national communications network was inaugurated under the 1932 Australian Broadcasting Commission, a national automotive industry (with the amalgamation of General Motors and Holden) opened in 1931, and Australia hosted the British Empire Games in 1938. One indication of the nation's self-confidence was the appointment of its first Australian governor-general, Sir Isaac Isaacs, in 1931. Howard Florey won the Nobel Prize for discovering penicillin in 1945. The dominant symbol of the nation's progress was the construction of the Sydney Harbour Bridge, completed in 1932. Artists like Grace Cossington-Smith and photographers like Max Dupain featured this in work that echoed European cubism and futurism, signifying the country's participation in a modern industrial age.

Modernity was also having its effects on the domestic front. Popular magazines between the two world wars drew material and style from both British and American publications, and cartoons often featured 'the new woman' usurping men's privileges. Women were increasingly depicted in office work and department stores. Hollywood gossip entered public discourse and modern domestic appliances were advertised. All this was encapsulated in the 1933 appearance of the still running *Australian Women's Weekly*.

Politically, the three decades from 1920 were characterised by turmoil. The government sought to modernise Aboriginal people by assimilating them into white ways, starting actively to abduct Aboriginal children and place them in foster care or institutions, creating what would later become known as 'the Stolen Generation'. Aboriginal tribes, forced into reserves and fringe urban areas as low-paid labour, began creating pan-Aboriginal groups. The Aborigines Progressive Association declared a Day of Mourning in 1938 and a national paper, *Abo Call*, appeared in the same year. At the other end of the social ladder, Australia's landed gentry and middle-class entrepreneurs felt threatened by the international proselytising of communism. The Great Depression saw a growth of left-wing political activism inspired both by local inequalities and fascist adventurism abroad. Robert Menzies's federal government banned the Australian Communist Party in 1940. In 1934, the European journalist Egon Kisch was invited to address anti-war and anti-fascist meetings in Australia and made headlines by defying a government ban on his landing. He jumped from ship to wharf and delivered his talks with a broken leg (fictionalised by Nicholas Hasluck in *Our Man K*, 1999). Fears of fascist fifth columns in Australia were equally strong (as reflected in D.H. Lawrence's *Kangaroo* and the disruption of the opening ceremony for Sydney Harbour Bridge by a soldier representing the right-wing New Guard). All this led to wartime shifts towards Labor governments (under John Curtin, 1941, and Ben Chifley, 1945) during which time banks and industries were nationalised.

Although World War One continues to be celebrated as the time when Australia began to think of itself as a nation, World War Two had a much more direct and lasting effect on the country.

Australia joined the anti-Nazi alliance in 1939 because it was still tied politically and culturally to Britain, and again it sent troops to the other side of the world, but when it needed to defend itself, it became clear that Britain (embodied in Churchill) was quite prepared to sacrifice its colonies to serve its own interests. After Japan entered the war in 1941, there were over a hundred attacks on Australian territory, most notably the bombing of Darwin in 1942, and a bloody jungle campaign against Japanese troops in New Guinea stalled actual invasion.

In 1948, Australian citizenship was recognised as separate from British. The war effort shifted Australia's economy into industrial production, and with that, an even greater concentration of people into urban areas. In geopolitics, however much the Japanese were hated for their brutal treatment of prisoners of war, their military conquests forced Australians to take Asians seriously and to broaden their view of their place in the world. Some Australians, including writers T.A.G. Hungerford and Hal Porter, gained firsthand experience of Japan as members of the post-war occupation force. When the United Nations was set up, social reformer Jessie Street and Labor minister and lawyer H.V. 'Doc' Evatt were delegates and Evatt helped draft the UN's Universal Declaration of Human Rights. Also important in the long run was the alliance with the United States in the Pacific campaigns. American troops were stationed in Australia (reflected in Thomas Keneally's novels *The Cut-Rate Kingdom* and *An Angel in Australia*) and both politics and culture began to turn away definitively from old colonial ties. ANZUS, a trans-Pacific military alliance consisting of Australia, New Zealand and the United States, continues to shape Australia's international relations.

CULTURAL CONTEXT

The 1920s and 1930s featured documentary writing that built up a collective awareness of the land as a vast and varied whole. Travelling through the interior and the tropical north was neither common nor easy, but photography and printing had improved and the widely read *Walkabout* (a kind of Australian *National Geographic*) was founded in 1934 to encourage development of the outback. Popular writers like Ion Idriess and Frank Clune travelled about recording legends and life in remote communities. Novelists like Katharine Susannah Prichard, Kylie Tennant, Ruth Park, Dymphna Cusack and Ernestine Hill provided fictionalised reports of bush workers, Depression struggles, urban slums and development projects, showing Australia as replete with human drama and history.

Art played a part in shaping new visions of Australia. In 1938, the Contemporary Art Society was founded in opposition to the Australian Academy of Art. As with European modernism, young Australian artists looked to 'primitive' cultures for their design and aesthetic drive. Reports, photos and museum exhibits made more white settlers aware of an Indigenous presence, and painters like Margaret Preston began using ochre colours and Aboriginal motifs in their work. Arrernte man Albert Namatjira took up watercolour painting mid-1930s and his landscapes became icons in many suburban homes. Poets also began using images and words from Aboriginal cultures to connect with 'the spirit of the land'. The trend was formalised by Rex Ingamells, who coined the term Jindyworobak (meaning 'to join up') and published his ideals as *Conditional Culture* in 1938. There was an element of paternalistic conservation in this, as most people (encouraged by Daisy Bates's memoir *The Passing of the Aboriginals*, also 1938) believed that tribal cultures would fade away under the impact of Western civilisation.

The years of the Great Depression consolidated Australia's image as an outdoor culture focussed on physical prowess rather than intellectual accomplishment. The racehorse Phar Lap became the working man's darling. Les Darcy, a boxer, became a national hero, and test cricket was enshrined as a national sport, embodied in Don Bradman and highlighted by heroic resistance to England's unsportsmanlike 'bodyline' bowling in the 1932 test series. A sense of Australia being an international innocent subject to more devious larger countries was strengthened when both Phar Lap and Darcy died in the United States, possibly because of match-fixing rackets.

At the same time, there was a sense of the former colony reaching a cultural 'critical mass'. The Fellowship of Australian Writers was founded in 1928, originally in Sydney, but soon with other state branches. The FAW fought against censorship, and in 1939, persuaded the government to upgrade the Commonwealth Literary Fund from a small pension for indigent aged writers to a series of grants enabling authors to produce books and to give lectures on Australian writing. In 1930, historian Keith Hancock published a cultural survey, *Australia*, and H.M. Green produced *An Outline of Australian Literature*. One indication of a national literary culture having 'arrived' was the first collection of stories in a series called *Coast to Coast* (1941); another was P.R. 'Inky' Stephensen's *Foundations of Culture in Australia* (1936), supplementing critical commentary by Vance and Nettie Palmer and Miles Franklin, and the appearance of key literary journals: *Southerly* (in Sydney, 1939) and *Meanjin* (Brisbane, 1940, moving to Melbourne, 1945).

From 1930, Sydney-based publisher Angus & Robertson produced a significant proportion of Australian literary work, though most publishing continued to occur in the UK. The Australian (later, National) Book Council began in 1945, supporting the publishing industry and founding an award for children's literature a year later. The war increased American interest in Australia and C. Hartley Grattan published *Introducing Australia* in the US in 1942. By this time, Errol Flynn (known for his role in Charles Chauvel's 1933 film *In the Wake of the Bounty*) and several Australian actresses had become Hollywood stars. Australia's literary ties with America were, however, curtailed in 1947, when Britain and the US signed a Traditional Markets Agreement. Britain retained publishing control over its former colonies. This meant that Australian work would almost always have to go through London in order to reach New York and the world.

The war years cut Australia off from European imports. Reduced book supply created a need for more local production and the war itself inspired literary efforts for some time. Education programmes for young men in the services and for those working on the home front were backed up with radio shows about reading and writing, and literature became something everyone could be part of. This helped to promote Australian writing, but it also encouraged a patriotic egalitarian scorn for elitist style and 'disloyal' social criticism. Wartime conditions also allowed government censorship that restrained literary expression for decades after. Writers like Sumner Locke Elliott, Eric Rolls, David Campbell, Geoffrey Dutton, Patrick White and James McAuley served in the military and others like Kenneth Slessor and Charmian Clift worked as journalists for the armed services. Poems, novels, plays, short stories and memoirs often depicted conflict on the front line (as with the 1950 best-selling novel *A Town Like Alice* written by Nevil Shute and popularised as a feature film), but also depicted social change in the major cities as the result of American troops being stationed there. Their smooth manners, smart uniforms and better pay generated excitement in many young women, hostility amongst Australian troops, and worry about declining moral standards in the wider community. The era was captured in the novel *Come In Spinner* (1951), jointly written by Dymphna Cusack and Florence James. War also initiated the shift away from Anglo-Celtic hegemony: in 1940, Britain sent Australia a boatload of European refugees (later known as 'the *Dunera* boys'), many of whom became leading artists and intellectuals, and, though government assistance for British migrants continued, a programme of encouraging migrants from continental Europe began in 1947 that would change the food habits and provincial attitudes of everyone.

PROSE FICTION

J.M. Harcourt, a journalist in Western Australia, achieved notoriety in being the first author to be banned after the 1933 formation of the Commonwealth Book Censorship Board. His 1934 novel, *Upsurge*, was deemed indecent, not just for depicting the licentious lives of Perth's idle rich, but because it showed the harsh conditions of workers and because it recorded police brutality towards protesters and communist organisers. The censorship board sought to uphold staid values of family life based on the kind of male sexism that the novel shows as permeating all classes including the revolutionary movement. *Upsurge* mixes slabs of didactic history and political comment with dramatic episodes centred on women workers, commerce, the legal system, the smart social set, and direct action communism.

The general tendency to worker-centred writing did not necessarily carry a political edge: it merely documented the nature of the Australian economy, still centred on farming, mining, timber-getting, and other modes of manual labour like loading ships and building railways. Miles Franklin's *All That Swagger* (1936) is one example. Social critique leavened with a romance or a family saga and some colourful country types to supply humour and villainy was the standard model for Australian fiction at the time. Kylie Tennant's *Foveaux* (1939), for instance, is a close-up of an inner-city suburb of Sydney, with a bishop and the well-to-do at the top of the hill and factory workers at the bottom. The story follows a cast of colourful characters as the district undergoes changes, making way for the motor car and a new kind of suburbia. Tennant's *The Battlers* (1941) follows the struggles of Depression-era 'travellers' camping out, cadging work, moving on to a new town to get government rations, drowning their troubles in pubs, going mad with starvation, and finding ways of supporting each other despite continual fighting among themselves. One point of interest in this characteristically picaresque novel is the idea that, despite racial prejudice, battlers both Black and white are definitive of Australia as opposed to the machines and politics of city life.

Xavier Herbert's *Capricornia* (1938) is another picaresque tale interested in the place of Aboriginal peoples in a future Australia. The book is a rambunctious mix of epic, idiom, anger, preaching, tragedy and celebration of the wild life of northern Australia. Herbert stripped away the romance of popular travel writing and was controversially frank about racial prejudice and the exploitation of Black women and workers. His world is one of random accident in which nature as much as human malignity determines what happens.

Other writers asked questions about the nature of the new nation by looking back to its origins. Combining elements of the convict novel and the saga of settlement, Brian Penton's *Landtakers: The Story of an Epoch* (1934) is a bleak account of the brutish conditions of pioneering in Queensland around 1840. It shows a rudimentary society beset by mistrust, deceit, theft and violence in which only the fit and ruthlessly self-centred survive. There is no mateship and nature is harsh. The central character arrives as a young scapegrace of English gentility and is steadily hardened by his fellows and by fate. He kills Aboriginal people, fights with his neighbours, marries out of desperation rather than love, and steadily loses his dream of returning to polite society 'back home'. Any human feeling renders him vulnerable to exploitation and the law continues to trap survivors of the convict system and those who shelter them. Like Joseph Furphy, Penton reproduces the speech of Scots, Irish and others to the point of stretching readers' comprehension and many scenes are so staccato that meaning must be inferred from indirection and truncated utterance. Apart from the implied criticism in the naturalistic display, the main critique of the settler comes from a disaffected ex-convict: he denounces pioneering destruction of the land with no thought for the future of the country.

A more measured inspection of Australia's foundations was Eleanor Dark's *The Timeless Land* (1941). It departed radically from white histories by imagining Aboriginal perceptions of the arrival of the First Fleet. Dark followed Henry Handel Richardson in seeing the sprawling new society in a huge continent as requiring an equally extensive fictional treatment, going on to complete a trilogy with *The Storm of Time* (1948) and *No Barrier* (1953). National construction is also the focus of M. Barnard Eldershaw's *A House Is Built*, published in London in 1929, then reprinted by the Australasian Publishing Company through the 1940s. Its two authors (Marjorie Barnard and Flora Eldershaw) avoided the standard rural settings and depicted the economic progress of Sydney in a Jane Austen-like set of interconnected personalities centred on one family. The novel also shows the restricted circumstances of urban women (rather than the hobbledehoy bush girl) and continues the debate about whether Australia should be 'tamed' to fit a British social standard, or whether that standard should be adapted to suit Australian life. Family fortunes fluctuate along with national changes, as when the gold rushes take men from the city. The family patriarch sets up a chain of stores selling supplies to miners and his daughter is able to apply her domestic management skills to the family business.

The Barnard–Eldershaw duo went on to record the effects of the Great Depression. They tried to avoid the fate of *Upsurge* by presenting worker desperation and its underlying causes as scenes in a book being written at a future time. Its author inhabits a sparse outback in a utopian commune otherwise subject to totalitarian governance from a central power. Despite this distancing strategy, the board of censors demanded modifications before *Tomorrow and Tomorrow* (1947) could be published. The title's original three 'tomorrows' from the Shakespearean quotation were restored when the unexpurgated edition appeared in 1983.

Also dealing with the effects of economic hardship and the attractions and dangers of ideological commitment, Christina Stead wrote *Seven Poor Men of Sydney* (1934). This novel escaped censorship by not showing mass action, and indeed, its interest is as much in character as in politics. Stead showed a modernist exploration of the mental processes of people as well as recording their outward dialogue and behaviour. She went on to write her most acclaimed novel, *The Man Who Loved Children* (1940), a trenchant portrait of gender relations that showed the connection between language and power in a family ruled by an ostensibly benevolent tyrant. Because she was living in the US, she disguised the autobiographical elements of a Sydney upbringing to suit her American publisher, and a combination of publishing regulations, the war and her astringent depiction of suicide and children rebelling against parents, meant that her work failed to attain its proper place in Australia until much later. Then it would be praised for its attention to emotions and its Joycean experiment with the father's use of 'baby talk' to subdue his family.

Eleanor Dark's *Prelude to Christopher* (1934) was a homegrown application of modernist elements that attracted many women writers. The title refers to a character that never appears in the book except as a hint at what might develop once its plot reached resolution. The story is prefaced by the opening bars of Tchaikovsky's sixth symphony, the so-called 'Pathétique', which sets up a resonance anticipating the novel's tragic end. The narrative occurs over four days, in which a man is hospitalised following his car accident, but the whole story stretches from around 1910 to around

1920 and occurs in the thoughts, memories and conversations of the patient, his mentally troubled wife, his staid mother, a nurse, and one of the doctors in the country hospital. It is a blend of *Anna Karenina*, Sigmund Freud, social Darwinism and Virginia Woolf, and is centred on debates over biology versus social conditioning, science versus emotion, idealism versus human nature. It is clearly anti-war and complexly ambiguous in dramatising the logic, ethics and human impact of eugenic selection. Works like this did not gain recognition until much later; modernism's multiple viewpoints and stream of consciousness in mentally unstable protagonists made stories hard to understand and, to the conventional reader, slightly distasteful if not also unpatriotic.

The golden age of the short story in Australia is usually located between 1880 and 1918. The bush ballad was often a short story in verse, and prose stories were sketches of social situations and colourful characters in a largely rural world. They normalised realism, humour, dry irony and occasional touches of gothic malevolence. Dickensian sentiment and the mechanics of plotting evident in popular writers like American O. Henry shaped Australian taste, though more literary-minded writers used Balzac, Zola and Chekhov as models. The longevity of many of Australia's 1930s writers kept social realism in play over three decades. Short story tradition was embodied in Walter Murdoch and Henrietta Drake-Brockman's 1951 Oxford University Press collection, *Australian Short Stories*. This book created a canon of social realism and folkloric tall story yarning typified by titles such as Henry Lawson's 'Send Round the Hat', Lance Skuthorpe's 'The Champion Bullock Driver' and Dowell O'Reilly's 'Crows'. The selection ended at 1946, major names among the twentieth-century writers being Katharine Susannah Prichard, Alan Marshall, John Morrison and Gavin Casey.

The Tracks We Travel was a series produced by the Australasian Book Society. The publisher produced cheap editions to promulgate the style and ideas of the communist realist writers group. The series appeared in 1953, 1961, 1965, and again in 1976. Editions included work by people writing poetry as nationalist Jindyworobaks (Flexmore Hudson, Roland Robinson and Nancy

Cato), but otherwise comprised politically committed writers like Prichard, Casey, Marshall, Morrison, Frank Hardy, John Manifold, Judah Waten, Dymphna Cusack, David Martin and Dorothy Hewett. Others less politically partisan but working with social realism were also included (Vance Palmer, Dal Stivens, Frank Dalby Davison).

Peter Cowan came to national attention in 1944 with his collection of short stories, *Drift*, and continued to publish over four decades. He began work as a labourer during the Great Depression, served with the air force in World War Two, then taught in schools and at the University of Western Australia, where for many years he edited the literary journal *Westerly*. Though his writing retains a realist hold on social situation and natural setting (influenced by John Steinbeck and Ernest Hemingway), it concentrates on atmosphere and fluctuating emotional states that respond to subtleties such as a woman's change of voice when she has a cold or the condensation on a cold car bonnet. Cowan aligned himself for a while with the modernist 'Angry Penguins' group, and there is a touch of T.S. Eliot's 'Preludes' in his stories of desultory encounters in boarding houses at the ragged edges of cities. His sentences are crafted to slow things down and suggest a submission to arbitrary fate, frequently portraying a suppressed struggle against the drab banality of suburban life. In the title story of *The Empty Street* (1965), the tale of a serial killer is stripped of drama as we see an ordinary office worker, tied to an embittered wife, seeking to convert his hobby of orchid growing into a new life as a horticulturalist. The murders occur offstage so that we are not totally sure what is going on, and even the final arrest is almost incidental as we see the protagonist placidly working in a nursery alongside a woman who intuits his inner troubles but can also sense his calm as he fulfils his dream. In retrospect, we can see Cowan's work very much centred on male characters, women being the objects of their momentary longing or hostility.

Writing by women continued through the inter-war and wartime eras. Australian modernity included an increasing female work force, as reflected in Kylie Tennant's novel *Ride On Stranger* (1943), but literary works by women (Barnard, Dark,

Stead, Prichard, Tennant, Franklin, Cusack) were constrained by normative masculine values (outdoor work, public issues, physical action). As a result, only a few women achieved literary recognition and the 'feminine' internal lives explored by modernism would not be 'discovered' by scholars until men like Patrick White authorised it and feminism created the intellectual space for it to be critiqued on its own terms.

Popular fiction marks the boundaries of capital-L Australian Literature but sometimes crosses into its space of scholarly interest. Contemporary recognition of gay and lesbian rights has allowed the rediscovery of journalist Frank Walford's sensation novel of 1933, *Twisted Clay*. Set in the Blue Mountains at the edge of Sydney's suburban sprawl, a tormented lesbian girl becomes a serial killer before committing suicide. Adelaide, for some reason, has produced a number of crime writers, the most successful of whom pre-war was Arthur Gask. He published for thirty years from 1921, mainly a series centred on Inspector Gilbert Larose, and earned praise from H.G. Wells. Helen Simpson reversed the immigrant trajectory of crime writers, moving from Sydney to London, where she was friends with Dorothy L. Sayers. Simpson wrote *Boomerang* (1932) and achieved some fame for *Under Capricorn* (1937) when Alfred Hitchcock filmed it in 1949.

Poetry

H.M. Green declared that before the 1950s there was little regard for the Australian novel: poetry was the only form that commanded literary respect. Lyrics appealing through image and verbal music were appreciated but verse with some philosophical depth was most valued. A major event among poets in the 1930s was the coming together of the Jindyworobaks, a loose group of writers centred on Adelaide. South Australia had had administrative control of the Northern Territory for many years, and there was a steady traffic of workers, missionaries, painters and adventurers between the southern capital, the 'Red Centre' and 'the North'. Absorbing some of the studies of central Australian Aboriginal groups via museum collections and writings from anthropologists, Rex Ingamells, Ian

Mudie, Flexmore Hudson, Roland Robinson and others sought to bring the colours and language not just of the bush, but also of Indigenous Australia into literary parlance. Critics disparaged them for 'decorating' white poetry with barely understood exotica but the 'Jindys' were a catalyst for greater appreciation of Aboriginal culture and for finding spiritual, not just economic, resources in the land.

Other poets were more concerned to connect Australian culture with its European antecedents in order to establish a continuity of artistic tradition in a country still seen as without any cultural foundation of its own. Rosemary Dobson's first collection *In a Convex Mirror* (1944) includes verse meditations on or inspired by paintings by Breughel, Vermeer, Botticelli and the 'Lady and the Unicorn' tapestries. Robert D. FitzGerald writes poems about Montaigne and Caesar and another about his Irish ancestor Mary Ann Bell ('Legend'). His 'Essay on Memory' (1937) warns against clutching the bones of a ghost and threats of war and chaos, but the poet also takes delight in rain and sunshine and stages a joyous revolution:

>   We'll make fabulous
> this world, in honour of them who gave it us,
> not just the Nelsons, Newtons, of our race,
> the Phillips grounding at a landing-place
> continent-wide, but all whom violence of mind,
> violence of action, gave such singleness
> that if they did but grow, ambitionless
> except to live in the sun, they served their kind

Such a vitalism of 'good effort' redeems the loss and failure of the past and 'builds upward' to a humanist future 'pregnant with daring and with destinies'. As with many aspects of Australian culture before the Second World War, this could be taken as liberal utopianism or crypto-fascist Nietzschean hubris. Either way, it is a triumphalist vision of white settler nation-building that battles against the haunting of Old World ghosts.

In contrast to Hugh McCrae's satyrs, FitzGerald produced a more sober and localised version of classical tradition in *The Greater Apollo* (1927):

> I look no more for gods among
>   The lace-like ferns and twisted boughs,
>   And little care though these should house
> The riddles when all life has sprung: ...
> ... Pan, Jehovah, Brahma, Thor—
>   The man-made gods of earlier days.

Like many of his fellow 'new world' poets, FitzGerald seeks to hack out his own sense of life's meaning; he seeks 'no longer to divide / being from that which gives it place' and posits 'a greater Apollo' manifest as cosmic infinitude while being content to find that revealed in nature: 'It is enough that trees are trees / that earth is earth, and stone is stone.'

A third poetic wrestling match with tradition and its lack dramatised the explorations that fed into the making of Australia. Dubbed 'voyager poems' by Douglas Stewart, these included Kenneth Slessor's 'Five Visions of Captain Cook' (1931), Stewart's own verse dramas (*The Fire on the Snow*, 1941, about Antarctic exploration, and *Ned Kelly*, 1942), William Hart-Smith's sequence on Christopher Columbus (1948), Rosemary Dobson's *The Ship of Ice* (1948), FitzGerald's *Heemskerck Shoals* (1949)—about Abel Tasman *not* discovering Australia, but heading on to New Zealand and Fiji after landfall in Tasmania—and Francis Webb's treatments of sailor-settler Ben Boyd (1949) and the explorer Ludwig Leichhardt (1952). The theme persisted into the 1960s with Rex Ingamells's *The Great South Land* (1951) and FitzGerald's *Between Two Tides* (1952). Webb would return to explorers in 'Eyre All Alone' (1961), and James McAuley encapsulated lost visions of a new Eden in 'Captain Quiros' (1964). The link between history and literature is indicated in the ending of the first section of Slessor's evocation of Cook's voyages: 'So Cook made choice, so Cook sailed westabout, / So men write poems in Australia.'

One theme that connected strategies for constructing an Australian poetic tradition was time. The weight of history sat with an Old World laden with a thickness of culture; new Australia was open to the future, but its present lacked a history of its own (white society mostly ignoring the Aboriginal past). There is also an interest (manifest in Slessor's evocation of Cook's pioneering calculations of longitude from chronometers) in the modern distinction between mechanical 'industrial' time and human experience of fluctuations and flows in temporal progression. This is clear in Slessor's elegy for a drowned friend, 'Five Bells' (1939), which begins:

> Time that is moved by little fidget wheels
> Is not my Time, the flood that does not flow.
> Between the double and the single bell
> Of a ship's hour, between a round of bells
> From the dark warship riding there below,
> I have lived many lives, and this one life
> Of Joe, long dead, who lives between five bells.

Slessor is arguably the most important poet from this period, not just because he plugged into national cultural constructions of history and scene (as with his 'South Country' and 'North Country'), but because he ranged across several styles of verse, moving successfully into imagist and modernist modes, mastering a rhythmic flow of blank verse, and finding a much less essayistic way to philosophise than FitzGerald. Early experiments in responding poetically to music turn into visual evocations of Sydney harbour that incorporate ideas as well:

> I saw Time flowing like a hundred yachts
> That fly behind the daylight, foxed with air; ...
> So Time, the wave, enfolds me in its bed,
> Or Time, the bony knife, it runs me through ...
> So water bends the seaweeds in the sea,
> The tide goes over, but the weeds remain. ('Out of Time')

Slessor's serious poetry stopped with his *One Hundred Poems* (1944), a definitive conclusion that allowed students to study his oeuvre with confidence, and his poems are still studied in schools and universities. Other poets like Judith Wright and R.D. FitzGerald continued to write for many more years, some finding fresh topics and styles, others honing the same set of skills and ideas. Rosemary Dobson differed from Slessor in presenting time as personal duration—the human life cycle, seen mostly from the perspective of an ageing and melancholy parent. One widely anthologised treatment of the theme was FitzGerald's 'The Wind at Your Door'. This appeared in 1952 but draws on his earlier thinking about memory and time. His medical ancestor oversaw the flogging of convicts, and the poet asks what kind of ethical obligations stem from acknowledging such a legacy. It is a question that later manifests in relation to white settler obligations arising from a history of death and dispossession inflicted on Australia's First Peoples.

The continuation of the landscape lyric is part of the lasting quest of Anglo-Celtic and European immigrants to discover a mode of antipodean belonging. This moves away from bush romance into a more georgic celebration of settled rural life, represented well by David Campbell's work. Campbell came from an established farming family, and in his first collection (*Speak with the Sun*, 1949) writes about droving, country horse races, storms and birds. Some poems (like the rollicking 1951 'Windy Gap', which ends 'And so I sing this song of praise / For travelling sheep and blowing days') draw on the bush ballad tradition, while others ('Night Sowing', 1950) are more meditative, in keeping with some of Douglas Stewart's reflections on nature in *The Dosser in Springtime* (1946). Campbell's poems are, however, more centred on family and connection to the soil and an inhabited landscape. Arguably, Stewart had more impact as a literary editor than as a poet, though his verses are treated with respect for their craft and gentle lyricism. Campbell develops a wider range over time, hinted at in the ironic title of a 1950 poem, 'A Cow in a Sonnet', and confirmed by city poems such as the 1953 'Bondi Tram'.

Despite an increasing homeliness in relation to the natural world, a strand of gothic unease continues to run through some verse. It reflects awareness of the harshness of Australia's mostly dry continent, seen in Slessor's 'huge abraded rind' of drought-stricken 'Crow Country' and Judith Wright's repeated images of bony ridges and dust. Beneath this there is an existential fear, imaged forth in vast spaces of land and sky. Slessor's night dissolves everything until there is only 'the quiet noise of planets feeding' ('City Nightfall'), or 'tunnels of nothingness, / ... / Infinity's trapdoor, eternal and merciless' ('Stars'). FitzGerald positions himself in a modern universe of astronomical dark expanses and the enigmas of quantum physics—'a placeless dot enclosing nothing'

('The Face of the Waters'). To this we might add another disturbance. FitzGerald sees a 'moonlight acre' beset by 'dark trees' that truss up the sentry wind and silently invade 'the moon's unguarded country' ('Invasion'); Slessor's 'South Country' concludes with 'a bony ridge' against the sky in which scene 'dwindled hills' seem to be 'a knob of skull, / Feeling its way to air' pushed up by 'something below'. This chthonic threat is given historical form by Judith Wright, who began to confront violent extermination of native tribes in her family history. 'Bora Ring' (1944) and 'Nigger's Leap: New England' (1945) show white society haunted by repressed knowledge of persecutions in which 'their blood channelled our rivers, / and the black dust our crops ate was their dust'. FitzGerald's menacing dark trees are the white settler's fear of Aboriginal attack, inverting the larger 'invasion' that refigures Slessor's 'knob of skull' as an actual human cranium surfacing as witness to past massacres. These poems anticipate the double-edged slogan subverting Australia's bicentenary celebrations in 1988: 'White Australia Has a Black History'.

War poetry mostly did not find publication until servicemen returned home, though there were military publications that included occasional literary pieces and a collection, *Poets at War* (1944). Civilian poets in Australia did refer to the war, as in Rosemary Dobson's 'Australian Holiday, 1940', which contrasts a sunlit peaceful beach with the darkness and death of war overseas. Judith Wright's 'The Company of Lovers' (1942) and 'The Trains' (1943) also show the effects of war on the home front. Two war poems that have been preserved through several anthologies are Kenneth Slessor's 'Beach Burial', written in 1942 while he was reporting on the North African campaign, and David Campbell's 'Men in Green', written in 1943. Slessor draws on Wilfred Owen's First World War poems, emphasising the pathos of war dead, and Campbell, who served in the air force, recalls flying soldiers into New Guinea and collecting the wounded they were relieving. He depicts the latter as being hunted by the brutal jungle terrain rather than as fighting other humans.

The war heightened ideological conflicts between socialists and conservatives. Politics became entangled with literature, as seen in the 1944 'Ern Malley hoax'. Two poets with classical tastes and anti-communist opinions spent their spare time in Army Intelligence constructing a pastiche of *Waste Land*-style verse from randomly selected sources. They invented a working-class author and had his equally fictitious sister mail her 'discovery' of his work to the most assertive magazine for experimental writing. Max Harris, editor of *Angry Penguins*, published the poems, hailing them as Australia's emergence from dreary convention into cosmopolitan modernism. The hoax has since served to inspire more verse, scholarship about the place of counterfeiting in Australian art and culture, and a novel by Peter Carey (*My Life as a Fake*, 2003). The immediate outcome of the hoax, however, was to consolidate a general 'common sense' suspicion of anything 'arty', and Harris joined a long line of publishers and writers charged with obscenity, Malley's poems containing swear words and supposed mention of sex.

More restrained, but startling at the time for her critical inspection of the legends of pioneering settlement and for her woman-centred outlook, Judith Wright's collections marked a turn in Australian poetry: *The Moving Image* (1946) and *Woman to Man* (1949). Wright continued to produce work of sufficient variety of theme and for so many years that she will be mentioned in subsequent chapters as well, but in the 1940s, she celebrated 'my blood's country' (a line from 'South of My Days') by depicting characters from bush society: wanderers ('The Idler'), ne'er-do-well British aristocracy ('Remittance Man'), and old farming families dreaming of their youth ('The Hawthorn Hedge', 'Brothers and Sisters'). These and her most anthologised poem, 'Bullocky', create a sense of pioneering folk history that is both a substitution for and a continuation of European tradition (the poems refer to the Trojan wars and the Bible, and echo Dylan Thomas, T.S. Eliot and W.B. Yeats). Wright's figures, however, are not the entirely loveable or heroic types of nationalist bush tradition, and her natural world is not a bucolic idyll: snakes are a threat and wild dogs die violently ('The Killer', 'Trapped Dingo'). Her verse becomes distinctive when she deploys the imagery of nature to suggest a vision of life that approaches mysticism but is fundamentally anchored in the body and an awareness of 'deep time' manifest in ancient stones and plants. 'The Cycads' and 'Flame Tree in a Quarry' illustrate such consciousness, and Wright goes further to connect the fires driving evolution to the mystery of conception and birth. The cell serves her as an image linking plants with the visionary poet's room or mind and, in *Woman to Man*, to the female body housing the cell/seed that is both in and out of time, both emerging to life and dying. The poems are remarkable for being the voice of a pregnant woman as well as for making poetry out of a biological process.

DRAMA

New technology frequently develops by exploiting older material, and radio in 1937 dramatised the comic rustics 'Dad and Dave' from Steele Rudd's *On Our Selection*. Locally written one-act plays were increasingly produced, including for radio, and Sydney Tomholt published ten of his in 1936 as *Bleak Dawn* (the title play being about a woman who is forced to separate from her impossible husband but who still yearns for his company). *Blue Hills*, a radio serial by Gwen Meredith, became a staple of lunchtime listening for decades and centred on the increasingly complex relationships of a farming family living somewhere back of Canberra as members engaged with social change.

Following interest in the north of Australia and its masculinist frontier, Henrietta Drake-Brockman, herself from a pioneering pastoral family, wrote *Men Without Wives* (1938). This was performed in Sydney and won the Commonwealth Sesquicentenary Prize for a play. Like Prichard, Drake-Brockman mentioned white male predation on Aboriginal women but indicated that this arose from an absence of white women who would civilise lustful men.

The New Theatre League was formed by left-wing writers and actors who wanted something more artistically structured than the 'agitprop' plays performed around the country on the backs of trucks and in Depression camps. Its production of American Clifford Odets's anti-fascist play *Till the Day I Die* was shut down in 1936 after the German ambassador applied pressure. Some of the New Theatre's work showed injustices of racial prejudice. George Landen Dann's *Fountains Beyond* (1942) depicted poor living conditions of Aboriginal 'fringe-dwellers' in Queensland and the tragic effects of white exploitation of corroborees as touristic dance shows. A strike by Aboriginal workers in Western Australia inspired a dance drama, *White Justice* (1946), and Oriel Gray staged *Burst of Summer* on the same topic in 1959. The New Theatre also provided opportunities for women to express radical ideas about gender equality.

When the war took many men overseas, women writers had more room to work for radio and the stage. Catherine Duncan, Oriel Gray, Betty Roland, Miles Franklin and Dymphna Cusack all wrote into the 1950s, Roland's 1942 *A Touch of Silk* remaining a distinctive contribution. She anticipated later migration stories in having a French woman marry a soldier, who takes her back to the bush and away from the luxuries of Europe. Cusack wrote with political purpose and her *Pacific Paradise* (1955) opposed nuclear testing, while *Morning Sacrifice* (1942) advocated for education reform in its depiction of the downfall of a sensitive young teacher under pressure from a rule-bound institution.

Little theatres proliferated through the inter-war period and Doris Fitton's Independent Theatre in Sydney had a major success with Sumner Locke Elliott's *Rusty Bugles* (1948). Elliott provided a realistic picture of the boredom and squabbling in a Darwin military camp. His reproduction of soldier's slang and swearing brought on a police order to close performances, but public protest allowed it to continue with some of the language toned down. The Independent Theatre lasted for forty years.

CHILDREN'S LITERATURE

Australian children mostly read British stories, often of an 'improving nature', either in school magazines or received as Sunday School prizes or compendia of tales and poems prepared for the Christmas market. Especially during the Great Depression, families could not afford luxury items, and children would often leave school with six years of primary education to work as labourers, so literary reading for children was not a huge market. Nonetheless, young readers developed into adult readers, and Australians continued to buy more books per head than many other ex-colonies. Their appetite for something other than Enid Blyton and English boarding-school tales inspired Eustace Boylan to write *The Heart of the School: An Australian School Story* in 1920. Writers for adults, like E.V. Timms and Frank Dalby Davison, occasionally wrote for children, Davison's *Dusty, the Story of a Sheep Dog* (1946) being popular. A popular series began in 1945: *Smiley* by Moore Raymond told of the comic scrapes and sentimental tragedies of a loveable ragamuffin. The book was adapted for film in 1956.

If girls devoured Mary Grant Bruce's Billabong series, boys followed the Sexton Blake detective-thriller books. This was a British phenomenon, but between the wars included many titles by Australians R. Coutts Armour and John G. Brandon. An outlier in this period is P.L. Travers's *Mary Poppins* (1934) in that the popular series had no Australian content, and the author's origins in Queensland were not discovered until years later.

The general popularity of anthropomorphised animals in children's literature (*Peter Rabbit* for example) inspired some successful characters in Australia: Blinky Bill (a mischievous young koala) and the Muddleheaded Wombat (popularised in a 1940s national radio serial) were the stars of this period. Blinky Bill reflected the Depression era. His adventures, written by Dorothy Wall, appeared in 1933, 1934 and 1937, and Blinky lives on as the icon of Australia's republican movement. Ruth Park's Muddleheaded Wombat tales were collected in print in the 1960s. They resemble England's Paddington Bear series in cataloguing comic adventures of misunderstanding or bright ideas that are disastrously implemented.

Australian writing attempted contact with the culture of its First Peoples, usually by appropriating traditional stories as 'fairy tale' entertainments. Another common ploy was to insert cute Aboriginal children into bush adventure fiction, often as guides and saviours to white children. Frank Dalby Davison allowed two Black children their own adventure in *Children of the Dark People* (1936), as did Mary and Elizabeth Durack in *The Way of the Whirlwind* (1941), both books using animals and spirits of place as fantastical helpers.

Chapter 5

Prosperity to Vietnam
1950–1965

Social and Political Context

After losing to Labor during the war years, Robert Menzies led a new Liberal Party and became prime minister in 1949, preserving much of the social welfare ethos promulgated by Labor but with a conservative free-market capitalist overlay. Australia under Menzies remained very much dominated by British decorum (the new Queen Elizabeth making a triumphal tour of the country in 1954). Even as Australian cinemas became the monopoly of Hollywood, until the 1970s everyone would stand to the playing of 'God Save the Queen' at the start of each show. After the disruptions of war, the accent was on social calm and economic prosperity. Industry was turned over to improving domestic life, with mass production of electric stoves, refrigerators, washing machines and a national car, the Holden. 'The Australian Dream' was realised for many in the form of a brick or timber single-storey home on a quarter-acre block of land that would comprise a front lawn and a backyard with fruit trees and a vegetable garden. Iconic inventions such as the Victa lawnmower and the Hills Hoist rotary clothesline signified an era of prosperity and suburban expansion. Australia showed its confidence in the international arena by hosting the Olympic Games in Melbourne in 1956, an event that helped instigate the beginning of television broadcasts.

The destruction of Hiroshima and Nagasaki created an international race to match American nuclear power, especially in the Soviet Bloc and also by the British government, which carried out nuclear testing in Australia's Montebello Islands and on the Nullarbor Plain at Maralinga, showing colonialist disregard for Aboriginal peoples and Australian servicemen, who were exposed to fallout. Worldwide dread of atomic warfare prompted popular protest movements against the arms race.

After the war, Australia was aware that it needed to be more self-sufficient and worked to broaden its economy. New mines were established producing mainly iron ore but also silver, lead and zinc, gold, and bauxite. Power for industrial expansion would come from coal mines and from large-scale hydroelectric projects in Tasmania and the Snowy Mountains. Science and engineering were built up, and Australia began rocket testing and satellite tracking, playing a role in the moon landing later on. Medical research and the creation of a strong public health system was spurred along by an epidemic of polio that paralysed many children through the forties and fifties. Limiting intellectual progress was the fact that children, especially in rural areas, would often leave at the end of primary school, and many more go to apprenticeships or jobs with an 'Intermediate Certificate' halfway through secondary schooling, only a few completing their 'Leaving Certificate' and fewer still matriculating with the subjects and grades sufficient to get them into university, even though more universities were being set up.

All this development required labour, and fear of invasion spurred by the war produced a 'populate or perish' policy that (with the ongoing concern for maintaining a cohesive—read 'white'—society) led the government to sponsor immigration by Europeans impoverished by the war. The nation's population reached ten million in 1959: very little still for a large landmass but a lot more than ever before. Australia had managed to maintain its agricultural sector, sending food parcels to a Britain still on rations through the 1950s. A 'Sunny South' replete with apples, dried fruits and pineapples became Australia's dominant image, one that Donald Horne labelled 'The Lucky Country' in his 1964 book of the same name. Horne was being ironic, as he saw prosperity producing smug complacency and condescension toward 'New Australians' who were expected to assimilate to an Anglocentric norm. Patronage of the 'Third World' operated via Colombo Plan scholarships to study in Australian universities. Assimilation was the policy for the Indigenous population as well.

Australian unions supported Indonesia's rejection of return to Dutch rule, but otherwise the country joined the Southeast Asia Treaty Organisation and fought with the US in the Korean War, with the British in Malaya against communist guerrillas, and with Malaya against Indonesia's 'Konfrontasi' aggression. Menzies tried to outlaw membership of the Communist Party, but was defeated, though a regime of surveillance of suspect citizens began that found its justification in 1954 when a Soviet diplomat, Vladimir Petrov, defected and gave information about espionage. The Communist Party of Australia in any case declined once members saw Stalin's tyranny and Russia's suppression of Hungary in 1956. National unity was strong enough for Rupert Murdoch to found a national newspaper, the *Australian*, in 1964. However, a period of political upheaval that accompanied the beginnings of major social and cultural changes was ushered in when Australia's defence treaty with the US led it to send 'advisors' to South Vietnam in 1962 and then troops in 1965.

Cultural Context

In 1961, the birth-control pill became available to women. Suddenly, a strongly patriarchal culture that had confined women to 'home duties' in support of working husbands and had bound them to sex as the means to produce children was confronted with individuals who could indulge in sex for pleasure with no fear of unwanted pregnancy, and who could refute any argument that they could not be given a job because they would only leave to have children. The beginnings of a new feminism were also linked with a growing anti-war movement. The left mixed with concerned citizens of all political sympathies who feared devastating outcomes of a nuclear arms race. This was brought home to Australians by Nevil Shute's novel of atomic Armageddon, *On the Beach* (1957), an international success as a film (1959) that featured antipodeans awaiting the end of everything as war and radioactive clouds moved south. A stronger international awareness and an increasing number of university-educated young people prompted discontent with settled parochial ways, and student magazines began to question convention.

Oz magazine, founded in 1963, deliberately set out to shock, and the Beatles' tour of 1964 confirmed staid parents' fears that a new generation of teenagers had emerged wanting more from life than a brick-veneer cottage and boiled 'meat and three-veg' dinners. Such suburban conventionality was satirised from 1955 onwards by Barry Humphries's stage persona, housewife Edna Everage (her name punning on a pretentiously 'English' pronunciation of 'average'). The opening up of narrow ideas of morality and decorum was signalled in the unbanning of *Lady Chatterley's Lover* and *Lolita* in 1965.

In literature, Cold War politics hardened a division between liberal humanist realism and socialist realism. Writers associated with the Communist Party of Australia (K.S. Prichard, Jean Devanny, Frank Hardy, Ralph de Boissière, Dorothy Hewett) subscribed to a worker-centred narrative that would expose the self-interest of bourgeois writing and the pernicious operations of big capital. More widespread was Australia's egalitarian ethos supporting a social welfare system using romantic if not sentimental depictions of people responding to social challenges as literary inducements to reform rather than revolution. Vance Palmer's 1948 novel *Golconda* exemplifies 'bourgeois' leftist social realism. The story documents the lives of an engineer working for a mining company, a union organiser, some independent fossickers (one of whom is a prophetic figure who has survived the failed utopian experiment in Paraguay), an enigmatic girl with artistic tendencies, a Greek entrepreneur, and so on. They come and go through the book as the mountain of silver and lead ore named after the legendary source of great wealth generates changes in community. The novel reflects national economic history and supports a broad ideal of collective well-being but its people are individuals driven by a Lawrentian concept of inner natural power that is ambivalent in its political outcomes. What can be noticed is that the open expanses of the outback are still seen as negating human purpose and that Aboriginal peoples are still either disregarded or disparaged.

Palmer's mining town includes several non-British characters, reflecting a social change that became visible everywhere during the 1950s. People with a range of languages, cuisines and literatures at their command began pushing back against the narrow materialism, bland diet and provincial outlook of a complacent Anglo-Australia. The cultural and linguistic exchange was humorously depicted in the best-selling novel *They're a Weird Mob* (1957). John O'Grady wrote it in the persona of an Italian immigrant, 'Nino Culotta', who tries to make sense of Australian mores and language. Its satire was inverted by Barry Humphries, who created the boorish 'ocker' Australian abroad, Barry 'Bazza' McKenzie. Humphries continued the habit of seeing Australia as an ignorant provincial outpost of anywhere, materially comfortable but culturally bankrupt (expressed in Robin Boyd's book *The Australian Ugliness*, 1960). Cheerful philistinism drove many arts workers overseas: Peter Porter, Sumner Locke Elliott, Clive James and Shirley Hazzard became permanent expatriates. Martin Boyd's novels of expatriation, *The Cardboard Crown* (1952), *A Difficult Young Man* (1955), *Outbreak of Love* (1957) and *When Blackbirds Sing* (1962) were praised by Australian critics. Popular writer Morris West stayed abroad for many years relying on foreign settings for reader appeal, as with his depiction of Naples in *Children of the Sun* (1957) and the Vatican in *The Devil's Advocate* (1959) and *The Shoes of the Fisherman* (1963).

With the exception of Angus & Robertson, Australian publishing was still mainly school-text centred or run by offshoots of London firms staffed largely from the home office. There was no significant literary agency in Australia until Curtis Brown established a Sydney office in 1967, and the Fellowship of Australian Writers did not operate as a forceful 'peak body' until it established the Australian Society of Authors in 1963. Nonetheless, the 1950s and early 1960s were a time when pioneering efforts to construct a self-respecting national culture began to see some success. In 1949, Sidney Nolan exhibited his 'Ned Kelly' paintings in Paris, generating a sense of international recognition, and Percival Serle produced a *Dictionary of Australian Biography*. Vance Palmer canonised bush writing in *The Legend of the Nineties* (1954), and in 1957, the first major national literary prize, the Miles Franklin Award for fiction depicting some aspect of Australian life, was won by Patrick White for *Voss*. 1958 saw the publication of Russel Ward's *The Australian Legend* and Arthur Phillips collected his essays in

The Australian Tradition. This circulated his much-quoted model of the colonial 'cultural cringe' (nothing could be good unless approved of by Europe, or conversely, our new world could beat Old World decadence at everything).

The increasingly professionalised group of Australian literary critics split between nationalists and 'universalists', both factions in opposition to the writers and journalists continuing to produce popular rather than literary work and both still to some extent dependent on overseas recognition of Australian writing. Thus, a 'nationalist' novel about father–son relationships in a struggling family of itinerant bush workers (Jon Cleary's *The Sundowners*, 1952) could be successful abroad as colourful exotica from the far-flung reaches of the British Empire but too much local idiom or politics might get it dismissed as merely of 'anthropological' interest. On the other side of the critical industry, a 'universalist' like Patrick White could be praised as doing new things with modernist fiction or denigrated as just a colonial imitator of Woolf and Joyce.

Strengthening the feeling that Australia was achieving its own national culture, the Children's Book Council of Australia was founded in 1945, and, following the establishment of the Australian Elizabethan Theatre Trust in 1954, the National Institute of Dramatic Art (NIDA) opened in 1958. That in turn developed the Old Tote Theatre (1963). The first university-level major sequence of Australian literature courses was offered at Canberra University College (later the Australian National University) in 1955, and G.A. Wilkes was appointed to a Chair in Australian Literature at the University of Sydney in 1962, the same year that Manning Clark published the first volume of his *A History of Australia*. A two-volume edition of H.M. Green's *History of Australian Literature* was published in 1961, when *Australian Book Review* also appeared. Between 1950 and 1964, new journals *Overland*, *Quadrant*, *Westerly*, *Australian Letters* and *Poetry Australia* commenced publication. Writers began to publish critical essays and monographs: for example, Judith Wright on John Shaw Neilson and Charles Harpur in 1963 and her book *Preoccupations in Australian Poetry* in 1965. The National Library in Canberra and the still-running Festival of Arts in Adelaide opened in 1960. In 1963, the scholarly journal *Australian Literary Studies* appeared, followed a year later by Geoffrey Dutton's substantial edited collection *The Literature of Australia*.

Dutton is something of a bridge between two phases of Australian literary culture. Like Patrick White, with whom he was for many years good friends, he came from an 'establishment' grazier family. He served in the air force during the war, studied at both the University of Adelaide and Oxford, and returned to write novels, stories and poetry (two collections are *Night Flight and Sunrise*, 1944, and *Night Fishing*, 1960). He is most remembered as a promoter of literary culture, editing the journals *Australian Letters* and *Poetry in Australia* with Max Harris. He wrote studies of Patrick White and several artists, recorded interviews with many writers, and with Brian Stonier and Max Harris republished many of the country's novels and significant non-fiction under their Sun Books imprint, founded in 1965. Though Dutton did teach at the University of Adelaide for some years, he embodied an earlier age of the practitioner enthusiast rather than the era of the academic critic.

Prose Fiction

Katherine Susannah Prichard's *Winged Seeds* (1950) provides a useful example of socialist realism in contrast to the social realism of Vance Palmer's *Golconda*. Set in the 1930s (later than *Golconda*) it also depicts a mining community, this one being the more established goldfields town of Kalgoorlie. Prichard's communism demanded that she show class warfare dividing society and she inserts the spectre of the Spanish Civil War as threatening Australia with a fascist-led return to global conflict. The author gives us a lecture on every page about this, about the unhealthy work conditions of miners, the exploitation of women and the dangers of abortion, the abysmal living conditions of Aboriginal fringe-dwellers, and so on. She tries to compensate by overlaying the didacticism with a hectic set of romances, just as jarring to the contemporary reader's ear. Interestingly, like Palmer, she introduces a young woman with artistic aspirations who disturbs the social fabric. However, her character is not Palmer's mysterious isolate in tune with the bush;

she is a cosmopolitan 'new woman' who sympathises with leftist causes but treats everything in Kalgoorlie as a touristic source of colourful material.

The core of realism and literary investment in the nation's development persisted, but things were changing. If the Ern Malley hoax delayed poetry's turn to modernism, the novel had been steadily applying some of its techniques (mental processes, multiple points of view, symbolic and sensory imagery, rhythmic sequences of prose). One sign of change was the awarding of the Miles Franklin prize for fiction to Patrick White's *Voss*. This, and the overseas recognition that led to White's becoming Australia's first Nobel laureate for literature in 1973, made his work a literary touchstone for critics.

In Patrick White's first published story (1937), an ageing colonel returned from service in India has intimations of some fuller mode of existence beyond the everyday. This can be touched on only in visions; otherwise, 'Only in dissolution is salvation from illusion'. Such a Manichean struggle between sordid fleshly mortality and the mind intuiting a transcendent wholeness would remain a feature of White's work through his fifty years of writing. Finding the words to express the vision of a select few and the struggle to uphold that vision amid the indifference and scorn of materialist society led White to adapt the techniques of Eliot, Joyce and Woolf to convey a sense of Australia's elusive soul. His style and metaphysical interest made him at once eccentric and exemplary. Such a position is given fictional form by visionary misfits like the four 'riders in the chariot' (in the 1961 novel with that title), the intellectually challenged Waldo in *The Solid Mandala* (1966), and the struggling artist at the centre of *The Vivisector* (1970).

After *The Aunt's Story* (1948)—a difficult work in that it centres on the impressions of a probably demented woman in European and American settings unfamiliar to most Australian readers—White published *The Tree of Man* (1955). This was recognisably a saga along the lines of *The Fortunes of Richard Mahony*, charting changes through flood and fire from pioneering settlement to suburban and urban life. However, it was unique in giving inner mental and emotional lives to an otherwise inarticulate workman and his wife.

Their perceptions of the land and each other are rendered through images resonant with symbolic associations.

Voss (1957) tells a story of heroic land exploration, modelled on the historical figure of Ludwig Leichhardt. However, the externals of heat and hardship are subordinated to an examination of the psychology and will of the visionary individual behind the hero figure of history and legend. Voss is both scapegoat and monster to Sydney's brittle society. He and his soulmate Laura know that real truth lies in mystical communion and self-sacrifice. The bush strips the explorer bare until he finally attains release when ritually killed by Aboriginal men, at which moment his spirit inhabits the land. Laura intuits his death and later comments: 'Knowledge was never a matter of geography ... It overflows all maps that exist. Perhaps true knowledge only comes of death by torture in the country of the mind.' Freud, Woolf and Bergson informed White's perspectival narratives and stream of consciousness passages, which track quests for self-knowledge. As he announced in an essay 'The Prodigal Returns' (1958), White sought to do away with 'the dreary dun-coloured' documentary realism of most Australian fiction. In doing so, he might construct myths on which a more sophisticated Australian culture could develop.

White's semi-rural life at Castle Hill west of Sydney becomes the setting for several of his works. In fiction, it first appears in *Riders in the Chariot* (1961), the title referring to the biblical chariot of fire that appears in a whirlwind and carries prophet Elijah up to heaven (2 Kings 2:11). This intertext is melded with Daniel's fiery furnace and Ezekiel's vision of wheels and angels. In the shallow materialistic world of Australian society (encapsulated in the name of a town, Barranugli), four misfits become White's equivalents of Elijah. Miss Hare is an aged eccentric, living on a family allowance in Xanadu, the mouldering estate of her excessive, poetically minded father, scion of a rich Sydney wine merchant. The 'grey, raggedy, native scrub' has overrun the property and Miss Hare also becomes 'speckled and dappled, like any wild native thing', more inclined to love nature than people. Mordecai Himmelfarb is a Jewish refugee working in a factory that makes bicycle lamps. His self-effacing love for all humanity is tinged with guilt over the loss of his wife to the

Holocaust, and he knows that he will suffer, as he does under the xenophobia of two 'respectable' women and the mindless humour of his workmates, who crucify him at Easter. He is tended to by Mrs Godbold, a laundry woman living in a tin shack on the edge of town, and by Miss Hare. The scene of his death is captured in paint as a pietà of Christ's deposition by Alf Dubbo, an Aboriginal fringe-dweller artist who stores up memories, dreams and biblical reading, possessed by the need to compose them in a surrealist mix akin to paintings by two of Australia's leading artists at the time, Sidney Nolan and Arthur Boyd.

In *The Eye of the Storm* (1973), Elizabeth Hunter, once a member of the landed gentry and Sydney society, is bed-ridden from a minor stroke. She is the centre of a swirling circle of carers and family but not, however, a *still* centre. She is fractious and vicious, though aware of her own shortcomings, drifting through memory and visits from her grown children in an attempt to analyse and break through the constraints, habits and disappointments of life. 'The worst thing about love between human beings', she says, is that 'when you're prepared to love them they don't want it; when they do, it's you who can't bear the idea.' The book contains some of White's most finely honed prose delineating this truth in Mrs Hunter's sharp interactions with the spiritually attuned Sister de Santis, the Jewish housekeeper Mrs Lippmann, the family lawyer Mr Wyburd, her daughter Dorothy, unhappily married to French nobility, her egotistical actor son Sir Basil, and others summoned up in reverie. Elizabeth recalls a family holiday on an island off the Queensland coast in which she survives a hurricane's battering. Throughout the novel, people and circumstance similarly harry and slash at protective carapaces until some core truth of the self is exposed and a moment of calm attained.

The sixties saw the last gasp of socialist realist writing. Frank Hardy's *Power without Glory* circulated more or less clandestinely in Melbourne once it appeared in 1950 with the Australasian Book Society. This was because the book became subject to a libel trial that skirted around its exposé of real-life con man, mobster and political influencer John Wren. It was 600-plus pages of dramatised documentary aimed at showing the corruption inherent in capitalism and revealing the intricacies of faction fighting across both left and right of Australian politics from 1890 to 1950. The novel was published again in the UK a decade later and finally made it into an Australian Classics series in 1972.

Hardy encouraged Dorothy Hewett, another Communist Party member, to write *Bobbin Up* (1959), a depiction of the lives of women workers at the Alexandria Spinning Mills in Sydney. Rather than a solemn polemic against capitalist exploitation of labour, Hewett produced a lively mosaic of voices (modelled on Dylan Thomas's *Under Milk Wood*) that retains a romantic 'vitalist' colour, interspersed with a cinematic collage of advertising signs, popular tunes, and small differences of class and architecture in down-at-heel inner-city Sydney. She focuses on the dreams and personalities of the women with whom she worked amid the dreary repetition and squalid facilities of a 'sweatshop', and shows the pervasive oppression of women by men of all classes with a frankness about bodies and sex that offended many, including the male-dominated socialist left. Recurrent mention of Sputnik sailing overhead puts immediate circumstance into global-historical context, giving some characters hope in the ultimate success of the proletariat. However, women striking for better working conditions are warned that 'it will be a long wait'.

One of the left-realists was Judah Waten. His novel *Alien Son* (1952) marks the beginnings of what became known as 'migrant' and then 'multicultural' writing in Australia. Previous fiction had acknowledged the presence of non-Anglo ethnicities in the British settlements (notably Eve Langley's 1942 *The Pea Pickers*, which featured Italians and Indians), but they had been depicted from the outside as colourful supplements to the white nation. Waten links a collection of vignettes showing the restless lives of a small Jewish community in a foreign land, struggling to make a living on the fringes of society, trying to preserve language and culture, arguing amongst themselves and worrying that their children will be absorbed into secular Anglo-Australia. The tales are told by the son of one family, who becomes increasingly distanced from his parents' world while being ashamed of his role as critical onlooker. *Alien Son* echoes the world of Irish slum life in Ruth Park's

The Harp in the South (1948) and *Poor Man's Orange* (1949) without the sunnier romance, and contributes to the identification of migrant writing with autobiographical documentation, although Waten's narrating voice is a literary construct.

Another writer who was a forerunner of 'migrant' or 'multicultural' writing was David Martin. Originally from Hungary, he worked as a journalist in England and India before moving to Australia. *The Young Wife* (1962) details the lives of Italian and Cypriot communities in Melbourne. Anna travels to Australia to marry. She is caught up in old politics, new loves, and tragedy possibly redeemed in the birth of her child. Martin's international reach is matched by Ralph de Boissière, who came to Australia from the West Indies and wrote *Crown Jewel* (1952), a fictional history of labour struggles in Trinidad.

Linked to *Alien Son* and a number of other novels by centring on a narrator with artistic ambitions who follows his vocation at the cost of preserving ties to family, class and religion is George Johnston's *My Brother Jack* (1964). This book became popular as a portrait of Australian society from immediately after World War One to the end of World War Two. Full of vivid detail and energetic drive, its appeal lies in its celebration of the narrator's brother as quintessentially Australian. Jack is a larrikin enthusiast, boxer, and hard worker, but a feckless adventurer, almost dying as he wanders about looking for work in the Great Depression. He eagerly enlists in the war effort and is loyal to family and his bookish brother David. As Jack gradually subsides into settled life, David slowly rises to a successful career as a journalist and war correspondent, becoming the adventurer that Jack wanted to be. The book gains depth by this largely autobiographical narrative being shown as a fictional construct and by brother-narrator-writer David interposing reflections on the workings of memory and his own shameful subterfuges and betrayals as he pursues his career. For a decade at least, *My Brother Jack* enjoyed both popularity and scholarly respect. It echoed Patrick White's more stringent exposé of the egotism of the artist, connected with widespread experience of war and its aftermath, and tapped into the 1960s discontent with the bland uniformity of suburban life.

Several writers were marked at the time as Patrick White's successors. Christopher Koch's *The Boys in the Island* (1958) earned him nomination for his symbolist evocations of elusive reality beckoning from behind a luminous façade of landscape and provincial distance. Koch's theme of colonial consciousness as a kind of gnosticism derived largely from his doubled 'exile', not only as an heir to English and Irish culture in Australia, but also as a Tasmanian separated from 'the mainland'. Randolph Stow was another 'next Patrick White'. *A Haunted Land* (1956) and *The Bystander* (1957) show both a rhapsodic appreciation of natural beauty and the underlying violence of usurping land and beating it into submission to found a squatter dynasty. All of Stow's early work rests on his own family history in Western Australia, and *The Bystander* in particular reveals both the prejudice of British settlers against other European immigrants and the hostility of pioneer materialists towards men with artistic sensibilities.

To the Islands (1958) was Stow's breakthrough novel. It is based on his own time on a northern mission station, where he developed his skills as a linguist and observed at close hand how Aboriginal communities lived and interacted with whites. The title refers to the mythical islands in Aboriginal lore to which souls of the dead go. Stephen Heriot established a mission in the bad days of 'frontier warfare' to protect Aboriginal people from massacre. His tough rule and the tropical heat and dust have exhausted him, and he is outraged by the new generation of Aboriginal youth who challenge his authority. Thinking he has killed one young man, he flees into the bush as both penance and a quest to bond with the land and its ancient soul. His Lear-like struggle to retain any faith becomes a figure for white settler guilt and for a more general existential confession of human violence. There is a *Voss* element in the romantic elevation of the extreme personality, but no elevation of the sufferer to any redemptive vision. Heriot never escapes 'being foreign', even though he arrives at a point of proximity with Aboriginal culture and the natural world.

Stow explored the principles of Taoism in the mysterious allegory that is *Tourmaline* (1963), a story of a religious cult in an isolated outback town. *The Merry-Go-Round in the Sea* (1965) has been his most popular book. It centres on seven years of Rob Coram's life from age five and conveys in fine detail his perceptions of the world and the densely woven fabric of his extended family, who boast several generations as landed gentry. Rob's hero worship of his cousin Rick Maplestead becomes key to the movement of the story. Rick joins the army in 1941 and spends the next five years 'off stage', seen only in vignettes of suffering as a prisoner of war. He returns but is unable to settle and finally decides to leave for Europe. Rob, feeling betrayed, faces the end of childhood and departure to boarding school. The book's appeal lies in many lyrical descriptions of seasons and the natural world. It also stands out because it gives the 'empty', history-less Australian countryside a thickly populated and historied texture.

Thea Astley is worthy of note for several reasons. Firstly, she wrote often about small-town life in tropical Queensland and its Pacific neighbours (not Sydney suburbs or the outback); secondly, she frequently depicted the fractious relationships between white and Indigenous peoples; thirdly, she developed an astringent tone and spiky style that aligned her with the young men hailed as Patrick White's successors. Her style, however, was all her own, and it took some time for her work to attract appreciative readers, despite Astley becoming (with four wins) the most successful contender for the Miles Franklin Award.

Astley began as a poet in Brisbane. Her early novels reflect the life of many young women of the 1950s sent as teachers to country towns: drab boarding houses, predatory men, parochial rectitude and gossip, and dreary classroom routine. In *Girl with a Monkey* (1958), one such teacher returns for one day to the town she has just escaped to collect her things. In this brief present, we are taken through her memories, discovering the antipathetic headmaster, the enervating heat, and the tedium that has led to her affair with a council labourer. He has become too serious for her and the narrative is infused with tension as she tries to avoid his probable violence before she catches the train to her new placement. The book relies on atmosphere: sunlight on tin roofs, dust, desultory conversation, a radio playing 'the plagal cadences of Delius'. It shows an author in love with the sound of words ('gobemouche', 'fribbling', 'sarmentose'). As with most of Astley's writing, irony is a double-edged tool, cutting into social pretention and ignorance but also biting back on its protagonist, the young teacher here having little other than book learning to raise her above those she is fleeing from. *A Descant for Gossips* (1960) also pillories small-town pecking orders of doctors and bank managers, their backbiting wives, and cruel bullying among school students. Astley's generally bleak view of the world is one element that prevented her work from becoming popular except among a scholarly few.

The Well Dressed Explorer (1962) is a more humorous 'biography' of a romantic egotist who stumbles charmingly and with innocent ruthlessness from one infatuation to another because he cannot do without being admired by women. Interest lies in Astley's dissection of the male psyche, in George's romance with the Catholic faith and his rather convenient use of confession to assuage his guilts, and in the inventive metaphors scattered through the text. Astley is as tough on her women characters as on her men, but in this book is less caustic, injecting wry epithets ('polite George', 'old stickler George!') that could come from George's own thoughts, others' ironic assessment of him, or the external narrating voice. The prose is orchestrated into long sections of descriptive narrative breaking into staccato one-word sentences. The effect is to make one aware of how we act out our lives, even to ourselves, and how the novel is always a staged artifice, even when it looks like simple mimesis.

The Slow Natives (1965) centres on a teenager veering between love of his parents and loathing for their conventional suburban life exacerbated by disgust at his mother's affair with a neighbour. His long-suffering father reflects Astley's interest in music: he is an examiner of young piano players across the country towns of Queensland. Nuns are legendary for teaching music in small towns and he becomes involved with the spiritual crisis of one with ambition to be a passionate musician. Desire, passion, idealism, all raise characters above the banality of life but expose them to attack from boorish neighbours, without the consolation of some White-like redemption through suffering.

Elizabeth Harrower returned to Sydney after years in London, where she wrote *Down in the City* (1957) and *The Long Prospect* (1958). Her work is noteworthy for its avoidance of rural settings and for its attention to the inner life of women. *Down in the City* starts with its Sydney setting, counterposing the seedy world of Kings Cross racketeers, foreigners, 'mascaraed women and powdered men', and the 'peaceful high-walled streets, the tennis courts … the white-brick blue-roofed mansions' of harbour suburbs. It then presents a series of cinematic clips—conversations among factory girls, socialites and movie-goers as the city day waxes and wanes. Within this panorama, a girl raised in isolation in a rich 'high-walled' home encounters a self-made entrepreneur and denizen of the rented apartments of Kings Cross. They are each fascinated by the difference of the other and marry. The book follows the peaks and troughs of their relationship: she, suddenly confined to domestic duties and obligations to neighbours who tyrannise with kindness or emotional need; he, patronising but resenting her privileged background while trying to take on its style. There are only muted dramas (Stan goes back to a casual girlfriend, the wife's reserve defeats gossipy interference, an emotionally erratic late adolescent breaks free of a neighbour's influence and takes on an Italian boyfriend). The interest lies in delineation of the adjustments and self-justifications of the central characters and how their relationships ebb and flow in keeping with the time of day and the humid summer heat.

Harrower reflected her London sojourn in *The Catherine Wheel* (1960) and returned to Sydney life in *The Watch Tower* (1966). The latter depicts two young women abandoned by their widowed mother (who is used to colonial life in India and goes 'home' to England). They are adopted by their employer who proceeds to trap them in a cycle of domestic violence. The action lies predominantly in the ups and downs of a poisonous group psychology. Felix, a petty small-business patriarch who can only feel happy demeaning those dependent upon him, despises them for being powerless and makes economically damaging decisions to punish his wife and her younger sister, leading to further cycles of his own shame and rage. Clare, the younger sister, has an artistic temperament that affords her emotional epiphanies, and she gradually breaks free from her sister's pragmatic but always tense submission to her husband.

Because they did not take on the public themes of male-centred national history, Harrower and Jessica Anderson were not hailed as Patrick White's disciples and had to wait for critical acclaim. *An Ordinary Lunacy* (1963) launched Anderson's novel-writing career. It has the same interest in women's mental states but adds dramatic flair to Harrower's style, drawing on the author's previous work in radio plays to open chapters with rapid dialogue. Anderson counterpoints social satire centred on a fashionable interior designer who survives by her wits with the brief love affair between her lawyer son and a fragile woman. The latter's remarkable beauty enmeshes her in dependent relationships that produce her husband's suicide (murder?) and later her own. The lawyer ends his infatuation and the book with a thought that applies to all the women in the story: 'how easy it was to strike an attitude, and how difficult to sustain it'.

In 1965, the first novel to be published by a Black writer appeared. Identified as an Aboriginal person at the time, Colin Johnson wrote *Wild Cat Falling*, a naturalistic story of a hipster youth released from prison, mixing with urban fringe Aboriginal people and indulged by university students because of his Camusian existentialism. His self-presentation as a born outsider and rejecter of society's lies propels him into trouble and, before being arrested again, he finds a more positive sense of identity through his uncle putting him in touch with country and Dreaming mythology.

Interest in women's writing has generated retrospective admiration for the work of June Healy, Pat Flower and Patricia Carlon, all of whom, between the late 1940s and the 1970s, wrote psychological thrillers rather than detective mysteries. Reflecting Australia's turn away from British culture, a long-time best-selling Australian writer masqueraded as an American, 'Carter Brown', who wrote over 300 pulp stories about dead and dangerous dames and tough-guy gumshoes. The counter to this was Jon Cleary's *You Can't See Round Corners* (1947), which, though published in New York, established the 'mean streets' of Sydney as a fitting location for crime writing. Cleary's battered investigator, Scobie Malone, in a later series, was a model for subsequent Australian PIs.

Coast to Coast was a series of collections of short stories published from 1941 annually until 1973 by Angus & Robertson. Its literary editors, Beatrice Davis and Douglas Stewart, both curated issues, as did a succession of writers (Frank Dalby Davison, Vance and Nettie Palmer, Barnard Eldershaw, Dal Stivens, Henrietta Drake-Brockman). After 1960, new writers Hal Porter, Thea Astley and Frank Moorhouse edited volumes along with literary editors like C.B. Christesen and Clement Semmler and scholars Leonie Kramer and A.A. Phillips. In the earlier editions, Brian James's stories were regular inclusions. His unsentimental tales of country life collected in *The Bunyip of Barney's Elbow* (1956) continue the comic yarn tradition. Germans and Irish populate poor farm holdings and depleted gold-mining towns, playing tricks on each other, revenging insults, and dealing with strangers who come and go. Irony is the dominant tone, and stories peter out as people disappear to the city or life just goes on regardless.

Hal Porter's work is quite different. He shows the difficulty of shaping a tidy literary history. Like Peter Cowan, he produced his first book of short stories in the 1940s, but moved into poetry, autobiography and novels, before publishing story collections in 1962 (*A Bachelor's Children*), 1970 (*Mr Butterfry*), 1974 (*Fredo Fuss Love Life*) and 1981 (*The Clairvoyant Goat*). This meant that his influence on the genre was not felt until much later than Cowan's and he appeared among younger writers whose concerns he did not share. Like Cowan, Porter was a modernist, but of a more poetical bent. *A Bachelor's Children* brings together stories mostly set in the 1920s and written in the thirties and forties. They have the same quality as early Slessor poems and Lindsay paintings in being theatrical, full of decoration and hectic style. Adults recall childhood encounters with eccentric aunts, uncles and local identities, recording in minute detail fashions and furnishings mysterious in their variety and obsolescence. Fanciful metaphors and words like 'atrabilious', 'mesembrianthemum', 'flagitious', 'miniver' and 'dundrearies' give the effect of Oscar Wilde mixed with Katherine Mansfield. The frequent attention to women was a change from previous writing, though the attitude towards them tends as much to mockery as to sympathy. *Mr Butterfry and Other*

Tales of New Japan provides an update on Somerset Maugham, with worldly-wise but only half-aware white men trawling the seedy bars and hotel lobbies of the world. The attitude is of self-critical supercilious wonderment towards the foreign. A stagey frisson of queer sexuality, dramatic style and unusual settings provided some glamour for Australian readers inured to 'kitchen sink' realism.

POETRY

The change in Australia's sense of its poetic output can be seen in differences between two school textbooks: one, appearing in 1958 (*The Poet's World: An Anthology of English Poetry, Australian Edition*, edited by Englishman James Reeves with an Australian section corralled at the end selected by a Professor of English at Melbourne University); the other, *The Progress of Poetry*, seven years later. This was edited by a lecturer at Adelaide University and a school teacher, and mixed in all the major Australian poets with British and American work. In 1965, Angus & Robertson also published a series, 'Australian Poets'. In many titles, living poets selected from their own work and provided an introductory essay. Poets featured were Charles Harpur, Bernard O'Dowd, Henry Kendall, Mary Gilmore, John Shaw Neilson, Victor Daley, A.D. Hope, James McAuley, Judith Wright, R.D. FitzGerald, Rosemary Dobson and Douglas Stewart. The series provided cheap study materials for the increasing numbers of university courses in Australian literature.

Judith Wright produced her second phase of poetry through this period. *The Gateway* (1953), *The Two Fires* (1955) and *Birds* (1962) were followed by the selection *Five Senses* (1963). *The Other Half* (1966) signalled the next stage in her career, appearing in the year her husband died. She continued to work her set of images linking a romantic view of nature to a darker vision of Australian climate ('Drought Year', 'Flood Year', 'Eroded Hills'), revisited legends ('Fire at Murdering Hut'), and explored the paradox of creative energy being also torment, birth being also entry into mortality ('The Cedars', 'The Cicadas'). Love promised some transcendent union or justification ('The Pool and the Star', 'To a Child',

'The Gateway'). Some of Wright's bleaker outlook stems from awareness of nuclear risk ('Two Songs for the World's End', 'The Two Fires') and there are notes of Buddhist influence in attention to self and the disturbances of action and utterance ('Return', 'For Precision', 'The Flesh'). There is also a gradual freeing up of metre and rhyme patterns and an increasing attention to individual items in the natural world ('Phaius Orchid', 'Scribbly Gum', 'Brush Turkey'). At the same time, the poet begins to meditate more on her art: 'these shapes that spring from nothing, / ... / a rhythm that dances / and is not mine' ('Five Senses'). Poems in *The Other Half* reflect social change in Australia, titles like 'To Another Housewife', 'Cleaning Day', 'Eve to Her Daughters' and 'Typists in the Phoenix Building' indicating Wright's feminist sympathies. Her protest against environmental damage is seen in the self-accusation of 'The Document' (remembering a sale of coachwood trees during wartime) and 'Turning Fifty'. Like the parrots outside her window, the poet says she will

> ... show my colours too.
> Though we've polluted
> even this air I breathe
> And spoiled green earth.

Francis Webb began writing in his twenties, and was influential on later poets who saw him marking a shift away from lyrical documentation of the land via a mix of late-Eliot style, pub idiom, and the decorative 'stagey' imagery of early Slessor. Webb wrote several verse dramas for radio and presented his longer poems as though he were directing a play. Strongly influenced by Browning's dramatic monologues, with touches of Hopkins, Lowell, Rilke and musical topics, Webb was first celebrated for his 1948 collection *A Drum for Ben Boyd*. This was a set of impressions of the legendary settler-entrepreneur, possibly a piratical slaver. A chorus of journalists lament being unable to get at reliable informants, and a variety of Boyd's acquaintances provide sketches, all pointing to the impossibility of pinning down into history a mythic character ('truth itself is a mass of stops and gaps'). The success of this perspectival and sceptical treatment of Australian history prompted Webb to repeat it in *Leichhardt in Theatre* (1952), his version of *Voss*, similarly drawing on exploration diaries but adding the imagined mental life of the subject (the 'ache within the symbol'). Stage performance blends with musical form: Charles Sturt's failure to find the mythic inland sea is 'an impasse at the centre' that is merely an 'overture' to the symphony of Leichhardt's expeditions. Webb's favoured style is eleven-syllable or longer-lined blank verse using internal rhyme and end assonance and interspersed with shorter rhymed stanzas. His religious beliefs (he wrote a 'Canticle' to Saint Francis and Saint Clare) generate meditations on suffering, and his last major work to recreate settler history ('Eyre All Alone' in *Socrates*, 1961) presents a mind grappling with exhaustion and the desert rather than a national hero. The poem also recognises that Eyre owed his success to his Aboriginal guide, Wylie. Webb's focus on 'the gimbals of unease' on which our lives swing encapsulated for many the modern angst that Australia's still strongly pastoral poetry did not engage with. This is most evident in the later poems (*The Ghost of the Cock*, 1964) about electric shock therapy and experiences in a mental hospital. Webb's collected poems appeared in 1969.

 A.D. Hope became publicly known as a poet when he published *The Wandering Islands* in 1955 and *Poems* in 1961, though his poems had circulated among friends since the 1940s. His most distinctive verse took the form of satirical reworkings of European myth informed by a Freudian view of sexuality and by a vision of Australia populated by complacent hedonists who at some limit realise the horror of their empty lives. Don Juan pursued by all the women he has seduced and by his own satiation and disgust is a cryptic comment on the adolescent sexuality expressed in Norman Lindsay's art and the national cult of physical health and beauty matched only by interest in material wealth. There was a certain shock value in poetry openly discussing sex and rewriting biblical figures. Hope was a university lecturer in English and put his reading to use in shaping tight rhymes and witty phrases in the style of Dryden and Pope, but with a strong element of Byron in both form and content. With characteristic irony, his most famous poem, 'Australia', allows that a redeeming culture for a new country might emerge not from inherited European 'chattering', but from some prophetic vision born out of experience in the ancient desert heart of the continent. Even then, however, that vision is expressed in biblical language.

Hope's verse for a decade or more became the overseas voice of Australian poetry in Commonwealth literature classes, no doubt because it represented (like Nissim Ezekiel's verse, for example) a mode recognisable from standard studies of English poetry with added touches of regional expression. In Australia, Hope's work attracted attention for its wit. He derided the 'bush ballad' tradition in 'A Letter from Rome', grumbling: 'Australian poets, if they ever tried, / Might show at least a rudiment of brain', but at the same time, his poems celebrated passion, both physical and emotional. He praises human drives but deplores their effects: lust, violence, commercialised banality. Deploying his customary irony, he sets up a 'Conversation with Calliope', lamenting a prosaic modernity that disallows heroic epics by using the style and length of epic verse. Acknowledging all such contradictions, he declares in 'An Epistle from Holofernes' that poets will continue to tap into some revivifying subterranean stream:

>If in heroic couplets, then, I seem
>To cut the ground from an heroic theme,
>It is not that I mock at love, or you,
>But, living two lives, know both of them are true.
>There's a hard thing, and yet it must be done,
>Which is: to see and live them both as one.

Less essayistic poems leave us with a mood provoking thoughtful response to a subject, as in 'The Death of a Bird', 'Man Friday', and the lament for species extinction, 'Moschus Moschiferus'. Hope continued to write for many years, his *Collected Poems* appearing in 1966 and again with more work in 1972, followed by *A Late Picking* (1975), *Antechinus* (1981), *The Age of Reason* (1985) and *Orpheus* (1991). He was an important reviewer of Australian writing, some of his critical work collected as *The Cave and the Spring* (1965). Editions of selected work kept appearing until his death in 2000.

Other academics were also producing books of poetry in this period. Now known mostly for his role in the Ern Malley hoax and for his founding editorship of *Quadrant* magazine, James McAuley followed up on his 1946 collection *Under Aldebaran* with

A Vision of Ceremony (1956) and *Captain Quiros* (1964). The latter long poem captured attention because it fitted with other works about key events in national history. As his second title indicates, McAuley adopted formal devices to construct a measured outlook on life, drawing on adherence to Catholicism as a conservative ritual holding modern chaos at bay. He went on to publish *Surprises of the Sun* (1969) and *Collected Poems* (1971).

Another Catholic professor, Vincent Buckley, questioned whether Australian literature could or should be taught as its own subject in universities, but his teaching and poetry nonetheless built up a coterie of writers in Melbourne and his *Essays in Poetry, Mainly Australian* (1957) was an important map of Australian work, as was his study of Henry Handel Richardson. Buckley's own work was informed by his Irish roots and Melbourne surroundings, his first collection, *The World's Flesh* (1954), also declaring his religious attachments. Connection to European literary tradition is suggested in *Arcady and Other Places* (1966), and *The Golden Builders* (1976), perhaps his major work, is a series of reflections on urban development, the nature of particular suburbs like Carlton and Fitzroy, and on his father dying of a stroke. Like his academic-poet colleagues, Buckley favoured regular metre and rhyme, but has a more relaxed voice than McAuley and less satiric bite than Hope. He did, however, critique politicians (seeing a Cold War demagogue behind each one) and was suspicious of leftist writers ('On Being an Anti-Communist Poet: This Hurts Me More than It Hurts Yevtushenko'). Two other important collections among his extensive output are *Masters in Israel* (1961) and *Late Winter Child* (1979).

Any country's poetic output will include quiet achievers who gain respect but only acceptance for one or two pieces in anthologies across time. Sydney-based poet Bruce Beaver shared with Francis Webb a history of psychiatric imbalance that sent him to a cure labouring in rural New South Wales until he settled on poetry and journalism. He produced his first collection of poems in 1961 (*Under the Bridge*), followed by *Seawall and Shoreline* (1964)— gentle poems in a variety of stanza forms, mostly unrhymed and in 'his own' voice remembering rural work or recording scenes from his life centred on Sydney's beach suburb of Manly. Beaver's breakthrough as a major literary voice did not occur until the 1970s. Two other quiet achievers were Elizabeth Riddell and John Blight. Riddell wrote technically accomplished ballad-form verse that gave stories a glow of symbol rather like Neilson's lyrics. Blight was valued for his unusual focus on sea life rather than the land, and for packing his observations and thoughts into sonnets that used enjambment to produce a relaxed meditative tone. His best-known poem is 'Death of a Whale', in which he notes how we lament the death of one small thing but turn away from large-scale disaster.

Bruce Dawe for most of his working life taught in schools rather than universities and wrote about lives in suburban Australia rather than striving after a philosophy, a portrait of the bush, or a theory of art. His poems date from the mid-fifties, and he adopts a colloquial register, borrowing the tone and some of the form of popular ballad tradition (as in 'The Last Romantics', about the romance of cowboy movies) to reflect ironically on the foibles of ordinary Australians and their national enthusiasms. His early work is collected in *No Fixed Address* (1962) and *A Need of Similar Name* (1965). The usual poetical apprentice work is sharpened up in evocations of Friday nights at the boxing ring ('There Was a Time') or the humour of a letter answering a job ad ('Ghost Wanted; Young, Willing'). 'Enter Without So Much as Knocking' orchestrates different voices as a Greek chorus telling us about a baby who enters the world of hospital machinery and grows to lose his dreams in a welter of radio competitions, commerce, civic commands and survival: 'I'm telling you straight, Jim, it's Number One every time / for this chicken, hit wherever you see a head and / kick whoever's down'. A car crash puts the speaker back in hospital and then the cemetery: 'permanent residentials, no parking tickets, no taximeters / ticking, ... // ... Silence.' Irony and references to popular culture become a hallmark of Dawe's work. Many poems originate in comments from friends, reviewers and items in the news. The last inspired a subtle protest against capital punishment ('A Victorian Hangman Tells His Love') and Dawe's air force service and news broadcasts increasingly direct his attention to Asia ('Butterworth Road') and to the war in Vietnam ('The Saigon-Dalat Night-train Runs Infrequently...'). His most anthologised poem in this context is 'The Not-So-Good Earth', in which Uncle Billy watches television reports of famine in China and the poem shows how newscasts can depersonalise human tragedy. An earlier poem, 'Guilt by Association', more overtly shows that we are complicit with history. Dawe continued to publish poems into the 2000s, increasingly critiquing topical issues such as the detention of refugees as 'illegal immigrants'.

Social movements bringing First Nations peoples into national visibility were matched by literary events. In 1964, Kath Walker, later to be known as Oodgeroo Noonuccal, published *We Are Going*, the first book of verse by an Aboriginal person. Dismissed by some as polemic and a naïve reprocessing of bush ballad forms, her work nonetheless had significant impact on Australian culture. Laments for loss of Aboriginal tradition were balanced with appeals for equal treatment of races. Walker became friends with Judith Wright and turned her early personal recognition of settler violence towards Aboriginal peoples into public and literary advocacy for Indigenous rights. She also inspired younger Aboriginal writers.

DRAMA

Australian theatre continued through the Vietnam War, though at a much-reduced rate of production. Popular modes, morale-boosting sketches and musical numbers were the main feature, with material still imported from Britain, plus increasing numbers of items being introduced from America, including 'classics' by Tennessee Williams and Arthur Miller. Radio drama remained a staple source of income for writers and actors for the next several decades. Many novelists (Vance Palmer, Morris West, Kylie Tennant, Dymphna Cusack, Ruth Park) and most stage writers also wrote for radio. Several men (Max Afford, Colin Free, Edmund Barclay, Peter Yeldham) and many women (Gwen Meredith, Oriel Gray, Catherine Shepherd, Pat Flower, Cathleen Carroll, Joy Hollyer) made long careers writing one-act plays for radio between 1940 and 1970, many without achieving fame on the stage or scholarly recognition.

Post-war society was much more self-consciously modernising and urban than previously, and the 'bush myth' was losing its power. The pathos of those caught in its thrall was captured in *The Summer of the Seventeenth Doll* by Ray Lawler. Itinerant workers on northern sugar cane farms come down to Melbourne for their annual carouse with their barmaid girlfriends only to realise that they are all getting old and the romance of their carefree lifestyle has worn off. The play premiered in 1955 and was an immediate success, touring the country and receiving critical notice in London. It conveyed the nostalgia for a golden past in common Australian speech and showed skill in modulating dialogue and mood within a tight structure. Its realism and evident interest in national identity preserved established conventions but concentrated on the interaction of individuals faced with a universal human predicament. Lawler also had *The Piccadilly Bushman* staged in 1959.

More contentious was Richard Beynon's *The Shifting Heart* (1957), which also made it to the London stage. It showed a marriage between 'Aussie' Clarrie and 'New Australian' Maria, their happiness spoiled by prejudices generated in the Second World War and the bashing to death of Maria's brother for daring to crash a dance claimed by Anglo-Australians as their own territory. Similar social critiques appeared from Oriel Gray (*Burst of Summer*, 1959) and Anthony Coburn (*Bastard Country*, 1963). Peter Kenna wrote several plays in this period but is best known for *The Slaughter on St Teresa's Day* (1959), which showed up the falsely romantic character of C.J. Dennis's urban larrikins in its depiction of working-class poverty, crime and gang violence.

After engagement in two world wars and continuing involvement in anti-communist conflicts (Korea, Malaysia), Australia officially fixed its identity around the figure of the warrior-hero. Younger Australians were questioning the whole militaristic myth, its degraded enactment in drunkenness and gambling after the Anzac Day marches, and the desirability of any conflict in a world threatened with nuclear annihilation. Alan Seymour ruffled feathers when he expressed all this in *The One Day of the Year* (1960), which adds class difference to generational conflict in that the young man questioning tradition has moved into a university education and away from his working-class parents.

The twin theatrical traditions of melodrama and naturalism gave way to new symbolic and impressionistic forms, most clearly in the plays of Patrick White. Returning from Europe and war to the complacent conventionality of suburban life in 'God's own country', White created characters blind to their own banal bullying awfulness but gave them appeal through framing them in stylised settings and a mix of colloquial and metaphorical language that allowed glimpses of tragic existential yearning. *The Ham Funeral* (1947) took a while to find acceptance, finally being staged in 1961. It featured rooms in a boarding house that symbolised different levels of existence, partly class marked, but mostly related to Jungian ideas of body, soul and anima. A Young Man shuttles between his landlady and an unseen girl idealised by him in an upstairs room. When he finally decides to meet her, the room contains only flowers, and he breaks through the walls of the set to seek maturity in the outside world. This staging, the symbolism and White's poetic language were not what audiences were used to, and *The Season at Sarsaparilla* (1962), with its depiction of metaphysical yearnings beneath ordinary suburban lives, and the ironic depiction of an intrusive do-gooder in *A Cheery Soul* (1963) provoked hostility amongst those who saw themselves and their values being derided. After *Night on Bald Mountain* reached the stage in 1964, it took revivals of the other plays in the 1970s to cement White's reputation as a dramatist.

This recognition was made more possible by a proliferation of theatres, both professional and experimental, in the latter half of the 1960s. A younger generation of playwrights started to appear before this (Jack Hibberd, Clem Gorman and, briefly, David Ireland), creating a basis for what would emerge as an eruption of 'new theatre' through the 1970s. During this time there was a growing interest in the Theatre of the Absurd and Theatre of Cruelty modelled overseas by Ionesco, Artaud, Grotowski and Peter Brook. These influences, and some dabbling in surrealism, meshed with older social realism to give a new rawness to exposés of national ideals like mateship and easy egalitarianism.

Children's Literature

After the war, Australian authors began to establish an international reputation for stories about Australian children in Australian settings. Publishing from 1948, Nan Chauncy celebrated life on an isolated rural farm in Tasmania, gaining national notice for *Tiger in the Bush* (1957) and *Tangara* (1960). Chauncy follows the nineteenth-century genre of adventures in nature, reproducing its suspicion of city life, but is an early includer of Americans, who take the place of English 'new chums'. Other rural romances came from Joan Phipson and Colin Thiele, the latter's *The Sun on the Stubble* (1961) being noteworthy for featuring the Barossa Valley community of German immigrants. Thiele featured South Australian settings, making the Coorong ocean lagoon, a pelican and a lonesome boy with an Aboriginal friend famous in his much-celebrated *Storm Boy* (1963). He also depicted the tuna fishing industry of Port Lincoln in *Blue Fin* (1969). Rex Ingamells tried a more realistic approach than previous children's books on Aboriginal subjects in *Aranda Boy* (1952). Eschewing the pastoral romance, Ivan Southall challenged his child protagonists, separating them from adults and easy survival by storm (in *Hills End*, 1962), bushfire (*Ash Road*, 1965) and plane crash (*To the Wild Sky*, 1967). Southall was also popular as the creator of Simon Black, an Australian pilot hero. Across this period, Eleanor Spence made her name writing for children, *The Green Laurel* (1963) being a modern family tale that does away with the old country–city binary. Alan Marshall established a trend of auto/biographical stories about overcoming adversity. His *I Can Jump Puddles* (1955) records his successful efforts to deal with country life despite having a leg crippled by infantile paralysis.

CHAPTER 6

Dissent to Dismissal
1965–1975

SOCIAL AND POLITICAL CONTEXT

Australia's entry into armed conflict in Vietnam was an extension of Cold War politics that set in train an end to Cold War thinking. It cemented ties between Australia and the US while inducing opposition to American power, and it reinvigorated the notion of Australian military prowess while questioning militarism. Australia had rejected mandatory conscription in previous wars, so the government resorted to a lottery to ensure recruitment. If your birth date came out of the barrel, you became a 'nasho' (someone doing national service), were given rapid training, and shipped off to messy jungle fighting. Opposition to both the means of selection and to the morality of the war led to public protest in 1964 and (following the example of the 1969 Washington Moratorium demonstrations) to a campaign of civil disobedience. Huge protest marches were met with police using tear gas—the first major civil conflict since the Great Depression. The 1950s respect for state machineries of order dwindled, backed by televised violence from the war zone, images of troops firing on protesters at Kent State University, and student unrest in Europe from 1968. The Vietnam War created the argument that people old enough to fight were also old enough to vote, and in 1973, Australia had reduced the voting age from 21 to 18, thereby enfranchising many who questioned national myths and political allegiances.

Regardless of anti-American sentiment, Australia's ties to America were strengthened by Britain's application for entry into the European Common Market in 1961, and its political membership of the EU in 1975. Suddenly, Australia's special relationship with its colonial 'parent', including special deals on agricultural trade and travel to Britain, ceased. Despite ongoing popular attachment to the romance of the royal family, young Australia stopped thinking of England as 'home'. The nation began issuing its own honours instead of accepting knighthoods and Commanders of the British Empire medals.

Shifts in social and political attitudes were impelled by other events. Within the country, the long reign of Prime Minister Bob (Sir Robert) Menzies came to an end. Menzies had been an enthusiastic monarchist, but Australia made a symbolic break with the past in 1966 when it converted its currency from pounds, shillings and pence to dollars and cents. By that year, despite past antagonisms, Japan had become Australia's leading trade partner and the nation was increasingly conscious of its place in South East Asia and the Pacific. When Malaysia's communal tensions led to race riots in 1969, many non-Malays migrated to Australia. The violent overthrow in 1973 of Salvador Allende's government in Chile led to an influx of a new group of migrants. Ongoing unrest in Indonesia and East Timor turned the Australian mind more towards the immediate region. Cyclone Tracy destroyed Darwin in 1974, focussing attention on the north of the country, otherwise neglected as a remote outpost of the nation.

Inside the country, campaigns against capital punishment saw the last hanging in 1967, and in that year the same kind of moral questioning, fuelled by America's civil rights movement, moved a strong majority of Australians to approve recognition of Aboriginal peoples as citizens of the nation with the right to vote. In the previous year, Gurindji stockmen working for a British-owned cattle station got tired of receiving only store supplies as payment and walked away to their tribal lands. This heralded a new era of activism for both proper working conditions and rights to hold traditional lands. Women played a large part in mobilising public opinion (Kath Walker and Faith Bandler being two writer-activists). Students and others organised a Freedom Ride, taking buses into country towns to desegregate swimming pools, hotels and public facilities. However, the federal constitution still left the Aboriginal population subject to government controls. In 1968, the discovery of Aboriginal remains and signs of ceremonial burial at Lake Mungo pushed back the verifiable date of human occupation of the continent, establishing a scientific basis for recognising that Indigenous Australians have the longest surviving culture in the world.

Agitation for social reform spread into other areas of life. Australia's union movement joined forces with community resistance against real estate 'developers' who were bulldozing historical buildings, taking over public parks, and pushing inner-city residents out to the suburban fringes. From 1971, Jack Mundey led 'green bans' that outlawed labour on many projects and laid the foundation for future environmental protection campaigns. Agitation against gender-based discrimination also gained force. Women sought the right to work after marriage, the right to legal abortion, to manage their own finances, and even the right to drink in hotels (considered a man's domain). Equal pay for doing the same work as men was legislated in 1969 and the Women's Electoral Lobby was founded in 1972. Germaine Greer became an international figure when she published her critique of patriarchy, *The Female Eunuch*, two years earlier. In 1975, *Hecate: A Women's Interdisciplinary Journal* appeared, and Anne Summers analysed sexism in Australian society in *Damned Whores and God's Police*.

In 1972, under the catchy song slogan 'It's time', a Labor government, led by the charismatic Gough Whitlam, was elected. A team of inexperienced idealists instituted rapid reforms: free tertiary education, the end to military conscription, special funding for schools in underprivileged areas, and recognition of the People's Republic of China. Restrictive immigration and assimilation policies were finally dismantled in 1974, replaced by 'Multiculturalism'— official recognition of the cultures and languages of migrant minorities. A movement began to return some lands to Aboriginal ownership and Australia relinquished its colonial administration of Papua New Guinea, taking it to independence in 1975. During this time, several states legalised abortion and consenting adult sex of any kind. Most of these reforms remain in place, but the government had little experience in economic management and the conservative opposition blocked budgetary process. The latter did a deal with the governor-general, who summarily dismissed the

Whitlam government in November 1975. Despite outrage at abuse of the Crown's powers and suspected connivance of the CIA, the conservative Liberal–National Party coalition was voted back into power, where it stayed for another decade, returning the country to a free-market, small-government regime. 'The Dismissal' remains a powerful legend in the public mind. Since then, politics has been heavily influenced by mining companies and global conglomerates.

Cultural Context

Awareness of Australia's increasing involvement in global social and political movements as an independent agent generated contradictory cultural impulses: on the one hand, there was a greater cosmopolitan openness to difference and a critique of the old myths of distant innocence and Anglocentric stability; on the other, there was a new nationalism that preserved many old assumptions. Studies in history and politics became popular as people sought to understand this change; Geoffrey Blainey's influential *The Tyranny of Distance* (1966) accompanied Manning Clark's volumes of history successively released from 1962 until complete in 1987.

From 1970 onwards, literary publishing and bookshops were beset by corporate takeovers that placed greater emphasis on global commerce than on national culture. Angus & Robertson tried unsuccessfully to break into the British book market, upheld its role as Australia's main promoter of a national literature, but ended up as a bookstore chain before being swallowed into HarperCollins. At the same time, funding from the Literature Board of the Australia Council for the Arts allowed some university presses (notably Queensland's) to boost their literary lists (UQP released Peter Carey's first book in 1974, for example) and sustained smaller operations such as Makar Press, Fremantle Arts Centre Press, McPhee Gribble, and Wild & Woolley (all beginning 1972–76). Literary magazines received funding to pay writers. There were experiments at getting stories back into newspapers (such as the supplement *Tabloid Story*, 1972–80, or later, *Australian Literary Review*). New alternative papers (*Nation Review*, *Adelaide Review*) carried literary content, and the burgeoning of the humanities and social sciences in Australian universities allowed for scholarly publications that included creative writing (such as *Southern Review*, beginning in 1963 at the University of Adelaide). Australian theatre received a huge boost when Currency Press, dedicated to the publishing of plays and theatre criticism, was founded in 1971. The Whitlam government established the Australian Film and Television School in 1973, while several state governments funded production units. They provided new opportunities for writers to earn a living and kept many literary classics in circulation as films. Most writers continued to earn very little from their writing though this was remedied slightly in 1974 when the government approved the Public Lending Right, paying for the use of books in public libraries. Whitlam was keen to do away with the image of Australia as a provincial and culturally barren place—an aim aided by Patrick White's winning the Nobel Prize for literature and by New South Wales's completion of the Sydney Opera House, both in 1973.

One aspect of Australian literature's development was the internationally emerging critique of teaching the British/European literary canon ('dead white males') in countries whose own languages and cultures bore little relation to what students were asked to read, and whose writing was often actively derided as 'sub literary' (usually by white male and often Oxbridge scholars). A loose coalition formed of younger academics from across the old British Empire, inspecting the textual dynamics and cultural politics of 'local' writing and promoting critical recognition of difference (racial, gendered, historical, aesthetic). The worldwide Association for Commonwealth Literature and Language Studies was founded in 1964, and held its second conference in 1968 at the University of Queensland with the theme 'National Identity'. Alongside this movement, Australia's older cultural nationalism gathered new impetus, modified to include writing by non-Anglo-Celtic Australians, by women and by Indigenous authors.

Prose Fiction

New novels that critiqued working conditions in Australia came from David Ireland, but by this time textual politics had shifted from realist class analysis to anarchic satire. Ireland's first novel, *The Chantic Bird* (1968), is a series of memories narrated to a would-be writer by an almost seventeen-year-old car thief, mugger, rapist and general delinquent. He claims to tell only those things that 'would be good for the readers' but presents a series of antisocial activities so relentlessly outrageous that at times they take on an air of farce. These culminate in the killing and butchering of the writer so he does not take control of the boy's story. This 'lumpy' tale mimics the erratic nature of the orphan boy's life. He sleeps rough, in hiding from any kind of authority figure, with occasional visits to his younger siblings (and perhaps his child) and their teenage carer (his lover?). The children bring out a kinder side to the narrator, and little Stevo's fairytale of 'the chantic bird', delivered in small instalments, acts as a foil to sordid life, and is a connective thread through otherwise random episodes and a reflection on the appeal of storytelling. The narrator cannot stand social structures that teach 'how to work for a boss' but any revolution is forestalled by his cynical view of humanity. His is 'a tale told by nobody … to show you what a silly thing it is to live'. The tale itself, however, has the energy of satire and picaresque variety, entertaining (and perhaps moralising) in its amoral excess.

At one point in *The Chantic Bird*, the narrator dreams of himself as a statue labelled 'The Unknown Factory Prisoner'. This supplies the title of Ireland's best-known book, *The Unknown Industrial Prisoner* (1971). It is a picaresque assemblage of vignettes that presents cartoon-like characters known only by their nicknames (Great White Father, the Volga Boatman, Samurai). Old-style allegory (and some biblical parody) mixes with Zola, Marx and occasional futuristic touches to present Australia (and human life in general) as a penal colony where everyone serves a life sentence labouring for a global corporation (here the Puroil refinery). Relief can be found in absurd hobbies (seeking God by crystal-set radio), tormenting each other, pilfering, drinking and sex. Ireland is distinctive for showing working life in all its ugliness but with an underlying fondness for odd characters and occasional bouts of lyrical effusion. ('At the water's edge, waves muttered little asides and slapped the stone slabs in irritation. Out on the bay, the hop and splash of mullet swimming for their lives.') As a long essay critiquing globalised capitalism, the book should fail as a novel, but the shortness of each scene and the variety of types lends a liveliness to the obvious message. There are some 'plot' developments, such as the steady diminution of one worker's body in successive amputations and a series of minor industrial accidents that build to an apocalyptic conflagration. Coherence is constructed from the framing but elusive presence of a mainly invisible worker who is writing a book 'to take apart, then build up piece by piece, this mosaic of one kind of human life ... to remind my present age of its industrial adolescence'.

Admired by some as an upended, darker modern version of the national novel of mateship, Ireland's inelegant form and political nihilism restricted his appeal, as did the sexism of his rough masculine world. *The Flesheaters* (1972) is another set of random sketches of incident and character, delivered by a hyper-aware and probably psychotic narrator who sees a Hieronymus Bosch world of carnal indulgence. Poverty is regarded as a congenital medical condition and unemployment a cause for psychiatric treatment. Characters indicate that everyone is crazy and that dreams and zany behaviour are the only sane ways of coping with life. Another zany is the central figure in *Burn* (1974), which turns to Aboriginal and mixed-race characters. Reading like a playscript rather than a novel, the text shows three generations fighting among themselves and against white society. They live in a shanty on a riverbank at the edge of a country town that wants to move them so the council can create a caravan park. The book ends with the uncertain prospect of a violent guerrilla action led by the father, whose memories of wartime experiences run through the dialogues. *The Glass Canoe* (1976) relocates Ireland's assemblage of short anecdotes and character sketches to Sydney's pubs and their world of tribal brawls, tales of sexual conquests and of sexually rapacious women, heroic drinking, and practical jokes. Essentially, Ireland's fiction is an updated urban version of the bush yarn and, in its working-class focus, is linked to the lighter work of Frank Hardy.

With a firmer hold on readers and scholars, David Malouf made his debut as a novelist with *Johnno* (1975). Not unlike George

Johnston's *My Brother Jack*, this tale of growing up in wartime Brisbane relies on the common device of a bookish narrator (nicknamed Dante) intrigued, harassed and led on by a more outgoing, rebellious companion. Opening with a distancing note of irony (Dante's father dies on the day he is given a clean bill of health), the story draws upon Malouf's own past, seen in his collection of essays *12 Edmondstone Street*. *Johnno* has the narrator returning from overseas to go through his father's house, where he finds a school photo of the trickster of the book's title. In the context of a provincial backwater where 'nothing extraordinary happened', Johnno offers drama and leads the push for Australian youth to go abroad and seek authentic being. After time in the Congo, Johnno moves to Paris, where Dante meets him, having taken up a teaching job in England. Over a series of travels, Dante watches his friend become increasingly erratic and inebriated, tormented by the gap between his idealism and existential rootlessness. Baudelaire is mentioned in passing. The two eventually return to Australia, Dante content to dwell in non-exotic Brisbane, Johnno going bush to work and dying in a possible suicide, having failed to live up to his models of Nietzsche and Schopenhauer. Dante closes the tale back among his father's books and memories of the Great Depression. He concludes, 'Maybe, in the end, even the lies we tell define us. And better, some of them, than our most earnest attempts at the truth.' This idea would inform many of the writers of the next generation.

Thea Astley's *A Boat Load of Home Folk* (1968) reminds Australians of their links with the Pacific. It interleaves short chapters switching between the present and pasts of characters sojourning on a tropical island. Each section is figured as a set of (anti-touristic) postcards that show everyone arriving at deflating self-knowledge, death, or both. Tensions build along with the weather until a cyclone hits the island and the sojourners take their own ruin home, leaving the ruin of the colonial settlement. No one gets off lightly in Astley's books. A jaundiced authorial outlook is, however, offset by moments of natural beauty.

Astley had musical training and places European classical pieces (Bach and Delius) in opposition to popular tunes, highlighting the lack of intellect and culture in Australia's mediocre suburbs and barbarous rural towns—given allegorical names like Grogbusters and Glittertops. In *The Acolyte* (1972) we see the two musical modes coming into alignment as a blind pianist fuses the classics and jazz to compose musical evocations of Australian life that are both satiric and tributes. Devotion to a superior of some kind runs through many of Astley's novels and here a bored young man aware of his limited talents becomes scribe, manager and dogsbody to the genius composer as well as part-time lover of that unruly man's women. The first-person narrative charts his increasingly disgusted self-awareness in the languor and rotting excess of the tropical setting. Astley deploys echoes of poets (Slessor and FitzGerald's 'The Wind at Your Door') to demonstrate the compelling disastrous nature of genius and to skewer the parasites of the 'arts industry'.

Increasingly, Astley focused on Australia's handling of a history of settler abuse of the Indigenous population. *A Kindness Cup* (1974) draws on a historical massacre of Aboriginal people by white townsfolk in up-country Queensland and turns it into a 'problem play'. A country teacher returns after twenty years to a celebration of town settlement led by a squatter turned politician and a former policeman who had led a posse of whites in the 'dispersal' of a tribe. The teacher wants to expose this outrage, engages support from the town printer, and they prosecute their plan against the wishes of a landholder who had been maltreated for warning the Aboriginal people. The book asks whose interests are being served by suppressing or revisiting inconvenient truths and ends with the townsfolk closing ranks against the two 'troublemakers'. It is a compact text in control of its material, but ambiguous in its message: clearly the actions of brutes and hypocrites are not to be condoned, but they seem to be untroubled by their misdeeds and the agents of white guilt and justice are either ineffectual or too passionately tied to personal vendetta.

Another writer who was hailed as 'the next Patrick White' was Thomas Keneally. Like Thea Astley and Morris West, Keneally inserted Catholicism into the largely Protestant landscape of Australian fiction, beginning with *The Place at Whitton* (1964), a sensation novel in which a hedonist would-be witch seeks out a turncoat murderous priest to perform dark rites. Critics noted the unusual combination of thriller and theology and some dramatic phrasing. Keneally turned his own experiences of seminary training into satiric use in an exposé of hypocrisy and pride amongst senior clergy, *Three Cheers for the Paraclete* (1968). He also produced a largely autobiographical novel of wartime childhood, *The Fear* (1965), featuring a weak bully who terrorises his family and escapes self-accusation by fanatical devotion to the communist cause. Keneally 'arrived' with *Bring Larks and Heroes* (1967), which won the Miles Franklin Award. It explored the beginnings of colonial Australia in lyrical prose that infused bare survival in a new land with moral dilemmas about preserving individual integrity in opposition to a brutal convict system. Keneally gathered a reputation for unpredictable shifts in output, such as *A Dutiful Daughter* (1971), arguably the first magic realist novel in Australia, and *Blood Red, Sister Rose* (1974), a fictionalised tale of Joan of Arc. *Gossip from the Forest* (1975) was a dramatic interplay of characters negotiating the armistice that ended the First World War. Keneally's second major success, both in terms of sales and critical regard, was *The Chant of Jimmie Blacksmith* (1972). Based on the historical manhunt for the Governor bothers, the novel dramatises the long pursuit, showing the mixed motivations of a cross-section of white society and exploring Jimmie's mental state. In the end, his brother is shot and a wounded Jimmie is captured. He awaits hanging as the rest of Australia celebrates Federation. The novel works with ironic counterpointing of characters and viewpoints and implies that the new nation carries a legacy of racial violence to be confronted and atoned for.

Harry Heseltine's 1976 *The Penguin Book of Australian Short Stories* marked a shift in style and content when it went beyond echoing the 1951 Oxford list to showcase work by Hal Porter, Patrick White, Elizabeth Harrower, Desmond O'Grady, Thelma Forshaw, Frank Moorhouse, Michael Wilding and Peter Carey. When Kerryn Goldsworthy selected material for her Dent/Everyman's *Australian Short Stories* (1983), she repeated the Penguin list, adding Catherine Helen Spence, Ethel Anderson, Christina Stead, Elizabeth Jolley, Morris Lurie and Murray Bail. As well as the new material from younger writers, it is worth noting Goldsworthy's retrospective inclusion of women.

This decade saw the rebirth of the short story, influenced by American writers like Hemingway, John Cheever, Raymond Carver, Robert Coover and Richard Brautigan, by the French nouveau roman, and by the popularity of Borges. Two influential editors were Frank Moorhouse and Michael Wilding, who in their own work depicted the 'new wave' of Sydney-based bohemians living a hedonistic life of road trips, communes, drugs and sexual adventure. 'The Beats' were models, and both Wilding and Moorhouse have stories recording an abortive attempt to organise a wake for Jack Kerouac. Moorhouse came from the country to work as a journalist and described the new 'urban tribe' in hectic and explicit prose. His books—*Futility and Other Animals* (stories, 1969), *The Americans, Baby* (stories, 1972), *The Electrical Experience* (novella, 1974), and many subsequent titles—were collections of what looked like short stories, but they dealt with the same cast of characters, dryly exposing fake intellectuals, phoney radicals and opportunistic lovers while mocking the materialistic world of their parents and 'the system'. Moorhouse's writing had an element of scandal in that its characters were identifiable real friends and enemies, though his narrator undercuts sensationalism with deadpan commentary and a world-weary tone. The stories attracted critical regard as 'discontinuous narrative' that cohered into a loose novelistic form.

Michael Wilding was a lecturer at Sydney University, and his stories are a more measured version of the same scenes; both he and Moorhouse are presences throughout *Aspects of the Dying Process* (1972). Wilding captures the sun-drenched hedonism of Sydney's beach culture and his alter ego writes up a slow contemplation of sexual pleasures and hesitant engagement with free-wheeling social connections, all laden with literary quotations. His second collection, *The West Midland Underground* (1975), includes remembrances of rising as a scholarship boy from England's working classes and moves to metafictional fragments and conceptual play, similar to Peter Carey's work. ('The Man of Slow Feeling', for example, imagines someone who can only receive the sensations of an experience hours afterwards.) Wilding goes on to write satirical novels such as *Living Together* (1974) and *The Short Story Embassy* (1975). The latter reads like an absurdist play and parodies famous short story writers and the literary politics of Australia. The 'embassy' allows writers to send rejection letters to publishers and editors seeking their work instead of the other way around.

A new era of short fiction was marked by *The Most Beautiful Lies*, edited by Brian Kiernan in 1977. (The title was taken from a tribute to Australia by Mark Twain.) Along with pieces from Wilding and Moorhouse, it included stories by Morris Lurie, Peter Carey and Murray Bail. Lurie worked in advertising alongside Carey and Barry Oakley, and like Oakley, produced comic tales, in his case often featuring Jewish characters, that updated earlier yarning traditions. Bail and Carey were different in that they had imbibed more of the fabular influences from abroad and (especially in Bail) some of the estrangement of the word that came with linguistic theories. A kind of philosophical metafiction resulted, as in Bail's 'Zoellner's Definition', in which dictionary definitions of words ('face', 'ear', 'nose', etc.) are deployed to compile a 'portrait' of Zoellner, making us aware that the writer is constructing something that is nothing but an image set made only of words. Bail's 'Portrait of Electricity' has a museum guide conduct the faithful past an increasingly absurd collection of items from the life of a famous person, pointing to our desire for intimacy with others and the past, only available as tiny hints from signs that are not the reality they signify. It prefigures Bail's humorous novel *Homesickness* (1980), which follows a mixed group of Australians trooping through a bizarre assortment of overseas museums.

Carey is generally more flamboyant in finding some uncanny or dramatically compelling image or situation through which to flaunt literary invention while making some criticism of the social order. In 'Do You Love Me?' a recognisable world is refigured into one where cartographers are employed by the state to make annual maps of the country, a 'census' that lets everyone know 'exactly where we stand'. Science is connected to nature rituals: a good mapping produces a bacchanalian Festival of the Corn. However, blank spaces on the map start to get bigger, and buildings and people begin to fade and disappear, producing mass panic. The narrator wills himself to love his cranky cartographer father, who nonetheless becomes invisible, leaving his mother asking with some concern, 'Do you love me?'. This is typical of Carey's blend of conceptual symbol (maps signifying the impossible goal of mimesis), references to realities like Shell Oil and ironing, elements from science fiction, and a moral tag. The story is characteristic of his second collection, *War Crimes* (1979). His first, *The Fat Man in History* (1974), supplied the stories selected in *The Most Beautiful Lies*, the most famous of which has been 'American Dreams'. In this, a quiet man in a small town has builders erect a large wall behind which he constructs a scale model of the town's people and buildings. When it is revealed, townsfolk debate whether it is a tribute or an act of revenge, as they see themselves estranged and uncover images of secret goings-on. They have thought of real life as being elsewhere and represented by American media, and this inauthentic living results in their becoming a tourist attraction wherein the model assumes an authoritative fixed reality that subsumes real temporal change. Carey remains hostile throughout his career to cultural colonisation (despite his later move to New York) but the story also rehearses another key theme: art's relation to reality, and how we read texts.

Shirley Hazzard commenced her literary career with a short story collection, *Cliffs of Fall* (1963), followed by a novel, *The Evening of the Holiday* (1966), and another story collection, *People in Glass Houses* (1967). Apart from their virtues of careful style and nuanced capture of unspoken flows of emotion, these works are important as symptoms of a new internationalism in Australian culture. Perhaps influenced by White's Nobel Prize and by the general turn to American literature, readers and critics were now able to accept work set in Italy, England and the US by an expatriate writer who appeared in the *New Yorker* rather than the *Bulletin*. Hazzard specialises in young women who slip almost passively into love affairs with pleasant men who carry a strong sense of male entitlement and an inability to tolerate wounded pride. Things fall apart with no great drama, but the women are left emotionally drained. Protagonists generally have a keen awareness of the shifting tones of relationships and are often able to talk about feelings, though without the ability to withstand the fading of connection.

Overshadowed by this 'revival' of story were migrant voices, some of which received more attention later. Pino Bosi, a journalist of Italian origin, published in both Italian and English, his story collections including *The Checkmate and Other Stories* (1973). He also wrote poetry, biography and a novel, *Australia Cane* (1971). Greek-Australian Vasso Kalamaras wrote in her mother tongue, also across several literary modes, her sixties story collection *Other Earth* appearing in translation in 1977, and *Bitterness* in 1983.

If Morris West was Australia's best-selling international success of earlier times, Colleen McCullough was his successor in the 1970s. While she worked in medical research in London and at Yale, she penned her first novel, *Tim* (1974), then produced her all-time hit, *The Thorn Birds* (1977). Based on her own upbringing in western New South Wales, this romance of country, Catholic guilts and passion sold so well she was able to become a full-time writer, producing, amongst other books, *The Ladies of Missalonghi* (1987).

POETRY

It is difficult to shape tidy literary-historical periods, since several poets (Gilmore, FitzGerald, Wright) continued to write for a very long time. Some (Wright in particular) reshaped form and theme several times in the process. Nonetheless, a new era of poetic production is reflected in titles like *New Impulses in Australian Poetry* (1968), edited by Rodney Hall and Thomas Shapcott, and *Modern Australian Poetry* (1970), edited by David Campbell. Despite the Ern Malley hoax, writers actively negotiated with the legacy of 'the moderns'. *The Faber Book of Modern Verse* had been a standard university text and its 1965 second edition added to the canonical trio of Yeats, Eliot and Pound (and the always influential Hopkins and Dylan Thomas) the voices of W.H. Auden, Philip Larkin, Ted Hughes, and Americans such as William Carlos Williams, Robert Lowell, Sylvia Plath, and the Black Mountain poets. The old pictures and philosophising in tidy verse that seemed to come as anonymous pronouncements became personal, colloquial engagements with the messiness and present objects of modern life. This newness was consolidated in Australia by the arrival of Donald Hall's *Contemporary American Poetry* after 1962.

Robert Adamson took over the long-running *Poetry Magazine* and renamed it *New Poetry* in 1970. As major publishers were taken over by international corporations, they began shedding their poetry lists. However, the increasing numbers of university-educated people and the availability of Arts Council funding ensured a continuing supply of writers and a growth in small presses and magazines. Some, like *Makar, Mok, Free Poetry, Leatherjacket* and Five Islands Press, were devoted entirely to poetry. The sense of a national collective of professional writers was reflected in the formation of the Poets' Union in 1977. That collective was both incestuous (reading and publishing each other's work) and riven by disputes. These gave some glamour to poetry but prevented any cohesive 'schools' from forming. The energising if contradictory mix of the new is seen in Tom Shapcott's *Australian Poetry Now* (1970). To work by Bruce Beaver, Bruce Dawe, Chris Wallace-Crabbe, Les Murray, Geoffrey Lehmann and Shapcott the poet, Shapcott the editor threw in David Malouf, Sylvia Kantarizis, Judith Rodriguez, Rodney Hall, Andrew Taylor, Roger McDonald, Robert Gray, Peter Skrzynecki, Rhyll McMaster, J.S. Harry, Richard Tipping, John Tranter, R.A. Simpson, Robert Adamson, Michael Dransfield, Vicki Viidikas and Alan Wearne—to list only those with some lasting hold on the cultural mind. It can be seen that the national corpus of poetry was still mostly male, with a few non-Anglo-Celtic names now being included. The background to these writers also reflects the domination of Melbourne and Sydney, something other cities fought against. *Makar* was located in Brisbane and the Friendly Street small press was established in Adelaide. Perth, Newcastle and, later, Wollongong developed their own writing circles and publishing outlets as well, nearly all having some attachment to a university.

Bruce Dawe continued to write, producing *An Eye for a Tooth* (1968), *Beyond the Subdivisions* (1969) and *Condolences of the Season* (1971), with the first edition of his widely read anthology

Sometimes Gladness appearing in 1978. The titles indicate his wit and a hesitant humanist optimism constrained by the pathos of human failings, impatience with injustice, and despair over repeated resort to war. His accessible work has been undervalued for its tendency to rely on content rather than style but became a staple of high school syllabuses. In some ways Dawe was a forerunner of the more critically praised Les Murray, though he is closer to A.D. Hope in his quick satiric responses to social situations. Dawe remained popular and continued to publish poems until his death in 2020.

Gwen Harwood commenced her public career as a poet with *Poems* (1963), though individual poems began appearing from around 1940. She began writing in Brisbane and ended up in Tasmania, from where she became famous for rude poetic gibes at editors and critics who dismissed her as a 'housewife' writing from the regional margins about women's experiences. Two books appeared in the 1960s, a selected collection in 1975, followed by *In Plato's Cave* (1977), *The Lion's Bride* (1981) and *Bone Scan* (1988), and a collected edition in 1990. Best known for sharp depictions of female experience (in particular, 'In the Park', in which a mother at the end of her tether says her children have eaten her alive, and 'Mother Who Gave Me Life'), Harwood also focuses on philosophy and music ('Beethoven, 1798', 'New Music', 'Divertimento', and libretti for the composer Larry Sitsky). Drawing on the ideas of Wittgenstein, the poet takes the separation of word and its referent as a sign of mortality but also as the gap that allows healing song to be more than mere instinctual utterance. Like Wright, Harwood retains conventional stanza and rhyme patterns (reworking Bible passages, old Scots ballads and sonnets, and connecting pastoral tradition to her Tasmanian environs). Harwood also creates dramatic sequences from the lives of an ageing and world-weary lothario, Professor Eisenbart, and an ineffectual music teacher, Professor Kröte, both affronted by careless youthful beauty and provincial ignorance. At times, Harwood sounds like A.D. Hope (to whom she pays tribute, along with Heine, Rilke, James McAuley and Philip Larkin).

Peter Porter also stuck to conventional poetic forms and wry commentary on life and is of note for marking a broadened national spirit that allowed expatriate Australians space in local discussions. Porter's work circulated mainly in Britain (his 'Annotations of Auschwitz' plugging into a post-war angst) but steadily drew attention in his homeland, often for his poem about Australia's best-known racehorse, 'Phar Lap in the Melbourne Museum', which ends, 'It is Australian innocence to love / The naturally excessive and be proud / Of a thoroughbred bay gelding who ran fast.' Porter's name now marks a national prize for poetry.

Bruce Beaver's *Letters to Live Poets* (1969) consolidated his growing reputation, establishing his hallmark mode of poem series (the *livre composé*): sonnets, odes, meditations, many inspired by Rilke, and redolent of the confessional tone of Lowell, but without the psychodrama. 'Letter VIII' sums up his work: 'I can barely name six kinds of bird / and seven kinds of flower. Some poet. / I concentrate on humans and the absurd.' *Lauds and Plaints* (1974) opens up the spacing of his previous blocks of long lines while also working towards a more imagist compression into short lines. There a zen-like calm often framing his middle-aged reflections on 'the human ache'. This collection was influential for its move away from 'poetical' qualities to a relaxed everyday voice and because it made poetry an international literary conversation rather than a mimesis of Australian nature and mores. Beaver's interaction with works of art and other poets, interspersed with small moments of domestic companionship continues in *Odes and Days* (1975).

Les Murray has to be Australia's most significant poet of modern times, if only for the volume of work produced, but also for his distinctive take on Australian culture, his international reputation, and his editing and anthologising of other poets. He first published with Geoffrey Lehmann (*The Ilex Tree*, 1965) and produced a book of verse every two or three years until his death in 2019. This output included two novels in verse, *The Boys Who Stole the Funeral* (1980) and *Fredy Neptune* (1998). Allowing for some opening up of stanza forms and a late move into short poems, Murray's style and themes remained consistent across his oeuvre. He became known popularly as 'the Bard from Bunyah', his hometown in the north of New South Wales that was settled by loggers (see 'Driving through Sawmill Towns') and dairy farmers ('The Butter Factory').

He draws on family stories and local folklore ('The Mitchells') to create a mythos of the rural battler with echoes of Wordsworth's romance of a dignified peasantry. Murray preserves the bush ballad form (including celebrations of bushrangers), while turning it to serious reflections on lives shaped by the Great Depression and two world wars ('Lament for the Country Soldiers'). Lyrics often capture scenes from nature and accompany bucolic accounts that invoke Hesiod and Virgil's *Georgics*. Murray's debunking humour is evident in the title *Lunch and Counter Lunch* (1974), the latter term being a cheap meal available in a pub. He can also produce effective epigrams (as in 'Company': 'Where two or three / are gathered together, that / is about enough').

Humour blends into essays on the laid-back culture of popular Australian life in 'The Quality of Sprawl' and 'The Dream of Wearing Shorts Forever'. These poems show Murray's love of the long line, which reveals a taste for the epic drawn from Old English poems and Dylan Thomas, from his Scots ancestry and Aboriginal sources. The most famous example of this last element is Murray's rendition of holiday weekend traffic winding across the land of the Rainbow Serpent creation spirit, 'The Buladelah–Taree Holiday Song Cycle' (from *Ethnic Radio*, 1977). Elsewhere, Murray explores a kind of anthropological archaeology, attempting to link present white settler rural culture to Aboriginal land-use and back through other civilisations, as in 'Cattle Ancestor' or 'Walking to the Cattle Place', in which links are made between cattle farming and the cow-centred history of India back to Mohenjo-Daro.

Murray has been criticised for being too conservative (he was a committed Catholic who clung to traditional ideas about gender and rejected any notion of Australia being part of Asia), but he espoused his own kind of radicalism that derided the political correctness of both left and right, especially as voiced by urban intellectuals. His brand of rustic populism is expressed in *The People's Otherworld* (1983) and he performed his eccentric republicanism in *Subhuman Redneck Poems* (1996). The other key aspects of his work are a facility for striking visual analogy and a love of onomatopoeia, most startling in his play with syntax to express an animal mind ('Pigs', 'The Cows on Killing Day'). His early work as a translator led to translations, mostly of German poets, and reflections on the nature of signs that ranged from Chinese pictographs to computer icons ('The New Hieroglyphics' from *Poems the Size of Photographs*, 2002).

Open form free verse, concrete poetry and spoken word became new norms, accompanying a drive to take poetry back to 'the people', rejecting elitism and decorum. Coming from the same background of youth revolt, a few took the 'sex, drugs and rock and roll' ethos into a renovated romanticism, playing the part of 'The Poet' to the full and burning out bright but early. Michael Dransfield (*Drug Poems*, 1972), Charles Buckmaster and Vicki Viidikas are examples. Dransfield is the most influential of these three, owing to his ability to transmute the physical details of heroin addiction and the surrealist imagery of a drug trip into an imaginatively coherent sequence set in and around a mouldering mansion named Courland Penders that is left over from the faded squattocracy. The otherwise self-indulgent individualism of the addict turns into a symbolist allegory—a celebration infused with romantic nostalgia of how we have moved on from old privilege and a pastoral world—mixed with confessional realism depicting an urban squat.

Fitting in with the anti-establishment attitudes of the time, working-class and ex-jailbird voices gained a hearing. Peter Kocan produced *Ceremony for the Lost* (1974) and *The Other Side of the Fence* (1975) before moving into fiction and autobiography, and Robert Adamson began his longer poetic career with pieces depicting tough street life and the reading that sustained him in prison. *Canticles on the Skin* (1970), *The Rumour* (1971), *Swamp Riddles* (1974) and *Theatre* (1975) show a rapid progression from naturalistic description to meditative work anticipating his long fascination with bird life and fishing. References to Mallarmé, Shelley, Hart Crane, Robert Creeley, John Ashbery and 'Robert Duncan's course of plain speaking / set to my own measure' accompany awareness of the potential to become inauthentic through playing up the roles of either 'crim' or 'poet'. 'The Rumour' is a sustained exploration of words, things and the muse, and how an order might be apprehended without it being any narrow dogma ('the law' becomes a metaphor for some shape to the universe).

Kath Walker published her second book of verse, *The Dawn Is at Hand* (1966). This was a more assertive set of verses than her first collection. As a pioneer of Aboriginal literary writing, she was joined by Jack Davis from the other side of the continent. During the 1960s, Davis wrote poems recording his life as a boy raised on the Moore River reserve and later as a stockman in the north of Western Australia. 'Desolation', 'Aboriginal Reserve' and 'The Drifters' echo the laments of Kath Walker's verse. 'Slum Dwelling', 'Prejudice' and similar titles critique the social status quo. He adds pen portraits of Aboriginal people ('The Black Tracker', 'The Artist', 'The Aboriginal Stockman', 'Urban Aboriginal'), and poems about nature. These were collected as *The First Born* (1970), sometimes given 'literary' flavour by including antiquated 'biblical' English. Davis's poetry became more lyrical over time, save for occasional hard-hitting attacks on white oppression. *Jagardoo* appeared in 1977.

Drama

Radio plays continued to be a significant part of dramatic writing through this period. Some of the more notable writers are Mona Brand, Jennifer Compton, Leonard Radic, Shan Benson, Tess Brady and Elizabeth Jolley. Staged drama in this period was, by contrast, undergoing radical change. In 1966, Jane Street Theatre was founded in Sydney as an experimental offshoot of the Old Tote Theatre Company, which itself morphed into the Sydney Theatre Company in 1968. Jane Street received a grant from the Gulbenkian Foundation to commission new Australian plays. It took its actors from the drama school at the University of New South Wales and staged works by Thomas Keneally, David Williamson and Dorothy Hewett. It also revisited older Australian plays (Edward Geoghegan's *The Currency Lass*, Rodney Milgate's *A Refined Look at Existence*), and went on to stage the popular *The Legend of King O'Malley*, written by Michael Boddy and Bob Ellis, in 1970.

Three plays marked a radical shift in Australian theatre. One was the staging of the American anti-war rock musical *Hair*, with naked actors (1969), signalling the arrival of a more libertarian counter-culture and a departure from British traditions. This was preceded by Alex Buzo's *Norm and Ahmed*, which exposed the racism lurking behind paternalistic bonhomie towards non-Anglo immigrants and ended with some violently profane language (1968). The other play was Jack Hibberd's *Dimboola* (1969). It consolidated a taste for 'cabaret' theatre by pulling audiences into the action and incorporating vaudeville or circus-related routines. *Dimboola* has audiences eating at tables as though guests at the chaotically farcical wedding reception being acted out. It became a hit with amateur groups and became a feature film in 1978.

Buzo went on to create *Rooted* (1969), a rapid-fire dialogue in which a middle-class man proud of his material possessions becomes a modern-day Job stripped of everything by Simmo, a demonic paragon of Aussie masculinity. We never see this malevolent force, but he takes the man's wife, takes over his apartment, and (abetted by a crowd of Job's-comforting 'friends') seems to be driving him relentlessly into utter destitution. The play showcases Buzo's ability to catch idiom and move us from social satire towards something like Beckett's existentialist darkness.

Buzo's *The Front Room Boys* (1969) was a satire of public service functionaries, *The Roy Murphy Show* (1971) brought out the infighting and commercial interests behind television sports commentary, and *Tom* (1972) attacked advertising agencies. *Macquarie* (1972) was an historical drama about the colony's controversially innovative governor. Keeping up the acerbic comedy of social analysis, *Coralie Lansdowne Says No* (1974) is set in the rich playground of Sydney's northern beaches. The sharply witty Coralie affects a 'women's lib' independence, keeping rich men at a distance while living off their hospitality. She is increasingly beset by visitors until she finally gives in to her inner anxieties and outer precarious lifestyle, accepting the proposal of a supposed poet from Canberra with a wryly resigned, 'You'll do.'

Jack Hibberd's *White with Wire Wheels* (1967) satirises male competition and yuppie pretensions. His *A Stretch of the Imagination* (1972) has an ageing hermit who parades his classical education between bouts of scatological humour. As he recalls his life, he invokes and destroys the common attributes of Australian culture, slogging on from day to day in grimly comic stoicism.

Hibberd went on to produce versions of Gogol and de Maupassant, adding touches of knockabout irreverence.

A 'new wave' of more popular, more political theatre moved down from the proscenium arch stage 'into the round' and was boosted by the creation of new companies and venues—in Melbourne, La Mama (1967) and The Pram Factory (1970); in Sydney, the Nimrod Theatre Company (1970) and The Stables (1975). As some names suggest, the action was no longer in grand palaces of culture, but in spaces where anything could be devised.

Barry Oakley wrote *The Feet of Daniel Mannix* (1971) about the controversial Irish Catholic archbishop of Melbourne who publicly opposed conscription in World War One and was connected with conservative Catholics splitting from the Labor Party. More interested in the lives of ordinary working-class Catholics, Peter Kenna wrote *A Hard God* (1973), depicting the Cassidy family's 1940s struggles to survive tragedy owing to industrial accidents. It shows union activism and the uneasy exploration of homosexual desire in the younger generation. Ron Blair followed up this Catholic theme with *The Christian Brothers* (1975), an exposé of the brutal schooling meted out by that teaching order, but softened by the sole actor, an aged priest struggling to hold to and communicate his sense of religious calling.

Beginning his career in Adelaide, Steve J. Spears wrote musicals and satirical shows noted for their harsh tone. His best-known play remains *The Elocution of Benjamin Franklin* (1976): not the American, but a boy who destroys his transvestite elocution teacher. Spears went on to work mostly in children's television, but continued to produce irreverent theatre pieces, like *Froggie* (1984), about a poet with no arms, and the more serious *Glory* (1988) about a woman subsiding into Alzheimer's confusion.

John Romeril was another of the younger Melbourne writers producing left-nationalist material that used popular folklore, song and vaudeville irreverence. He often worked collaboratively and was a pioneer in the community theatre movement. The title of an early play, *Whatever Happened to Realism?*, indicates the shifts occurring at the time, though stylistic change was only part of the story—the play was part of an anti-censorship push following the arrest of the cast of Buzo's *Norm and Ahmed* for using indecent language. *Chicago, Chicago* (1970) had cardboard cut-out characters and actors who changed roles, so that we are never clear what is 'real' (a depiction of the chaos of the 1968 Democratic Convention in Chicago) or what is the fantasy of a psychotic individual. Romeril's most highly regarded work has been *The Floating World* (1974). A veteran of World War Two embarks on a package tour to Japan that allows gibes at commercialised popular culture and drives the protagonist steadily into memories and psychosis.

Following social reforms inspired by feminism, women objected to the domination of theatre by brash young male writers producing male-centred stories. Women in the Australian Performing Group staged *Betty Can Jump* in 1972, and later left to found the Melbourne Women's Theatre Group.

The most visible woman in theatre, though, was the older writer Dorothy Hewett. Between 1967 and 1975 she wrote eight plays, the most notable being *This Old Man Comes Rolling Home* (1967) and *The Chapel Perilous* (1971). The first is set in Sydney's urban slums and is a bleak depiction of the vortex of poverty, working-class solidarity, family ties, early pregnancies, alcoholism and petty crime. Its naturalist portrayal is leavened only by the relentless optimism of the father of the family, Tom Dockerty, and recourse to fragments of popular song and poetry.

Hewett's second play, *Mrs Porter and the Angel*, is a grotesque satire featuring crazed academics, two students and a 'camp' couple, in which all kinds of sexual acts are mentioned, a mad wife cooks her baby to please her husband's demand for a roast dinner, and imaginary dogs pursue each other throughout. Subtitled 'A Modern Fairytale in Two Acts', it draws on Beckett, *The Waste Land* and surrealist ideas, and either confused or offended many when it opened in 1969, though like the first work, it is clearly infused with sexual energy and general vitality pushing against oncoming age and death, and carries a clear message that women are trapped in patriarchal society.

It was the third work that brought together themes and techniques in a manner more appealing to audiences. *The Chapel Perilous* drew on Hewett's own childhood and schooldays, reflecting her isolated upbringing in which books provided inspiration and consolation. Sally Banner rebels against her schooling and the staid sexual mores of her time, setting herself up as a heroine on a quest for self-determination and artistic recognition. In scenes that are sometimes literally carnivalesque, Sally's pursuit of her genius and carnal fulfilment (mostly disappointing) is counterpointed by commentary from teachers, fellow students, lovers, political activists and her parents. Loudspeakers, masks and Greek chorus singing of popular songs chart Sally's doubtful progress in cycles of retrospect through school, war years and leftist protests, to some degree of literary renown. She donates a stained-glass window to her old school and we are left wondering at the end whether she makes any submission, token or genuine, to social convention.

The most enduring and successful male dramatist from the 'new wave' of Melbourne playwrights is David Williamson. For three decades he has been Australia's most productive playwright, with international recognition and feature films made of several of his plays. After a teaching career in thermodynamics and social psychology, he wrote a comic piece, *The Coming of Stork* (1970), connecting with the sexual revolution of youth culture, but went on more seriously to write *The Removalists* and *Don's Party* in 1971. Both plays have become school texts and are regularly re-staged.

In many ways, Williamson's work updates the satires by Barry Humphries of 1950s complacent materialism, this time exposing the crass underbelly of 1970s young adults who are climbing into the professions and business with nothing to anchor them other than a love of beer and an obsession with sex. They are the ugly Australians of the new middle class that defines mainstream Australia. The early plays are all male-centred: women increasingly seize upon the freedoms of the post-pill sexual revolution and the ideals of feminism, but they usually function as agents of desire and angst amongst the men around them. There is usually an outrageously frank lecher who highlights the more cautious and hypocritical sexism of his mates and challenges the self-protective hauteur and anger of the women. Often someone will begin telling home truths or spilling what friends have been saying behind someone's back, and then everyone buys in to protect themselves or establish dominance over the group. *Don's Party* dissects a group of 'friends' gathered to watch a national election count on television. Most hope that Whitlam's Labor Party will end years of conservative government, but the politics is sidelined by a wife-swapping swill of bitchiness and latent despair that shows what follows once libertarians get jobs, marry, and acquire real estate.

All of the early plays received attention—praise and shock and prudish disapproval—for their Wilde-like repartee, their unremitting display of mores most people knew of but didn't talk about, and the inclusion of crude language. *The Removalists* was Williamson's first international success not just for these qualities, but because it tackled another social phenomenon widely acknowledged but rarely revealed: the corrupt edges of the police force. Williamson takes a sergeant and his newly graduated constable and puts them into a case of domestic violence. The sergeant offers to help a battered wife move out of her house, hoping to gain sexual favours from either her or her sister. The husband comes home unexpectedly, and his aggressive outrage leads to him being handcuffed and beaten up. Eventually, the women leave and the young constable, emotionally unhinged by his boss's relentless psychological manipulations goes wild and causes the death of the husband. The sergeant, ever looking after his own interests, refuses to cover it up, and the play ends with the young policeman fighting him so that it will look like they were both attacked and had to respond in kind. The removalist of the title is hired to shift furniture and is a bleakly neutral 'technologist' moving in and out of the central drama. The play's strengths are in its interconnection of male power, state power, and different personal responses to those, and its skilful orchestration of shifts in the focus of violence from one combination of characters to another. Williamson also produced a semi-farcical tale of a returned soldier from Vietnam, his girlfriend, the man who has taken his place while away, and an incompetent robber in *Jugglers Three* (1972).

The seventies saw the first plays performed that came out of prisons. These are best represented by the work of Jim McNeil's *The Chocolate Frog* (1971), *How Does Your Garden Grow?* (1974) and *Jack* (1977). He shows not just the harsh institutionalised life of inmates but also the sexual and emotional relationships that develop between them and sometimes survive when men are released. Law reforms removing the criminalising of homosexuality enabled public recognition of gay life and one of the earliest plays reflecting this was Martin Smith's *Love Has Many Faces* (1970).

The pioneering work for the stage by an Aboriginal writer was Kevin Gilbert's *The Cherry Pickers* (1971), which depicted the struggles of Aboriginal itinerant labour. Inspired by this and the general upsurge of activism by First Peoples, Bob Maza and others established the National Black Theatre in Sydney in 1972. Maza collaborated with actor Jack Charles to create *Jack Charles Is Up and Fighting* in the same year. Perhaps the most successful Aboriginal work of this period was Robert Merritt's *The Cake Man* (1975). The play opens with a 'first contact' scene in which a soldier, a priest and a settler kill an Aboriginal father and the settler inveigles the wife and her son to go to a mission reserve by offering them cake. Later, in that reserve outside the bounds of a town, a mother dreams of a Santa Claus figure who will appear one day to deliver plenty to Black folks. Her son pilfers lumps of coal from a white man in the town and when the man brings the law to the mission, he is shocked at the sight of a baby being raised in squalid poverty. The next time the son goes on a raid, the man gives him a box of food and is hailed by the mother as the 'cake man'. Later Aboriginal work (such as Gerry Bostock's 1976 production *Here Comes the Nigger*) would not resort to such a happy ending.

CHILDREN'S AND YOUNG ADULT LITERATURE

Children's literature had been for the most part written by adults as 'improving' tales to socialise young readers into an orderly genteel world. By the 1970s, teachers realised two things: that many texts reproduced tacit prejudices of class, race and gender, and that most children relished seeing their own worlds—warts and all—in the books they read. Amid outcry from conservative adults, books for young readers began to include swear words, and show children being critical of their elders. Urban poverty, conflict and less than desirable parents feature in L.H. Evers's *The Racketty Street Gang* (1961) and Reginald Ottley's *The War on William Street* (1971). Stories also began to include 'difficult' characters other than the little saints and lovable rascals of earlier writing for children. H.F. Brinsmead in *Pastures of the Blue Crane* (1964) creates an unsympathetic protagonist who has to struggle to find happiness alongside an equally unpopular adult and in new surroundings. The plot includes discovering an ancestry racially different from the mainstream. Patricia Wrightson's *I Own the Racecourse!* (1968) centres on an intellectually challenged boy. David Martin's protest novel *Hughie* (1971) shows an Aboriginal boy encountering the colour bar and becoming part of the historical movement to desegregate country swimming pools.

CHAPTER 7

Multicultural to Bicentenary
1975–1988

SOCIAL AND POLITICAL CONTEXT

Until the mid-seventies, Australia had been a fundamentally working-class society and manual labour was still the general norm. At home, laundry would be done in a 'copper' boiling tub, cooking often still on a wood stove, and toilets would be a small shed in the back garden over a pit or a drum that would be emptied by the council 'dunny man'. Over time, urbanisation and the social welfare system enabled increasing prosperity, higher levels of education and civic improvements, until a higher standard of living centred on suburbia and the middle class was taken for granted. Rural life and economic struggle retained its hold on the national imagination but was no longer a meaningful reality for an increasingly comfortable suburban middle class. Agriculture itself became more mechanised and family farms gave way to corporate ownership.

Economic stability allowed greater tolerance for social reform and the arts. This was perhaps most evident in South Australia, where Don Dunstan (premier, 1967–68 and again 1970–79) removed electoral rigging, lowered the voting age from 21 to 18, legalised consenting homosexual relationships, opposed the death penalty, appointed a female judge, supported Aboriginal land rights, and pushed the national Labor Party to abolish the White Australia Policy. He also inaugurated the South Australian Theatre Company and the South Australian Film Corporation and built a Festival Centre to further strengthen Adelaide's Festival of the Arts. In 1976, Pastor Doug Nicholls became the first Aboriginal governor of any state.

By contrast, Joh Bjelke-Petersen, premier of Queensland, suppressed civil liberties, maintained oppressive controls over the state's Aboriginal population, did deals with mining, gambling and real estate, and interfered with Whitlam's federal government. He made Queensland an isolated bastion against 'socialist tyranny' while gerrymandering the electorate. He was not alone in corruptly exploiting commercial opportunities. Many 'developers' amassed personal fortunes from investment, real estate and mining, especially in Western Australia. Some of these, like Alan Bond (founder of Australia's first private university) and the Nugan Hand Bank, pushed the boundaries too hard, leading to bankruptcy and exposure for malpractice. The eighties were a time of boom and bust, the boom encapsulated in Australia's winning the America's Cup in 1983 with the latest in yacht racing technology. The commercialisation of everything was marked by Kerry Packer creating World Series Cricket in 1977. Amidst unbridled exploitation of nature for profit, people began protesting against forest logging and defeated Tasmania's efforts to drown trees and Aboriginal sites under dams for hydroelectricity.

In 1980, Aboriginal people at Noonkanbah protested over mining on a sacred site. In 1982, Hermannsburg mission folk gained freehold title to their land, and the Indigenous people of Maralinga had their land returned to them in 1984 after a clean-up of radioactive waste left by British nuclear testing. A year later, Ayers Rock (Uluru) was returned to Aboriginal custody, and in 1988, Imparja, an Aboriginal-run television station, was opened in Alice Springs. However, the law operated in discriminatory ways against Indigenous people. Frequently, bush folk visiting towns and drinking in public spaces were locked up, whereas whites would be given a warning or a fine. In gaol, despair, neglect and violent attack from police regularly resulted in deaths. In 1987, a 'Black Deaths in Custody' Royal Commission conducted an enquiry, making recommendations to improve race relations that in many instances remain unimplemented.

In 1983, Bob Hawke won Labor government. Although he was a Rhodes Scholar, Hawke projected an image of the knockabout beer-drinking Aussie and, having worked his way up through the union movement, he was able to set up a Prices and Income Accord, which brought employers and workers together to negotiate fair conditions under government arbitration. For some time, this reduced loss of productivity through strike action. Hawke also re-established Whitlam's nation-wide funding for health care under the Medicare system. However, he also began the privatisation of government assets on the advice of his treasurer, Paul Keating. Keating saw the need to free up Australia's old protectionist economy; he floated the dollar and opened markets to global trade.

Just prior to the bicentenary of Australia's colonisation, several events marked a new era in Queensland. Premier Joh Bjelke-Petersen retired in 1987, at which time the Fitzgerald commission of enquiry exposed corruption among the state's police and politicians. New systems of probity and progressive reforms were adopted. Brisbane reinvented itself as a cosmopolitan city when it hosted a World Expo in 1988. The bicentenary completed a process of national assertiveness. In 1984, 'Advance Australia Fair' replaced 'God Save the Queen' as the national anthem. Two years later, Australia broke with the British legal system by making its own High Court the ultimate site of appeal. A new Parliament House was opened in 1988. General celebrations of the founding of the nation were countered by Aboriginal groups marching under banners protesting against 'invasion day'.

Cultural Context

The youth revolution activists of the seventies became suburban parents, and there was a sense that Australian culture was part of world cultural exchange. Thomas Keneally won the Booker Prize in 1982 for *Schindler's Ark*, a novelised oral and documented history about a German con man and the many Jews he saved from Nazi persecution. The book started an ongoing debate about the nature and ethics of 'faction' and the appropriate handling of Holocaust (and by extension, Aboriginal) history. The Booker win put Australia on the world literary map, and international visibility was reinforced by popular music, which exported bands such as AC/DC and INXS, and singers like Olivia Newton-John and Kylie Minogue. On television, *Neighbours* became the most popular 'soap' serial and spread to Britain. *Gallipoli* marked a new wave of Australian filmmaking, and the National Gallery of Australia opened in 1982.

The trend to establish autonomous Australian branches of major publishing houses continued and there was a boom in Australian literary publishing. New magazines and small presses like Tasmania's *Island* (1979), Sybylla Press (1976), *Scripsi* (1981) and Five Islands Press (1986) appeared. Arguably, this outbreak of cultural confidence was its own downfall, producing too much writing for the market, and too much of average quality. However, major work came from a wider range of publishers: Helen Garner and Tim Winton, for example, got their break thanks to McPhee Gribble. Mergers and takeovers were happening, though. McPhee Gribble was swallowed into Penguin Australia, now itself part of an even larger global combine. Some companies survived as niche brands (Sybylla was a feminist press and became part of Spinifex publishing). The 'boom' attracted private sector interest, and in 1980, food manufacturer Vogel created a prize for new work that launched many careers over the next decade. Governments also took an interest, New South Wales beginning a cultural 'arms race' among the states by inaugurating its Premier's Literary Awards in 1979.

The academic study of Australian literature assumed more influence in shaping the field than had been the case when magazine editors and journalist reviewers acted as guides to reading. In 1977, the Association for the Study of Australian Literature was founded. Writing by 'new Australians' was by this time sufficient for scholars to begin teaching 'multicultural' courses. In 1984, Manfred Jurgensen established *Outrider*, a magazine focused on writing by and essays on cultural minorities. Work dispersed across small publications was collected into anthologies, notably Peter Skrzynecki's *Joseph's Coat* (1985). Sneja Gunew's essay 'Framing Marginality' in *Southern Review* (1985) set the terms of academic discussion, leading to her anthology with Jan Mahyuddin, *Beyond the Echo: Multicultural Women's Writing* (1988) and to her collaboration with Kateryna Olijnyk Longley, *Striking Chords: Multicultural Literary Interpretations* (1992).

Scholarly work came together in *The Oxford History of Australian Literature* (1981) and the first edition of *The Macquarie Dictionary*, based around Australian usage of English. The *History* was compiled largely by academics imbued with tones of authority and a sense of duty to establish a canon on solid 'universalist' literary value. However, both society and literary studies had so changed that single views setting up hierarchies of cultural value were being replaced by assemblages of essays representing the national literary scene as a 'horizontal' mosaic of varied colours, as seen in Laurie Hergenhan's collection for the bicentenary, *The Penguin New Literary History of Australia*.

The lead-up to the bicentenary saw a wave of historical work that filled in the gaps and silences in earlier studies that emphasised white settler 'progress', the bush, and (male) mateship. In 1981, Drusilla Modjeska published *Exiles at Home*, a study of Australia's women writers. Robert Drewe's debut novel, *The Savage Crows* (1976), dramatised the suppressed story of colonial violence against Tasmania's Aboriginal peoples, while Eric Rolls's *A Million Wild Acres* (1981) anticipated a general questioning of European modes of farming and concern about ecological imbalance. Rosa Cappiello's satirical fiction/documentary *Oh, Lucky Country* (1984) overtly attacked the myth of 'god's own' country benignly welcoming 'new Australians' (and challenged the national monologic Anglophone culture by appearing first in Italian). Kevin Gilbert edited *Inside Black Australia* (1988), showcasing Aboriginal poetry.

Cultural successes started to wane as panic set in over global amalgamations of publishing companies. Governments turned to economic rationalism with accompanying cuts to the arts, and 'Australian Literature' seemed to disappear as universities diversified their subject offerings to include cultural studies, women's studies, Indigenous studies, and so on. However, courses in creative writing were being created, producing an ever-increasing number of writers. Deregulation and amalgamation of publishing opened opportunities for international deals so that genre fiction by Australians could become international best-sellers. Commercially based festivals along with prestige-based state prizes spread around the country, giving public profile to the arts. All this favoured a general turn from high culture to 'middlebrow' literature within a global mass market that provides ongoing spaces in which literary innovation can survive.

PROSE FICTION

Jessica Anderson showed her versatility in moving from a psychological thriller marked by colourful eccentrics (*Last Man's Head*, 1970) to a historical novel (*The Commandant*, 1975). The latter explored personalities as shaped by the convict system, in particular the legendary martinet Captain Logan, who had control of the first penal colony in Moreton Bay, now Brisbane. He is seen through the eyes of the settlement's women. Anderson's big success was *Tirra Lirra by the River* (1978). This novella was hailed by feminists for its portrait of a woman beset by male expectations but finding ways to remain independent. It depicts an old woman reflecting on her life, partly in reverie during a bout of pleurisy. Nora has been a dreamy girl living through books (visions of Lancelot and Camelot) and, like Tennyson's Lady of Shalott, trapped indoors with embroidery as her only artistic outlet. At eighty, she returns to her family home and the tropical colour of her old Brisbane garden next to the river of her youth. Her life has been spent fleeing from 'greyness': drab provincial convention, domestic servitude to a tedious husband in Sydney, struggle through wartime London. Her story is framed by a tacit quest to find a memory of her father, killed in the First World War, and some emotional reconciliation with her dead sister. Nora finds female companionship and finds satisfaction and salary in dressmaking. Anderson is able to shock readers by speaking coolly about abortion, suicide and murder as manifestations of female suffering, despair and rage.

Anderson's *The Impersonators* (1980)—published in America as *The Only Daughter*—also won the Miles Franklin Award, but is a more conventional family saga, centred on the double marriage of a malevolent invalid patriarch, his previous and current wives, and their extended family of children. Anderson captures in detail the street life around some of the nicer suburbs of Sydney, the corrupt business practices of some of the wealthy, the fetish of having a house with harbour views, and attitudes to the rise and fall of the Whitlam government. A book of stories set in her Queensland childhood and in her adult world of Sydney (*Stories from the Warm Zone*, 1987) and the novels *Taking Shelter* (1989) and *One of the Wattle Birds* (1994) added to Anderson's writing for radio and television.

Olga Masters and Elizabeth Jolley were examples of the 'late blooming' writer. Masters detailed the struggles and desperation of women in country towns and their children. Her major works were the story collection *The Home Girls* (1982) and the novel *Loving Daughters* (1984). Jolley managed a longer career than Masters and harboured a greater, if always restrained, sense of the absurd, crossed with a taste for the grotesque. She ventured into depicting queer relationships among women: schoolgirl infatuations and older women yearning for female companionship. Starting with radio plays, some poetry and two collections of short stories during the 1970s, Jolley moved to novels: *Palomino* (1980), *The Newspaper of Claremont Street* (1981), *Mister Scobie's Riddle* (1983) and *Miss Peabody's Inheritance* in the same year. *Milk and Honey* (1984) has a boy with musical talent adopted into the claustrophobic Austrian migrant family of his cello teacher. To an accompaniment of Beethoven, Brahms and Rilke, he is sucked into marriage with the daughter and contrives an affair with a more down-to-earth Anglo-Australian woman. He loses his hand trying to save a mad aunt from a fire; his wife is engaged in an incestuous relationship with her intellectually challenged brother, has an intellectually challenged daughter, and probably kills her husband's lover. The only people content at the end are the two simpletons, who find menial jobs in a mental institution.

Foxybaby (1985) led up to Jolley's most famous work, *The Well* (1986). Hester, an ageing and sharp spinster, inherits her father's farm and takes on a sixteen-year-old orphan as companion. It is debatable who is exploiting whom, and Hester tries to educate her pop-music and movie-loving protégée while indulging her enough to keep her around. One evening, young Katherine drives home and hits something they think is a man and Hester drops the body into an old well. Katherine thinks the man is still alive and contrives a romantic fantasy that she will rescue him and they will marry, even though local gossip says he was an itinerant thief who has stolen Hester's cash. The older woman puts paid to romance by having the well sealed. A visiting novelist enthuses about the characters and stories to be found in country towns, and the tale closes with the prospect of Katherine heading to America with her long-time pen pal and Hester starting to tell a scary ghost story to her neighbour's children—one that sounds like the tale we have just read. *The Sugar Mother* (1988) is more humorous. A childless academic, whose wife (ironically a gynaecologist) goes overseas on the conference circuit with a possibly lesbian colleague, is besieged by his lower-class English neighbour who foists, along with charitable hot meals, her nubile daughter on him as a surrogate mother ('sugar mother'). He is charmed into love and into thinking that his wife will be delighted to be presented with a baby on her return. Jolley is skilled at having us both mock her satiric targets and squirm while waiting for the inevitable disenchantment.

Helen Garner had a more dryly caustic view of human foibles. *Monkey Grip* (1977) focuses on the bohemian share houses of Melbourne during the social experiments of the counter-culture generation. Like Moorhouse and Wilding, Garner also works with real-life characters and short stories patterned into linked novels. Unlike the Sydney men, she refuses to romanticise the partner swapping and drug culture, seeing the cost it has for women. She shows dispassionately the sordid side of fringe life and the confused passive aggression of people finding themselves entangled in a mix of reality and idealism. *Monkey Grip* explores ties between love and drug addiction contrasted with the everyday need to put food on the table and get the kids to school. In the two novellas *Honour & Other People's Children* (1980), Garner shows the delicate emotional plays of a divorcing couple, their daughter and the husband's new partner (at a time when divorce was still socially stigmatised). She also creates one of her key figures: the woman who finds herself older, unpartnered and childless, and who gets to be 'auntie' and 'house mother' to assorted drop-outs, single mothers and their children. Satiric depictions of no-hoper hippies and layabouts and middle-class families clinging to dreams of rebellion appear in *The Children's Bach* (1984) and reach a kinder apotheosis in the novel *Cosmo Cosmolino* (1992).

Less lasting in influence than Jolley or Anderson, but well regarded during the eighties was the fiction of Barbara Hanrahan. It operates at a quirky angle to reality while yet being based on the author's experiences. Marketed as fiction, but primarily autobiography, Hanrahan's *The Scent of Eucalyptus* (1973) and *Sea Green* (1974) tell a tale of growing up in a female household in 1940s Adelaide, both mother and grandmother being poor and widowed, the latter caring for her sister, forever 'young' with Down syndrome. This is followed by the writer's voyage to London to continue her art training (Hanrahan was a well-regarded printmaker). The narratives operate through a schizoid alternation of adult narrator and child character, both feeling simultaneously in and out of the society described. There is a fascinated horror of bodily intimacy, a detached suffering of sexual abuse at the hands of male relatives, and a haunting awareness of death. The narrator protects herself with a barrage of obsessively documented details of clothing, food, advertisements and household goods, but suffers bouts of anorexia, an abortion, and dependence on males who are otherwise feared.

Hanrahan displaced her personal anxieties onto artwork and fiction grounded in colonial Adelaide's genteel conventionality with side visits to Britain or New Zealand. Idyllic gardens or wooded enclosures are imbued with a gothic Midsummer Night's Dream of crippling ideals and lurking threat, flouted and twisted passions. Her first novel, *The Albatross Muff* (1978), precedes *Where the Queens All Strayed* (1978), *The Peach Groves* (1980), *The Frangipani Gardens* (1980), *Dove* (1982), *Kewpie Doll* (1984), *Annie Magdalene* (1985), *A Chelsea Girl* (1988), *Flawless Jade* (1989) and *Good Night, Mr Moon* (1992). A sense of duplicity in others is expressed in images of dressing up, game-playing, circuses and sideshows. Hanrahan published two sets of stories: *Dream People* (1987) and *Iris in Her Garden* (1991), plus an autobiography, *Michael, Me and the Sun* (1992).

Shirley Hazzard certainly attended to the lives of women. Her protagonists provide sardonic views of male privilege and bureaucracy, but from a cooler cosmopolitan standpoint. Hazzard worked in the UN and travelled in Hong Kong, China and Europe, settling eventually in New York. Her watershed work was *The Transit of Venus* (1980), the title invoking Australia's foundation myth of Cook's voyage to Tahiti that led to his 'discovery' of the Great South Land. This national allusion pulled readers into an extended saga of love affairs and loveless people centred on three Australian women who go to England. The book's flair rests on the author's love of language and knowledge of literature. A character arrives at a country house on a dramatically 'wild and stormy night'. As he waits to be received, he finds a Bulwer Lytton novel on a table. Doomed love affairs carry allusion to *Tess of the D'Urbervilles* and Hardy's poems. A play of shifting viewpoints and implied mental processes appropriate to a modern novel come from a nineteenth-century observing voice that takes a phrase and turns it into sardonic comment: 'Those peering into the oven of his career would report, "Christian is rising", as if he were a cake or a loaf of bread.' The title's historical reference becomes a metaphor for the disturbing passage of passion through lives. There is consummate control over material and witty intelligence, but also a cleverness that scores points off characters. A quiet feminism is summed up by one character: 'Women have to go through with things. Birth, for instance, or hopeless love. Men can evade forever.' *The Transit of Venus* followed two novels, *The Evening of the Holiday* (1966) and *The Bay of Noon* (1970), both reflecting the author's life abroad. Hazzard continued to attract readers across the forty years of her writing, but a protracted gap in her fiction prevented widespread fame until *The Great Fire* (2003), partly dealing with the bombing of Hiroshima and Nagasaki, won the Miles Franklin prize.

Along with Robert Drewe, Tim Winton has redirected literary attention from the bush to the coast. Winton began his writing career by winning the Vogel prize for a first manuscript for *An Open Swimmer* (1982). This was followed by *Shallows* (1984), a dramatisation of social tensions in his early hometown of Albany, where Australia's last whaling fleet ran up against 'green' protests. Winton has become popular partly because he gives sympathetic attention to the male worlds of physical activity, while attending to the 'softer' side of life: family, care for nature, spiritual yearnings.

He continued the tradition of social realist short stories with a lyrical tone in *Scission* (1985) and *Minimum of Two* (1987) and began his writing for younger readers with *That Eye, The Sky* (1986). Contact with working-class society injects an edge of violence into many of Winton's novels, and he produced a thriller, *In the Winter Dark*, in 1988.

Important for its signalling a literary turn towards Asia, Christopher Koch's *The Year of Living Dangerously* appeared to considerable acclaim in 1978. It is set in the last years of Sukarno's rule in Indonesia and uses the Hindu-derived Javanese shadow-puppet drama as a metaphor for political struggle. Koch weaves in his interest in Australia's lingering colonial attachments and stumbling efforts to find an independent identity. The book's complex layering is matched by Brian Castro's mix of historical novel and identity quest centred on Chinese migration to Australia, *Birds of Passage* (1983). A group of novels more centred on adventure-romance in foreign parts appeared at this time, two of the more complex being *Monkeys in the Dark* (1980) and *Turtle Beach* (1981) by Blanche D'Alpuget.

Gerald Murnane has both puzzled and intrigued readers with his unusual mix of dreams, fixations from childhood (Catholic doctrine, games of marbles and horse racing), and philosophical meditations. He takes on the role of an Australian Borges, creating conceptual fables that remain clearly anchored in reality, but nested narratives rehearse the limits of realism. Hailed by some as a stylist deserving of the Nobel Prize, Murnane was awarded the Patrick White Prize in 1999 for writers of merit who had not been accorded due recognition. *Tamarisk Row* (1974) and *A Lifetime on Clouds* (1976) are novels of childhood and adolescence. In the latter, Adrian Sherd enlivens his daily round of suburbia and Catholic indoctrination in St Carthage's College by constructing a fantasy life wherein he travels the USA along with three girls who alternately tease and throw themselves into sexual escapades with the ever-virile youth. These dreams he rationalises as acceptable alternatives to sinful indulgence in real-life lust, and the novel revels in fine details of the 1950s everyday—reading the sports pages and comics in the paper, doing homework, listening to the radio, mother making an album of magazine cut-outs featuring the royal wedding. Amongst the humorous depictions of teenage boys tormented by sexual urges there are moments of reflection on the illusion of desire and representations of it. Adrian takes a magnifying glass to a photo of a nude only to have her disappear in a mass of small dots.

The Plains (1982) was Murnane's breakthrough work. It appeared to invoke the approved icons of 'the bush' and the squatter or 'cattle baron'. Clearly located in the wheat and grazing western district of Victoria where Murnane spent childhood years and where he returned later in life, the novel defamiliarises its setting, turning laconic graziers into feudal heads of dynasties and the plains into a mirage that these lords of the land mull over, constantly defining its qualities and refusing any definition of them. Murnane has fun parodying the literary pursuit of a national soul. A young filmmaker goes inland to gain sponsorship from one of the squatters so he can carry out research into the region and produce a film showing something that no one has detected about the plains before—not a mimetic capturing of detail but a play of light that transforms materiality into a dream image. After twenty years, he is still searching, ultimately settling on a quietist ideal of silence in which perfection lies in potential and perception is forever encircled by the deformations and mirages of its own operations. *Landscape with Landscape* (1985) and *Inland* (1988) continue such themes, the first title indicating Murnane's penchant for the *mise en abîme* that both preserves and mocks mimetic realism. Tropes are reworked in short stories (*Velvet Waters*, 1990), another novel, *Emerald Blue* (1995), and a collection of essays, *Invisible yet Enduring Lilacs* (2005).

David Malouf came into his own as a novelist with *An Imaginary Life* (1978). Roman poet and mythographer Ovid is banished to the boundaries of the empire because of too pointed satires. At the edge of the steppes, he has to learn new languages—of the tribe he lives among and the natural world he is surrounded by. He captures and tames a child raised by wolves, trying to teach him to speak, but also learning through him to appreciate nature and the limits of power and humanity. At the end, the boy leads Ovid to a romantic union with the forces that animate all of life. The book was a refreshing departure from Australian social realist narrative and yet provided an allegory of how 'exiled' white colonists might come to terms with antipodean difference. In *Fly Away Peter* (1982), this is envisaged through birdwatching. Squatter's son Ashley befriends labourer Jim and hires him to record the birds on the coastal wetlands on his property. The birds also link them to a woman photographer, and, when officer Ashley and private Jim 'migrate' to First World War battles in Europe, birds provide a sustaining connection between the hemispheres. Jim is killed, leaving photographer Imogen wandering an Australian beach mourning. But she is given a vision of grace when she captures the image of something magical: a youth in harmony with natural forces, surfing the waves.

Malouf entered his 'middle period' with *Harland's Half Acre* (1984). This presents a fictional biography (based on the painter Ian Fairweather) of a boy from rural Queensland learning to define himself in opposition to his charming but ne'er-do-well father. Harland survives the Depression and puts his drawing skills to work in the city, learning to paint as he does so. He dreams of buying back the extensive farmland his improvident forebears have lost, but ends up a hermit on Bribie Island, looked after by young surfers and the lawyer son of a family that buys Harland's paintings. The imaginative centre of the book is the mystery of how art transforms brute experience (the murder-suicide of two of Harland's friends, for example). Harland's transpositions of tropical vegetation into cubist compositions 'proclaim a people's identity in a place it scarcely knew existed'.

Patrick White, in his memoir *Flaws in the Glass* (1981), said that his writing was 'a means of introducing to a disbelieving audience the cast of contradictory characters of which I am composed'. The idea of a multi-faceted, shape-changing personality is developed in his later work and is foreshadowed in *A Fringe of Leaves* (1976). Based on Eliza Fraser, the historical survivor of shipwreck and life with Aboriginal people, this novel begins with the gossipers of conventional society asking whether Mrs Roxburgh 'is a lady'. That person starts life as a Cornish farm girl, marries into polite society, is seduced by her husband's brother whom they visit in Van Diemen's Land, then shipwrecked off the coast of Queensland.

An Aboriginal tribe tolerates Ellen's presence as she is stripped of all signs of Western identity (save for her wedding ring, which she ties to her 'fringe of leaves' waistband). She is reduced to such hunger that she gnaws a possibly human bone discarded from a possibly cannibalistic funeral rite. Ellen is led back to white settlement by a convict with whom she forms a loving relationship, and faces return to civilisation with feelings of entrapment. Her story asks us where the bases of identity and the limits of humanity can be found, and what civilised culture consists of. Despite its good intentions, the book has been criticised for its largely negative depiction of Aboriginal life.

More overtly interested in the personae wrapped about our 'self', *The Twyborn Affair* (1979) begins with redoubtably British Miss Clitheroe and Australian merchant millionaires the Golsons travelling 'on the Continent', where they encounter the ancient Greek Mr Vatatzes and his younger paramour, Eudoxia. Eudoxia turns out to be a cross-dressing male, son of Mrs Golson's lesbian lover who is married to a cross-dressing judge in Sydney. Eudoxia reappears as Eddie, a war hero returned home, who escapes Sydney to labour on a pastoral property. He has two sexual encounters, one with the station-owner's wife and the other with the male manager. In the third section, Eddie turns into Eadith Trist, madam of a London brothel to the gentry. White is brutally honest about the fleshly side of mortality and deft in tracing the emotional complexities of relationships as shifting personae circle each other in a quest for some kind of redeeming love. He closes off his lifetime fictional output with the supposed diaries (edited by family friend Patrick White) of a multi-ethnic shape-changing and seemingly demented woman, Alex Xenophon Demirjian Gray, titled *Memoirs of Many in One* (1986).

A younger generation of novelists was spearheaded by Peter Carey, who published *Bliss* in 1981. The book contains most of the author's motifs and themes: the family small-town service station and tinkerers with mechanical devices; well-meaning but befuddled men pushed along by ruthless women; capitalism, particularly as represented by con men and Americans; the power of story and the appeal of its fakery. The evil city is opposed to the more salvific bush, though the latter can be mocked for harbouring hippies with fatuous 'alternative' beliefs. Carey worked in advertising and at one point moved to a rural commune on the tropical north coast of New South Wales and *Bliss* translates this background into the story of Harry Joy, whose near-death experience leads him to believe that the world and his dysfunctional family are actually hell and that the products he has successfully advertised are causing an epidemic of cancers. He is placed in a psychiatric institution and eventually joins a free-loving 'earth mother' who collects honey and makes pots in the bush. Carey mixes humour with an often-grim view of society and sets lyric passages against fast-moving colloquial dialogue and some touches of Latin American fantasy.

It is this last element that drives Carey's next book, *Illywhacker* (1985). An illywhacker is a carnival spruiker whose slick hyperboles entice people to buy. Herbert Badgery, the central figure in a picaresque epic, confesses to being an inveterate liar, and spins the tale of his life that is also a comic romp through an unofficial Australian history. There's a Badgery in Patrick White's *The Tree of Man*, and Carey can be read as providing an irreverent counter to the solemn pioneering of White's protagonists. Carey's Badgery is a salesman who wants Australia to produce its own products. His dreams and failures extend the more limited world of *Bliss* out to a view of global capitalism that leaves Australia as a cage of curiosities catering to foreigners.

Oscar and Lucinda (1988) brought Carey international attention when it won the Booker Prize. Like many other works of 1988, it questioned Australia's official history. It also wonders what gets transported from England and how it is transformed in the process. Actions arise from chance and the rubbing together of mismatched forces: fundamentalist religion versus Anglican doubt, scientific taxonomy versus the fluctuations of gambling, conventional gender roles countered by forceful female personalities. Nothing is what it seems: passion is both admirably energising and dangerously extreme; the hard father is a loving man who lacks the means of showing it; glass is both beautiful and functional, solid and liquid; a clerk is a heroic explorer in disguise; a heroic explorer is a ruthless megalomaniac; a cleric is an innocent weakling who unwittingly creates chaos around him. Oscar overcomes torment to do something extraordinary out of love for Lucinda (floating a glass church upriver to his country parish), though it is another woman who founds on him the family that leads to the narrator, who writes the novel as his exploration of a complex parentage.

Thea Astley continued to produce acerbic counters to the national legends of prosperous farming and happy egalitarian mateship. *An Item from the Late News* (1982) centres on a squatter's daughter with artistic aspirations who returns as a teenager to her tiny town of Allbut (all but not there) and is attracted to a hippy pacifist who has set up a bomb shelter and garden on the outskirts of town. The townsfolk mistrust him for being on friendly terms with Aboriginal folk, and he is demonised as a pervert for being found comforting a young girl after she has been raped by a local thug. The artist narrator records her own betrayal of the man out of jealousy. Astley creates an air of ritual tragedy echoing Lorca's dramas. A Christmas tradition of men donning horns and battling in the street makes hermit Wafer a sacrificial victim, town violence echoed in allusions to world events. The narrator says, 'And in the end the landscape wins', an idea common to Australian writing.

Astley returned to a Pacific setting in *Beachmasters* (1985). Loosely based on a historical secessionist movement in Vanuatu, the novel orchestrates three voices (English, French and 'Seaspeak' or Bislama creole) belonging to the various communities that find themselves tied to the beauty of the tropics and a messy history. This time it is not tourists who are the focus, but mixed-race Islanders caught between late-colonial political chicanery and indigenous desire for self-determination. The oldest planter sums up both an existential and aesthetic position that underpins the fluctuations of history: 'Trying to carve out a good sentence. There's little else to do.'

It's Raining in Mango (1987) is a set of stories that are independent but also interconnect as episodes in an extended family history that reflects some of Queensland's past. Rednecks, hippies, Aboriginal peoples, returned soldiers, prostitutes, gold miners, sugarcane farmers—all struggle along in the tropical heat amid floods, brawls, massacres, protests against forest logging, and war. Time is fluid and there is a mixture of fatalism and rage that nothing changes. A feisty married couple is described as 'united by the vitality of loathing', which characterises Astley's work: a lively loathing of ignorance, violence, laziness, patronising priests, racism, sexism and bad spelling, matched by a fascination with the people touched by all these qualities and the conditions.

By the mid-1980s, a new generation of university-educated writers was more attuned to literary theory and cultural studies. A mixing of genres and writing aware of its own contingencies of production and fictive status appeared in novels by Tom Flood, Peter Mathers and Dal Stivens. The cryptic title of Flood's *Oceana Fine* (1989) alludes to a strain of wheat. Murder mystery frames old tropes (city boy encounters gothic threat in country; the romance of settler farming versus harsh economics; realistic depiction of picaresque wanderings on the frontiers of mining and farming between the wars), but these are subverted. Picaresque wanderings become those of women, not men; white storytelling melds with Aboriginal creation story; history is not a narrative of noble Anglo-Celt pioneering. 'Histories'— plural—is the title of not one but two chapters, different versions of the same events appearing as two columns of text. The opening chapter is tellingly labelled 'Lie of the Land'. History becomes story, and story is presented as a collage of official reports, family legend, local folklore and the narrator's memories of childhood. The text confronts readers with their own responsibility to make sense of conflicts, multiplicities and unresolved endings. It parades an intertextuality—Penelope pursued by suitors, Medea and Colchis, *Moby Dick*, Lewis Carroll, Biblical creation and apocalypse—that is complicated by Flood's personal intertext: the book reflects his labouring in Western Australia's wheatfields, the home country of his mother, Dorothy Hewett. Peter Mathers's *Trap* (1966) likewise destabilises narrating positions. A claustrophobic community fired by millennial intensities of gnostic mania is also an allegory of reading that undoes the singular author-ity of the text.

Unlike many of the American examples inspiring Australian postmodernism however, these books often retain a thread of serious social commentary. Flood's *Oceana Fine* makes reference to historical events such as the Poseidon mining boom of 1968 and raises concerns about agribusiness trying to control patents for crops. Dal Stivens's early experiment *A Horse of Air* (1970) was an indirect comment on species loss and contains overt denunciation of the Vietnam War. Other experimental writing has been inspired by feminist and gay politics, including Jan McKemmish's *A Gap in the Records* (1985) and Marion Campbell's *Lines of Flight* (also 1985). Campbell spent time in France and her thickly textured stream of consciousness novel depicts a young Australian woman developing her painting skills there. She mixes with students discussing the latest ideas about language and gender and shows up the workings of the art world as she tries to keep sliding free from all kinds of entrapment while retaining her capacity to express feminine desire and make her own artistic statement.

Carrying a hint of self-correction in the light of feminism and new literary theories, David Ireland produced two new novels: *A Woman of the Future* (1979) and *City of Women* (1981). The latter imagines Sydney as a space from which men have been banned but the women's world is just a mirror image of a standard 'ocker' (demotic Australian) patriarchy. *City of Women* finds connection with other Ireland novels in its quest for love and meaning in an otherwise bleak or absurd world. *A Woman of the Future* makes this more apparent and links the protagonist's search for understanding and self-determination to her nation's sense of itself in the world. The body of the nation is perhaps as anxious and unstable as the bodies surrounding protagonist Alethea; they begin to lose bits or mutate, producing extra limbs, coins and trees, and Alethea herself gradually turns into a leopard. Allegory points to the suppressed rage of women subjected to male arrogance and sexual predation, but as Alethea asserts her freedom to use boys and men, she also becomes an item of sexual trade. Feminist demonstrators are depicted as irrationally violent and Alethea is a maneater, undercutting any real gender critique.

In keeping with Aboriginal protests against bicentenary celebrations, Colin Johnson changed his name to Mudrooroo Narogin (the Noongar word for paperbark and his registered place of birth). He had followed up on his first novel with *Long*

Live Sandawara (1979), another naturalistic depiction of urban rebelliousness but grounded on the real history of Western Australian outlaw, Jandamarra. In 1983, Johnson joined those revising official histories by publishing *Doctor Wooreddy's Prescription for Enduring the Ending of the World*. Using diaries and records from nineteenth-century Tasmania concerning George Augustus Robinson, the self-appointed 'conciliator' between settlers and 'blacks', the author imagines the world of Indigenous Tasmanians, focusing on Wooreddy and his wife Ludjee. Wooreddy is a 'clever man' shaman presented as a philosopher doctor. His mix of mockery, spells and stoicism allows for critique of 'Fada' Robinson and protest against white invasion. For the bicentenary, Mudrooroo revised his own work. *Doin' Wildcat: A Novel Koori Script* shifts the literary language of his original novel into colloquial Black English and an older Wildcat looks on at the changes to his work as it is filmed by a Jewish American and criticised by younger Black actors.

Meanwhile, an Aboriginal woman had found book publication. Monica Clare's *Karobran* (1978) combined autobiography with fictional techniques. More overtly novelistic, though also deriving from personal experience, Archie Weller's *Day of the Dog* (1981) revisited the life of poverty, petty crime and incarceration that Black youth seemed to be condemned to. Eric Willmot fictionalised the life of the man who tried to resist the first occupation of Sydney. *Pemulwuy: The Rainbow Warrior* appeared in 1987.

A book that caught attention in the 1980s was Beverley Farmer's *Milk* (1983). Though there are stories set wholly in Australia and centred on male characters, most of the collection is based on the author's four years living in Greece with her Greek-Australian husband and his family. The experience is imagined more fully in Farmer's novel *Alone*, published in 1980. Tensions in family relationships exacerbated by cultural differences are coloured by melancholy and loss. A woman teaches herself to ice-skate while her lover takes his wife to New York and then decides to end the affair; a wife waits for her son taken to Greece by his father; another watches her Greek husband succumbing to the advances of a younger Greek woman; a woman records the loss of her mother as she is worn away by cancer. We might think that the effect would be maudlin but there is a toughness behind the observing voices and their worlds are full of light and sensory images (food is a feature). Feelings are set against the physical presence of bodies recorded in detail. Mirrors and later work around water imagery—in the novel *Seal Woman* (1992) and the compendium *A Body of Water* (1990)— lent themselves to interpretations based on theorists like Lacan and Irigaray. The closeness between stories and autobiography appealed as well to critics revaluing crossed boundaries in studies of 'life writing' (work by Gillian Bouras and Charmian Clift being similar cases).

Susan Hampton's *Surly Girls* (1989) included some poetry but comprised mainly short stories driven by a feminist social critique. Her work can be read alongside Jessica Anderson's *Stories from the Warm Zone and Sydney Stories* (1987) and Helen Garner's *Postcards from Surfers* (1985). Elizabeth Jolley's short stories also sit with this group, *Five Acre Virgin* (1976), *The Travelling Entertainer* (1979) and *Woman in a Lampshade* (1983) being her best-known collections. *Bearded Ladies* (1984) introduced Kate Grenville to Australian readers and her stories published in the bicentenary year as *Joan Makes History* are a feminist rewrite of the approved national story. Grenville went on to write *Lilian's Story* (1985), a fictionalised account of the abusive childhood and eccentric adulthood of a Sydney identity that was followed by the imagining of her abusive father's psyche, *Dark Places* (1994).

Story collections became fewer until *Inprint: The Short Story Magazine* (1977 to 1986) appeared from Western Australia and Bruce Pascoe published the series *Australian Short Stories*. *Inprint* gave space to 'migrant' writers such as Lolo Houbein, Serge Liberman and Zeny Giles. Bruce Pascoe founded Pascoe Publishing in 1982 and produced sixty-five story collections up to 1998. The first issue brought together David Ireland, Frank Hardy, John Clancy and the comic writer Barry Dickins. Subsequent issues included new names like Tim Winton, Beverley Farmer, Garry Disher, Gillian Mears, Steven Carroll, Carmel Bird, Amy Witting, Ruby Langford, Kevin Brophy and Merlinda Bobis. From 1999, another series took over. *The Best Australian Stories*—for most of its life coming from

Black Inc. publishers in Melbourne—got well-known writers to select from the previous year's books and magazines.

Endorsed by South African writer Alan Paton and published in America, *The Track to Bralgu* came out in 1978. This collection of tales incorporated northern Aboriginal myth and fantasy, forcefully revealing the damaging impact of colonisation and uranium mining on Indigenous lives. Purportedly written by an Arnhem Land Aboriginal person, B. (for the morning star, Banumbir) Wongar, the collection followed *The Trackers* (1975), a short fantasy-SF protest novel. This mix of Orwell and Kafka presents an assimilated Chinese-Australian whose skin gets darker until he has to flee north to join persecuted Aboriginal families. It was followed by another story collection, *Babaru* (1982), and a trilogy (*Walg*, *Karan* and *Gabo Djara*, 1983–87), again exposing the malign effects of uranium mining. Wongar entered the nation's long history of literary hoaxes when he was revealed as a migrant from Serbia, Streten Bozic. Bozic had lived for some time among Indigenous tribes. He went on to write his life story in *Dingoes Den* (1999), revealing interesting links to Miles Franklin, Alan Marshall and the socialist realists.

In 1980, the American publisher McGraw Hill started business in Australia and published *The Dying Trade* by journalist Peter Corris. It presented Sydney as the equivalent of San Francisco and a place of competing interests, different ethnicities, sport and corruption. It began a long-running series featuring Cliff Hardy, a tired, ironic private eye, who set the modern benchmark for Australian crime writing. From the 1980s onwards, there was an upsurge in novels featuring female investigators, some of them receiving scholarly attention (Gabrielle Lord, *Fortress*, 1980; Jan McKemmish, *A Gap in the Records*, 1985; Marele Day, *The Life and Crimes of Harry Lavender*, 1988). McKemmish shows up the silences and ambiguities in documentary evidence, thereby pointing to the gendered biases of written history.

POETRY

Three anthologies defined changes in post-1960s Australian poetry: John Tranter's *The New Australian Poetry* (1979), Susan Hampton and Kate Llewellyn's *The Penguin Book of Australian Women Poets* (1986), and Kevin Gilbert's *Inside Black Australia* (1988).

Tranter assembled twenty-four poets from 'Australian poetry's most exciting decade'. In that sense, the book belongs in the previous chapter, but the 'generation of '68' experimentalists and counter-culture rebels shaped writers from subsequent periods. The poets in this collection are the equivalent of the Moorhouse-Wilding-Carey cultural shift in fiction and the 'new wave' in theatre. Influenced by popular music, drugs, and gathering protests against war, censorship, and sexual prudishness, poets (while often declaiming against American imperialism) drank in the rhetorical drive and freer forms of Ginsberg, Ashbery and Frank O'Hara, and worked in an awareness that they were not producing Art conveying timeless Truth and Beauty but messing about with words to create a textual artefact and a reading experience. Tranter saw all this as a rebellion against the material and attitudes taught in university departments of English. Of his selection, Bruce Beaver, Rae Desmond Jones, Nigel Roberts, Michael Dransfield, Vicki Viidikas, Robert Adamson, Martin Johnston, Jennifer Maiden, Charles Buckmaster, Kris Hemensley, Philip Hammial, John Forbes, Laurie Duggan, Alan Wearne, John A. Scott and Tranter himself have maintained a presence in the national literary consciousness.

Tranter's collection was typical of national anthologies in foregrounding male voices (only Viidikas and Maiden were women). Susan Hampton and Kate Llewellyn realised that any accurate reflection of Australia's poetry scene would have to start with a specialist showcase. Arguments about activist sympathies overlooking lack of artistic merit continued but sounded increasingly hollow as the variety and liveliness of women's writing became evident. Their collection included ninety-one writers, half of whom now appear regularly in national anthologies. Hampton and Llewellyn revived interest in work by Zora Cross and Lesbia Harford, and confirmed the canonical status of Mary Gilmore, Judith Wright, Gwen Harwood and Rosemary Dobson, giving prominence as well to Kath Walker (Oodgeroo), Judith Rodriguez, Pam Brown and Ania Walwicz.

Elitist aestheticism, even when it took the form of anti-conservative experiment, excluded Aboriginal voices from the national poetry hoard on the grounds that they were too confined to protest and obsolete popular forms. Kevin Gilbert's selection of Black poetry showcased its power, breadth and depth, leading to inclusion in national anthologies as a natural part of Australia's literary production. Gilbert signalled the importance (and survival) of Indigenous languages, and alongside known poets (Jack Davis, Oodgeroo/Kath Walker) introduced new voices (Charmaine Papertalk-Green, Eva Johnson, Archie Weller, Joy Williams, to name only some). They were not confined to protest but also celebrated traditions, laughed at life, and made 'whitefella' words over into 'blackfella' idiom and rhythms.

Tranter mentions the advent of the small offset litho press, the Gestetner printer and the electric typewriter as facilitating quick, cheap publication of chapbooks and little magazines. Leading publishers (University of Queensland Press, Angus & Robertson, Heinemann) were still producing poetry while small presses (Hale & Iremonger, Hyland House, Five Islands Press, Paper Bark Press) and regional publishers (Wakefield Press in South Australia, Fremantle Press in Western Australia) added to cooperatives (Collective Effort Press) and self-publishers. Computers and the internet began to extend the publication and imaginative reach of poetry from around the mid-1980s. Poets who had been scrounging American and European books suddenly found they were in easy contact with both writers and editors overseas, gaining access to international magazines such as *Salt* (UK) and *Poetry* (US). In Australia, *HEAT* and *Boxkite* produced a cosmopolitan selection of writing.

The private experience of silently reading printed text behind which the writer remained a shadowy presence mutated into public readings. In some ways, this provoked a more page-centred poetry of shape and space; in others, it led to an evanescent poetry that had its life mainly in performance: breathing, cadence, volume control. The changes are clear in Penguin's *Off the Record* anthology (1985). Showing all the hallmarks of desktop computer design, with margins going wild, a variety of fonts and whole pages given over to repeated words, the book also came with a disc of spoken poems. The populist trend is hinted at by the inclusion of 'Tom, the Street Poet', and the editor, 'Pi O', typically introduces himself with deflating mockery in sans serif as 'a famous poet'; 'he has a business card which says so'. The sans serif script expresses the demotic attitude of work from this period. Of the eclectic selection, survivors in the national literary archive include Eric Beach, Jenny Boult, Pamela Brown, Joanne Burns, Larry Buttrose, Lee Cataldi, Anna Couani, Chris Mansell, Billy Marshall-Stoneking, Graham Rowlands, Gig Ryan and Ania Walwicz.

John Tranter opposed poetry as romantic personal expression (one poem asserts 'The Failure of Sentiment and the Evasion of Love'). Theoretically aware (he invokes Leavis, Sartre, Foucault and Barthes), Tranter takes a 'cold eye' and an increasingly cynical persona to the influence of French symbolists, English modernists and the neo-romanticism of Australia's counter-culture. He works with the street culture of toughs, prostitutes and drug-taking that his companion poets (Dransfield, Forbes) deal in, but adds the cafés, jazz, fast cars and planes of New York style, as well as an awareness of 'third world' politics, especially in South America (influenced by Neruda and others). Tranter published *Red Movie* (1972), *Crying in Early Infancy* (1977) and *Dazed in the Ladies' Lounge* (1979), much of the contents available in *Selected Poems* (1982). Though his poems sound colloquial and ironic and look like the free verse of his fellow poets, Tranter's are generally stripped of illusory glamour and play across constructed identities. In 'Memoirs of a Forty-Year-Old Revolutionary', the 'I' is 'a wasted thirty-two', 'thirty-four', 'perhaps I'm a woman, thirty-eight, a tiresome traveller / with a suitcase full of dumb disguises'. Another poem is titled 'Waiting for Myself to Appear', as though the self exists only in the development of the poetic text. Some poems feed back onto the Sydney literary scene (Frank Moorhouse gets a mention, and his docu-fiction is redolent of Tranter's work). Others about writing poetry rely on surrealist images, fragments and non-sequiturs, but usually carry a sense of deliberate formal shaping, including a long experiment with the sonnet form. Tranter mocks poetic posing while drawing attention to his own posing (as in 'The

Alphabet Murders'), appropriating B-grade movies, noir detective fiction, and pop songs.

Alan Wearne generally eschewed the free verse open-form style of those influenced by the Black Mountain poets and other Americans, preferring to develop the ballad tradition into something that carries the speech and attitudes of modern urban Australia as well as satiric gibes at politics. In this, he was closer to Bruce Dawe than to many in Tranter's anthology. Wearne began writing in the seventies with *Public Relations* (1972) and *New Devil, New Parish* (1976) and continues to publish, but his major work comprises verse narratives: *The Nightmarkets* (1986) and two volumes of *The Lovemakers* (2001, 2004). These bring together monologues from and portraits of assorted Melbourne types, from drug barons and prostitutes to suburban couples and merchant bankers.

Possibly the most representative of the '1968 generation' is John Forbes. He relates to drug-culture hedonism not as a neo-romantic poetic vocation but rather as simply part of urban contemporary life. With one eye on the inner-city street and another on the television, Forbes presents a chaotic bombardment of images from popular culture, literary tradition and global politics as a symptom of living in 'The Age of Plastic'. Poems suggest that an engaged not caring is the only way to cope with a media onslaught of violence and absurdity that poetry must recycle in trying to shape into significance. Forbes writes mostly about the sun-drenched grit and glamour of Sydney while largely doing so from a flat in Melbourne, the city-centric viewpoint underpinned by debts to Frank O'Hara. The titles of early collections indicate something of his tone: *Tropical Skiing* (1976), *On the Beach* (1977), *Stalin's Holiday* (1980), *Drugs* (1981) and *The Stunned Mullet* (1988). Poems work with incongruity, filmic reference that includes the idea of nuclear end times, anti-conservative anti-Marxism, and colloquial jokiness suggesting a mind surprised and overwhelmed. Several poems labelled 'The Joyful Mysteries' attest to his Catholic schooling, though he eschews any religious belief, preferring to reflect his reading of philosophers such as Quine, Blanchot and Richard Rorty. One of his most anthologised poems, 'Four Heads and How to Do

Them' (classical, romantic, symbolist, and conceptual), is a clever synopsis of Western poetic history that presents his own work as both erudite and mocking.

Jennifer Maiden has sustained a long career as novelist, painter and poet, living on the western edges of Sydney. Starting with *Tactics* (1974), she produced five more books up to the bicentenary. She presents the domestic intimate world of female frustration and incipient violence in relationships, sometimes with allusions to Greek myth. Gradually, pieces grow longer: 'Fabrics', using the associations of 'mordant', strings together seemingly random patches of imagist notes (a child in a pram, a photo of the corpse of a Jewish rebel against the Romans, a cave filled with explosive gas). Longer lines of more narrative drive develop, though twists of phrase and jumps in 'plot' make reading a challenge. *The Occupying Forces* (1975) is a dystopian landscape in which two female partisans are captured by male invaders. Death and loss haunt much of Maiden's work; poems address teenage anorexia, juvenile detention, and, increasingly, national and world politics. In *The Trust* (1988), the poem 'Language' begins, 'I need to learn a language but not English / or at present any further maidenese.' This heralds a move to less obscurity and more open lines of often humorous incongruities.

Bruce Beaver kept on producing collections: *Death's Directives* (1978), *As It Was* (1979) and *Selected Poems* (also 1979), followed by *Headlands* (1986) and *Charmed Lives* (1988). He has increasingly adopted a mix of prose and long-lined verse, a feature of *As It Was*, which is a memoir of vignettes ('Beginnings', 'The Poems', 'Bucolics') punctuated by photographs. The poet's neuroses are recorded and the 'bucolics' sketch the farm work he did for some years as therapy ('Pea Picking', 'Herding Cows', 'Ploughing and Swearing').

Beaver's mix of autobiography, lyric and photo essay anticipates Laurie Duggan's *The Ash Range*. This 1987 book is a memoir of place rather than person. It is a regional history of the farm and forest districts of southeastern Victoria. Duggan ranges from geology, Aboriginal myth and Scots migration to accounts of fire, flood, massacres of local tribes, gold mining and crime. It is poetry by design: a bricolage of quotations from navigators, explorers, local newspapers and diaries. Text is set around the margins of pages amid lots of white space and photos, sometimes rearranged into verse-like lines and occasionally supplemented by the poet's own versified commentary.

Duggan's turn to memoir verse is echoed in the work of Robert Adamson, who, through *Cross the Border* (1977) to *Where I Come From* (1979), steadily hones his work down to short deadpan lines recording images of his family past. *The Law at Heart's Desire* (1982) takes us to *The Clean Dark* (1989), hailed as a major work and the end point of *Selected Poems 1970–1989*. With some forays into Charles Olson's open form, but mainly in short stanzas and short lines holding a lyric rhythm, the poet takes stock of where and how he lives. Poems seek a kind of present transcendence that immerses him 'in a language / we speak trees in' or in the being of a bird. Increasingly we find love poems amid the calm of the observer who has 'discovered the secrets / of description by simply living here', though there is also an opening out to 'conversations' with other writers (Robert Duncan) along with awareness of the Aboriginal presence in the landscape.

The New Australian Poetry is heavily Sydney-Melbourne focused. Richard Tipping might well have been included, but he lived in Adelaide. After some early printed work (*Soft Riots*, 1972; *Domestic Hardcore*, 1975), Tipping created 'word poetry' by altering signage (a direction to the airport became 'airpoet'; a botanical gardens tree is labelled 'Poet Tree') and by carving punning words in stone as public sculpture. Also from Adelaide, Geoff Goodfellow found that the new romanticism and push for a national culture of the 1970s created room for worker poets renovating the bush ballad. Two of Goodfellow's best-known collections are *No Collars, No Cuffs* (1986) and *Bow Tie and Tails* (1989). Another poet working with 'streetwise' experience and straightforward colloquial language is Rae Desmond Jones (*Orpheus with a Tuba* and *The Mad Vibe*, 1973; *Shakti*, 1975; *The Palace of Art*, 1981). He applies sharp wit to pithy lines of lively visual similes, moving from politics and rough sex to the literary scene. 'You have to be tough to be a poet', for example, notes that 'it doesn't help to be drunk or stoned / Because the smart ones aren't / & they form gangs'. His later work is selected in *It Comes from All Directions* (2013).

Another poet who might well have been included in a book of 'new' poets was J.S. Harry. She published only a few collections spaced over three decades but had a quiet influence. Her first book, *the deer under the skin*, appeared in 1971, followed by *Hold for a Little While and Turn Gently* (1979), *A Dandelion for Van Gogh* (1985), *The Life on Water and the Life Beneath* (1995) and a *Selected Poems* (also 1995). Combining Olson's open form and E.E. Cummings's wordplay, Harry alternates lyric descriptions of moments in a life with allusions to ancient Egyptian myth, the key interest being in natural cycles and modern disruption of harmonious relations between mankind and a plethora of plants, birds and animals (from cockroaches to elephants). She is not a romantic; her poems usually centre on hunting, fishing and violence, using short, choppy lines that shift us from immediate detail (a mouse, say) to Einstein and space exploration. Her deadpan tone hides tacit social critique, particularly in showing gaps between abstract principles and real bodily experience and the power of 'the word-knife' to connect the two. There is a strong undercurrent of gender violence, her most anthologised poem ('tunnel vision') being a harsh scene of sexist graffiti surrounding the screaming figure of a rape victim running through city traffic.

Pam Brown has published relentlessly through chapbooks and small presses. Taking part in the drug-taking bohemian counter-culture ('I Remember Dexedrine'), Brown works with epigrammatic short poems processing the motifs of popular films and songs (one collection is titled *Country and Eastern*, 1980). Tough love poems are tinged with surrealist satire. Increasing in length and moving into prose (particularly in stanzas recording her time in Vietnam), Brown's poems take a cold look at her life as she ages ('it started with noise / and ends with worry'), ruefully confessing at one point, 'and of course I have become / the wholly romantic poet'. Brown's early work is collected in *Selected Poems 1971–1982* (1984), her later phase seen in *THIS WORLD / THIS PLACE* (1994), and lines and narrative open up into more playful but also more pointed commentary on the contemporary art scene, global media and corporate economics (*text thing*, 2002).

Many older poets adjusted their work to suit the times or reflect new phases of personal quests. In *Alive* (1973), Judith Wright reviews aspects of climate change and sets up a parallel between her house and her ageing self, accepting a 'symbiosis' that envisages both depletion and survival. This collection includes 'Two Dreamtimes', her now well-known address to her Aboriginal friend Oodgeroo. In *Fourth Quarter* (1976), the poet berates herself: '"Concentrate, woman, concentrate." Free verse is harder to bring off than rhyme'. She doesn't give up on rhyme completely but does move to a freer flow across irregular stanza lengths. Wright composes letters to other poets and revisits some of her influences (Yeats, Old English metaphor, Traherne, Keats, Blake). She returns to Eve as a rebellious figure while still attending to Aboriginal presence ('The Dark Ones') and to wildlife ('Platypus'), and opens up a more autobiographical strand ('Moving South', 'Unpacking Books'). In her collection *Phantom Dwelling* (1985), she reprises thoughts on her lineage ('For a Pastoral Family'). Her environmental activism continues (seen in 'Rainforest' and 'Notes at Edge'), but she makes a startling move to the form of the ghazal and an affinity with Sufism. Other poets persisting into later life are Gwen Harwood, Peter Porter, Thomas Shapcott, Rowland Robinson and David Campbell.

Dorothy Hewett is (to quote her autobiography title) a 'wild card' in the country's literary pack, having published novels, short stories, poetry and playscripts, theatre criticism and life writing. Her work began with poetry (in 1938 when she was fifteen), which she produced until her death in 2002. Her colourful life of communist activism and bohemian living gave her a reputation for both scandal and ebullience. This is reflected in her two major poetry collections *Rapunzel in Suburbia* (1975) and *Alice in Wormland* (1987). These are flowing free verse showing both a frank directness and a theatrical artifice. Vernacular vignettes of often squalid Australian life are cobbled into myths blending the reading matter of a lifetime. It all builds towards a corpus that records a lifelong lust for both sex and love and endless falls into disappointment.

There is a naturalistic cataloguing of period bleeding, fornication, abortion, drugs, suicides, the egotistical angst of male poets, and uncomfortable situations late in life when the poet finds herself in the same room as her husband, her ex-husband, her ex-lover and their two wives ('Re-Union'). In the end, there is the realisation that the dream of recovering the garden of childhood with its ideal imaginary friend is an impossibility that 'must always be lost / & found & lost again' ('The Infernal Grove').

Hewett's legacy was to some extent inherited by Kate Llewellyn. Without the political commitment of her forebear, Llewellyn came to literature later in life as a country girl with a background in nursing. She adopted a no-nonsense tone and dramatised her persona in frank admissions of female desire, anger, and disbelief in the patriarchal aspects of biblical and classical traditions. Patronised as 'shrill' and artless, her work was regularly excluded from anthologies until feminism forced a shift in Australian culture. After *Teeth and Other Verses* (1965), Llewellyn gained some visibility with *Trader Kate and the Elephants* (1985). She continues to publish poems and has developed a strong reputation as a writer of memoir that includes meditations on life, nature writing and verse, beginning with *The Waterlily: A Blue Mountains Journal* (1987).

Robert Gray's books of verse run from the early 1970s (*Creekwater Journal*, *Grass Script*) through to the 2000s (*Selected Poems 1963–83*, *The Skylight*, *Piano*, *Certain Things*, *Afterimages*) editions of selected and collected work appearing up to 2014. He wrote a well-regarded autobiography, *The Land I Came Through Last* (2008). Gray's reputation was consolidated mainly in the 1980s, for work characterised by lyric pictures of fields and farms, particularly in northern New South Wales, rendered with a dispassionate tone and notable for inventive imagism. Gray has written on John Shaw Neilson, has debts to Thomas Hardy's verse, and evinces occasional touches of Heraclitus, Dylan Thomas, Buddhism and the Old Testament. He had a strict religious upbringing and asserts his adult counter-belief in atheistic existentialism. There is a predilection for the fourteen-syllable line and couplets that are carefully managed to sound like prose, as befits a writer who says, 'Our only paradise is the ordinary'.

Geoffrey Lehmann edited an anthology of Australian poetry with Gray that became a byword for conservative taste. Lehmann's own work after his 1960s debut with Les Murray honed blank verse and took on unusual topics such as the world of ancient Rome in *A Voyage of Lions* (1968) and *Nero's Poems* (1981). *Ross's Poems* (1978) and later work (such as in *Spring Forest*, 1992) continued an engagement with rural life (despite Lehmann being a city lawyer and tax consultant) and with the lives of his forebears, his father in particular. His *Collected Poems* (1997) was reprised in 2014 to include later work, by which time he had taken up rigorously factual self-portraits composed as one would a painter's portrait and travel tales.

People who would attract regular interest thereafter are Jamie Grant, Dorothy Porter, Andrew Sant and Anthony Lawrence, Rory Harris, Chris Mansell, Graham Rowlands and Kevin Hart. Translations became more common, including of Australian writers like Vasso Kalamaras and Dimitris Tsaloumas, who published in both Greek and English in Greece and Australia. Other 'migrant' or 'multicultural' poets working in English also feature in the eighties. 1989 saw Peter Skrzynecki and Anna Couani still publishing, while 'π.o.' ('Pi O', Peter Oustabasidis) developed his transcriptions of creolised 'wog' English in *Fitzroy Poems*, and Ania Walwicz confirmed her reputation as an acerbic experimentalist in prose poems of 'migrant english' with the appearance of *Boat*. π.o., as a self-declared anarchist, plays across styles, moving into concrete shape-poems that pun verbally and visually across all the characters on the keyboard, mix Greek and English, and even incorporate Chinese characters (*Big Numbers: New and Selected Poems*, 2008).

Migrants from Europe resented ignorance and disparagement of their rich cultures and often recreated their pasts while denouncing prejudice. Their work took time to be appreciated as more than only protest and autobiography. One example is the work of Antigone Kefala. A Romanian Greek who migrated to New Zealand and then Australia, her work was largely disregarded as lacking affect and style (it worked with de Chirico-like surreal images linked with Greek myth). After her prose fable *The Island* (1984) received favourable attention, her verse—*The Alien*, 1973; *Thirsty Weather*,

1978; *European Notebook*, 1988; *New and Selected Poems*, 1992 (in bilingual edition as *Poems*, 2000)—came to be valued for its careful, pared back craftedness and exploration of estrangement as part of the human condition.

Mark O'Connor's work is worth noting because of its engagement with environmental issues. After early poems of travel in Europe, he contracted residencies to write about the Great Barrier Reef (*Reef Poems*, 1976; *Poetry and Pictures: The Great Barrier Reef*, 1985) and the Monaro high country and Blue Mountains (*Poetry of the Mountains*, 1988). His residency at the Museum of Victoria resulted in *The Ship Trans-Time: Words for a Museum* (1989). *The Eating Tree* appeared in 1980, followed by *The Fiesta of Men* (1983), and in 1989 he produced *The Great Forest*. His writing strips away romantic anthropocentrism while sometimes preserving nationalist sympathies. In 'The Pairing of Terns', O'Connor admits that the attempt to communicate the worth and vitality of nature as nature can be managed only via metaphors. One of his most successful pieces is the narrative sequence 'Planting the Dunk Island Botanic Gardens', in which he revegetates a tourist resort island, inspired by the hermit memoirist E.J. Banfield. O'Connor went on to produce *Firestick Farming* (1990), *Tilting at Snowgums* (1996), *The Olive Tree* (a collected edition, 2000) and *Pilbara* (poems about the northwest of Australia, 2009).

John Kinsella came to notice in 1989 when *The Book of Two Faces* and *Night Parrots* appeared. The latter plugged into the tradition of explorer poems with a sequence about the lost gold prospector Harold Lasseter, but its interest in endangered species and land degradation attracted interest and he has gone on, informed by Buddhism, to write both poetry and prose about rural life and living in harmony with animals and the land. He incorporates concepts from science, self-reflexive critique of writing, his family's history of farming, and analysis of the capitalist machine. Works like *The Silo* (1995), *Counter-Pastoral* (1999), *Doppler Effect* (2004), *The New Arcadia* (2005), *The Land's Meaning* (2012), and *Graphology Poems 1995–2015* (2016) mount a deconstructivist attack on the romantic lyric. They dismantle the 'sovereign subject' of much nature writing, and question writing itself as a vehicle of colonialism and the ravages of the Anthropocene. Apart from his environmental concerns, Kinsella has been an important figure in giving Australian poetry international reach. He worked at Cambridge University and in the US, and edited the international poetry magazine *Salt*, which, as a publishing house, has introduced a number of Australian poets to overseas readers.

There has been a loose ensemble of 'university poets' (teachers in English departments) following on from Hope, McAuley and Buckley. They include Andrew Taylor, Vivian Smith, Jennifer Strauss, Syd Harrex, Norman Talbot, Philip Mead, Fay Zwicky, Dennis Haskell, Chris Wallace-Crabbe, and more recently Kate Lilley. Their work spans several decades and crosses into the age of creative writing teachers, a notable member of this group being Ron Pretty. Besides his own extensive output, Pretty founded poetry magazines and Five Islands Press, promoting the work of many contemporary writers. The dominant mode in this group has been modernist ironic blank verse, though some, like Harrex, also mined a long and broad seam of the sonnet.

The most productive and anthologised of this group has been Wallace-Crabbe. He rose to a personal chair in the English department of Melbourne University, with stints in the US, Italy and beyond. His first publication was *In Light and Darkness* (1954) and he is still writing. Poems about nature appear throughout his work but use scenes as an occasion for philosophical musings. In poems like 'A Wintry Manifesto' he works towards a rationalist humanism that goes on to celebrate the world of things and seek out sources of joy in the here and now. Later collections are titled *The Thing Itself* (2007), *The Domestic Sublime* (2009), and *The Foundations of Joy* (2013). With this thought-poetry goes a playfulness and wit (hinted at in titles such as *The Emotions Are Not Skilled Workers*, 1979, and *The Amorous Cannibal*, 1985). Form remains a touchstone, as suggested by 'Homage to Mondrian', which is a sonnet of spare half-lines. *The Rebel General* (1967) signalled a turn towards politics, though poems about memory and childhood run through all of Wallace-Crabbe's books, as does a concern for connections between reading and actual experience. Travel sketches recording his US visits shift to a more direct personal voice and a looser style with some prose poems. A generally urbane tone draws energy from colloquial phrases, as in collections called *For Crying Out Loud* (1990), *By and Large* (2001) and *Telling a Hawk from a Handsaw* (2008).

Colin Johnson/Mudrooroo reimagined Aboriginal oral epic in *The Song Cycle of Jacky* (1986)—'Jacky' being a derogatory label for any Aboriginal man. The cycle shows the prejudice towards and maltreatment of Jacky but also presents him as a trickster who knows how to slide past misfortune and mock white society. Mudrooroo published another song cycle, dramatising his own travels in an allegory of bird migration, *Dalwurra: The Black Bittern* (1988). Other collections of note by Black writers appearing during the eighties include *Black Man Coming* (1980) by Gerry Bostock, Robert Walker's *Up, Not Down, Mate: Thoughts from a Prison Cell* (1981) and Maureen Watson's *Black Reflections* (1982). Jack Davis's *John Pat and Other Poems* appeared in 1988. The title poem commemorates a death in police custody that sparked off a national enquiry into treatment of Aboriginal people in the prison system. To protest the colonialist bicentennial celebrations of 'settlement' (or 'invasion'), Kath Walker changed her name to Oodgeroo (paperbark tree) Noonuccal (her language group).

Aboriginal poetry, like much other poetical output, consists often of self-published and small-press work and a lot of anthologised pieces otherwise scattered through magazines (Eva Johnson's poems fall into this group). Frequently we find only one publication from a writer who is moved to record personal pain or to protest ongoing oppression and then returns to the daily struggle and/or social activism, as with Norman E. Rosas's *Poems from the Heart* (2000) or Cec Fisher's *Unity Now* (1991).

A prominent Aboriginal figure was Kevin Gilbert. He was born by the Lachlan River in New South Wales and, after years in an orphanage and in rural work, he began reading and writing during an extended gaol term. He emerged to take an active role in land rights agitation, helping set up the Aboriginal Tent Embassy outside parliament, and demanding a treaty between the government and a sovereign First Nations people. His politics are evident in his poetry: *People Are Legends* (1978), *Flashes of Essence* (1991),

Child's Dreaming (1992) and *Black from the Edge* (1994). Gilbert also includes lyrical evocations of country ('Tree', 'Taipan'), extends his concerns to nuclear threat ('Won't You Dad?'), and has a light touch in mixing free verse with rhyme.

Gilbert's anthology *Inside Black Australia* included the work of Lionel Fogarty. With a reputation as young radical emulating America's Black Power movement, Fogarty has become the most prolific of Aboriginal poets, and arguably the most interesting. As his titles demonstrate, he has broken free of the standard forms to work with his mother tongue (Waka Waka) into which he mixes a lexis and syntax that is partly his own and partly a transcription of 'mission' English and creolised Aboriginal English. His first collection, *Kargun* (1980), was followed by *Yoogum Yoogum* (1982), *Kudjela* (1983) and *Ngutji* (1984). He went on to publish *Jagera* (1990), *New and Selected Poems: Munaldjali Mutuerjaraera* (1995), *Dha'gun Jabree Djan Mitti: The More Complete Works of Lionel Fogarty* (2007), *Yerrabilela Jimbelung: Poems about Friends and Family* (2008), *Connection Requital* (2010), *Mogwie-Idan: Stories of the Land* (2012), *Eelahroo (Long Ago) Nyah (Looking) Möbö-Möbö (Future)* (2014), and *Harvest Lingo* (2016). Fogarty's corpus is an important assertion of the survival and literary adequacy of Indigenous languages and a challenge to white readers to approach Aboriginal culture on its own ground. Poems range from polemic ('Fuck All Departments', 'Rules for Radicals', 'Spirits to Malcolm X', 'Black Suicides') to celebrations of people and folklore ('Remember Something like This') and Black womanhood and country ('Kurumba'). The default style is Ginsberg-like free verse 'rant', but in Fogarty's own crafted poetic voice.

DRAMA

This period saw a 'second wave' of theatre work. It included emerging 'multicultural' voices, work dramatising regional histories and the continued push, influenced by Brecht and Pinter, away from old social realist work. New theatres like Playbox (Melbourne), Sidetrack (Sydney), Hole in the Wall (Perth), Belvoir Street Theatre (Sydney) and the Red Shed (Adelaide) declared their 'fringe' experimentalism, some being linked with student productions at universities and colleges.

A new presence was Stephen Sewell. Mostly working around Sydney, he mixed his Catholic upbringing with Marxist ideas, and wrote *The Father We Loved on a Beach by the Sea* (1978). Politics became more central to his work, *Traitors* (1979) depicting the conflict between Stalinists and Trotskyites. *Welcome the Bright World* (1982) shows a man caught up in German politics in the late 1970s, while his most remembered work, *The Blind Giant is Dancing* (1983), dissects the faction fighting in Australian left-wing politics as old unionists are replaced by career politicians who will sell their principles to succeed. He intercuts the Australian action with pictures of global poverty and conflict and mixes into the male world of power plays questions about feminism. *Dreams in an Empty City* (1986) was followed by *Hate* (1988) and Sewell became famous for his epic social analyses lasting up to four hours.

Michael Gow's *Away* (1986) has been a staple of high school study, partly because of its deployment of Shakespeare as a frame around the stage action. A school performance of *A Midsummer Night's Dream* opens a tale of three families: the headmaster and his wife; a working-class migrant, wife and son; and a middle-class man with a snobbish wife and rebellious daughter. They head off to different locations but, after a storm that borrows from *The Tempest*, all end up together on a beach. In the process we learn of the neurosis of the headmaster's wife, grieving over her son killed in Vietnam, the hidden anguish of the actor son of migrants, who has an incurable disease, and the desperation of the snob wife to fight free of her poor origins. The play ends with a mix of fatalistic optimism and a passage from *King Lear*. Gow also wrote *The Kid* (1983), *Europe* (1987) and *1841* (1988), the last being a view of early colonial society that bicentenary audiences found inappropriately critical.

Some commentators see this period characterised by a greater international outlook. Coming from New Zealand via Canada, Alma De Groen did not feel tied to national themes and settings and came up with *The Rivers of China* (1987). It dramatised Katherine Mansfield's time at the Gurdjieff Institute in 1922, juxtaposed with a future Australian society run by women. In one half, Mansfield realises the sexist aspect of Gurdjieff's philosophy, and in the other, her male channeller has to decide whether to assert his male self and remain enslaved in the matriarchy or hold with his female persona and die of her illness. De Groen also wrote *The Joss Adams Show* (1970), *Perfectly All Right* (1973), *Going Home* (1976), *Chidley* (1976), *Vocations* (1982) and *The Girl Who Saw Everything* (1991). Her consistent interest is in gender relations. Tony Strachan drew attention to Australia's colonial presence in Fiji and Papua New Guinea in *Eyes of the Whites* (1981). Roger Pulvers's *Yamashita* (1977) depicts the vested interests at work in the war crimes trial of the Japanese commander. Pulvers's work incorporates elements of Japanese theatre. From another direction, German Peter Handke has influenced Louis Nowra's plays.

Nowra also goes international in setting one of his early works in nineteenth-century Paraguay. This unusual location is partly explained by Australia's failed utopian venture there, though *Visions* (1978) concentrates on the dictator Lopez and his Irish paramour as they overreach in seeking to build a great city and fall to an ignominious end in Paraguay's dry interior. If Nowra is interested in the use of power, he centres that on how we use language, as suggested by the title of the Pinteresque play *Albert Names Edward* (1975). *Inner Voices* (1977) has courtiers coaching the mute child prince Ivan so they can put him on the Russian throne. Once there, the boy takes his revenge on his tormenting manipulators and retreats into the voices in his head. *Inside the Island* (1980) was followed by Nowra's best-known early work, *The Golden Age* (1985). In this he invents a creolised English for a group of escaped convict offspring raised in isolation in the Tasmanian bush. Their discoverers split between romanticising them as noble savages and conducting experiments on them as genetic curiosities, the two attitudes framed by the Second World War and the politics of eugenics. Nowra had a success in the bicentenary year with his stage adaptation of Xavier Herbert's sprawling novel *Capricornia*.

Dorothy Hewett continued writing for the stage, her collected plays being published in 1992. Her predilection for lively musical theatre found widespread approval in *The Man from Mukinupin*

(1979), which plays on a typical place name from Western Australia and the slang for misbehaving (mucking up). Hewett's most notable theatre pieces (she also wrote for radio) were *The Tatty Hollow Story* (1974), *Joan* (1975), *The Golden Oldies* (1976), *The Beautiful Mrs Portland* (1976), *Golden Valley* (1981) and *Song of the Seals* (1983). Hewett incorporates aspects of Ibsen and, as in *The Tatty Hollow Story*, creates surrealistic effects as the somewhat spooky figure that everyone talks about appears as a despoiled mannequin, dramatising the hollowness of the identities that society projects onto us.

David Williamson's early plays can be quite long with many scenes. Gradually he honed work into two-act dramas with a few central characters. *Travelling North* (1979) was successful in Australia and London, was filmed in 1987, and set for school study. The play draws upon the habit of retirees to set off around Australia towing caravans, usually moving to somewhere warm. Frances, a divorcee in her mid-fifties, teams up with Frank, a widower in his seventies, and they head north from Melbourne to the horror of Frances's two daughters. They are scandalised by the unmarried liaison, worried that Frances will end up looking after a geriatric. Daughter Helen is also cross that she is losing a mother who has done a lot of her housekeeping and babysitting. There are comic moments: when Frank and Frances arrive at their ideal getaway cottage, they are beset by a well-meaning neighbour who insists on building them a massive barbecue. Frank himself becomes a figure of both fun and pathos as he badgers the local doctor about his health, researches his own cures, and quietly gives in to heart disease. Williamson injects some political comment when Frank and neighbour Freddy disagree over the wisdom of having troops in Vietnam. There is a slight feminist element in showing Frances restless for city art shows and family contact while Frank is happy fishing every day. In the second act, we see Frances sorting out her relationships with her daughters. Frank is now hospitalised in Melbourne and is desperate to have Frances drive him north again, but once there, she has to go back to comfort Helen whose husband is leaving her. Ironically, the hostile Helen has been funding her mother's life in the north. Frank satisfies Frances's wish to marry, takes her to an art show in Sydney, and, as the promising new era of Gough Whitlam's Labor government approaches, dies. Frances resolves to continue travelling north on her own. *Travelling North* is a tidy, feel-good drama; it provoked complaints that Williamson was watering down his art to produce a commercial product. Criticism coincided with Williamson's move away from his Melbourne origins to live in Sydney and write about a flashier side of Australia's new capitalist adventurism. *Emerald City* (1987) draws on traditional rivalries between the two cities (one supposedly cold, wet and morally earnest, the other sun-drenched and hedonistic) and addresses suggestions that he had compromised his artistic integrity.

Patrick White continued his attack on suburban mores and conventional piety in *A Cheery Soul*, written earlier but not getting notice on the stage till 1979. He deplored the emphasis on commercial success in Australia, writing 'morality plays' such as *Big Toys* (1977) and *Signal Driver* (1982).

Themes of women's struggles to keep custody of children, survive poverty, resist sexual predation, keep jobs, and get promotion made it to Australian stages supported by such groups as Home Cooking Theatre (Melbourne) and Women on a Shoestring Theatre (Canberra). Sydney-based Jennifer Compton created work mostly linked to the women's movement (as suggested by her *No Man's Land*, 1975, later known as *Crossfire*). After *All Good Children Go to Heaven* (1973), she went on to write about Hitler's lover Eva Braun (1978), and *All the Time in the World* appeared in 1986. Other feminist work from this period includes Jennifer Claire's *The Butterflies of Kalimantan* (1983), Suzanne Spunner's *Running Up a Dress* (1986), and Doreen Clarke's *Bleedin' Butterflies* (1980). Feminist solidarity included recognition of lesbian relationships as depicted in Alison Lyssa's *Pinball* (1981) and *The Boiling Frog* (1984).

Australia's new multicultural policy opened a space for assertions of non-Anglo-Celtic experience. There had been a long tradition of Yiddish drama in Melbourne, and Italians and Greeks post-war set up their own cultural networks, as with Doppio Teatro, an Italian group performing in both English and Italian. Theodore Patrikareas had his 1960s work in Greek translated later as *The*

Promised Woman, *The Uncle from Australia* and *The Divided Heart*. Vasso Kalamaras also wrote plays in Greek, the translated *The Bread Trap* being performed in Perth in 1983. Janis Balodis, of Latvian origin, came out with *Too Young for Ghosts* (1985), followed later by *No Going Back* (1992) and *My Father's Father* (1996), in which tales of immigrant families are intercut with segments from Ludwig Leichhardt's explorations.

Aboriginal playwrights gained inspiration from Western Australian Jack Davis, who wrote a trilogy, *Kullark* (1979), *The Dreamers* (1982) and *No Sugar* (1985), followed by *Honey Spot* (1987). These placed in counterpoint social realist family dialogues from the 1930s, scenes of first contact between white and Black folk, and a mix of dream and myth, all centred around Perth and the infamous Moore River Settlement. Eva Johnson, from South Australia, wrote her first play in 1979 (*When I Die You'll All Stop Laughing*) and went on to create *Faded Genes* (1981), *Onward to Glory* (1984), *Tjinderella* (1984)—a Black version of the Cinderella story—and *Murras* (1988).

LIFE WRITING

'Life writing' re-entered the literary fold when feminism brought critical attention to bear on journals and letters by women. Opening for question what made it into historical record or literary publication raised further questions about how we construct auto/biographies. Two texts can be mentioned as signalling an Australian turn to (self-)conscious biographical writing: Brian Matthews's book on Henry Lawson's mother, *Louisa* (1987), and Drusilla Modjeska's account of her own mother, *Poppy* (1990).

Matthews begins in conventional manner with the subject's birth details, but immediately falls into 'Notes towards an alternative text'. The writer details his despair as he realises both the paucity of material for researchers of subaltern lives and the temptations for the biographer to fill gaps or tidy up hearsay. To allow for a controlled imagining of possible truths, the writer sets up a 'diary' of commentary on his research and writing but cannot find the right tone or balance. He invents meta-personae: 'the biographer' and an alter ego Owen Stevens. The book's subject will be approached indirectly via Louisa's daughter, Gertrude. Her reliability as a witness can be assessed by Stevens, whose comments can then be evaluated by 'the biographer'. Biography becomes a fragmented multivocal affair. Louisa emerges as a dramatic teller of tales and energetic campaigner for votes for women, beset by male persecutions and family frustrations, with elements of her personality left open to debate. Despite all his careful strategies, the biographer confesses his inability to capture his subject:

> When, as biographer, for example, I record Louisa's victory over the New South Wales Typographical Association, I do so with some elation in the writing. I am elated for her. ... I don't know if she was elated, and I couldn't prove that she was. ... I empathise with an emotion I assume must have existed. ... Where does that leave the truth?

Modjeska begins her narrative with a chapter labelled 'Family' and ends with one labelled 'Friends'. Psychoanalysis blends with feminist theory to present three generations of women whose weeping accompanies their births of daughters. The imprisoning consolations ('cure and poison both') of being 'an ordinary family' shape mother Poppy's mental fragility and her daughter's drive to discover what went wrong. Telling the mother's story requires gathering disparate reports from others and creative invention to fill gaps in them. That supplementation leads the biographer (fractured as Drusilla and Lalage, her mother's name for her) to meditate on her own investments and projections. The silence of unreachable pasts is also figured as 'the enigma, and therefore the power, of the silent feminine'—the enforced silence of a mother whisked away into a mental hospital, the strategic silences of the same woman divorced and building a career in social work while becoming the lover of a priest; the silences between her daughters and within the writer herself. Modjeska's untangling of mysteries draws upon her wide reading: Luce Irigaray, Christa Wolf, Cora Kaplan, and a list of 'literary madnesses'. The writer comes to accept her mother's comment that she has used feminism as a way of protecting herself from men, and we catch glimpses of her parallel story of hesitant and failed relationships.

Such works added creative flair to life stories. More straightforward was *A Fortunate Life* (1980), the best-selling autobiography of poor bush worker and war veteran, Albert Facey. Other works came from Aboriginal women. Sally Morgan's *My Place* (1987), for example, wove together quest narrative, multi-generation family voices, pathos and humour, and motifs from nature and Aboriginal lore. The mix of biography and autobiography pointed to the unspoken stories and pain of Aboriginal history across generations and constituted a collective story rather than a set of individual tales. This is reflected in the mother-daughter auto/bio collaboration *Auntie Rita* (1994) by Jackie and Rita Huggins, and Ruby Langford's *Don't Take Your Love to Town* (1988), which sparked a sharp debate about the proper relationship between Indigenous writer-subjects and white editor-scribes.

CHILDREN'S AND YOUNG ADULT LITERATURE

Mem Fox began a stellar career writing picture books for younger readers with her all-time hit *Possum Magic* (1983). For older children, Eleanor Spence entered the difficult area of 'social problem' novels. *A Candle for Saint Anthony* (1977) not only depicts the post-war multicultural mix of European migration but also includes a tentative homosexual attraction between two teenage schoolboys. Ruth Park produced a popular time-travel story that takes young readers into the slum tenements of Sydney (*Playing Beatie Bow*, 1980). Robin Klein scandalised many with her dark novel about children caught up in a religious cult (*People Might Hear You*, 1983). Books about multiculturalism, urban poverty, teenage pregnancy, youth suicide and drug culture proliferated, running the gamut from rebarbative didacticism to depressing naturalism. Other books turned to fantasy. Victor Kelleher, in *The Master of the Grove* (1982) and *Taronga* (1986), worked with both prehistoric hunting society and futuristic settings. Gillian Rubinstein attracted attention for incorporating the new cyber-world into an adventure tale, *Space Demons* (1986), in which characters spin in and out of the computer games they play. Patricia Wrightson attempted to get close to an indigenous sense of an animate land in *The Nargun and the Stars* (1973) and went on to create a 'Dreaming' fantasy adventure centred on an Aboriginal youth, Wirrun (*The Ice Is Coming*, 1977; *The Dark Bright Water*, 1978; *Behind the Wind*, 1981). Chthonic creatures, dangerous to humans because indifferent to their existence, have to be managed into uneasy quietude. Genuine Indigenous folk story was popularised by illustrated books, notably Dick Roughsey's colourful series about the Rainbow Serpent and other creation stories, starting in 1975 and running through the 1980s.

CHAPTER 8

Deregulation to GFC
1988–2008

SOCIAL AND POLITICAL CONTEXT

In 1991, Paul Keating replaced Bob Hawke as prime minister. Keating was an anomaly: a boy from the working-class western suburbs of Sydney who wore Armani suits. He had a gift for verbally skewering his opponents and achieved some progressive social changes while further opening up Australia's economy to globalised markets. He set up a compulsory superannuation scheme for all workers and redirected the nation away from its old British ties, favouring links with the Asian region and the possibility of becoming a republic. (The Australian Republican Movement was founded in 1991.) Keating continued naval and air support for the American invasion of Iraq, and in 1992, introduced a mandatory detention period for asylum seekers. Following the global stock market crash of 1987, unemployment was high, and with deregulation of the market, local manufacturing declined. By this time, Mitsubishi and Toyota dominated the car market and there was a major strike by airline workers. However, Keating's Labor government won praise for 'pump priming' the national economy, insulating Australia against the economic downturn. Despite this, ongoing privatisation of government assets and large-scale selling of forest products and minerals overseas inspired the creation of a new political party, the Greens, in 1992.

After a campaign by Eddie Mabo and supporters both Black and white, the High Court of Australia in 1992 ruled in favour of Mabo's claim to his people's traditional ownership of land in the Torres Strait. This overturned a legal doctrine that had become popular myth: that Australia in 1788 was *terra nullius*—generally understood to mean that the continent was empty and awaiting occupation. It really meant that legally it contained no recognisable authority with which the British could treaty, so that native claims to land were extinguished by white settlement. Also in 1992, the prime minister delivered his 'Redfern Speech'. Redfern is an inner suburb of Sydney heavily populated by Aboriginal people, and the speech publicly acknowledged their historical dispossession and maltreatment. A year later, the Keating government passed the Native Title Act, allowing Aboriginal land claims to be lodged.

Conservatives and mining companies responded to the Mabo case by creating fear among white Australians that they would 'lose their backyards' to Aboriginal people. This fear, and radical left disapproval of Keating's economic policies, led to the election in 1996 of a Liberal–National Party coalition led by John Howard. His government would last for eleven years. A clever strategist, Howard worded a referendum on whether Australia should be a republic in a way that ensured a 'no' vote and he increasingly accommodated far-right opinion once populist agitators began to be voted into federal parliament. Legislation was passed to protect pastoral leases by declaring that they could coexist with Indigenous land claims. The loudest of the new populists was Pauline Hanson, who founded her own One Nation party and complained about 'special treatment' of Aboriginal people, about Australia being 'swamped by Asians' and, eventually, about its being invaded by Muslims. Hanson came from Queensland, popularly regarded as a 'redneck' state. The stereotype was perpetuated when Australia moved to put the clocks back an hour in summer, but Queensland refused, farmers arguing that 'daylight saving' would unsettle dairy routines and extra sunlight would fade the curtains. Western Australia also refused, creating four Australian time zones in summer, with Perth four hours behind Sydney.

Just before the change of government, Labor's attorney general established a commission of inquiry into the removal of Aboriginal and Torres Strait Islander children from their families. Led by Sir Rowland Wilson and Aboriginal activist Mick Dodson, the inquiry collected official reports and heard personal testimony showing that state and federal governments had approved the forcible abduction of children from their families across three generations. At best, the policy intended to improve the lot of underprivileged children by inducting them into the ways of the dominant society, but reality meant harsh institutions, sexual abuse and exploitative use of inmates as domestic and rural labour. The process was genocidal in concentrating on 'half-caste' children, who were deemed educable, with the explicit aim of 'breeding out' any ties to Indigenous family, language and culture. Testimony to the commission made clear the emotional trauma and cross-generational family dysfunction caused. The 1997 *Bringing Them Home* report on the 'Stolen Generation' led to a shift in the general attitude to Indigenous affairs. However, worried by the legal and economic consequences of admitting to past guilt, Prime Minister Howard refused to offer an official apology.

In 1996, strict gun controls were legislated following a massacre of tourists at the Port Arthur convict settlement in Tasmania. In the same year, the Howard government passed a Workplace Relations Act that undid Bob Hawke's policy of collective bargaining over pay and conditions for workers. Howard's act was a union-busting tool that encouraged companies to offer individual contracts. In 1998, Patrick Corporation, which controlled most of the docks, put its staff on casual contracts lacking the protections the Maritime Union of Australia had fought for. When workers protested, Patrick locked them out. Union picket lines were violently broken up by 'security guards' in balaclavas. Howard's attacks on worker rights gradually destroyed a history of social welfare and union solidarity that had protected living standards.

Howard's conservative coalition directed its politics towards what he called 'aspirationals': small-business owners and tradespeople who sought greater material prosperity and who were more interested in tax cuts than supporting public funding for schools or unemployment benefits. 'Freedom of choice' became justification for removing regulations controlling banks, environmental degradation and overseas investment in Australian agriculture and mining. Publicly owned services (the post office, electricity supply, freeway construction) were partially or fully privatised.

This commercialisation of everything was accompanied by moments when the costs of development were recognised. Asbestos mining had supplied building materials for Australia's post-war reconstruction but was discovered to cause severe lung disease. Products started to be banned in 1991, ending in a total ban in 2003, and awareness of industrial pollution and the effects of smoking led to many reforms.

Sydney hosted the Olympics in 2000. This created a surge in international tourism in Australia. Alongside parading national icons (whip-cracking stockmen, Ned Kelly, the suburban lawnmower), it also showcased Aboriginal culture in its opening and closing ceremonies. One of the performing bands, Midnight Oil, added an unscheduled political note by wearing black T-shirts with 'Sorry' printed on the front. This criticism of Howard's refusal to apologise to First Nations peoples was amplified by a huge 'reconciliation' march across Sydney Harbour Bridge, with a plane etching 'Sorry' in the sky above.

During the late 1990s, many Timorese refugees fleeing Indonesian-instigated violence were welcomed to Darwin. This sympathy for refugees changed, however. In August of 2001, the Norwegian freighter *Tampa* rescued around 400 Afghan asylum seekers from a sinking boat. It was boarded by Australian special forces and prevented from entering Australian waters, ultimately landing at Christmas Island because of illness on board. Norway correctly protested that exclusion violated UN regulations, but the government pushed through a Border Protection Act, excising outlying islands, so that 'boat people' could not claim asylum by landing on Australian soil.

The September attack on New York's Twin Towers created popular fears that refugees from Middle Eastern war zones would include terrorists. Howard exacerbated this concern when he falsely claimed that asylum seekers had thrown their children overboard from a 'people smuggler' vessel in order to force their rescue rather than letting the navy turn their boat back to Indonesia. Refugees were described as 'queue jumpers' and 'illegals' and despite humanitarian protests no government has had the courage to dismantle the system of turning back boats, detaining refugees in gaol-like 'camps', and removing many to overseas sites for indefinite periods. Popular hostility to 'boat people' intensified when tourist sites in Bali and the Australian embassy in Jakarta were bombed in 2002. These events allowed civil rights in Australia to be abrogated in the name of anti-terrorism protections. Immigration and Customs was converted into a militarised Border Force that has been impervious to public scrutiny. Muslim youth in Australia felt increasingly harassed and white Australians became more suspicious of brown faces. When 'Lebanese' men went to Cronulla beach in 2005, local 'Anglos' brawled with them and this was a visible end to the ideal of multicultural harmony.

By 2007, enough discontent over restrictions of civil liberties, erosion of job security and government alliances with big corporations had built up for Kevin Rudd to lead the Labor Party to electoral success. Some of the more extreme elements of the Howard era were wound back, but Labor did not hold power in the Senate. Rudd became unpopular but has gone down in history for his 2008 public apology to the 'Stolen Generation' of Aboriginal people, and for opening up serious debate about climate change.

Cultural Context

Conservative free-market economic rationalism became ideological gospel. Egalitarian reforms based on feminist and postcolonial theories were defamed as 'politically correct' socialist tyranny, and the Howard government turned culture away from collective good to individual interest. Australia unwittingly promoted this American-influenced change when its research organisation, the CSIRO, patented its prototype for wi-fi (1996, confirmed by an international lawsuit in 2009), prompting the internet and smartphone revolution. Despite turning everyone into atomised units of media consumption, this technology did enable the wider circulation of scholarship, stories and verse via websites.

'Neo-liberal' commercialisation sparked active opposition. Labelled 'the culture wars' by the press, it centred on arguments over Australian history. Howard wanted the colonising myths of peaceful settlement and civilisational progress to be perpetuated; he lamented what he called 'black armband' accounts of suffering inflicted on convicts, Aboriginal peoples and the environment. These had been set forth by people such as Henry Reynolds, who, from 1981 onwards in *The Other Side of the Frontier*, *The Whispering in Our Hearts* and *Why Weren't We Told?*, exposed the fact that there had been a protracted undeclared war of violent confrontations between settlers and Aboriginal people. In 2002, Keith Windschuttle, who had denounced 'the postmodern turn' in historical work as political interference in a supposedly objective study of records, published *The Fabrication of Aboriginal History*. He argued that there had been fewer Indigenous deaths than claimed and that no official policy authorised killings or removal of children. 'Black armband' historians called this 'whitewashing' history, and many poems, novels and plays have engaged with questions of evidence, interpretation and the responsibilities of present generations for past failings.

In literature, an important publication was Mudrooroo's *Writing from the Fringe* (1990), later revised as *Indigenous Literature of Australia: Milli Milli Wangka* (1997). It challenged Black writing to move beyond autobiography, social realism and protest to more complex assertions of a non-white world view incorporating 'Dreaming' consciousness. Mudrooroo labelled this mode 'maban reality'. His work was complemented by Anita Heiss's study of Indigenous publishing, *Dhuuluu Yala: To Talk Straight* (2000), and by her collaboration with Peter Minter and Nicholas Jose to produce the *Macquarie PEN Anthology of Aboriginal Literature* (2008).

Changes in theories of literary study and history were highlighted by the issue of *The Oxford Literary History of Australia* (1998) edited by Bruce Bennett and Jennifer Strauss. This was a more kaleidoscopic and extensive set of essays that challenged the rather patrician uniformity of the 1981 *Oxford History of Australian Literature*. Despite economic challenges, literary publishers continued to emerge: Brandl & Schlesinger in 1994 and Giramondo a year later. Giramondo survived by connecting to university teaching and it emphasised new and experimental writing, its big success occurring when Alexis Wright's *Carpentaria* (2006) won awards and international praise.

The push to maximise profit margins as publishers became part of global corporations led to a proliferation of 'middlebrow' writing and best-sellers. Previously, someone who put out a book a year was suspected of being a popular hack; now key figures were expected to have a new novel at least every two years. Writers were increasingly encouraged to take an active role in promoting their work, with reputations moving towards the poles of either 'celebrity' or 'hermit' authors. (In Australian fiction, Bryce Courtenay sits at the popular end and Gerald Murnane at the literary hermit end of the spectrum.) Australian publishers attended international book fairs and courted success that would once have been viewed as impossible. Australian children's literature made sizeable inroads on the overseas market. Globalisation had become sufficiently embedded in Australia for Scribe, founded in the 1970s in Melbourne, to become a publisher of overseas work, including translations, and sell titles back to the UK and USA.

The Australian government encouraged international reach, funding translation of texts and visits by artists of all kinds to festivals around the world. This was seen as 'soft diplomacy' and support was provided to develop overseas centres for Australian Studies. Those in China were bolstered by Prime Minister Rudd's breaking Australia's monolingual habit when he showed that he spoke Mandarin. Government support for the arts saw a brief boom in Australian filmmaking, with international hits like *Strictly Ballroom*, *Muriel's Wedding* and *Priscilla, Queen of the Desert*. Australian film workers (Baz Luhrmann, Hugh Jackson, Guy Pearce, Nicole Kidman, Cate Blanchett) gained entry to Hollywood. At the same time, globalisation increased the power of large operators, so that Fox Studios was able to open a production facility in Sydney, diverting a lot of Australian talent into working on American blockbusters.

Teaching creative writing courses in universities and the availability of writers' grants led to more literary output. Journals specific to the craft of writing (such as the online *TEXT*) encouraged a shift from literary analysis towards artists' statements and ficto-criticism. Arguably, this has injected a greater self-consciousness and conceptual underpinning to literary writing. Equally, there has been a growth of courses in script writing that have encouraged more people to work with television and film productions and to write for podcasts and 'new media'.

In 1995, a major literary scandal sparked cultural debate. A novel manuscript awarded the Vogel prize went to publication in 1994 and won the Miles Franklin Award. *The Hand that Signed the Paper* told how Ukrainians brutalised by famine and oppressed by Russians took part in Nazi massacres of Jews. In the book, a university student finds her uncle (and potentially her father) facing prosecution for war crimes and assembles accounts from her family to make sense of it all. The text recreates the wartime attitudes of many Ukrainians, and the book itself was read as anti-Semitic. It did suggest that trials for war crimes were undesirable impositions of contemporary morals on quite different past situations, but the attitudes and editing of the young narrator place some distance between implied author and the historical views collected. Argument over the supposed morality of the book spilled over into questions about the ethics of reproducing racism or trying to avoid responsibility through 'postmodern' textual play. Debates were exacerbated by strands of plagiarism in the novel, further fuelled by the discovery that the author was not a Ukrainian with an authentic attachment to her sources. Not just using a nom de plume but publicly enacting a Ukrainian identity, author 'Helen Demidenko' turned out to be Helen Darville, the child of English immigrants.

The effect of all this (other than resuscitating discussion of Australia's obsession with literary hoaxes) was to consolidate popular suspicion of clever literary structuring and scholarly authority (the Miles Franklin judges were mostly university lecturers). The scandal focused on identity politics and the ethics of representing 'the other'. Darville managed to offend both Jews and Ukrainians and embarrassed those who espoused progressive cultural views. 'Anglo' conservatives were able to use Demidenko to claim that multiculturalism had become a sacred cow protecting 'ethnic' writing from proper literary judgement.

Prose Fiction

The year after the bicentenary, Peter Goldsworthy published his best-known work, *Maestro*. This relatively short novel captured the national imagination because of its teenage 'getting of wisdom' plot and its unusual setting in tropical Darwin (with contrasts to staid Adelaide). It rehearsed themes of Australian innocence versus European tragedy, pop versus classical culture, and the ruthless dedication required to become a leading artist compared to the human ties that leave most of us as more likable second-rate achievers. Goldsworthy has been a literary all-rounder, with eight books of poetry (notably *Readings from Ecclesiastes*, 1982; *This Goes with That*, 1991; *Anatomy of a Metaphor*, 2017), several collections of short stories (from *Archipelagoes*, 1982, through *Little Deaths*, 1993, to *Gravel*, 2010) and a series of novels. Goldsworthy combines a detached observation of human foibles with satiric wit, and his scientific interests (rooted in his medical training) led him to a comic fantasy about cloning, *Honk If You Are Jesus* (1992), and *Wish: A Biologically Engineered Love Story* (1995), depicting a love affair between a man and an ape. His most recent novel, *Minotaur* (2019), is a thriller about a blind detective exacting revenge on the criminal who blinded him.

Thea Astley continued to experiment with form and the limits of realism. *Reaching Tin River* (1990) begins with the narrator offering a number of alternative openings. These are all reprised during the course of the story, which has the narrating young wife escaping an oppressive marriage to pursue historical research into a small-town pioneer. She becomes increasingly obsessed until her experience and the diaries of her subject seem to show a time warp of mutual haunting. Music and Euclidean geometry are integrating leitmotifs. *The Multiple Effects of Rain Shadow* (1996) is set around Palm Island, a 'native reserve' cum prison in Queensland that built its own community out of fragments of Aboriginal tribes shipped there by the state. It sets up differing perspectives on a central moment of crazed violence (historically real, circa 1930). The story and its aftermath are recorded by itinerant whites working at the edges of officialdom and their accounts are interspersed with a 'chorus' in Aboriginal creole. Pathos and tragedy wash across frustrated anger at racism and patriarchy and ineffectual protests against 'the system'. Astley signed off with *Drylands* (1999), for which she won her fourth Miles Franklin Award. It is a set of nested stories, all recording life in another nasty rural town by the woman running the newsagent shop. Elegantly constructed, it rehearses the difficulties of beginning to write and ends by asserting that there is no ending. We sense the author's rage against small-town life in which everything is mindless and mean, most women are victims and all men are bullies with tendencies to mob violence. The only exception is the figure of the artist/writer, like all Astley's other creative onlookers, complicit in the entropy that pulls everyone down.

Elizabeth Jolley established herself as a teacher of creative writing and found a way to integrate her short stories into novel form. *My Father's Moon* (1989) draws on her experiences as a schoolgirl and then wartime nurse in England, tracking the protagonist's love for another (mostly imagined) woman and her seduction by a surgeon and his society wife. Vignettes of varying length are linked by the motif of her father consoling her loneliness with the idea of sharing 'his' moon, and by recurrent musical references. Indeed, Jolley goes on to create a symphonic weaving of leitmotifs in three movements, adding *Cabin Fever* (1990) and *The Georges' Wife* (1993). The protracted monologue reprises sentences from previous books and charts the struggles of a single mother through post-war rationing and careers as hospital aide, housekeeper and live-in mistress to Mr George, finally emigrating to Australia when her lover gains work there. Jolley concluded her opus with *The Orchard Thieves* (1995), *Lovesong* (1997), *The Accommodating Spouse* (1999) and *An Innocent Gentleman* (2001).

If Jolley is known as a West Australian, Marion Halligan is identified with Canberra, where she helped found a regional writing group. She has specialised in 'quiet' books of largely middle-class and suburban settings, though *Spider Cup* (1990) paralleled the journey of self-discovery of an Australian woman going through divorce with a love-and-vengeance tale of a seventeenth-century French noblewoman. Like Jolley, Halligan deploys subtle ironies to dissect the power of husbands and explore possibilities for women to find liberation. She also produces lyrical evocations of gardens and attends to 'female' crafts like cooking and dressmaking, as in her most complex work, *The Golden Dress* (1998). One of her best-sellers was a literary whodunnit spiced with a bit of queered romance, *The Apricot Colonel* (2006).

Gender and sexuality are the focus of Mary Fallon's *Working Hot* (1989) and Sue Woolfe's fiction. Fallon achieved a certain notoriety for her lesbian content, and her multi-voiced narrative enacted questions of how we read or dismiss bodies and texts. Woolfe depicted women fighting to be accepted as part of the art world and as mathematicians (*Painted Woman*, 1989; *Leaning towards Infinity*, 1996). Linda Jaivin extended Fallon's foray into erotica with *Eat Me* (1995) and wrote humorous 'pop' fiction with titles like *Rock and Roll Babes from Outer Space* (1996) up to *The Infernal Optimist* (2006). Jaivin had built a reputation as a journalist with expertise on China, something matched by Nicholas Jose, whose multi-stranded novel *The Red Thread* (2000) is a Chinese love story.

David Foster attracted attention for his novel *The Pure Land* (1974), which works with photography and the scenery of the Blue Mountains. Matching Jaivin's spoof humour and adaptation of popular genre fiction, but with an anchor in classics such as *Faust*, Virgil and Voltaire, Foster has since cultivated dark satires. *Plumbum* (1983) catalogues the farcical adventures of a heavy metal band escaping dull Canberra to wrestle with the perils of Sydney and Calcutta. Later, a postman uses his knowledge of a small community to solve murders (*Dog Rock: A Postal Pastoral*, 1985). Foster resolutely lampooned the 'political correctness' of feminism and related 'middle-class' concerns, the title *Testostero* (1987) indicating his fictive sympathies. Later, he created his major—certainly lengthy—work, *The Glade within the Grove* (1996). In it, he displays his interests in martial arts, masculinity, music, the classics, religions, the wonder of forests and Australia's history of rapacious land use.

Peter Carey amplified the darkness evident in his short stories in *The Tax Inspector* (1991). In the working-class western suburbs of Sydney's light industry belt, a young woman audits a failing car repair and sales business. The book is about corruption: gangsters and real estate sharks at one end of society and psychopath teenagers and squalor at the other. Cars, petrol and oil are metonymic of all the pollution of modernity, and the Catchprice family is completely dysfunctional owing to toxic chemicals and generational abuse of children. The grim tale and its unfashionable setting turned some readers away from Carey, who by this time had moved to New York. Distance allowed him to think globally, and the result was *The Unusual Life of Tristan Smith* (1994). It is a complex allegory that has not received its due as a *tour de force* gesturing to *Midnight's Children* and *The Tin Drum*. The story centres on bohemian affairs in a leftist theatre troupe into which the misshapen dwarf protagonist Tristan is born. His little community is enmeshed in the politics of Efica, an island half, seeking independence from its larger neighbour, Voorstand. There, Efica's small-time agitprop group has its equivalent in a large bread-and-circuses industry clearly modelled on Disneyland. Carey fuses aspects of islands under French control with apartheid South Africa and undertones of American influence over Australia.

Carey has been successful in connecting with the wider Anglosphere while keeping up links with his homeland. In one of his reinventions of literary history (*Jack Maggs*, 1997), he writes back to Dickens's *Great Expectations*, having the transportee Magwitch return to seek out his (ungrateful) protégé only to become the subject of Dickens's obsession with hypnotism. A more complex mix of Frankenstein, Maughamesque colonial romance and the infamous Ern Malley hoax is *My Life as a Fake* (2003). The same messing with fact and fiction occurs in *The True History of the Kelly Gang* (2000), which won the author his second Booker Prize. Carey uses the self-justifying Jerilderie Letter of Australia's most famous outlaw to reconstruct the letter's semi-educated Irish voice and have Kelly tell us his life in letters to his (fictional) wife and child. He pulls in newspaper cuttings, diary jottings and notes, annotated by an archivist. The papers have been collected by the schoolteacher who betrayed the Kelly gang to the police. He deposits his collection in a state library to reveal 'the true story' of one of the nation's most persistent legends. Carey's version of Ned can be compared with Jean Bedford's *Sister Kate* (1982) and Robert Drewe's *Our Sunshine* (1991) as well as Douglas Stewart's verse drama.

Carey's own progress from a small-town car yard to international literary fame is ironised in *Theft: A Love Story* (2006), in which a butcher's son becomes a tormented genius painter caught up in the machinations of collectors and the global art market. Carey reworks his Kelly ventriloquism in the voice of the painter's intellectually challenged brother, and throws in another of his deceptive, tough women, part Australian, part New York art dealer. It is a tongue-in-cheek mystery, a popular romance and a social critique.

A new voice emerged in the bicentenary year that was only fully heard in 1992 when Alex Miller's *The Ancestor Game* appeared. Miller arrived from England as a teenager and worked on Queensland cattle stations before moving to Melbourne, where he became a teacher, an art dealer and part of the theatre scene. The nature of painting—and writing—is a central theme in *The Sitters* (1995) and *Prochovnik's Dream* (2005), crossing with the mysteries of personality, love, and what drives us (*Conditions of Faith*, 2000). *The Ancestor Game* explores the deracination and quest for belonging of the migrant. An emigré British academic meets an art teacher born in China but educated by a German and at a Ballarat boarding school. They contrive a testy friendship in which the former tries to assemble an account of the four generations of Fengs based on the novel/family history written by his friend's grandmother and the diaries of the German mentor translated by his artist granddaughter. The novel won the Miles Franklin Award for its carefully counterpointed structure and play between modes of constructing history.

The two books that consolidated Miller's reputation as an Australian author were *Journey to the Stone Country* (2002) and *Landscape of Farewell* (2007). In these, he returns to his youthful experiences of rural Queensland, but pushes into the complexities of history and race relations. In *Journey to the Stone Country*, a Melbourne academic is suddenly dumped by her husband and flees to join an old friend who is doing archaeological assessments of sites earmarked for mines or dams. Her Aboriginal colleague grew up alongside her on remote cattle stations where one grandparent married an Aboriginal woman while his neighbour massacred her relations. The two share a love of the land and struggle to find ways to acknowledge the violent past while learning to live with each other and resettle a long-abandoned farm. The book could be criticised as a feel-good story of reconciliation for settler Australia. *Landscape of Farewell* is a corrective to such a reading.

An old German academic plagued by family silences about what his father did during the war is challenged by a young Aboriginal scholar to engage properly with the history of massacre that he toys with. He goes to Australia and meets her uncle (Dougald Gnapun, who appears in the previous novel). The two old men establish a friendship and eventually Dougald requests Otto to write down the story of his great grandfather, leader of a historic massacre of white settlers in the nineteenth century. Otto dramatises his account, entering into the tale, and thinks about how the writer has to (mis) appropriate historical record as his own to make it come alive. Other white writers might well have sparked a storm of outrage for daring to write on behalf of Black people, but Miller has been credited with careful management of his material, and for showing that an apology is only the beginning of honest confrontation with the past and commitment to some form of restitution for its victims.

In 1991, Tim Winton came out with what is often voted Australia's favourite contemporary novel. *Cloudstreet* evokes the riverside setting of Perth and relates the story of a lively if unruly family in a rambling share-house at the edge of the city. The story captures the knockabout glamour of the rambunctious poor, injecting a stream of consciousness in the mind of an autistic child and revealing the haunting of the house by ghosts of Aboriginal people once brought there to be trained up in white mores. The very popularity of this novel kept Winton at the edges of critical regard for some years, as did his focus on male experience in an age of feminism, but he has continued to sell well, forcing serious analysis from critics interested in masculinity and how the spiritual is dealt with in an often relentlessly secular society.

The Riders (1994), set mostly in the Ireland of Winton's forebears, is about father-child love and a desperate search across Europe for the wife-mother who abandons them. Winton received more attention for his next two books, *Dirt Music* (2001) and *Breath* (2008). He specialises in damaged or trapped people who bounce off each other in attempts to find 'a pure part' of themselves realised in moments of 'grace' often linked with some 'holy' place in the natural world. Winton has a gift for capturing the laconic repartee of workers and using popular modes (action adventure, road journeys, surfing lore) as a basis for serious discussion of how we push at limits to escape the ordinary or try to live down our pasts. During this time, Winton also consolidated his reputation as a writer for children, with comic works such as *The Bugalugs Bum Thief* (1991) and a number of books about would-be hero Lockie Leonard (1990–97). Short story writing continued, collected as *Blood and Water* (1993) and *The Turning* (2004).

Beginning with a short story collection, *The House of Breathing* (1992), Gail Jones has become a leading novelist at the 'high literary' end of the fiction spectrum. She follows on from David Malouf's rhythmic prose and resonantly symbolic motifs, adding an artistic self-awareness. A feature of Jones's fiction is its international outlook: stories are set in London, Paris, Bombay, Tokyo, Berlin, Palermo. *Black Mirror* (2002) places a young Australian woman, Anna, in London. She is writing the biography of an expatriate painter and is about to interview her before she dies. Victoria, as a marginal colonial, has mixed with the surrealist artists of Paris. Through her, we see the pretentiousness, sexism and racism of the leading lights of the time. She herself plays outrageous roles to confuse her interrogator (whom she mocks, turning her name into textually significant distortions: anamorphic, analeptic, anachronistic). The women discover each other's backgrounds in Kalgoorlie, share a female-artistic desire to break free of male provincial society, and through a texture of literary reference (Ern Malley, Baudelaire, Pound, Benjamin) and motifs from Victoria's paintings (stars, fires, mirrors, hands), the mysteries of surrealist composition are shown to inhere in memory and the trauma of a lost mother.

Sixty Lights (2004) is another recovery of history with a feminist touch. It goes further back in time, using *Jane Eyre* and *Great Expectations* as reference points. An orphaned brother and sister shuttle between England and Australia. Jones jumps between the children's present and their parents' previous present, at times looking forward in what is a characteristic tense in all the novels: 'Years later … in a pleat in time, Lucy wakes'. Lucy both moves and is fixed in time, eventually becoming a photographer (a woman entering a man's space and converting a 'science' into an art form).

She seeks 'an image that will stand in for me' that will be 'flecked with time'. On a sea voyage, Lucy is seduced by a British officer and lives with an 'uncle' in Bombay, where as a free-thinking 'colonial' she outrages Raj society. She returns to London to enjoy 'new woman' freedom in community with her married brother before she dies in childbirth.

Dreams of Speaking (2006) is a meditation on the nature of modernity. The invention of cellophane, aeroplanes, cars, cinema, radio, the telephone, neon lights, photocopying, bar codes, space travel and the internet become the subject of books being written by Alice and Mr Sakamoto, an acquaintance Alice meets in Paris after leaving her Western Australian origins. Modernity both speeds up time and freezes it. Doubling and repetition become leitmotifs—the book ends with Alice's sister asking her to tell the story of Mr Sakamoto, which we have already been reading. Gaps and silences infuse the narrative with melancholia. Alice is lonely overseas and discovers that she was adopted; Mr Sakamoto has lost his mother and his family has suffered in the bombing of Nagasaki; Alice mourns his death soon after she visits the family in Japan. The life of the narrative is as much in its texture of resonances as in its content.

Sorry (2007) maintains Jones's style but addresses matters of social import. The title points to protests against the conservative government's refusal to apologise for the policy of removing children from Aboriginal families. A British man trains as an archaeologist and moves his family to northwest Australia to study Aboriginal people. His wife goes slowly mad from isolation and his emotional bullying. She quotes Shakespeare as a buffer against and commentary on life. Their daughter, Perdita, becomes friends with the 'blacks' attached to the cattle station they live on, as well as with the deaf-mute son of the station owners, and with Mary, the Aboriginal teenage house help. Perdita's father is killed while sexually abusing Mary, who is taken off to prison. Perdita develops a stutter that pushes her into silence, but in Perth she locates Mary and discovers Billy, her mute friend, learning to communicate through sign language. Perdita is also taken to a psychologist who teaches her to use Shakespearean iambics as a means of overcoming her mutism, during which she confronts what has traumatised her. She realises that Mary is innocent and has protected Perdita, who had blindly killed to protect Mary. Mary refuses offers to bring her justice and dies before Perdita can say sorry. A book about what can and cannot be said, about the shape of feelings and the consolations of literature, *Sorry* has been praised for its examination of white guilt and its refusal of any easy reconciliation.

Another 'stylist' is Michelle de Kretser. Her first novel, *The Rose Grower* (1999), is set in a provincial town during the French Revolution, reflecting the author's time living in France. Her second book, *The Hamilton Case* (2003), is a mix of Naipaul's *The Mimic Men*, Rushdie's *Midnight's Children* and a range of detective novels. It is set in colonial Sri Lanka, de Kretser's birthplace. The author refuses categorisation as an ethnic minority author, though *The Lost Dog* (2007) explores migrant identity. Tom, a young academic in Melbourne writing a book on Henry James, experiences the gaps and overlaps in time and memory that the city presents to the newcomer. He tries to live down his poor Anglo-Indian background, links up with an East Asian-Australian artist whose play between painting, photography and the 'junk' of modernity reflects her elusive self and the mystery of a lost husband. Tom's protective façades are shattered when he 'goes bush' to write and his dog runs away. In the search for the pet, he finds the emotional strength to be able to support his ageing neurotic mother. It is a complex book, working as much through kaleidoscopic fragments and mood as through plot.

Richard Flanagan gained attention as a Tasmanian-based writer with his *Death of a River Guide* (1994). It reflected the movement to save the island's forests and rivers from development and impressed with its echoes of Carlos Fuentes and the mental processes of a character either dying or dead—in this case a kayaker trapped underwater. Flanagan followed up with *The Sound of One Hand Clapping* (1997), a saga of a migrant worker on Tasmania's hydroelectric construction scheme and his daughter. He then changed course again, producing *Gould's Book of Fish* (2001), a fantastical reworking of Tasmania's convict-era history based on real people and an actual book illustrating antipodean marine life.

A faker of antiques for the tourist trade finds one version of the original covered over with writing, loses it, but is so taken with the stories that he writes down what he remembers. It is a forged tale by a forger that contains faked documents and invented legends and exposes the horrors of convict suffering and massacres of Aboriginal tribes. The twists and turns of the story question Voltaire's rationalist enlightenment, the reliability of official histories, and the function of art and literature. *Wanting* (2008) is a quieter, more pathos-laden exploration of the adoption of an Aboriginal girl by Governor and Lady Franklin. They experiment with educating her as a 'white' but abandon her to racist colonial society when they return to England. This tale is set against Dickens's passion for his mistress and his play about Franklin's doomed Arctic expedition.

In 1992, Andrew McGahan won the Vogel Literary Award for his first novel, *Praise*. This represented an Australian 'grunge' genre stripping all romance from an urban drug-taking counter-culture. After the rampant greed of the eighties economic boom, money trumped ideals, and drugs and sex became commodities exploiting and exploited by young adults at the bottom of the social ladder. McGahan followed up with *1988* (1995), a crime thriller *Last Drinks* (2000) and *The White Earth* (2004), which won the Miles Franklin Award. This depicts the many aspects of attachment to place. A boy is caught up in his great uncle's obsession with holding on to a ruined Queensland grazing property. It shows conservative reactions against Native Title legislation and includes gothic elements that connect to violent 'Black dispersals' during white settlement. McGahan followed up with *Underground* (2006), and in *Wonders of a Godless World* (2009) ventured into science fiction fantasy. He also wrote a series of adventure fantasy novels for young adult readers and several plays. His last adult novel was another crime plot, *The Rich Man's House* (2019).

While these younger authors were making their mark, David Malouf continued to write, producing *The Great World* (1990), *Remembering Babylon* (1993), *The Conversations at Curlow Creek* (1996) and *Ransom* (2009). The first title refers both to the great world beyond small-town rural Australia and to a disused fairground in Singapore where Allied troops assemble following surrender to the Japanese in World War Two. The two protagonists are then interned in Changi prisoner-of-war camp and sent off to starvation and labour in the jungle building the Thai–Burma railway. The book explores the mysteries of 'body knowledge' and a mateship that bonds two quite distinct personalities. It shows how imagination, dream and memory sustain people through torment. Fundamentally a realist saga, the novel continues previous interests such as how maps and naming take you beyond your immediate world and also confirm your place in it, and the troubled relationships between sons and fathers.

Remembering Babylon recaptures the symbolist music of *An Imaginary Life* and asks how white settler Australia might connect with the land and Indigenous culture. In mid-nineteenth-century 'frontier' north Queensland, a girl and her brother are playing when a figure silhouetted by the sun appears. The boy, empowered by his whiteness and gender, raises a stick to his shoulder, and the figure shouts, 'Do not shoot. I am a B-b-british object!' This creature of imperial power is Gemmy Fairley, a much-abused London urchin, shipwrecked in Australia, then taken in by Aboriginal tribesmen. He is sheltered by the children's Scots parents, but though he gives the hamlet's parson a vision of the new land, other locals are threatened by Gemmy's ties to 'savages' and by his example of the fragility of identity and the limits of language. He is roughed up and eventually disappears. Years later, we meet the two children of the opening scene, one living as a nun for whom her hives of bees provide a vision of perfect community, the other a senior politician in the state parliament, weary of conflict. Mention of massacres of Aboriginal people by cattlemen is offset by memories of Gemmy and the two look to love and 'a kind of praying' that will balance the swings of history.

The setting of *The Conversations at Curlow Creek* is a hut in the wilds of New South Wales where a soldier attends a captured bushranger on the night before his execution. Themes include the determinism of circumstance and how history transmutes into legend. Soldier Adair is remade in folklore as 'O'Dare' in a counter-factual romance of heroic bushrangers. Malouf returned to the European classics with *Ransom* (2009), a gentle (and quite short) reimagining of the *Iliad* in which king Priam humbles himself before Achilles to reclaim the body of Hector.

Kate Grenville produced *The Idea of Perfection* in 1999. This was a nicely modulated rural romance featuring feminism's claiming of textile craft as art. It is centred on two diffident characters who bond over the fate of an old timber bridge slated for replacement. Together they put life back into the dying town they have retreated to. Grenville's book was matched a year earlier by Murray Bail's *Eucalyptus*, which nested a set of stories from around the world in the fairy-tale format of a father setting an impossible challenge for suitors to his daughter. The winner will be the one who correctly names all the species of eucalypt on his property. The book plays games with critics' demands for Australian novels to be both universal and local, and with the emphasis on nature as a defining characteristic of the nation. Both novels support the idea that middlebrow romance fiction is the new (old?) centre of Australian writing.

Steven Carroll has not made a huge splash in the waves of literary history, but garnered admiration for his Glenroy trilogy: *The Art of the Engine Driver* (2001), *The Gift of Speed* (2004) and *The Time We Have Taken* (2007). Glenroy is a suburb that in the first novel is only just being developed on the fringes of Melbourne. The trilogy follows the growth of a young boy and of Australia during post-war modernisation, ending with Glenroy celebrating its centenary. Carroll differs from the generally hostile literary attitudes towards suburbia. He shows the dreams and disappointments of people as they move between moments of contemplation and the relentless flow of time. A boy enacts the tedium of suburban life by repeatedly bowling a ball against a wooden fence, but he is dreaming of becoming a cricketer famous for perfect deliveries. His father is an alcoholic who harbours an ideal of a perfect art of driving trains. Women nurse dreams of perfect loving relationships while living the drudgery of domestic labour. Glenroy incorporates migrants from England and Europe, and despite petty fears and jealousies, develops into a community. In *The Lost Life* (2009), Carroll's impressionist fugue textures become a riff on T.S. Eliot's 'Burnt Norton' in which a young couple are briefly caught up in the poet's unhappy emotional life and discover how contradictory moods can flitter together through the day, while music, gardens and love can provide moments of transcendental vision.

The 1990s were a watershed for Aboriginal fiction. Mudrooroo (accepting his literary project as Aboriginal regardless of questions raised in 1997 about the writer's identity) published *Masters of the Ghost Dreaming* (1991), a sequel to *Doctor Wooreddy*. Mudrooroo again rewrote his first novel as *Wildcat Screaming* (1992). This focused on the protagonist's time in gaol, injecting Foucault's ideas on surveillance and institutional power and Bentham's enlightenment reason manifest in the convict prison as a panopticon. After this, came a series of fantasy horror novels (*The Kwinkan*, 1993; *The Undying*, 1998; *Underground*, 1999; *The Promised Land*, 2000). They bounce off Conan Doyle, Bram Stoker, the Eliza Fraser story, and elements of Native American and West Indian shamanic beliefs. His books become increasingly odd and disturbingly misogynistic. Sam Watson's *The Kadaitcha Sung* (1990) also sets up a fantastical conflict between good and evil based on traditional shamanism but grounds it in gritty but sexist depictions of Black struggles for survival in Brisbane. The move away from social realist protest was further marked by Archie Weller producing a post-apocalypse fantasy fable, *Land of the Golden Clouds*, in 1998.

Kim Scott began his fictional output with *True Country* (1993) and gained widespread recognition for *Benang: From the Heart* (1999). *Benang* deploys something close to the 'magic realism' of many postcolonial writers. His 'spirit child' protagonist starts to literally float free as he probes the real history of himself, his mother(s) and his Aboriginal heritage. He has been alienated from Indigenous roots by white settler patriarchs who deliberately have offspring from native women over successive generations in order to breed out Blackness in the district. The boy gains power over his decrepit grandfather, inflicting violence on him in return for what he and others suffered. Both narrative and house become fragmented as the boy wrecks walls and shreds (real) documents of white history and regulations controlling race relations in Western Australia. Scott's work to resuscitate the Noongar language becomes apparent in the more lyrical *That Deadman Dance* (2010), which traces the collaborative period of first contacts between Aboriginal people, sailors and farmers, and laments the gradual closing of minds as white settlement becomes self-sustaining. Scott is unique as the only Aboriginal person to have won the Miles Franklin Award twice. Other work includes *Kayang and Me* (2005) and *Taboo* (2017).

Melissa Lucashenko began her career in fiction with *Steam Pigs* (1997), a naturalistic account of a teenage Aboriginal girl who escapes her family and small-town racism for the working-class grind of Logan in Brisbane's outer suburbs. Sue picks up occasional work while living with her brother and supporting his two children. She quarrels with him and moves in with Rog, who, though pale-skinned, has Aboriginal family. Seeming to provide security and love, Rog also has a short fuse, and beats Sue up. She meets up with a lesbian couple who educate her in feminist and racial politics. They get her into university, where she discovers a new awareness and self-respect. The book's realistic depiction of aimless circling is leavened by ironical humour about the lot of Australia's underclass and by demotic language that includes Aboriginal words.

Also in 1997, Alexis Wright published *Plains of Promise*. This was a complex structuring of voices that blurred realist narrative with fantastical reveries, and it dared to critique urban Black activists for sexist behaviour. Initially confusing, it eventually was seen to express the trauma of a mother and its transmission to her offspring. Its modernist elements were more visible in the epic *Carpentaria* (2006), shaped by Wright's reading of international postcolonial writing. Both novels are set in the author's birth country, the Waanyi riverine 'gulf' region of north Queensland. Hard-hitting criticism of white prejudice, police oppression and the invasion of multinational mining corporations is mixed with conflict between different modes of Aboriginal survival (resistance, complicity and hybrid cultism), and mythic agency vested in land, river and sea. The epic is narrated through a fusion of old men talking and the voice of the country itself. Despite its length and complexity, the book quickly achieved national and international success.

Another success was Tara June Winch's *Swallow the Air* (2006). This linked stories into a lyrical 'wandering girl' quest for family roots that included depictions of childhood by the sea, poverty, drugs and racialised sexual abuse. Vivienne Cleven's *Bitin' Back* (2001) won the David Unaipon Award for its mix of serious discussion of non-standard sex roles and small-town farce. A young star footballer suddenly takes to wearing dresses and inhabiting the persona of writer Jean Rhys. His mother has to cover his tracks to avoid scandal and find out what is going on. Jared Thomas also works the young adult–adult crossover format, and explores questions of gender and sexuality with *Calypso Summer* (2002).

Like *Bitin' Back*, Marie Munkara's *Every Secret Thing* (2009) is full of humour. The novel shows the (thinly disguised Tiwi) inhabitants of a northern island rambunctiously 'humbugging' the Catholic priests and nuns who seek to civilise them. Knockabout picaresque misadventures close on a sad note as people realise how much they have become reliant on white ways and alcohol. Anita Heiss also used comedy to break down stereotypes of Aboriginal women. Her adult romances along the lines of *Sex and the City* feature a professional woman negotiating a mesh of expectations from men, both Black and white, as she travels the world in *Not Meeting Mr Right* (2007), *Avoiding Mr Right* (2008), *Manhattan Dreaming* (2010) and *Paris Dreaming* (2011).

The 1990s saw a generation of migrants freed from the survival phase of resettlement beginning to write long fiction with ties to Asia rather than Europe. Adib Khan, originally from Bangladesh, published two melancholic novels capturing diasporic experience: *Seasonal Adjustments* (1994) and *Solitude of Illusions* (1996). He followed up with the more upbeat *The Storyteller* (2000), and a compelling treatment of Australian soldiers in the Vietnam War coping with return to civilian life. *Spiral Road* (2007) reprises the plot of his second book, with a secularised librarian returning to his family in Dhaka. He becomes caught up in cross-generation conflicts between old feudal privilege and urban commerce, the pull of the past (in which he fought for independence from Pakistan) and his nephew's present involvement with a terrorist group. Christopher Cyrill produced *The Ganges and Its Tributaries* (1993) and *Hymns for the Drowning* (1999). Cyrill is an admirer of Gerald Murnane's fiction and works a similar vein of nostalgia expressed as cool assessments from an onlooker on life. Increasingly, migrants were fleeing conflict in the Middle East and subject to rigid policies of exclusion and detention. Fiction depicting the motives and suffering of asylum seekers began appearing, notably, Eva Sallis's *Hiam* (1998) and Tom Keneally's *The Tyrant's Novel* (2003).

The big hit of this era from the perspective of multicultural writing was Yasmine Gooneratne's *A Change of Skies* (1991). Gooneratne is a scholar well versed in Jane Austen and produced a comedy of manners in which Sri Lankan couple Bharat and Navaranjini Mangala-Davasinha try to assimilate into Anglo-Australia as Barry and Jean Mundy. The book has some pointed satire of conservative white attitudes to Asian immigration. Gooneratne also published a memoir, *Relative Merits* (1986), another novel, *The Pleasures of Conquest* (1996)—set in the Democratic Republic of Amnesia and parodying colonial adventure romance—and a collection of stories, *Masterpiece* (2002).

Unlike the cheerful dynamo that is Navaranjini in *A Change of Skies*, the women in Chandani Lokugé's *If the Moon Smiled* (2000) and Suneeta Peres da Costa's *Homework* (1999) experience isolation and mental breakdown in the alien society they move to. Lokugé went on to publish *Turtle Nest* (2003) and *Softly as I Leave You* (2011), the former depicting gender prejudice, the fragility of adopted children seeking their roots and the corrosive effects of tourism in Sri Lanka. *Homework* mixes pathos with satiric humour and a touch of magic realism, as a young girl with a critical eye learns to fit into Australian society and tries to sustain her disintegrating family. Similar attention to the children of migrants and inter-ethnic relationships can be found in Hsu-Ming Teo's *Behind the Moon* (2005), which followed *Love and Vertigo* (2000).

Prior to these dark views of diasporic lives, Beth Yahp came out with *The Crocodile Fury* (1992). This mixed memories of childhood in Malaysia with Malay and Chinese folklore to tell the tale of a girl, her mother and grandmother, all connected to a rambling haunted house at the edge of the jungle. Once the palatial home to which the grandmother was assigned as child servant, it is now a school run by nuns where the unwed mother-daughter works and the granddaughter is a scholarship student. The narrative circles around as warnings about spirits overlap with fears of male predation and conflict between soldiers and communist 'bandits'. Pent-up 'crocodile' fury gathers force, revealing facts about all three women. Simone Lazaroo, also with origins in Malaysia, grounds her work in histories and experiences of growing up and characters' attempts to find some kind of equanimity amid the disruptions of migration. Her novels are *The World Waiting to Be Made* (1994), *The Australian Fiancé* (2000), *The Travel Writer* (2006), and a tale of cooking, tourism and terrorist insurgence set in Bali, *Sustenance* (2010).

A different immigrant is John Coetzee, who moved from South Africa to Australia in 2002, the year before he won the Nobel Prize. Coetzee has rapidly been accepted, in part because he began linking novels to Australia. *Elizabeth Costello* (2003) features a crusty older Australian woman writer who travels the globe giving talks about 'posthuman' ethics and eluding attempts to identify her with her textual persona or pin her down to narrow interpretations of deliberately ambiguous statements. *Slow Man* (2005) builds on Coetzee's own bicycle accident, bringing Elizabeth and a couple of European migrants in as irritating carers, exploiters and interlocutors during his convalescence. Fiction and memoir merge in a series: *Boyhood* (1997), *Youth* (2002) and *Summertime* (2009), collected as *Scenes from Provincial Life* (2011). *Summertime*, for example, has a biographer citing Coetzee's diaries (that refer to the writer as 'he') and interviewing women who were important to him. This happens after 'Coetzee' has moved to Australia and died, and characters debate the reliability of the novelist's self-presentation. Coetzee adds social critique and essay to his deconstruction of realism and the sovereign self in *Diary of a Bad Year* (2007). He expands a dream-like scene from *Elizabeth Costello* into a meditation on migration and Lacanian lack in the otherwise puzzling philosophical parable *The Childhood of Jesus* (2013), extended into a trilogy: *The Schooldays of Jesus* (2016) and *The Death of Jesus* (2019).

Immigration is matched to a lesser extent by emigration, some writers maintaining Australian credentials by either continuing to set stories in the homeland or by publishing with an Australian company. Peter Carey is the best-known of these, but a strong presence has been Janette Turner Hospital, also resident now in the United States after time in Canada. Her first novel, *The Ivory Swing*

(1982), is set in India, where she lived with her husband for some time. Australian-based novels are *The Tiger in the Tiger Pit* (1983), *Borderline* (1985), *Charades* (1988), *The Last Magician* (1992) and *Oyster* (1996). *The Last Magician* is notable for its futurist dystopia set in Brisbane, with resistance coming from an underground alliance of feminist and Aboriginal rights activists. Turner Hospital went on to write a harrowing tale of terrorist hijack, *Due Preparations for the Plague* (2003), and *Orpheus Lost* (2007). Geraldine Brooks is another Australian novelist resident in the US. *March* (2005), a novel about the Civil War, won the Pulitzer Prize.

Crime fiction continued to stretch its generic boundaries, with more female investigators from Susan Geason (*Shaved Fish*, 1990), Finola Moorhead (*Still Murder*, 1990) and Kerry Greenwood. Starting with *Cocaine Blues* (1989), Greenwood developed a best-selling series centred on Phryne Fisher, a sophisticated flapper who escapes from British aristocracy into ambulance driving during World War One, then migrates to Melbourne. There, she takes on a Chinese-Australian lover, a couple of working-class assistants and two adopted girls, and solves a host of mysteries, flouting patriarchal and social conventions in the process. Greenwood's books are popular entertainments; Peter Temple broke through the fence between literary and popular when *Truth* won the Miles Franklin Award in 2010. It followed titles in his popular Jack Irish private investigator series set in working-class Melbourne, beginning with *Bad Debts* in 1996. Solid achievement in the crime genres also came from Gary Disher, John Carroll and Philip McLaren (*Scream Black Murder*, 1995; *Lightning Mine*, 1999; *Murder in Utopia*, 2007). McLaren is Aboriginal, includes Indigenous politics in his plots, and has become better known in France than in his homeland. He began his career with a historical novel about race relations, *Sweet Water, Stolen Land* (1993).

This phase of Australian fiction can be rounded off with the publication of *The Slap* (2008) by Christos Tsiolkas. He specialises in family hostilities, sordid grunge scenes of drugs and sex, and a trenchant class analysis of urban Australia. His protagonists endeavour to piece together selves fragmented by multiple ethnicities and clashes over attitudes, ambitions, sexual preferences, religions and capitalism. Rage and shame fuel extreme behaviours in a dystopian multicultural society, whether it be in modern Australia or a Europe haunted by histories of violence and betrayal. Tsiolkas's first novel, *Loaded* (1995), is famous for launching Russell Crowe's career in the film version, *Romper Stomper*. Tsiolkas's other work includes *The Jesus Man* (1999), *Dead Europe* (2005), *Barracuda* (2013), and a gritty imagining of a young Saint Paul tormented by the fleshly excess of Greco-Roman paganism, *Damascus* (2019). He has also written plays and two collections of short stories: *Sticks and Stones* (2012) and *Merciless Gods* (2014), as well as a monograph on Patrick White.

Almost every major novelist at some point issued a story collection. David Malouf, for example, is at his best with shorter works that capitalise on his penchant for resonant symbolic imagery and rhythmic patterning. He published a set of three novellas, *Child's Play, Eustace, and The Prowler* (1982), and the story collections *Antipodes* (1985), *Untold Tales* (1999), *Dream Stuff* (2000), *Every Move You Make* (2007) and *Complete Stories* (2007). Thea Astley at times builds her novels as episodic compendia of tales and followed the story collection *Hunting the Wild Pineapple* (1979) with *It's Raining in Mango* (1987), *Vanishing Points* (1992), *Coda* (1994) and *Collected Stories* (1997). Janette Turner Hospital received positive attention for her collections: *Dislocations* (1986), *Isobars* (1990) and *North of Nowhere, South of Loss* (2003), her work showing interest in chaos theory and fragile fluctuating connections.

One discernible pattern in short story history is that a small publisher appears, issues a half-dozen titles, then disappears. The anthology has been a more lasting outlet for stories, variously featuring work from creative writing classes, Aboriginal writers, women writers, regional writing groups, as well as multicultural writing, writing about AIDS, disability, the environment, and so on. Frank Moorhouse, editing the 2004 *Best Australian Stories*, lamented a decline in publishing outlets for the form, but Robert Drewe three years later was celebrating the many magazines accepting material (the old standards plus new ones such as *HEAT*, *Going Down Swinging*, *Sleepers Almanac* and *Kill Your Darlings*). A few mainstream publishers (Black Inc., University of Queensland Press and Penguin) still issued story collections and Ginninderra and Affirm presses have become dedicated publishers of single-author story collections, with Spineless Wonders publishing on the internet.

Short story lists demonstrate how international Australian writing has become, with tales in Spanish (María Eliana Rojas), Greek (John Vassilikakos), Vietnamese (Phan Lac Phuc), Italian, Polish, French, and other languages. Popular romance stories (Rachael Treasure a regular proponent) and science fiction are significant components of English-language production, the latter genre featuring Greg Egan, Damien Broderick, Terry Dowling, Alex Hammond, Ben Chessell, Stephen Dedman, Jack Dann and Lucy Sussex. Many story writers also write novels and plays, while poets also work in short fiction, and there is considerable blurring of categories from prose poem to story to novella through to novels with episodic structures.

Between 2000 and 2020, the writers most frequently selected in the annual *Best Australian Stories* series have been Marion Halligan, James Bradley, Liam Davison and Cate Kennedy. Halligan dryly exposes sexist older men and their hapless but ironically aware wives and lovers. She also deploys a gothic colouring to bring out subtle nuances in relationships. Davison's first story collection appeared in 1989, a collected edition coming out in 2001. He, like most others, adopts a plain realist style, but specialises in coastal rural settings, with young males recalling childhood and coming to realise adult realities. Bradley put out a collection, *Beauty's Sister*, in 2012. Cate Kennedy has been a consistently visible story writer, poet and editor, with two story collections: *Dark Roots* (2006) and *Like a House on Fire* (2012).

Books of short stories do not always lead to national recognition. Michel Faber has four collections, but he migrated to Scotland after thirty years in Australia and has mostly published there. Gerard Windsor stayed put and has always commanded an audience for his stories, though he has turned to autobiography (growing up Irish Catholic) and novels. His first collection, *The Harlots Enter First*, appeared in 1982, followed by *Memories of the Assassination Attempt* (1985) and *The Mansions of Bedlam* (2000). Other regulars on the story-writing scene have been John Clanchy, Laurie Clancy,

Matthew Condon, Nick Earls, Carmel Bird, Archie Weller and Mandy Sayer. One shift in literary topics was marked by Tobsha Learner, whose *Quiver* (1996), *Tremble* (2004) and *Yearn* (2011) brought otherwise popular modes of erotica and queer desire to literary attention. Andy Quan followed up on his books of poetry with *Calendar Boy* (2001), a story collection engaging with both Asian ethnicity and gay sexuality. David Brooks also stands out for his international, intertextual and theoretically informed writing—increasingly as poetry—that engages with the ethical treatment of animals. His story collections are *The Book of Sei* (1988), *Sheep and the Diva* (1990) and *Black Sea* (1997). Brooks exemplifies Moorhouse's notion of a 'looser' story form, with spaced sequences of 'syncopated' fragments in different type.

Australia's love-hate relationship with its major successes, especially if they involve people or works that move overseas, is reflected in regular tales of writers being better known abroad. One such is Matthew Reilly, an international best-seller of thrillers and young adult fantasy. Reilly has lived in America for some years and two successes are *Ice Station* (1998) and *The Tournament* (2013). Bryce Courtenay has been more appreciated in Australia. His global hit *The Power of One* (1989) accorded with the self-help ethos of a neo-liberal era, and his blockbuster books moved from his South African origins into a trilogy of Australian sagas, *The Potato Factory* (1995), *Tommo and Hawk* (1997) and *Solomon's Song* (1999). More 'upmarket', Colleen McCullough's Masters of Rome series appeared between 1990 and 2007, after which she rewrote Jane Austen in *The Independence of Miss Mary Bennet* (2008). Di Morrissey capitalised on travels with her diplomat husband to produce a romance adventure every year from 1991 (*Heart of the Dreaming*). Most books take an Australian to exotic locations like Burma and Malaysia. Also turning to fiction following work in advertising is Liane Moriarty. A string of novels following *Three Wishes* (2003) led to her international success with *Big Little Lies* (2014). The other international best-seller of this period is Markus Zusak's *The Book Thief* (2005), a crossover young adult–adult novel in which Death narrates the tale of a German town during World War Two, and a girl's bonding with the Jew her family hides in their cellar.

Poetry

There are only loose and shifting 'schools' in contemporary Australian poetry. Variety has perhaps been manufactured by creative writing courses in which students experiment with all forms, from sestinas to surrealist cut-ups. One trend culminates in *The Anthology of Australian Prose Poetry* (2020). Small magazines best show the eclectic spread, including shape poems, poems set out in double columns or separate squares that 'talk' loosely to each other, lots of white space and different fonts, and increasingly, lexis and symbols from the sciences. The default standard, however, remains irregular lines of left-justified free verse running for about a page, with the three-line stanza favoured by many. UQP, Five Islands Press, Picaro, Vagabond Press, Giramondo, and Puncher & Wattman are established poetry outlets, though journals have carried the weight of poetry publishing (*Jacket*, *Cordite*, *Otis Rush*, *Famous Reporter*, *Scripsi*, *HEAT* and *foam:e* adding to older titles).

A poet who has published extensively and won a handful of awards, but who rarely gets into anthologies is Peter Boyle. The anomaly is perhaps because of his close engagement with literature in Spanish and translation—reflected in titles like *November in Madrid* (2001) and *Reading Borges* (2007), though his first collection (*Coming Home from the World*, 1994) indicates an Australian base. Boyle's *Ghostspeaking* (2016) is a *tour de force* compendium of invented poets, mainly from Latin America. Boyle provides 'translations' of their work, biographical notes, interviews and fragments of their correspondence, capturing the range of styles of many known writers but also injecting his interest in Asian culture and criticisms of Australia's treatment of asylum seekers.

Rhyll McMaster was regularly included in anthologies. She won prizes early on for descriptions at once detailed and pared back ('Birds', 'Fox', 'The Loquat Tree'), and for imagistic memories from childhood in Brisbane ('Profiles of My Father'). Her focus on the natural world was sustained by sheep farming, and her nursing background inclined her towards topics linked to chemistry and psychology ('On a Glass Slide'). The personal, family life and medicine come together in a set of poems 'My Mother and I Become

Victims of a Stroke' in *Flying the Coop: New and Selected Poems* (1994). McMaster's first collection was *The Brineshrimp* (1972), then *Back Steps Lookout* (1977), *Washing the Money* (1986) and *On My Empty Feet* (1993). *Experiments and Games of Chance* (1994) was followed by *Chemical Bodies: A Diary of Probable Events 1994–1997* (1997), some collaborations on artist's books, then *The Elegant Rabbit and Other Poems* (2003) and *Late Night Shopping* (2012).

Across this period, Robert Adamson produced an autobiographical mix of prose and poetry, *Wards of the State* (1992), and poems in *The Brutality of Fact* (1993), *Waving to Hart Crane* (1994), *The Language of Oysters* (1997) and *Black Water* (1999), culminating in *Mulberry Leaves: New and Selected Poems 1970–2001* (2001). A reprise of his early 'tough' work moves into social critique and experiment with form ('Lozenge for Brennan', 'Lozenge for Mondrian'). Tributes to other poets (Francis Webb, Hart Crane, Les Murray, Charles Olson and others) appear, and his nature poetry moves closer to the objectivism of Louis Zukofsky. Bruce Beaver also continued writing into his later years, the results seen in *New and Selected Poems: 1960–1990* (1991), *Anima and Other Poems* (1994) and, posthumously, *The Long Game* (2005) and *Flautist in the Laundry* (2007).

Judith Beveridge's *The Domesticity of Giraffes* (1987) was followed by *Accidental Grace* (1996), *Wolf Notes* (2003) and *Storm and Honey* (2009). Eschewing poetry as the expression of one's own personality, Beveridge looks for language that conveys both music and emotion, concentrating mainly on the natural world. Favouring the linked three-line stanza of around eleven syllables, Beveridge varied her forms, occasionally turning to prose poems with surrealist touches, but mostly she uses clear language enlivened by inventive metaphors. She sets forth the other as observed image without attempting possession of it by the observer. The self is also distanced by voices of personae: Hannibal addressing his elephants; elephants 'talking' about humans; those toiling at the bottom of the economic ladder (many in India). There is also a long sequence on the life of the Buddha. Beverage acknowledges influences from Derek Walcott, Seamus Heaney, Carol Ann Duffy and Elizabeth Bishop.

Jennifer Maiden came out with *Play with Knives* in 1990, a thriller novel in which a therapist interacts with Clare, a sixteen-year-old who as a child murdered her siblings. It inspired later poems where the adult Clare marries George Jeffries and the two of them spark a long series of poems, each section having George wake up in different locations that allow commentary on politics and satiric conversations between political figures. *Mines* (1999) centres mostly on the poet's life by the Nepean River and Blue Mountains, her daughter's school events, and links with other poets (Dorothy Porter appears often). Her work talks about female experience, sex, reading, semi-precious stones, television watching and work with migrants in a Torture and Trauma centre. *Friendly Fire* (2005) takes in more international politics and invented conversations in conflict zones.

Porter herself produced a crime novel in verse, *The Monkey's Mask* (1994). She plays with the postmodern turning of investigation back onto the investigator, telling a tale of deception centred on lesbian desire with accompanying exposés of class difference and poseur poets. Porter's book mixed the hard-boiled genre with feminist assertiveness and tight imagistic verse. *The Monkey's Mask* is perhaps the only Australian poem other than 'The Man from Snowy River' to be made into a feature film. Porter's earlier collections often affected a tough 'butch' persona (*Little Hoodlum*, 1975; *Bison*, 1979; *The Night Parrot*, 1984; *Driving Too Fast*, 1989). She then produced a sequence, *Akhenaten* (1992), that dramatises the short and eccentric life of the Egyptian pharaoh. Porter continued to tell stories in verse, working with psychiatry, deep-sea biology and serial murder (*What a Piece of Work*, 1999; *Wild Surmise*, 2002; *El Dorado*, 2007).

John Forbes, before dying suddenly in 1998, published *Thin Ice* (1989), a *New and Selected Poems* collection (1992), *Troubadour* (1993), *Roman Poems* (1994), *Damaged Glamour* and *Humidity* (both 1998). His complete works came out in 2001. There is a shift towards academic theory (cultural studies, postcolonial analysis, queer theory), registered in flippant dramatised situations (furniture removals, domestic quarrels). Readers are left to 'to sketch yourself / because this poem lacks form & structure, / isn't going anywhere in fact'. 'Sydney Harbour Considered as a Matisse' mocks commercialised 'tourist art' and asks, 'Can art be good enough to save all this?'. The poem ends, 'Maybe just'.

Kevin Hart deserves mention for being one of the few Australian poets to work with overtly religious content tinged with his professional interests in philosophy. He began publishing in the mid-seventies (*The Departure*, 1975; *Nebuchadnezzar*, 1977; *The Lines of the Hand*, 1981; *Your Shadow*, 1984) and continues to publish (*Wild Track: New and Selected Poems*, 2015), but the bulk of his collections appear between *New and Selected Poems* (1995) and *Young Rain* (2008), with another selected collection, *Flame Tree* (2001). Hart is often linked with Alan Gould, both of them helping build the literary community in Canberra. Gould's work is distinctive for drawing on Nordic traditions, a result of his living in Iceland before migrating to Australia. His poetic output is sampled in *The Past Completes Me: Selected Poems 1973–2003* (2005) and he published *Charlie Twirl: Sixty-One New Poems* in 2017.

Joanne Burns collaborated with Pam Brown (*Correspondences*, 1979). Burns began publishing collections in the 1970s (with a characteristic edgy flourish evident in the title *Adrenalin Flicknife*, 1976) and still writes. After *blowing bubbles in the 7th lane* (1988) and *on a clear day* (1992), she produced *penelope's knees* (1996), *aerial photography* (1999), *people like that* (2001), *footnotes of a hammock* (2004) and *an illustrated history of dairies* (2007). Although the poet performs her work for radio, Burns's prose-like blocks of print do not have the look of performance poetry (which generally tends towards rap). Her poems are in lower case, with phrases punctuated mostly only with full stops. They are feminist for concentrating on details of the everyday (pockets, laundry, plastic bags, shopping). Burns will also skewer male privilege and critique consumerist society and the media's 'empty' smorgasbord of global violence and poverty. By *an illustrated history of dairies* (2007), Burns moved to depicting Sydney types: the socialite, the rock-band guitarist, and so on. Her prose poems devolve into strings of imagist fragments, though she returns to longer autobiographical pieces in which something more than cynicism shines through.

Gig Ryan was another *enfant terrible* in the heady days of seventies counter-culture, working in casual jobs, in bands, and on a feminist magazine. 'If I Had a Gun' was infamous for its uncompromising response to male power, echoed in her 1980 first collection, *The Division of Anger*. She has sustained a 'fringe' position as a plain-speaking recorder of inner-city life and critic of capitalism (*Heroic Money*, 2001) while increasingly engaging with classical themes and music. Other works include *Manners of an Astronaut* (1984), *The Last Interior* (1986), *Excavation: (arguments and monologues)* (1990), *Pure and Applied* (1998) and *Research: Poems* (1999).

Contemporary with Pam Brown, Diane Fahey completed a doctorate on Vincent Buckley and Gwen Harwood. She began publishing poems in the 1970s, her first book, *Voices from the Honeycomb*, coming out in 1986. An interest in insect life is made clear in *Mayflies in Amber* (1993), which devotes poems to ants, earwigs, silverfish and other tiny creatures. Fahey's second major interest is the Greek classics. *Metamorphoses* (1988) reworks the tales of Leda, Daphne and Ariadne from a woman's viewpoint. Ten years later, in *Listening to a Far Sea*, Fahey does the same for men: Heracles, Midas, Perseus. She also produced 'snapshots' of districts around her native Melbourne and continued writing for another twenty years, *Winter Solstice* appearing in 2008 and poems about birds, *The Wing Collection*, in 2011.

Jill Jones has produced books every year since her first collection, *The Mask and the Jagged Star* (1992), won the Mary Gilmore Award for poetry. Other key titles, several winning awards, are *Flagging Down Time* (1993), *The Book of Possibilities* (1997), *Screens, Jets, Heaven* (2002) and *Broken/Open* (2005). *Flagging Down Time* presents a crepuscular world of loneliness, longing, bars and taxis. A lingering formality of structure resolves into 'Eleven Fifteen', an elegant echo of the sonnet made up of eleven poems of fifteen lines each, in which the last line of one becomes the first of the next, all in the circled frame of 'There's no such thing as an innocent day'. By *Broken/Open* the lines have been pared back and the sense of a musing persona stripped away, leaving the poem as images speaking to each other. We glimpse the shadow of a feeling with no tangible referent. Cityscapes still hover and occasionally a 'voice' surfaces watching movies or out drinking or thinking about itself lying in the grass of 'this / my suburban dirt'. Lines and stanzas break open and coalesce, increasingly becoming debates with and assemblages of the work of other poets. Jones also co-edited with Michael Farrell *Out of the Box: Contemporary Australian Gay and Lesbian Poets* (2009), marking a major social shift in Australia.

Anthony Lawrence worked as a jackaroo (apprentice labourer) on country farms, then on fishing boats, and writes of his experiences in a style influenced by American moderns. He has also written poems about cricket and 'A Field Guide to Native Metaphor'. *Dreaming in Stone* (1989) is followed by *Cold Wires of Rain* (1995), *The Viewfinder* (1996) and *New and Selected Poems* (1998). Later work includes *Skinned by Light* (2002), *Bark* and *Magnetic Field* (both 2008).

John Tranter extended his postmodern approach to the poem as depersonalised wordplay. He experiments with a mechanics of 'translation' influenced by his close attention to computers. Either from his own transcription or via voice recognition technology, he takes the sounds of French originals and finds similar sounding words in English from which to construct a 'non-translation', or takes the first and last lines of stanzas in someone's poem and builds something quite different from them (as he does in 'The Anaglyph', a remix of John Ashbery's 'Clepsydra'). These poems are collected in *Starlight: 150 Poems* (2010). *Urban Myths: 210 Poems* (2006) selects from his many books following the 1982 *Selected Poems*. We see increasing attention to Eastern sources: Li Po, haiku, haibun. He is already starting to produce 'dubs' of other poets, as in 'Grover Leach', a tongue-in-cheek version of 'Dover Beach', and the irreverent 'After Rilke' ('I hate this place. If I were to throw a fit, who / among the seven thousand starlets in Hollywood / would give a flying fuck?').

Michael Farrell stands out in contemporary anthologies for preserving the unpunctuated lower case and slapdash irreverence of the 1970s. He combines serious critique (rewriting Kenneth Slessor's 'South Country' to show the silences about an Aboriginal presence) with interest in music and composer John Cage. His collections include *living at the z* (2000), *ode ode* (2002),

BREAK ME OUCH (2006) and *a raider's guide* (2008). Other poets of note building profiles during this period and continuing to write into the present include Bronwyn Lea, Maria Takolander, Peter Rose, Felicity Plunkett, Andy Kissane, Andrew Landsdown, Alex Skovron, Jamie Grant and Chris Andrews.

Once the Europe-origin 'multiculturals' established a literary base in Australia, voices from Vietnam and China began to find publication. One of the most energetic of these has been Ouyang Yu. He has been instrumental in promoting Australian literature in China and has anthologised Chinese writing in translation for the Australian market. Ouyang came to Melbourne to study Australian literary representations of Chinese people and created a reputation as an 'angry young man'. *Moon over Melbourne* (1995) raised eyebrows for refusing the persona of grateful immigrant, including a poem titled 'Fuck You, Australia'. His mostly irregular free verse continues to rage powerfully against stereotypes and put-downs of Chinese, but is also of interest for its agonistic self-analysis, and its frank exposition of sexual politics, particularly when the migrant male finds himself alone and lustful in a hostile land. Ouyang's work is most nuanced when depicting negotiations across disparate languages, cultures and facets of identity. He has published novels (*The Eastern Slope Chronicle*, 2002; *The English Class*, 2010; *Loose: A Wild History*, 2011; *Billy Sing*, 2017) along with a regular stream of poetry collections with telling titles such as *Foreign Matter* (2003). *The Kingsbury Tales* (2008) was an important collection.

Of Iranian origin, Ali Alizadeh is one of Australia's new generation of refugees from Africa and the Middle East. His poems in *eyes in time of war* (2006) are two-line stanzas of unrhymed blank and free verse that echo the form of the ghazal (some are reworkings of Attar, Hafez and Rumi). There are love poems and hard-hitting self-lacerating pieces showing the psychological damage to the unwelcome immigrant. Adam Aitken's *In One House* (1996) rehearses memories of Malaysian childhood among servants and analyses the underlying dynamics in poems like 'Post-colonial' and 'Orchid Weather', with later politics examined in 'Village Ways', 'What She Told Me of the War' and 'The Bad Women of Bangkok'. Aitken records the incongruities of banal modernity meeting history and tradition in tourist snapshots of Burma, Central Australia and Cambodia, and closes with 'The Empire of Signs', a lyric sequence bouncing off other poets and depicting young-adult life in the inner suburbs of Sydney, with a brief excursion to Bali. His first book of verse was *Letter to Marco Polo* (1985) and one of his most recent is *Archipelago* (2017), with *Impermanence* (2004) suggesting a characteristic sensibility.

Graeme Dixon's *Holocaust Island* (1990) won the first David Unaipon Award in 1989 for a first manuscript from an Aboriginal or Torres Strait Islander. Collections of note from the nineties include Burraga Gutya's *Ngali Ngalga (Let's Talk)* (1990), Joy Williams's *Blackberry's Child* (1991), Alf Taylor's *Singer Songwriter* (1992), Lisa Bellear's *Dreaming in Urban Areas* (1996) and John Muk Muk Burke's *Night Song and Other Poems* (1999). Prominent theorist and critic Romaine Moreton published her first book of poetry, *The Callused Stick of Wanting*, in 1995. Moreton's work matches political point with experiments in varying lines and opened up stanzas, and she followed up with *Post Me to the Prime Minister* in 2004. Kerry Reed-Gilbert worked in support of the social and literary aspirations of Aboriginal women and published her own poetry as *Black Woman, Black Life* in 1996. Her other collection is *Talkin' About Country* (2002). Literary academic Peter Minter continues to publish and began his career as poet with *Rhythm in a Dorsal Fin* (1995), followed by *Morning, Hyphen* (2000) and *Blue Grass* (2006). Minter's work inclines more towards a quiet lyricism and nature-centred subjects. With Nicholas Jose, Minter and Anita Heiss edited the landmark *Macquarie PEN Anthology of Aboriginal Literature* (2008), before which Heiss added poetry to her fiction with *Token Koori* (1998) and *I'm Not Racist, But...* (2007). Archie Weller also turned to verse with *The Unknown Soldier and Other Poems* (2007).

Next to Lionel Fogarty, the most prolific Indigenous publisher of verse is Sam Wagan Watson. Self-consciously adopting the profession of 'poet' and writing at times about the cost of distancing oneself from family and friends to write, Watson records the childhood pleasures and adult challenges of urban living in rented rooms and 'boneyard' fringe suburbs. He pens love poems to his muses, wryly reflects on wandering around to literary festivals and includes satirical pieces on racial politics ('Cheap White Goods at the Dreamtime Sale'). Watson also expresses concern at environmental degradation, especially as it applies to Brisbane's wetlands. A recurrent motif is minatory ghosts. Watson's collections in this period are: *Black Eye Junior* (1999), *Of Muse, Meandering and Midnight* (2000), *Hotel Bone* (2001), *Itinerant Blues* (2002), *Smoke Encrypted Whispers* (2004) and *Three-Legged Dogs and Other Poems* (2005).

A lot of Aboriginal verse echoes song (country and western being a major influence), and at the popular end of the poetry spectrum, musicians such as Archie Roach, Bob Randall and Kev Carmody are important figures. Roach published poetry as *You Have the Power* (1994); Randall's 'Brown Skin Baby' has become nationally known for summing up the pain of mothers forcibly separated from their children; and Carmody's 'From Little Things Big Things Grow' is an anthem for land rights activism.

Drama

David Williamson's work becomes a series of satiric analyses of Australia's cashed-up professionals and business folk. He mocks pretension, put-down and double standards. *Money and Friends* (1991) taps into the 1980s boom-and-bust era of speculative investments, mining and real estate development. A group of people who have bonded through having holiday homes at the same beach have their friendship tested when they are asked to help bail out the bankrupt 'nice guy' at the play's centre. It is typically well crafted with an ironic tying up of ends in which everyone gets their just desserts. Other plays from this period include *Top Silk* (1989) and *Siren* (1990). Less orderly is *Brilliant Lies* (1993), a case study of contemporary concerns about sexual harassment in the workplace. A young woman plans to sue her boss for making unwanted advances that force her to leave her job, but it turns out that she has a reputation for telling 'brilliant lies'. Her boss points out the double bind he is in (if he pays up, he's seen as guilty; if he doesn't pay up, his reputation is still damaged), but he is also lying when he denies molesting her. As the conflict develops, it turns out that every character is lying and the woman's family shakily accepts everyone's failings.

Dead White Males (1995) was written partly to counter 'politically correct' criticism of Williamson's work by academics. It features a professor spouting postmodernist theory and sexually exploiting his female students. *Heretic* (1996) dramatises the life of Derek Freeman, the anthropologist who rubbished a popular view of idyllic Samoan life expounded by Margaret Mead. *After the Ball* (1997) is a quiet two-act tragedy in which Australian audiences have reflected back to them their increasingly aged and mentally frail population and the struggles of adult children dealing with demented and dying parents and with each other. *Up for Grabs* (2001) turned a critical eye on the cupidity of art dealers and collectors. It was followed by a similar dissection of the infighting in the literary world, *Soulmates* (2002). His *Collected Plays* have been published in five volumes, lastly in 2019.

A different set of work about upper-middle-class lives, but without the comic-satiric attitude of Williamson, comes from Joanna Murray-Smith. Situations involving a moral dilemma (response to the Holocaust, a woman adopted out in infancy making a claim on her birth mother, an extra-marital affair) are mulled over by characters not entirely sure of what is going on, each with a reasonable position on the matter but perhaps not entirely honest about their own part in it. Action occurs mainly in an enclosed domestic space. Murray-Smith's plays are *Atlanta* (1990), *Love Child* (1993), *Honour* (1995), *Redemption* (1997), *Nightfall* (1999), *Bombshells* (2001), *Rapture* (2002) and *The Female of the Species* (2006). Three of her later plays are collected under the telling title *Stories of Love and Deception* (2015). Her work has been successful overseas, and she writes fiction as well.

Hannie Rayson had a success with *Hotel Sorrento* (1990). Three sisters gather at the family home in a beachside town south of Melbourne. Hilary has stayed at home caring for her son and father; Meg, a novelist shortlisted for the Booker Prize, lives in London with her English husband; Pippa is an advertising executive in New York. Interest in Meg's novel and its clearly autobiographical elements brings in Marge, a neighbour, and her long-time journalist friend Dick. It is a middle-class drama raising questions about Australian identity, family loyalty, and the ethics of using people's lives as material for novels or newspapers. It is also about ageing and memory. Melancholy (the title of Meg's novel) pervades the play as the family home is put up for auction, leaving Marge trying to capture the spirit of the place in her painting. Rayson also wrote *Mary* (1985), *Room to Move* (1986) and *Life after George* (2000).

The theatre scene was an active one through the 1990s. Stephen Sewell continued to write, coming out with *Hate* (1988), *Sisters* (1991), *King Golgrutha* (1991) and *The Garden of Granddaughters* (1993). Jennifer Compton wrote *The Big Picture* (1998), about women's desires and struggles against poverty. John Romeril staged *The Love Suicides* (1997) and *Miss Tanaka* (2001), while Michael Gow created *Furious* (1990), which depicts a successful playwright sapped of his drive by a crowd of fans and 'arts industry' leeches. Michael Gurr began his playwriting career with the sensational-sounding *Sex Diary of an Infidel* (1992). He asks political questions about the impact of neo-liberal capitalism (*A Pair of Claws*, 1983; *Underwear, Perfume and Crash Helmet*, 1994) and adds absurdist farces such as *Imitation Real* (1981) and *What You Wanted* (1983). Other major plays by Gurr are *Jerusalem* (1996), *Crazy Brave* (2000), *The Simple Truth* (2002) and *Julia 3* (2004). The tragic impact of AIDS was brought home to audiences in plays such as Alex Harding's *Blood and Honour* (1990) and Timothy Conigrave's *Like Stars in My Hands* (1997). A stage version of Conigrave's book about gay life, *Holding the Man*, appeared in 2006.

Louis Nowra created his best-known work, *Così* (1992), and earlier in the same year, the largely autobiographical *Summer of the Aliens*, in which he played himself as a teenager growing up in a bare, strange world. *Così* carries the same character into his university years, when he takes a job providing drama therapy in a psychiatric hospital and ends up trying to hold together a group of wildly zany people rehearsing Mozart's *Così fan tutte*. *Radiance* (1993) is well known thanks to a film version. Three Aboriginal half-sisters with different life stories gather for their mother's funeral, discovering family secrets and the town's long persecution of the mother. Nowra has been prolific, turning to satires of corruption in *The Temple* (1993) and *Incorruptible* (1995), a surrealist set of scenes from the Balkan wars, *Miss Bosnia* (1995), and a play about the violent life of a street-living teenager, *The Jungle* (1995).

New plays included Sam Sejavka's about drug culture (*In Angel Gear*, 1990) and Thérèse Radic's *The Emperor Regrets* (1992). Janis Balodis added *Heart for the Future* (1989) and *Wet and Dry* (1990) to his nineties work. Tess Lyssiotis founded the Filiki Players in 1984 to cater for Melbourne's large Greek community and wrote *Hotel Bonegilla* (1984) about one of the ex-army camps where immigrants were housed before finding homes of their own. Her trilogy about the Papageorgiou sisters—*A White Sports Coat* (1988), *The Forty Lounge Café* (1990) and *Blood Moon* (1993)—tells stories of arranged marriage, migration, struggles in small businesses and squabbles over family property. Ernest Macintyre had an established reputation in Sri Lanka, migrated to Australia, and wrote the satirical drama of migrant race relations *Let's Give Them Curry* (first staged as *Dark Dinkum Aussies* in 1981), plus 'problem plays' about the civil unrest in his homeland, *Rasanayagam's Last Riot* (1990) and *He Still Comes from Jaffna* (2000). Vietnamese immigration led to plays about the war and its effects. Duong Le Quy wrote *A Graveyard for the Living* (1996?), *Market of Lives* (1998) and *Meat Party* (2000), all translated from Vietnamese and published in 2002. Huong Nguyen, Phi Hai and others devised *Wild Rice* (1997) and Binh Duy Ta wrote *The Monkey Mother* (1998).

Regional theatre was developing. In Wollongong, Wendy Richardson commemorated a mine disaster (*Windy Gully*, 1987) and provided a woman's view of wartime life (*Lights Out, Nellie Martin*, 1990). Post-war labour in the Port Kembla steelworks is depicted in Katherine Thompson's *Diving for Pearls* (1991). Her *Barmaids* (also 1991) is a tribute to working-class women. Similar work based on historical documents and oral history developed in other towns outside of capital cities: Logan in Queensland and Parramatta in Sydney, for example. In Newcastle, *Aftershocks* (1993), a 'verbatim theatre' piece by Paul Brown and the Newcastle Workers' Cultural Action Committee, was composed from accounts of the town's earthquake in 1989 and staged in 1991.

Patricia Cornelius has had plays staged almost every year, sometimes collaborating with others (Andrew Bovell in *Who's Afraid of the Working Class?*, 1998). Aiming to show poor uneducated people without belittling or romanticising them, Cornelius's *Lily and May* was staged in 1986, and *Love* in 2005. The latter depicts two women in prison forming a lesbian relationship. One gets out, becomes a prostitute and takes a male lover, and they are joined by the other woman. Bald statements of love, concern over drug-taking, and jealousy of each other circle repeatedly until the prostitute falls ill, the male leaves for another woman, and the original two women are left bickering. It is spare and frank, stripped of grunge descriptions that might give colour to the scenes, and resisting any catharsis, but relies very much on the actors to supply intensity and emotional variations to the repetitious dialogue.

Nick Enright trained in New York before returning to Australia, where he has taught, acted and directed across the country. Writing plays began in 1973 with *Cupid in Transit*, followed by work in musical theatre and a comedy (*Daylight Saving*, 1989). He then wrote about the psycho-social impact of murder (*A Property of the Clan*, 1992, rewritten as *Blackrock*, 1995), about tracing children given out to adoption (*Chasing the Dragon*, 1998) and the ethics of filming children for television documentary (*A Man with Five Children*, 2002). Other works include *Mongrels* (1991), *St James Infirmary* (1992), his popular collaboration on a musical about singer Peter Allen *The Boy from Oz* (1998), and *Country Music* (2002).

For someone who is a medical general practitioner, Ron Elisha has been an extraordinarily productive playwright. Close to the sizeable Jewish community in Melbourne, he has worked around Holocaust memory, extremism and ethnicity. Plays include *In Duty Bound* (1979), *Blood Libel* (2004) and *Honour Killing* (2004). He also delves into historical topics, as in *Einstein* (1981), *Esterhaz* (1990, based around Haydn), *The Goldberg Variations* (2000), *Love Field* (2004, in which Jackie Kennedy and Lyndon Johnson fly out from Dallas with the body of JFK) and *Renaissance* (2005, Leonardo da Vinci awaits the death of a man so he can make anatomical drawings). *Freedom* (2006) enacts the crisis of a speechwriter and a therapist as the US president prepares to address the UN about

China. These are merely samples from a prolific career that includes writing for children and the screen.

Andrew Bovell began an award-winning career in film, television, fiction and theatre, initially with Melbourne Workers' Theatre, then the Melbourne Theatre Company. *After Dinner* (1988) opened at La Mama and toured the country. In the same year, he had premieres for *The Ballad of Lois Ryan*, about work in the trade unions, and *Ship of Fools*. His theatre adaptation of *Gulliver's Travels* (1991) included music and puppetry. It was followed by *Scenes from a Separation* (1995), written with Hannie Rayson. Another play about betrayals and infatuations with a mystery element, *Speaking in Tongues* (1996), became the feature film *Lantana*. Collaboration with Patricia Cornelius and others led to *Who's Afraid of the Working Class?* (1998) and *Fever* (2002). *Holy Day* (2001) contrasts two versions of racial conflict on the colonial frontier.

Jenny Kemp focuses on women's experience. She breaks her characters up into different aspects of their selves, creating a surrealist effect, with alternative outcomes swirling around a single event. *Call of the Wild* (1989), *Remember* (1993), *The Black Sequin Dress* (1996) and *Still Angela* (2002) are some of her plays. Also deploying mythic, slightly surrealist symbolism, with an erotic current running through, *Wolf* (1992) by Tobsha Learner is a tale of male sexual rapacity. It follows *Witchplay* (1987), about a fortune teller and Auschwitz survivor, and is succeeded by *Miracle* (1992), a comedy in which a supermarket checkout woman receives heavenly messages via her cash register. *The Gun in History* (1994) stages three different stories all relying on a Luger pistol souvenired from World War Two. *The Glass Mermaid* (1994) combines a tale of suicide and family mourning with sexual escapade and recovery from trauma by a refugee from the former Yugoslavia.

Daniel Keene started with La Mama and Playbox in Melbourne from whence his work has spread across Australia and on to America and France. *Cho Cho San* (1984) is a darker revision of *Madame Butterfly*. *All Souls* (1993) has the spirit of an old street-dwelling woman recounting stories of other lives on Walpurgisnacht. *To Whom It May Concern* (1998) has a dying man taking his intellectually challenged son around looking for somewhere to place him when he's gone. Other plays—most quite short—include *Terminus* (1996) and *A Glass of Twilight* (1997). Keene's work has appeared in suites, so that *Untitled Monologue* and *Night, a Wall, Two Men* plus *Scissors, Paper, Rock* and *To Whom It May Concern* along with *Kaddish* and *The Violin* and *The Rain* all appeared in 1998. Later works are *The First Train* (2001), *Half and Half* (2002) and *The Nightwatchman*, commissioned in French as *Le veilleur de nuit* (2005).

Ben Ellis combines political critique with imaginative storylines and surrealist combinations of narrative. After *Post Felicity* (2000), he wrote *Falling Petals* (2002), featuring three high school students desperate to do well in their final exams so they can escape from their country town. They gather under a Chekovian cherry tree, the falling leaves of which are symbolic of the growing number of child deaths from a mystery disease. Increasingly, the three students, and then their parents become ruthlessly fixated on surviving and escaping the town's quarantine. The play demonstrates the nasty side of economic rationalism and self-interest. Dialogue is intercut with actual court transcripts about refugees in detention camps and an uncanny absurdism is intensified by a vision of Australia invaded by penguins. The political effect of all this is debatable, but it is an entertaining piece, more engaging than most activist theatre. Three monologues were staged as *Eclipses* in 2002, and *These People* (2003) dissected suburban life. *The Captive* (2010) allegorises colonisation.

Brendan Cowell also combines humour with social comment. After *Bed* (2002), he had a success with *Rabbit* (2003). Later work includes *Morph* (2003) and *Ruben Guthrie* (2005). *Morph* is a *Godot*-like exchange between a seaman, later a body builder, and a ballerina. There is a good deal of erotic interplay and the overall point is the social stereotyping of body shapes and gender roles. *Ruben Guthrie* is a more multi-stranded story about a top advertising writer losing his job and girlfriend as he tries to give up drugs and alcohol in a world that is fuelled by both.

Aboriginal theatre had a strong showing in this period. Eva Johnson wrote *Mimini's Voices* (1990), *What Do They Call Me?* (1991), *Two Bob in the Quid* (1992)—in modern terms, two cents on the dollar, suggesting some significant shortcoming—

and *Heartbeat of the Earth* (1993). Bob Maza wrote *The Keepers* (1989), and Jack Davis came out with *Barungin: Smell the Wind* (1988), *Our Town* (1990) and *Wahngin Country* (1992). Staged in the bicentenary year, *Barungin* revealed a new edge in Davis's work by including a list of names of Aboriginal people who had died while in police custody. This was followed by the more upbeat 1990 musical *Bran Nue Dae* by Jimmy Chi, which used a lot of creole English, celebrated the multi-racial mix of Broome, and satirised racial stereotypes and white romanticising of Aboriginal culture. Jane Harrison's play *Stolen* (1998) depicted the life of Aboriginal children forcibly removed from their families to be 'whitified' in institutions. Harrison followed up with *Rainbow's End* (2005), an evocation of 1950s Victoria in which three generations of a family engage in protests over poor housing and worry over how romantic ties might clash with kinship regulations. Wesley Enoch created *Black Medea* (2000) in Sydney. David Milroy wrote *King Hit* (1997) about an Aboriginal boxing troupe and cattle station life in the Kimberley region of Western Australia. Tony Briggs wrote *The Sapphires* (2004), a feel-good story about his mother's singing group, which became the subject of a successful film.

The organising committee for Sydney's Olympic Games had a brief to promote different aspects of Australian culture. It sponsored a Festival of the Dreaming in 1997, which staged *The Seven Stages of Grieving* (1995) by Wesley Enoch and Deborah Mailman, *Box the Pony* (1997) commissioned from Leah Purcell, Deborah Cheetham's *White Baptist Abba Fan* (1997), Julie Janson's *Black Mary* (1996), and Josie Ningali Lawford's *Ningali* (1994). Apart from *Black Mary*, a historical drama about a Black woman involved in the white male business of bushranging, the other plays rely on a single actress recounting, with the aid of projected images and symbolic props, the sad and violent history of colonisation, family oral histories of struggle, and moments of public protest.

CHILDREN'S AND YOUNG ADULT LITERATURE

Young adult fiction, including thrillers and fantasy, with children's writing tending more to humour, are represented most prominently by Margo Lanagan and Andy Griffiths, Morris Gleitzman, Nadia Wheatley, Gary Disher, Paul Collins, Judith Clarke, Tristan Bancks and Sophie Masson.

A successful story of finding one's identity within Australia's Italian community was Melina Marchetta's *Looking for Alibrandi* (1992). It became a high school text and inspired a feature film. Emily Rodda reached an international market with a young adult fantasy series beginning with *Rowan of Rin* (1993), and Gary Crew estranges both past and future with heightened symbolism (*House of Tomorrow*, 1988; *Strange Objects*, 1990). Garth Nix's The Old Kingdom series—*Sabriel* (1995), *Lirael* (2001), *Abhorsen* (2003), *Clariel* (2014), *Goldenhand* (2016) and *Terciel and Elinor* (2021)—is successful internationally. These feature late-teenage girls as witch-warriors in a highly detailed set of societies that combine *Lord of the Rings*-style adventure with steampunk gadgetry, undead spirits, shamans, enchanting bells, Borgesian libraries, and so on. Isobelle Carmody enjoys an even more dedicated following for her Obernewtyn Chronicles, the first volume of which (*Obernewtyn*) she completed in 1987 at the age of fourteen. Six titles led up to *The Red Queen* (2015). She has written other fantasy series as well as science fiction and horror for adults.

John Marsden remains a best-selling author for high school readers. *So Much to Tell You* (1987) is the journal of a girl turned mute by parental conflict. We read over her shoulder as she learns to deal with trauma and find friends. *Dear Miffy* (1997) consists of letters to an ex-girlfriend from a delinquent boy who has attempted suicide. Marsden's greatest success has been his thriller Tomorrow series. *Tomorrow, When the War Began* (1993) starts with a disparate group of students on a camping weekend. They return home to find the country has been invaded and their town is a prison camp. War adventure, bush survival drama, interpersonal negotiations and teenage humour blend, with the narrator musing on ethical challenges. Seven titles up to 1999 have been followed by three more following Ellie, the central character.

Children's picture books have been a site for perpetuating the bush mythology and balladry of Australia, with works like *Mulga Bill's Bicycle* (2005) and tales of feisty grandmas on country farms.

They are a major export item, often featuring cute native animals, as in Pamela Allen's work and Jackie French's *Diary of a Wombat* (2002). Contemporary life for Aboriginal children is captured in Phillip Gwynne's *Deadly, Unna?* (1998) and in the comic *Yirra and her Deadly Dog Demon* (2007) by Anita Heiss, who also follows a strong line of life writing by Aboriginal women in her fictionalised history of a Stolen Generation girl, *Who Am I? The Diary of Mary Talence, Sydney 1937* (2001).

Genre bending and the turn to popular culture has expanded the literary field. One example of this is the work of Shaun Tan, which employs the fabular aspects of children's literature while addressing social issues: migrant identity, colonisation and animal rights. Tan collaborated with John Marsden to produce *The Rabbits* (1998). This has the format of a child's picture book and sets out an allegory founded on huge plagues of introduced species between the wars that also alludes to racial conflict. Tan's own work began with *The Lost Thing* (2000), a picture book depicting weird but vulnerable bio-forms in a dystopian steampunk landscape. A wordless graphic novel *The Arrival* (2006) gently depicts the othering of immigrants and the invisibility of non-normative bodies, while later work mixes stories with artwork to present the fantastic lurking in ordered suburban (adult) complacency and debates around animal rights (*Tales from Outer Suburbia*, 2008; *Tales from the Inner City*, 2018).

OTHER GENRES

Australia has produced piles of memoirs, family histories and autobiographies, but not all receive attention as literary works. One exception is *The Road from Coorain* (1989) by Jill Ker Conway. Her quietly elegant prose is memorable for providing an insight into the mores and struggles of farming and how rural life can shape personalities. It is also a commentary on environmental degradation resulting from unsuitable agricultural methods. It presents a model feminist tale of daughter and mother conflict and the drive to overcome masculinist discrimination. All these elements led the writer towards a distinguished academic career in America.

Another distinguished career, but in British television and literary journalism, was that of Clive James. He perfected the arts of the witty book review and interview, and in 1992 established an Australian readership with *Unreliable Memoirs* (1980). He created his persona as 'the boy from Kogarah' who battled his way from a single-parent working-class upbringing to international fame. James turned out some spoof 'epics' in rhyming couplets in the 1970s, then wrote more serious verse later in life, usually coloured by sardonic humour, as in *The Book of My Enemy* (2003). In this, a writer gloats when finding his rival's work on the remainders tray of a bookshop. James was diagnosed with an incurable cancer but increased his fame by surviving until 2019, as one poetry title put it, *Condemned to Life* (2015).

The First Stone (1995), subtitled 'Some questions about sex and power', started what has become Helen Garner's hallmark—a mix of personal reflection, investigative journalism and moral inquiry centred on a controversial topic. It reports on a case in which the master of a university college was accused of minor sexual harassment by two young women, who took the matter to the police. As a 'second wave' feminist, Garner could not understand the rhetoric of victimhood that required the women to go to law rather than directly challenge the purported perpetrator. Nor could she comprehend the doctrinaire hostility she encountered among 'third wave' women academics when she probed into the case. She examines all the structures and individuals involved without ever arriving at clear answers to her questions. The book radically divided readers, as did Garner's subsequent attempts to get into the minds of a murderer and a man who killed his children. She returned to autobiographical fiction with *The Spare Room* (2008), an exasperatedly humorous account of caring for a friend with cancer who drains all her supporters by refusing to accept that she is dying.

CHAPTER 9

GFC to Covid
2008–2020

SOCIAL AND POLITICAL CONTEXT

Labor's Julia Gillard replaced Kevin Rudd as prime minister in 2010 and introduced a tax on carbon usage to control carbon dioxide levels. She faced opposition from the media as well as her political opponents, partly because she was a woman, partly because her efforts to reshape immigration procedures and to offset the effects of the 2007–08 Global Financial Crisis had not been well thought through. Rivalry between Rudd and Gillard destabilised government sufficiently for Tony Abbott to lead the Liberal–National conservative coalition back into power in 2014. One of his first acts was to remove the carbon pricing policy. Abbott was a hard-line conservative. He tried to reinstate the British honours system and resisted legalising gay marriage (which happened following a national plebiscite in 2017). As with the Labor Party, coalition infighting resulted in rotating leaderships, Malcolm Turnbull displacing Abbott as prime minister in 2015. Turnbull's best efforts at moderate reforms were defeated by the hard right and he was displaced by Scott Morrison three years later. The stability of the long-established two-party system had collapsed, resulting in a more combative politics relying on the goodwill of smaller political groups and focused on short-term survival rather than serious policy planning.

The civil order fragmented under the impact of neo-liberal capitalism. Unbridled commerce led to mining corporations vandalising Indigenous sacred sites. Banks outsourced financial advice to customers, and agents on commissions pulled clients into loans they could not afford. At least one bank managed to continue to charge customers after they had died! It took a national commission of enquiry to expose all this. Other commissions revealed malpractice and profit gouging in private education and health care, in care for the disabled and in aged-care institutions. The most shocking result of all was the combination of internet extremism and anti-Muslim sentiment that prompted one young Australian to move to New Zealand and gun down worshippers in five mosques. Suddenly, everyone had to face the fact of racist white violence, now organising in a neo-Nazi and conspiracy-ridden underground. The land of mateship and a fair go for all had become a home for cells of populist resentment fanned by Trumpist rhetoric from the US and the negative effects of a globalised economy.

Some things appeared to be going well. Ken Wyatt, from Western Australia, was the first Aboriginal person to be elected to the national House of Representatives. He stood as a Liberal and has had portfolios in Health and Aboriginal Affairs. He has been joined since by Labor's Linda Burney. Such political progress has not been matched by social change. Rates of Aboriginal illness, suicide, incarceration, poverty and death in custody continue to far outnumber those in the rest of the population. A 2017 national conference at Uluru produced a 'Statement from the Heart' requesting a statutory body to represent Aboriginal voices to parliament, constitutional recognition of First Nations peoples, a treaty, and a structure enabling people to tell the truth of history. A national referendum (since defeated) was planned to address these demands.

2019–20 was, for Australia, a time of crisis. Both earlier and later than usual, bushfires burned across almost all states and territories, destroying forests, wildlife and towns on an unprecedented scale, and focusing public attention on climate change. The government was forced to recognise the need for action, though mining interests and 'climate deniers' have continued to stymie reforms. Fires were followed by floods and then Covid-19. A previously ideologically rigid free-market government found itself obliged to show leadership for the communal good. It imposed travel restrictions, closed places of public gathering and poured money into supporting those forced to give up work. However, its underwriting of sports and business failed to extend to universities, artists, writers, musicians and actors. Increased numbers of people at home with time on their hands or having to educate children created stronger demands on books and streamed television series, so creative writing did not disappear.

Although Australia remains notionally a Christian country, the church-going norm of the 1950s has given way to a statistically secular society, with religious belief splitting into many faiths: Christianity, Islam, Buddhism, Hinduism and Judaism being only the major ones. Christianity now encompasses Catholic, mainstream Protestant, various ethnic denominations of Orthodox churches, and a whole range of largely American-derived evangelical churches. The change has resulted in a trend to conservative attitudes, with Christian lobby groups presenting as an embattled minority, claiming that the godless hordes of politically correct socialists are denying them free speech and the right to discriminate against those they deem heathen. Within religious groups, there are battles over whether women can be ordained leaders, whether abortion is a woman's right or a sin, and whether non-heteronormative sexuality can be condoned.

Catholics were heartened by the canonisation of Australian nun Mary MacKillop. However, they also had to confront the heartless operations of the church as a self-protective institution when stories emerged of child sex abuse at the hands of priests and cover-ups by bishops. The Anglican church has also been a significant source of legal cases; indeed, any institution that ran schools and orphanages has been exposed as a base for abuses of power by paedophiles. As with domestic violence, for many decades, polite society did not mention it, and police did not interfere in 'private' matters. Increasingly victims have chosen to speak out and take matters to law, forcing a reassessment of national assumptions and values. (A fictional treatment of all this is Tom Keneally's *Crimes of the Father*, 2016.)

Years of economic comfort for most people and a creeping emphasis on individual interest have resulted in high expectations and a proliferation of 'causes' among minority groups. Politically, this has led to new 'single issue' parties split across the extremes of right-wing and left-wing platforms. A sense of instability has been exacerbated by the sudden realisation that Australia's exports of minerals and agriculture to China have made it the modern equivalent of the colony once reliant on wheat and wool exports to Britain. Australia sees itself as a middle-level power in the region with some leverage on international politics but opposing China's militarisation of the South China Sea, its treatment of its Uighur Muslims and detention of some Australians provoked a war of words and China's shutdown of sections of Australia's trade. This pushed Australia into closer ties with the US and new ones with India. An air of unease hangs over the once complacent nation.

Cultural Context

The return to conservative government and the shock of the GFC locked in an obsessive focus on the economy as the source of all value. Cultural activities were expected to pay their way: business plans became as important as creative visions, and money went to large operations with either mass appeal or snob value that could attract corporate sponsorship. Arts Council funding continued, but with budget cuts and a lot of attention to 'wasting the taxpayer's dollar'. Grants approved by the Australian Research Council were cancelled by ministers focused on 'useful knowledge' and the fields of science, technology, engineering, mathematics and medicine (STEMM). The government's Productivity Commission (mainly economists from the business sector) made repeated attempts under the rubric of buyer choice and free-market competition to remove all protections on Australian publishing. This threatened local cultural production with dumping from international conglomerates. Regulations requiring a percentage of locally produced material to be aired on television have also been challenged. Print culture survives but increasingly moves into performance and digital media, and production and discussion have begun to move away from formal structures (major theatres, academic journals, newspaper reviews) towards a DIY grass-roots mode (blogging, book groups, Instagram).

One turn in constructing Australian literary history has been the gradual bibliographic compilation of work by Australians not written in English and/or not published in this country. Such 'gap filling' in the national record occurs because of a general critical turn towards empirical studies aiming at 'big picture' mapping. This has become possible thanks to digital databases. Reformist literary histories have expanded to chart the mechanics of publishing and readership. The government and university-funded AustLit database of writers, writing and critical commentary and Trove, the National Library's 'wiki' project aiming to digitise all newspapers and magazines, enable studies of serialised fiction and magazine poetry, and publishing records show how important popular genres were, though they have been ignored in older literary histories.

Two seemingly contradictory publications can be sampled as characterising this period. Literary editor and reviewer Geordie Williamson lamented the decline in the study of Australian literature, championing some allegedly undervalued fiction writers in *The Burning Library* (2012), while three years earlier Nicholas Jose and others edited the compendious *Macquarie PEN Anthology of Australian Literature*, also published in the US by Norton as *The Literature of Australia*. Debates over the health or frailty of Australian literature continue as its study spreads out across departments of literature, creative writing, cultural studies, gender studies, Aboriginal studies, the environmental humanities and into yet more interdisciplinary guises.

One of the turns in literary criticism has been away from older nationalist frameworks to inspect the transnational networks that have always surrounded and penetrated the nation space. This not only means the influences from Europe (the supposedly nationalist *Bulletin* having included samples and reviews of French, German and Russian writing), but also the circulation of Australian authors and books overseas. The transnational turn can be represented by *Scenes of Reading: Is Australian Literature a World Literature?* (2013) edited by Robert Dixon and Brigid Rooney, and by work such as David Carter and Roger Osborne's study *Australian Books and Authors in the American Marketplace, 1840s–1940s* (2018). It is also manifest in critical discussion of Australian literature emanating from Britain, the US, France, Germany, Italy, China, India, Spain and elsewhere.

As an addendum to all the above, critics encouraged by the shifts in Australia's ethnic composition have extended earlier work on the literary engagement with Asia and have begun to look at links with India. This can be tracked back to colonial times, with John Lang writing from Bengal, and later Mollie Skinner and Ethel Anderson telling yarns based on their Indian sojourns as nurse and military wife. Later, we find novels by Hugh Atkinson (*The Pink and the Brown*, 1957), Christopher Koch's novel *Across the Sea Wall* (1965) and poetry by Colin Johnson/Mudrooroo and Vicki Viidikas. More recently, Inez Baranay's novel *Neem Dreams* (2003) found publication in India. After Mena Abdullah published her 1950s stories of diasporic life, a later generation of Indian Australians have occupied their own part of Australia's literary landscape. The development is marked by anthologies: *Of Sadhus and Spinners* (2009), *Of Indian Origin* (2018), special issues of *Southerly* (2010) and *Antipodes* (2011), and the compendium of essays edited by Amit and Reema Sarwal, *Reading Down Under* (2009).

Prose Fiction

Gerald Murnane enjoyed a resurgence of critical attention, particularly after a band of dedicated fans in 2017 went to his rural retreat in western Victoria for a conference on his work. Murnane had produced short story collections (*Velvet Waters* and *Emerald Blue*) and a book of essays in the 1990s, when he was taken on by the publisher of 'art' writing, Giramondo. He then published *Barley Patch* in 2009, a distinctive mix of fiction and essay, going on to write *A History of Books* (2012), *A Million Windows* (2014), *Something for the Pain: A Memoir of the Turf* (2015) and *Border Districts* (2017). In 2019, he put out a book of poetry (*Green Shadows*). Text Publishing reissued *A Lifetime on Clouds* in its Australian Classics series in 2013, and in 2019, it listened to Murnane's grumblings about how his first publisher had gutted the work and published the original full-length version of the novel as *A Season on Earth*.

Alex Miller followed up an interest in Tunisia evident in *Conditions of Faith* (2000), in which an Australian woman escapes her marriage by journeying there from France. In *Lovesong* (2009), he bases the story on a café in Paris run by Tunisian migrants. Into this world, stumbles an Aussie innocent abroad who falls in love with the daughter of the café owner. There is a plangent melancholy about Miller's writing that colours his carefully straightforward prose, but *Autumn Laing* (2011) has a sharper edge. An acerbic old lady looks back on her life, assessing the egotism of artists and the costs of passion. Miller captures the voice and crackly energy of his protagonist, providing a thoughtful assessment of love, marriage and career as based on the lives of Sidney Nolan, Sunday Reed, and their partners at the Heide arts community in 1930s Melbourne. *Coal Creek* (2013) also captures the voice of a character, this time a semi-literate bushman. He tells a Shakespearean tragedy of mismatched personalities, loves and locations in the backblocks of north Queensland. Miller added to his novelistic output (he has also written short stories, essays and biographies) with *The Passage of Love* (2017), a largely autobiographical meditation in which an old man in New York recalls his youth and discovery of reading and writing as a source of meaning in life.

Peter Carey by now has become a kind of Australian Dickens, with the same facility for dramatic circumstance, colourful rogues, direct 'speech', and concerns for social issues. *His Illegal Self* (2008) depicts a child of 1960s American radicals still in hiding. He is raised by his New York grandmother but impelled to drop out and go on the run (partly in search of his parents), until he ends up on a commune in Queensland. Alexis de Tocqueville's tour of the USA underpins *Parrot and Olivier in America* (2009), which debates the merits of democracy and 'enlightened' prison systems. There are tacit comparisons with Australian society emerging from its convict past. Carey messes with history by making the amanuensis for minor noble Olivier a sometime Australian who tinkers with what he writes and associates with artist fraudsters trying to make a living. One of them is a version of the nineteenth-century bird illustrator Audubon. Picaresque servant-scribe Parrot closes his narrative with a vision of an egalitarian world of opportunity, though one Frenchman's scornful prediction that a levelling democracy will end up electing a dictatorial fool gives Carey a moment of prophecy.

Add to these themes Carey's persistent fascination for mechanical gadgetry and you arrive at his next and strangest novel, *The Chemistry of Tears* (2012). Playing with elements of the

Brothers Grimm, with the manufacture of a silver swan automaton (now in the Bowes Museum), with Charles Babbage's calculating 'engine' that anticipated computers, and with Carl Benz's invention of the petrol-driven carriage, Carey tells a tale of three people made desperate by grief (for a dead lover, a chronically ill son, a drowned family), all finding consolation in making or curating ingenious machines. Their stories raise the question of how much these inventions are signs of artistic inspiration and how much they lead us into the 'satanic mills' of the Anthropocene. *Amnesia* (2014) updates the technology to drones and computers, linking contemporary concerns over surveillance with the legend in Australia that the CIA engineered the coup that ousted Whitlam's Labor government in 1975. Another naïve rogue (an old, drunk journalist) is hired to tell a tale (fake) that will free a girl (echoes of an Australian held in Guantanamo and of WikiLeaks) from persecution by big business and American state agents. Truth and lies switch places and young hackers end up saving the day. *A Long Way from Home* (2017) anchors exploration of gender roles and Aboriginal identity on the 1950s road race around Australia known as the 'Redex Trials'. Maps become a significant motif.

Richard Flanagan consolidated his reputation with *The Narrow Road to the Deep North* (2013), which won the Booker Prize in 2014. This story of his father's generation of prisoners of war used as slave labour to construct the Thai–Burma railroad for the Japanese reconfigures diaries and memoirs, but adds some fictive portrayal of the private flaws underlying public heroes and includes some investigation of the pressures and cultural vectors driving Japanese troops to treat their prisoners so harshly. Prior to this large book, Flanagan had written a thriller in protest at Australia's legislative overreaction to 9/11. *The Unknown Terrorist* (2006) shows a hapless night-club dancer caught up in unrelated criminal activity that becomes a media frenzy about terrorism.

Flanagan increasingly takes on the role of public intellectual, and this can result in overly didactic fiction. He moved away by returning to the theme of forgery with *First Person* (2017). The narrator-writer's subject is a con man, and the story asks not just what is true and what is not, but to what extent the subject's amorality starts to take over the writer depicting it. Flanagan goes on to write *The Living Sea of Waking Dreams* (2020), in which a woman believes she is progressively losing parts of her body in sympathy with the disappearance of all kinds of Australian wildlife. She, her stuttering underachieving brother and their go-getting venture capitalist brother debate the proper care of their frail mother, cruelly prolonging her life out of perverse love and neuroses arising from abuse of the boys in a Catholic school. The drama occurs against a backdrop of apocalyptic bushfires as we confront trauma, dementia, suicide, the dehumanising effects of the internet, and the fragile nature of love.

Kate Grenville created a furore with the first in a series of historical novels, *The Secret River* (2006). Fictionalising the story of an ancestor who 'took up' land on the Hawkesbury River during the convict era, the book shows the first contact between settlers and Aboriginal landholders, charting the misunderstandings and hostilities that lead to massacre and the troubled conscience of ancestor Thornhill as he becomes a 'pillar of the community' in New South Wales. The book garnered notoriety in part for being open to interpretation as excusing white occupation as a historical inevitability and more for the author's challenge to historians that novelists do history better. Grenville went on to write *The Lieutenant* (2008), *Sarah Thornhill* (2011) and *A Room Made of Leaves* (2020), all filling out the colonial record with more imagined characters taken from real life. Her historical fiction can be compared with Rodney Hall's Yandilli trilogy, *Captivity Captive* (1988), *The Second Bridegroom* (1991) and *The Grisly Wife* (1993), and Thomas Keneally's *The Playmaker* (1987).

Five Bells (2011) by Gail Jones is bathed in the sunshine of Sydney harbour. Based on the well-known elegy by Kenneth Slessor, the novel also includes a drowning, but plays a counterpoint of four characters whose paths cross on visits to Circular Quay. We discover their various stories of escaping violence and forgiving their tormentors. *A Guide to Berlin* (2015) also has origins in other writing—a young Australian visits the city looking for time to write and meets a group (Italian, American and Japanese) who tell their different stories, linked by a love of Nabokov's writing. Memory, also embodied in Berlin's ruined cityscape, serves as a marker of loss and a means of constructing continuity. Death and its concealment bring the realisation that the stories necessary to self-formation inevitably distort, censor and fail.

Jones modulates themes of death and survival through patterns of light and dark. In *The Death of Noah Glass* (2018) this is figured forth by two art historians, one male and Australian, the other female and Sicilian. He is fascinated by the clarity of Piero della Francesca's paintings, she by the darkness of Caravaggio's life and work. The Australian dies in Sydney and his troubled artist son travels to Sicily to determine whether his father was involved in art theft. With no definite answers, he returns to his sister, who is also decoding her father's clues to what he has left behind.

Michelle de Kretser's *Questions of Travel* (2012) places two stories in contrast to each other: that of a rootless cosmopolitan, essentially operating as a tourist overseas, and the past and present of a refugee from the horrors of Sri Lanka's civil war. After the short *Springtime: A Ghost Story* (2014), *The Life to Come* (2017) focuses on the subtle interactions of people, different emotions and opinions appearing as dialogues and circumstances shift. The unconscious racism of an otherwise liberal middle class is exposed in the process.

Centred on Australian life, Tim Winton wrote *Eyrie* (2013) and *The Shepherd's Hut* (2018). The former features the urban high-rise apartments that house the poor, the old, struggling single parents, and so on. A burnt-out environmental activist, separated from family and hitting the booze, takes refuge there and recovers his self-respect through trying to protect his neighbour from the stalking of a drug dealer. The latter novel also uses Australia's increasing drug trade as a plot device, criminals torturing a hermit priest who refuses to give up the young delinquent he has befriended after they both stumble on a desert drug lab. Winton deployed his talent for convincing dialogue to write for the stage, producing *Rising Water*, *Signs of Life* and *Shrine* (2012–13).

Sofie Laguna started as a successful children's writer then moved into adult fiction with *One Foot Wrong* (2008), followed by *The Eye of the Sheep* (2014). A story of transgenerational family violence and alcoholism, the latter creates the mind of an autistic boy who tries to make sense of life and control his erratic energy through reading home appliance manuals. His father beats his mother, his brother beats his father and leaves home, his father beats the younger son and leaves so as not to do worse, and his long-suffering mother falls into lethargy and dies of an asthma attack. The boy is taken into care, is manipulated by his foster 'siblings' into an adventure in which he finds his father and eventually settles with his father and uncle in an island retreat. A similar mix of pathos and humour, crime, love and dysfunctional family life in Brisbane's suburban slums given the young adult appeal of a streetwise idealist teenager, bildungsroman form, a bit of magic realism and a thriller plot came from Trent Dalton. *Boy Swallows Universe* (2018) was a huge success.

After *Steam Pigs*, Melissa Lucashenko went on to write young adult books. Their lighter touch informs later adult work, which gains tighter control of narrative. More Aboriginal language appears, with glossaries specifying sources. *Mullumbimby* (2013) mixes romance, horses, Aboriginal lore and the personal and collective politics of having a hold on land. The book keeps readers hooked with a varied cast of characters, lively colloquialisms and one-liners that draw on a wide range of global popular culture, from Bob Marley to Jane Austen. It carries strong messages about the emotional weight of history, partly figured in the protagonist's job maintaining the local cemetery. Lucashenko's work mixes race and sexuality, seen in the lesbian bikie protagonist of *Too Much Lip* (2018), a novel that combines small-town politics, the dark history of rural race relations, crime, romance and demonstrations of the transgenerational damage of child abuse.

Nearly all of these elements feature in Tara June Winch's *The Yield* (2019), which makes the recovery of Indigenous languages a central part of the story. The narrative is in three parts: a nineteenth-century missionary trying unsuccessfully to mediate between Black and white folk, a grandfather who has been compiling a Wiradjuri dictionary that includes glosses on cultural meanings, and his granddaughter returned from England for his funeral. She is faced with the impending loss of the family home to mining interests. Everything turns on her gathering evidence of long-term occupation of the land, which she does with the help of documents originating in the other two strands of the book. Her research uncovers a shameful family secret concerning the disappearance of her sister years before as well as the positive if unwitting contribution of white farmers. The latter's family history is also under threat from mining and they have unwittingly facilitated land rights claims by their past thefts of Aboriginal artefacts sent on to museums.

Another work deals with the intersections of race and sexuality in a more fabulising manner. *Heat and Light* (2014) won the David Unaipon Award for Ellen van Neerven. Comprising three sections ('Heat', 'Water' and 'Light'), the book is a collection of short stories centred on family and lesbian desire as framed by Aboriginal experience. The book has mainly attracted attention for its middle section, which weaves race and sexuality into a science fiction mode that blurs the 'species barrier', attacks anthropocentrism and expresses concern at environmental destruction.

Alexis Wright mirrors van Neerven's themes in *The Swan Book* (2013), highlighting another strand in common: migration and the oppression of displaced people. Some of the displacement is caused by environmental disasters, marginal groups being pushed into the wastelands and polluted swamps created by the dominant society. Woven into an amalgam of swan stories drawn from European culture, the black swans of Australia are linked with an Aboriginal girl traumatised into silence by a history of abuse. She is 'captured' as a wife by Australia's president (in this futurist dystopia, a sell-out Aboriginal man) but is able, with help from wise women and birds, to break free. The book is a complex mix of interests that continues to puzzle, intrigue and impress readers.

Wright's novel reflects a general turn in fiction towards 'cli-fi': fiction dealing with climate change and related environmental concerns. Some aspects of this are found in Greg Egan's science fiction, but more complex literary genre crossings occur in books like James Bradley's *Clade* (2015) and *Ghost Species* (2020), Josephine Wilson's *Extinctions* (2016) and Laura McKay's *The Animals in That Country* (2020). An ur-text for environmentally concerned fiction is George Turner's *The Sea and Summer* (1987).

More in keeping with the gentler, largely female-centred interest in wellness and healing after trauma is Amanda Lohrey's *The Labyrinth* (2020). This won the Miles Franklin Award and also sells well to book groups. It centres on a middle-aged woman whose son suffers mental breakdown and is gaoled for murder. She takes a cottage by the sea near the prison and remembers her own upbringing among the institutionalised patients of her psychiatrist father. She employs a migrant worker to construct a circular labyrinth as a healing walking path and connects with the local community in the process. Lohrey built a reputation as a politically engaged novelist, starting with *The Morality of Gentlemen* (1984) and *The Reading Group* (1989), but moved into other interests with *Camille's Bread* (1995). Lowrey also edited Tasmania's *Island* magazine.

One book that has since received a lot of attention is Charlotte Wood's *The Natural Way of Things* (2015). It mixes *Lord of the Flies* with *The Handmaid's Tale* and a world of reality TV shows and consumerism. Feminist rage at the treatment of women caught up in sexual scandal joins with an interest in the lives of plants and animals. Victims of sexual abuse are herded into a rural compound where they work as slave labour, they and their three warders becoming cut off from the world and increasingly reliant on trapping rabbits and collecting plants and fungi. One woman turns hunter and eventually escapes into the grassland camouflaged in rabbit skins. Her friend's romance of being rescued by a white horse proves delusionary, but when she is rescued with most of the other women she escapes back to the 'wilderness' rather than submit to social conditioning again.

With the same anger at male exploitation of women (especially Asian 'mail order' partners stereotyped by white men), Merlinda Bobis developed a reputation in Australia as a powerful performer of song and poetry, drawing on folk traditions from her native Philippines. She has gone on to write two collections of stories, *The White Turtle* (1999) and *Accidents of Composition* (2017), and a set of novels: *Banana Heart Summer* (2005), *The Solemn Lantern Maker* (2008), *Fish-Hair Woman* (2012) and *Locust Girl: A Lovesong* (2015). The last two develop a fabular magic realist mode. *Fish-Hair Woman* is the largest and most complex work, recording the violence of Filipino civil conflict and seeking a way to give testimony to the unspeakable, conveying both the horror of the violence and the painful silence of those traumatised by it.

Anger pervades a lot of writing by new multicultural voices of Middle Eastern heritage, in particular of young men who have grown up on the fringes of Sydney and Melbourne and have been stereotyped as rapists and thugs. Michael Mohammed Ahmad founded Sweatshop, a writing workshop in Sydney's western suburbs, from which he issued *The Lebs* (2018), a frank depiction of hypermasculinity and an attempt to fracture a homogenised view of Muslim youth. Its protagonist is an Alawite Muslim who wants to break out from his high school herd and discovers new hope in a drama group. This book was anticipated by Omar Musa, who mixed some grunge writing with hip hop to portray the underside of Canberra society in *Here Come the Dogs* (2014). Musa has also written two books of poetry.

Markers of transition in multicultural writing were the books by Nam Le (*The Boat*, 2008) and Tom Cho (*Look Who's Morphing*, 2009). Le attracted comment partly because of the international range of lyrically written short stories crafted in an American writing school, and mostly because of his subtle handling of textual politics. Refusing the pigeonholes of 'ethnic' and 'Vietnamese-Australian' writing, his major piece begins 'This story does not begin on a boat' but subtly turns a son's attempts to fight free of the family past into a means of telling his father's experience of oppression and risky refugee escape on a boat. Cho also breaks ethnic stereotypes, invoking a plethora of popular culture icons, humour and 'queer' experience to destabilise ideas of identity. His work was of particular interest for bringing back the postmodern aspects of Carey and Bail. In more traditional guises, story collections have also appeared from Debra Adelaide (*Letter to George Clooney*, 2013; *Zebra and Other Stories*, 2019), Robert Drewe (*The Rip*, 2008; *The Local Wildlife*, 2013; *The True Colour of the Sea*, 2018) and Georgia Blain (*The Secret Lives of Men*, 2013).

Despite Moorhouse's sense of a new looser form, the story has not shown significant experiment apart from staccato sequences of numbered sections, occasional forays into unusual speaking positions and semi-absurdist humour. An exception is the move to microfiction (stories one might compose on a mobile phone that blur into poetry's turn to the prose poem). One of the first publications demonstrating this is Susan McCreery's *Loopholes: Microfiction* (2016). Other changes have been mainly in content, with a comfortable middle class fixating on illness and growing old, though encounters with the poor, divorce and loss of loved ones often provide material, and capturing the argot of a subculture and the digital world marks some tales.

Tony Birch published his first story collection, *Shadowboxing*, in 2006, followed by another in 2009, and has gone on to create three more collections, most recently, *Common People* (2017). These have been well received for their tales of family, childhood and growing up poor on the fringes of Melbourne, with his Aboriginal heritage being kept as an often tacit part of the narrative. More overt in terms of racial politics is Jeanine Leane's fictionalised set of memoirs *Purple Threads* (2011) and Maxine Beneba Clarke's *Foreign Soil* (2014). Leane depicts the warmth of family amid the struggle to thrive by Aboriginal women in rural New South Wales. Of Afro-Caribbean lineage with an upbringing in the tough suburbs of western Sydney, Beneba Clarke pulls few punches, which she also delivers in later autobiography and performance poetry.

Roanna Gonsalves mixes protest, pointed satire and lighter humour in her depictions of Goan Catholic migrants moving to Australia (*The Permanent Resident*, 2016). An entirely different set of work comes from another (but older) Indian-Australian, Subhash Jaireth. With time in Russia and work in translation, he adopts a quiet, slightly melancholic literary style (*To Silence*, 2011; *Moments*, 2015), though he injects a little metafictional humour in stories like 'Jack and Jill'. With a reputation as a poet, Alex Skovron turned to the short story (*The Man Who Took to His Bed*, 2017). Michelle Cahill, also a poet, completed a story collection, *Letter to Pessoa* (2016). This was another wrestling match with the problematic of identity. The title alludes to the Portuguese modernist who wrote as multiple distinct personae. Exuding moods of longing and anxiety, the stories set up correspondences (letters and resonances) with Derrida, Conrad, Genet, Coetzee, Atwood and Woolf and range across a variety of overseas settings.

The ever-energetic John Kinsella added story collections to his books of poetry and longer fiction, the more recent of which are *In the Shade of the Shady Tree* (2012), *Tide* (2013), *Crow's Breath* (2015) and *Old Growth* (2017). Central to his work is the search for an ethical connection between humans and land, and this links him to books by Ceridwen Dovey (*Only the Animals*, 2014) and Joshua Lobb (*The Flight of Birds*, 2019). Other new voices of some note include Julie Koh (*Portable Curiosities*, 2016), Tegan Bennett Daylight (*Six Bedrooms*, 2015) and Pippa Kay (*Back Stories*, 2005; *Keeping It in the Family*, 2018). Danielle Wood keeps up the ongoing feminist revisionary project with *Mothers Grimm* (2014). Three other women writers who have been accorded literary recognition are Gretchen Shirm (*Having Cried Wolf*, 2010), Maria Takolander (*The Double*, 2013) and Paddy O'Reilly (*The End of the World*, 2007; *Peripheral Vision*, 2015; *It Happened Off the Leash*, 2016). As regular practitioners of note, we can add Susan Midalia (*A History of the Beanbag and Other Stories*, 2007; *An Unknown Sky*, 2012; *Feet to the Stars*, 2015) and Jennifer Mills (*The Lap*, 2007; *The Rest Is Weight*, 2012). Contemporary male story writers include A.S. Patric (*The Rattler*, 2011; *Las Vegas for Vegans*, 2012; *The Butcherbird Stories*, 2018), Will Elliott, Chris Leckonby, Ryan O'Neill, Chris Womersley and Tom Petsinis.

In 2012, Giramondo published *Stream System: The Collected Short Fiction of Gerald Murnane*. Kathleen Mary Fallon produced *A Fixed Place* (2019) and Janette Turner Hospital returned to the short story with *Forecast: Turbulence* (2011). Beth Yahp, long silent after *The Crocodile Fury*, came out with *The Red Pearl and Other Stories* in 2017. Her Asian-Australian presence was backed up by Alice Pung, who moved from fiction-shaped memoir (*Unpolished Gem*, 2006; *Her Father's Daughter*, 2011) into stories (*In a Heartbeat*, 2017). Mandy Sayer, writing stories from 2000, produced a new collection *Crime and Other Pastimes* in 2020, and in the same year Arnold Zable, a name from early multicultural writing best known for his novel *Café Scheherazade* (2001), published *The Watermill*. Elizabeth Tan received wide recognition for her collection *Smart Ovens for Lonely People* (2020), the title indicating a satiric view of our use of technology to solve social problems. Closing off this rapid history of short fiction, Louis Nowra, well known for his theatre work and memoir, published *Collected Stories* in 2019.

At the popular end of the literary spectrum, a new sub-genre of 'bush chick lit' has emerged—romances based on strong women running outback farms. This has been mirrored in crime writing, with Gary Disher producing a series centred on a country policeman in dry farm towns (*Kill Shot*, 2018; *Peace*, 2019; *Consolation*, 2020). Jane Harper's *The Dry* (2016) and *Force of Nature* (2017) were best-sellers. Australian residents writing thrillers set in their native Ireland are Adrian McKinty (*I Hear Sirens in the Street*, 2013; *In the Morning I'll Be Gone*, 2014; *Gun Street Girl*, 2015) and Dervla McTiernan (*The Ruin*, 2018; *The Scholar*, 2019; *The Good Turn*, 2020). Kate Morton studied Victorian and gothic literature and from 2006 has worked those fields to produce atmospheric women-centred romances of some sophistication, *The Lake House* (2015) being one of the most recent. Far from romance, but also internationally popular was Hannah Kent's historical recreation of the story of the last woman executed in Iceland, *Burial Rites* (2013).

Poetry

There are far too many poets emerging in the last twenty years to be fully catalogued in any meaningful way, and it is clear that there is little agreement among prize-givers and anthologisers about who the principal figures are. A history of the near present is obliged to concentrate on poets who have attained public visibility not only by persistent publication and winning awards, but also by standing out as editors of anthologies and reviewers in the major newspapers. One writer who ticks all these boxes is Sarah Holland-Batt, who remarkably ran a weekly column in the *Australian* explaining contemporary poems. Holland-Batt comes out of writing classes in both Queensland and the US, and won a bagful of awards for her first collection, *Aria* (2008), and the Prime Minister's Literary Award for *The Hazards* (2015). Her other books are *The Pocket Mirror* (2011) and *Fishing for Lightning* (2021).

Judith Beveridge added *Storm and Honey* (2009) and a 'new and selected' *Sun Poems* (2018) to her output so far. She also had a selection of her work published in the USA (*Hook and Eye*, 2014). She has developed a set of poems around fishing and marine life and continued her imagined life of the Buddha (*Devadatta's Poems*, 2014). Joanne Burns produced *amphora* (2011), *brush* (2014) and *apparently* (2019). Jill Jones added *Dark Bright Doors* (2010) and *The Beautiful Anxiety* (2013) to her corpus and *A History of What I'll Become* (2020) continues her preoccupation with time, perception and memory.

Jennifer Maiden pushed into international circulation with Britain's Bloodaxe Books publishing *Intimate Geography: Selected Poems 1991–2009* (2010), while issuing a book almost every year, from *Pirate Rain* (2009) to *The Espionage Act* (2020). *Liquid Nitrogen* (2012) continues and expands the George Jeffries and Clare 'story' already at work in *Pirate Rain*. The two have dreamlike adventures in locations of international disasters that have political implications for the reader. Increasingly, there are also 'diary poems' of autobiographical reflection, often including debate with her critics. *Liquid Nitrogen* sets up comic dialogues between Eleanor Roosevelt and Hillary Clinton, Aneurin Bevan and Julia Gillard, Dietrich Bonhoeffer and Kevin Rudd. The opening poem is typical in beginning with the writer's birth in the Year of the Ox: 'As an ox / I am alert to the point of twitching but / still trample through the difficult.' The liquid nitrogen of the book's title refers to the cooling of 'big data' CIA computers at Langley and US persecution of Julian Assange.

Maiden's work is an indication of how poetry remains a political medium. Some critics detect a shift towards the long poem, though that form has been around for some time. An ongoing concern is to fight free of the lyric, particularly in its pastoral mode. One experimental expression of this has been John Kinsella's 'graphology' poems, which break up into visual constructs that are 'translated' into drawing, and as environmentally invested work, hung on trees and inscribed in the land itself. As with work that mixes with musical performance (Jill Jones, for example, writing as part of a sound installation), such experiment is ephemeral and escapes anthologies. One interesting development is Stuart Barnes's 'redaction' poems, where he takes a known poem by someone else and blacks out sections of it to reveal a different though related verse within.

Anthony Lawrence has been prolific, poems regularly collected as *The Welfare of My Enemy* (2011), *Signal Flare* (2013), *Headwaters* (2016), *101 Poems* (2018) and *Time Machine* (2019). The titles reveal an interest in technology and *The Welfare of My Enemy* is a long poem in loosely rhymed couplets in which a series of voices (police, murderers, a sniffer dog, victims and their families) provide vignettes of the torment attaching to the many missing persons in Australia's past and present. Michael Farrell's 2019 collection is titled *Ashbery Mode*. Though published in the US, it deploys Australian colloquialisms—as in the poem 'Avago' (a common exhortation at sports matches or a doctrine of self-help propounded by conservative politicians). *Enjambment Sisters Present* (2013) indicates Farrell's work as a performance poet. Other titles are *Open Sesame* (2012), *Cocky's Joy* (2015) and *I Love Poetry* (2017). *Family Trees* came out in 2020. Ouyang Yu has published *Bilingual Love Poems* and *Self Translation* (both 2012), *Fainting with Freedom* (2015), and most recently, *Flag of Permanent Defeat* (2019), *Terminally Poetic* and *Living after Death* (both 2020).

Poems that show the process of present living rather than being discrete observations of external situations have become more common, with the work of Ken Bolton (following John Forbes and Frank O'Hara) providing frequently humorous and self-mocking instances of the spaced-out flow of a mind and voice wandering across past, present, friends, politics and reading. Bolton has been around for years, running two important small magazines in the 1980s (*Otis Rush* and *Magic Sam*) but still writing. His *Selected Poems 1975–90* came out in 1992 and his latest work includes *Lonnie's Lament: Towards a History of the Vanishing Present* (2017), *Starting at Basheer's* (2018) and *Salute* (2019).

A much younger writer is Jaya Savige, who won the Thomas Shapcott Poetry Prize for his first book, *Latecomers* (2005). Since then, he has published *Surface to Air* (2011), *Maze Bright* (2014) and *Change Machine* (2020). *Latecomers* deploys a terse wit and, at times, surreal imagism in open couplets, sometimes rhymed, and in longer-lined blocks that recall wartime manoeuvres and fishing on the poet's childhood island next to Brisbane. Poems combine consumer advertising with narratives of personal relationships that are cut into by violences of accident and world politics. There is an increasing interest in wordplay and reflections of European travel and art.

Michelle Cahill has become known as an advocate for multicultural minority writers, in particular those with roots in Asia, largely owing to her founding with Kim Cheng Boey and others the online magazine *Mascara Literary Review*. She herself is Indian-Australian by way of East Africa and Britain, and wrestles with the nature of identity and womanhood as they are lived in Australia, her view suggested in the title of her first poetry collection, *The Accidental Cage* (2006). There is an intensity of tactile and visual images that exude both musicality and a heightened fragile passion. Her second book (*Vishvarupa*, 2011) turns these concerns to critical recasting of Hindu deities and dogma. Her other collections are *Night Birds* (2012) and *The Herring Lass* (2016).

More recently, Shastra Deo, Indian-Australian with origins in Fiji, won the Thomas Shapcott Poetry Prize for *The Agonist* (2017). Interspersed with anatomical illustrations, the book takes up literary-cultural interest in the body as a site of harm, fragility, affirmation, identity and sexuality. Deo's terse surrealism presents dreams of threat and loss, and physical violence that requires rituals to keep body and soul together. She also considers the somatic aspects of language and the weight of diasporic being.

Judith Bishop started publishing poems in the 1990s but her first book, *Event*, did not appear until 2007, after which she published *Alice Missing in Wonderland* (2008), *Aftermarks* (2012) and *Interval* (2018). Words like 'frailty' and 'delicacy' are used to characterise her work, which is usually a meditation on the brevity of life and impressionist rendering of timeless moments infused with hints of personal relationships and historical ruptures (the Spanish conquest of Mexico). Hiatus, silence, breath, wind and qualities of light are common motifs, and as a linguist, Bishop also investigates communication across difference, the 'as if' of poetry being part of the attempt to connect.

Melbourne poet Jordie Albiston and Diane Fahey produced *The Body in Time / Nervous Arcs* with feminist press Spinifex in 1995. Albiston includes a sequence on Mexican artist Frida Kahlo. She favours historically based documentary writing and recreates letters from convict and early settler women in *Botany Bay Document* (1996). Later titles include *My Secret Life* (2001), *Vertigo (A Cantata)* (2007), *Euclid's Dog: 100 Algorithmic Poems* (2017) and *Element: The Atomic Weight and Radius of Love* (2020). Two other poets gaining attention in recent times are Bonny Cassidy and David McCooey. The latter published poems during the nineties and later a series of books: *Blister Pack* (2005), *Graphic: Two Sequences* (2010), *Outside* (2011) and *Star Struck* (2016). McCooey won the Mary Gilmore Award for his first collection of verse which contains a sequence 'Tasmanian Skies' stemming from his first teaching post. He has edited anthologies, while Cassidy became a regular reviewer. She completed a doctorate on the poetry of Jennifer Maiden and Jennifer Rankin and produced her own book, *Said to Be Standing*, in 2010. Later collections are *Certain Fathoms* (2012), *Final Theory* (2014) and *Chatelaine* (2017). Her writing evinces a critical engagement with feminist and postcolonial theory and settler–Indigenous politics.

Sam Wagan Watson kept Aboriginal poetry on the literary radar with *The Curse Words* (2011), *Love Poems and Death Threats* (2014) and *Monster's Ink* (2016). High rates of poverty, illness, suicide and imprisonment among Australia's Aboriginal population, raids on territory by mining companies and ongoing reluctance by government to recognise Indigenous sovereignty mean that Aboriginal poets still have much to protest about. Harm done to Stolen Generation children and their offspring is at the centre of Elizabeth Hodgson's *Skin Painting* (2008), winner of the David Unaipon Award in 2007. Yvette Holt won the same award in 2005 for *Anonymous Premonition*, published in 2008. Charmaine Papertalk-Green began writing poems in the 1980s and several appeared in *Inside Black Australia* as rhetorical questions about injustice and loss of culture. She has since published *Just Like That and Other Poems* (2007), *False Claims of Colonial Thieves* (2018) in collaboration with John

Kinsella, and *Nganajungu Yagu* (2019). The last is an interesting mix of letters from her mother to her younger self when she was training in Perth accompanied by reflections on them from the present. These take several forms, from 'vertical' poems to sequences of long-line stanzas, many with chanting refrains in the author's two languages. In the second half of the collection, the poet lists various questions from the Western Australia Natives (Citizenship Rights) Regulations Forms, all of which make citizenship conditional on forsaking contact with Aboriginal people and culture. Each is accompanied by a box in which a satirical or critical answer is provided.

The other leading Indigenous poet from the 2000s is Ali Cobby Eckermann. Her collections are *Little Bit Long Time* (2009), *Kami* (2010), *Love Dreaming and Other Poems* (2012) and *Inside My Mother* (2015). She has published two verse novels: *His Father's Eyes* (2011) for younger readers, and *Ruby Moonlight* (2012), which won the Kenneth Slessor Prize for Poetry. Much of her work records her journeys to reconnect with her birth family in the north and west of South Australia. *Ruby Moonlight* is a sequence of short verses of pared-back narrative, telling a tale of massacre from the 1880s and the subsequent survival of a young woman. *Inside My Mother* shows a growth of confidence in letting the imagery and situation carry a message. Poems retain a romantic vision of contact with nature (birds are a strong presence) while experimenting with forms and ranging across past and present, domestic and national topics.

Other Indigenous poets emerging in the new millennium include Natalie Harkin (*Dirty Words*, 2015), Brenda Saunders (*Looking for Bullin Bullin*, 2012; *The Sound of Red*, 2013), Julie Gough (*Shale*, 2018), Kerri Shying (*Elevensies*, 2018; *Knitting Mangrove Roots*, 2019; *Know Your Country*, 2020) and Phillip Hall (*Sweetened in Coals*, 2014; *Fume*, 2018). Better known for their fiction, Tony Birch published *Broken Teeth* in 2016, Ellen van Neerven, *Comfort Food* in 2016, and Jeanine Leane, *Walk Back Over* in 2018. Younger writers beginning their careers in these years, many with creative writing classes shaping their work, include Evelyn Araluen, Paul Collis and Elfie Shiosaki.

Drama

The push to commercialise everything from the 1990s onward resulted in theatres generally becoming either large-scale companies with corporate or state government backing or smaller niche operations, with some companies fading away altogether. At the smaller end, big-name authors and directors have been to some extent replaced by group-devised plays. Internationalisation and low budgets have led to local writing being supplemented by reworkings of European material and by 'translations' of earlier Australian literature. Kate Mulvaney has specialised in adaptations of classical plays and novels. One of her most successful works is the cheerful growing-up tale *Jasper Jones* (2016).

Typical of the 'devised' work of recent times is Raimondo Cortese's *Buried City* (2012). Cortese is merely the 'writer': his contribution is shaped by a 'concept and director' person and five 'co-devisor' performers. How change affects individuals, how we live alongside each other without really communicating, the nature of modern labour—all inform what gets written. This is then 'worked up' by the six actors (from a visibly wide range of ethnic backgrounds) and the director's role is to 'broker a set of relationships' that result in a swirling kaleidoscope of scenes described by the writer as 'ritual everydayness'. These are intended to 'give the audience a bigger role in reading what they see ... seeing the work as a set of questions.' The set is a scaffolding and back of a shed, and no cues are given to the sound or lighting designers or the 'singer-songwriter' as to how they should modulate our impression of 'Godot on speed' with a lot of supposedly naturalistic vulgar dialogue. It all clearly provides an energetic theatrical 'experience' but runs the risk of being incoherent.

Andrew Bovell's *When the Rain Stops Falling* (2008) is set in an Alice Springs of the future and had a London production. Bovell dramatised Kate Grenville's convict-era novel *The Secret River* in 2013, and the family drama *Things I Know to Be True* played in Adelaide and Sydney in 2016. Bovell's sometime co-writer, Patricia Cornelius has continued to create tough monosyllable titles (*Slut*, 2000, followed by *Shit*, 2015) and a string of other plays, her more recent published work being *The Berry Man* (2009), *Do Not Go Gentle* (2010), *Savages* (2013), and *Lovely, Lovely, Sometimes Ugly* (2019).

Daniel Keene remained prolific, staging *Life Without Me* (2010), *Boxman* (2011), *Dreamers* (2014), *Mother* (2015), *Wild Cherries* (2019) and *The Curtain* (2020). These works turn more to depicting poverty, refugees and disability issues. *Mother* sets up nine scenes in a monologue by an old vagrant woman, who gradually reveals her descent into alcoholism, institutionalisation and street life but clearly retains a degree of self-knowledge and fortitude. *The Long Way Home* (2014) was commissioned by the Sydney Theatre Company and the Department of Defence to record the wounds, physical and mental, of war veterans.

Michael Gow continues to write, his 2014 *Once in Royal David's City* beginning with an actor playing a theatre director who addresses the audience in Brechtian distancing directness: 'Welcome. Thanks for coming. I'm in an airport. The stage represents an airport.' Will and Jeannie tell us about their annual Christmas holiday rituals, a therapist attempts to get Will's father to read after he's had a stroke, actors bitch about each other while rehearsing *The Importance of Being Earnest*. Will recalls his visit to Germany on pilgrimage to Brecht's home but resists a teacher's invitation to talk to her students. Will's mother is in hospital, dying of cancer, visited by strangers. There are no clear structural divisions, and everything is permeated *ad nauseum* by recorded Christmas carols. Gow worked out the shape of the play as it was being workshopped rather than writing it as a set piece.

Van (Vanessa) Badham emerged as a new talent with *We Met at the Demo* (1996), a satire about students changing political views as they get older. Social critique continues with *The Wilderness of Mirrors* (1999), a thriller in which a woman becomes paranoid while hiding Burmese dissidents. Later plays include *Persae* (2005, a transfer of Aeschylus onto the invasion of Iraq), *Muff* (2009) and *The Bull, the Moon and the Coronet of Stars* (2013). The last of these has an artist working in the Ashmolean Museum, where she contrives an affair with a married staff member. The next scene puts her on a train heading to a new job in Wales. The third scene shows her teaching a women's art class in Wales, again having an affair with a man who becomes a life-drawing model for her bacchanalian art class. Originally a radio play, this work sets up overlapping voices, both as thoughts and speech, and turns each section into an archetypal ritual based on Ariadne and the Minotaur under the three signs of its title. Other plays include *Banging Denmark* (2019) and a stage version of Orwell's *Animal Farm* (2020).

Alana Valentine trained at the National Institute of Dramatic Art (NIDA) and has worked in radio, television and filmmaking. Her stage work begins with *The Conjurers* (1997). *Love Potions* (2006), about sensuality, food and sex, and *Savage Grace* (2001), about AIDS and euthanasia, were followed by *Run Rabbit Run* (2004). This composed verbatim interviews with club fans about the (later reversed) decision to exclude the South Sydney rugby league team (the 'Rabbitohs') from the national competition. In *Parramatta Girls* (2007), Valentine again shaped up verbatim reports of exploitation and abuse from former inmates of an institution for reforming delinquent girls that dated back to the 'female factory' housing women convicts. Other community-centred work stems from a flood in Katherine (*Watermark*, 2008) and a festival of knitted beanie hats in Alice Springs (*Head Full of Love*, 2010) as well as interviews with politicians (*MP*, 2011) and accounts by high school girls of their experiences online (*Cyberbile / Grounded*, 2012).

Valentine is a prolific writer, sometimes having four to six plays appear in one year. She increasingly collaborates with Aboriginal actors and informants (as in *One Billion Beats* with Romaine Morton, 2016, and the musical *Barbara and the Camp Dogs* with Ursula Yovich, 2017). Recent work includes *Letters to Lindy* (2016)—about the legal case and divisive media representation of Lindy Chamberlain, whose baby disappeared when her family camped at Ayers Rock/Uluru—and *The Sugar House* (2018). *Ladies Day* (2016) makes Valentine's verbatim theatre into a thematic device: an alter ego writer interviews 'drag queen' men who go to Broome's race day. Histories of oppression emerge alongside the female interviewer's own experiences of male power. Stories build to violent male-on-male rape and equally violent revenge, causing the interviewer to wonder about the veracity of her informants, one of whom tells her that the authenticity she wants to discover is really only confirmation of the stereotypes she seeks to break down.

Tom Holloway has attracted attention for his one-word-per-line Pinteresque dialogues in *Red Sky Morning* (2008), *Don't Say the Words* (2008), *Love Me Tender* (2010), *And No More Shall We Part* (2011) and *Forget Me Not* (2013). They convey an edgy toughness that spills over into impressionistic effects. The second play reworks Aeschylus's *Agamemnon* as three views of the same story. The audience doesn't know for some time whether it is watching an account of an actual event, a sexually charged word game, or two actors rehearsing lines. Suggestions of voyeurism within the scenes begin to spread out to include the audience.

Milk Crate Theatre is typical of many 'special interest' community groups (following on from the influential Theatre of the Deaf established in the 1970s). This particular group uses actors experiencing homelessness. *This House Is Mine* (2015) is a devised work coordinated by Maree Freeman that pulls together a sequence of tales about teenage psychosis, bullying, lesbian love, drug-taking, and so on, all resulting in socially marginalised and precarious lives. Inner states are indicated by video projection and the varied exchanges give liveliness to the production, though there is an underlying air of earnest didacticism. More effective as a theatre piece is Angus Cerini's *The Bleeding Tree* (2015), which attacks male violence against women, concentrating the theme on one woman's murder of her brutal husband. This is presented as a 'Greek' chorus of mother and two daughters whose rhythmic short lines interweave and rhyme to create a gothic ritual not unlike a dark fairy tale.

Suzie Miller, who otherwise works as a human rights lawyer, took up the story of a mother who was not permitted to hug her son before he was hanged in Singapore for carrying drugs. She turns this sad detail from history into a multi-stranded exploration of the importance of touch (*Caress/Ache*, 2015). Miller has worked in theatre in Canada, the UK and Ireland as well as Australia.

Aboriginal theatre has continued, increasingly crossing with dance and musical performance. Nakkiah Lui was discovered by a playwriting programme for young people known as 'The Voices

Project', which has collected work since 2011. Lui went on to stage *This Heaven* (2013), about Black deaths in custody, *Kill the Messenger* (2015) and *Black Is the New White* (2017). Leah Purcell staged her substitution of a Black woman for the heroic settler of Henry Lawson's story 'The Drover's Wife' in 2016.

Contemporary Australian theatre is unlikely to settle into tidy categories. However, it is clear that the place of women in society, domestic violence, queer sexualities, the persecution of refugee 'boat people', and minority voices are persistent themes. Asian, Pacific and Middle Eastern names have begun to appear alongside older European ones: Michelle Law, Natesha Somasundaram, Taofia Peleasa, Genevieve Chung and Yamana Fayed being only some. Those positioned more closely to the 'mainstream' who have produced several works include Seanna van Helten, Eva di Cesare, Kathryn Ash, Bill Reed, Keziah Warner, Noëlle Janaczewska, Vanessa Bates, Alison Croggon, Lally Katz and Emma Mary Hall.

Postlude

It is a contradiction in terms to write a history of the present; books must be listed with little sense of what their significance will turn out to be. We shall end with two books that appropriately deal in the ambiguities of time travel. They have much to say about Australia, if not also about contemporary society worldwide. *Factory 19* (2020) by Dennis Glover begins with a gambling tycoon who builds a modern art gallery in Tasmania and a prime minister who harasses his staff to the point of breakdown. Both are recognisable identities in real life, but the story moves on into a 'back to the future', or more accurately 'onwards to the past', tale in which the prime minister's hapless speechwriter has a public nervous breakdown and becomes a figurehead for a movement to reject the stranglehold of digital technology. The millionaire, having destroyed Tasmania's economy by closing his gallery, reappears and creates a utopian community based around a huge pre-war factory and the life and fashions of 1948 (before the RAND corporation commercialised computers). The book scores many satiric points against contemporary society, advocates for nostalgia (historical memory) as inspiration for social improvement, but of course shows the shortcomings of an uncritical reinvention of the past. The narrating speechwriter, now manager of the factory, is aware of the environmental and social hazards of the 1950s and records the collapse of his boss's ideal.

Glover's mix of social comment, fantasy, genre formulae and serious writing that looks both backwards and forwards is matched by the Tribe trilogy by Ambelin Kwaymullina. She has written many stories featuring Aboriginal culture for children and for her trilogy draws on Aboriginal totems, shamanic powers and creation spirits, on Western Australia's citizenship legislation that granted exemption from persecution to approved Indigenous people, and on A.O. Neville's 'protection' of the rest in government-run detention centres. *The Interrogation of Ashala Wolf* (2012), *The Disappearance of Ember Crow* (2013) and *The Foretelling of Georgie Spider* (2015) set a loose coalition of plant-people, hunters, and a youthful tribe with special abilities against a rivalrous alliance of cities that have outlawed them. Among all the bells and whistles of fantasy action adventure, the plot rests on being able to mind-map connections between past, present and future, with a message that it is choice and community that determine how multiple possibilities will resolve into disaster or salvation—determinants that also apply to literary history.

Glossary of Australian Terms

Many terms appearing in the text are glossed as they appear. Wider reading is likely to present many of the following idioms. The most authoritative reference work is *The Macquarie Dictionary*.

ambo: ambulance driver; medic
ankle biter: toddler; young child
banana bender: someone from Queensland
bastard: a term of both abuse and affection, the latter especially when prefaced by 'you old'
battler: a working-class individual fighting the odds
bikie: someone riding a large motorbike (often a Harley Davidson), usually wearing a leather jacket, and generally thought of as tough and possibly part of a gang
block: a small agricultural holding; government-allocated land for returned soldiers
bloke: man; fellow; chap; SIMILAR IDIOM: *cove*
bludger: someone who shirks work or lives on someone else's work
bogan: a low-class rather coarse person from the outer suburbs
boong: derogatory term for an Aboriginal person
break: a place where surfable waves rise and fall
brickie: bricklayer
bullocky: a man driving a team of oxen pulling a wagon laden with supplies or wool bales (bullockies are known for their swearing)
bush: uncultivated, undeveloped, sparsely populated region (similar to **outback** but not devoid of scrub and trees)
bushed: lost in the **bush**
cabbie: taxi driver
chalkie: teacher
check-out chick: a woman operating the till in a supermarket

chook: hen or rooster (often kept in backyards)
cobber: mate; buddy
cocky/cockie: someone eking out a poor living on a small holding; dairy farmer, fruit grower, etc.; ALSO: short for 'cockatoo'
cocky's joy: golden syrup; semi-processed liquid sugar (a proverbial staple for poor farmers)
coo-ee: a distance-penetrating call (useful if **bushed**)
copper: a large cauldron of beaten copper, suspended over a fire (used to wash one's clothes)
corroboree: a traditional Aboriginal dance
council: the third layer of civic organisation; an elected body governing a town and its surrounding district
country: (in modern usage) homeland; the specific area to which one has **Dreaming** and family ties
crook: ill (as in, 'I feel a bit crook')
croweater: someone from South Australia
currency lad/lass: someone born in Australia
cuz: cousin; ALSO: a general term of friendly address used mostly by Aboriginal people
deener: one shilling (twelve pence)
digger: ordinary soldier
do a U-ie: to make a U-turn
do one's block: to become very angry; to express rage; SIMILAR IDIOM: *do one's nana*
Dreaming: a broad term applied to set of cultural and spiritual beliefs held by Aboriginal peoples, encompassing stories about the creation and workings of the universe, codes of living in and interacting with the world, and related concepts and attitudes
drongo: a bird; ALSO: a stupid person
drover: a horseman herding sheep and cattle, often taking them long distances (thus becoming an *overlander*)
dunny: lavatory (until the 1970s, often a sentry box construction over a hole in the ground, or a removable can some distance from the house); SIMILAR IDIOM: *bog, loo*

expat: short for 'expatriate' (someone living overseas)
fair dinkum: true; genuine; SIMILAR IDIOM: *pukka*
fang it: to accelerate; to drive at speed
FIFO: 'fly in, fly out'—an itinerant worker (usually in mining)
firie: firefighter
flash: showy; gaudily dressed
flush: wealthy
garbo: garbage collector
goanna: piano
God botherer: a regular church-goer; religious proselytiser; SIMILAR IDIOM: *holy Joe*
greenie: someone supporting ecological sustainability
grey nomad: a retired person who travels the country with a caravan
grub: food
gubba: Aboriginal term for a white person; SIMILAR IDIOM: *kartiya, balanda, whitefella*
hang a right: to make a right turn
Hills Hoist: a rotary clothesline (and 1950s symbol of domestic civility), consisting of a metal pole with four arms (strung with wires) which could be raised or lowered
hit the skids: to apply the brakes
hooroo/ooroo: goodbye; SIMILAR IDIOM: *cheerio*
hubby: husband
humbug: to pester, usually with the aim of extracting food or money from someone
jake/she's jake: 'it's okay'; all right; under control
jumbuck: sheep
kangaroos in the top paddock: crazy; SIMILAR IDIOM: *bats in the belfry*
Koori: Aboriginal person from Victoria or New South Wales
lamington: a quadrilateral of cake coated with chocolate and dried coconut flakes
larrikin: anyone unruly, from a street gangster (originally) to a loveable clown

Leb: Lebanese; but generically, someone of Middle Eastern heritage

mallee: a low-growing tree with extensive roots; ALSO: the region it grows in (SA, VIC, NSW), legendary for the hard work required to clear its habitat for cropping

mob: a large herd of sheep or cattle (or kangaroos); ALSO: Aboriginal idiom for tribal, family or language group

mulga: a low-growing tree; the area in which mulgas grow; ALSO: somewhere remote, the **bush**

Murri: Aboriginal person from Queensland

Ned Kelly had a gun: said when someone is charging a large fee

never never: the far **outback**; SIMILAR IDIOM: *back of Bourke, beyond the black stump*

new chum: any new arrival to Australia

no worries: 'you're welcome'; 'I'm happy to do it'; SIMILAR IDIOM: *no probs*

Noongah/Noongar/Nyunga: Aboriginal person from Western Australia (but the term refers to other groups as well)

not the full quid: intellectually challenged; SIMILAR IDIOM: *a sandwich short of a picnic*

ocker: someone exaggeratedly Australian in speech and behaviour, usually also someone brash and crude

old lag: long-term convict

old man: father; ALSO: (sometimes) husband

on the wallaby: wandering around the countryside looking for work or food; SIMILAR IDIOM: *humping bluey, waltzing Matilda*

outback: dry (often desert-like) plains far inland, away from any towns

pavlova/pav: a meringue-base dessert filled with fruit and cream

perisher: a long journey through the bush without much water

piece o' piss: an easy task

piss off: 'go away' (said rudely); SIMILAR IDIOM: *on ya bike*

pissed off: angry; fed up

pissed: very drunk; SIMILAR IDIOM: *blotto, shickered, off one's face*

pissing down: raining hard

pollie: politician

pom/pommie: British person

quid: one pound (twenty shillings)
Red Centre: the central—largely desert—landmass of Australia, the epithet deriving from the colour of the soil; variously labelled *the dead heart, the back of beyond, the* **never never**
ringer: the fastest shearer in a shed; SIMILAR IDIOM: *gun*
rip: a strong current pulling swimmers out to sea
round: a set of drinks for one's circle of friends
run: a large parcel of land taken over for sheep or cattle grazing
sandgroper: someone from Western Australia
sanga: sandwich
schooner: large glass for beer
selector: someone who competed for a **block** of land offered by the state either for a small fee or free subject to a term for converting it to farming
servo: service station (a petrol pump, usually with a food outlet)
shanty: primitive building often connected with sale of liquor
shed: general storage building; a large outbuilding of tin sheets and timber designed for sheep shearing, sorting and packing wool
sheila: woman; SIMILAR IDIOM: *sort*
shout: to buy a **round** of drinks
skint: broke; without money
skip: Anglo-Celtic Australian person
sky pilot: priest; minister of religion
sparkie: electrician
spit chips: to be angry
sponge: a light fluffy cake (women in the 1950s would compete to produce the best sponge cakes)
spruiker: someone who stands outside a circus show or shop and shouts out the attractions inside to drum up custom
squatter: the (proverbially rich) boss of a large pastoral holding; originally, someone who acquired land simply by going beyond government limits and settling on it
station: a large agricultural holding and/or the homestead from which it is managed

stockman: cattle herder, similar to **drover**
stone the crows!: an expression of surprise or shock
stove: for many years, an iron box with cupboard-like compartments for baking and removable rings on top for boiling pots (fuelled by wood, possibly oil)
Strayan/Strine: mocking term for colloquial Australian English
strewth: an exclamation of surprise; 'gosh!'
swagman/swaggie: a wanderer camping out, carrying a bedroll (*swag*) and a pot for cooking (*billy*)
swimmers: bathing costume; SIMILAR IDIOM: *togs, cozzie*
take the piss: to make a joke; to mock or try to fool someone
tea: (when not referring to the drink) dinner
thongs: rubber sandals
transportation: historically, the shipping of convicts to the colonies
trap: police; SIMILAR IDIOM: *copper, trooper, gunjie, john, fuzz*
truckie: professional truck driver, especially for long-distance haulage
true blue: a loyal, patriotic Australian
tucker: food
ute: short for 'utility vehicle', a driver's cab with a tray behind for small loads (similar to the American pickup truck)
Vegemite: a brand of tar-like yeast-based paste rich in vitamin B, eaten on toast
walkabout: originally Aboriginal English for nomadic travel seeking food or visiting ceremonial sites; in general use, leaving work to go wandering
wog: derogatory term for someone with roots outside of western Europe, usually Italian or Greek
wowser: teetotaller; puritan; killjoy
yard: the 'Australian dream' became a bungalow on a quarter-acre block, with fruit trees and a vegetable garden plus play area at the back (*backyard*) and a smaller flower garden at the front (*frontyard*); in farming, a fenced-off area for sheep or cattle
zac: sixpence
zilch: nothing

Useful Resources

DATABASES

AustLit: The Australian Literature Resource is the main bibliographic source for creative and critical works, with biographical notes on authors, a dedicated section on Aboriginal and Torres Strait Islander writing, and notes for teachers. Some details are not yet filled in, and it does not cover much critical material published overseas. URL: austlit.edu.au.

Informit database includes back issues of many leading Australian journals. URL: search.informit.org.

Project Gutenberg contains over 300 Australian titles: most of the major exploration narratives, and fiction and verse by many key authors up to around 1920. URL: gutenberg.org.

SETIS has digitised many early texts and is available free through Sydney University's digital library. URL: digital.library.sydney.edu.au.

Trove database has digitised hundreds of early newspapers and is made accessible by the National Library of Australia and partner organisations. URL: trove.nla.gov.au.

In India, print material collections of varying extent are to be found in many departments of English. The more comprehensive ones are at the University of Madras, Dhvanyaloka library in Mysore, JNU in Delhi, and the Universities of Bankura and Burdwan in West Bengal.

JOURNALS

Antipodes
Australian Book Review
Australian Literary Studies
Coolabah (open access online)

Cordite Poetry Review (online)
Island
Jacket (poetry; archive accessible online via *Jacket2*)
Journal of the Association for Studies of Australian Literature (*JASAL*) (open access online)
Journal of the European Association for Studies of Australian Literature (*JEASA*) (open access online)
Meanjin
Overland
Quadrant
Southerly
Sydney Review of Books (online)
Westerly

REFERENCE BOOKS

The Macquarie Dictionary is the go-to reference for Australian idiom. Originally edited by Arthur Delbridge and published in 1981, updated several times.

The Australian Dictionary of Biography. Ongoing, first issued by Melbourne University Press in 1966.

Horton, David, ed. *The Encyclopedia of Aboriginal Australia*. 2 volumes. Canberra: Aboriginal Studies Press, 1994.

General Histories

Carter, Paul. *The Road to Botany Bay*. London: Faber, 1987.

Clark, Manning. *A History of Australia*. 6 volumes. Melbourne: Melbourne University Press, 1962–1987.

Keneally, Thomas. *Australians*. 3 volumes. Crows Nest, NSW: Allen & Unwin, 2009–2014.

Macintyre, Stuart. *A Concise History of Australia*. Cambridge: Cambridge University Press, 1999.

Reynolds, Henry. *The Other Side of the Frontier: Aboriginal Resistance to the European Invasion of Australia*. Melbourne: Penguin, 1990.

Cultural and Social Commentary

Blainey, Geoffrey. *The Tyranny of Distance: How Distance Shaped Australia's History*. Melbourne: Sun Books, 1966.

Dale, Leigh. *The Enchantment of English: Professing English Literatures in Australian Universities*. Sydney: Sydney University Press, 2012.

Davis, Mark. *Gangland: Cultural Elites and the New Generationalism*. Sydney: Allen & Unwin, 1999.

Docker, John. *In a Critical Condition: Reading Australian Literature*. Melbourne: Penguin, 1984.

Gammage, Bill. *The Biggest Estate on Earth: How Aborigines Made Australia*. Sydney: Allen & Unwin, 2013.

Hirst, John. *Sense and Nonsense in Australian History*. Melbourne: Black Inc., 2009.

Hodge, Bob and Vijay Mishra. *Dark Side of the Dream: Australian Literature and the Postcolonial Mind*. Sydney: Allen & Unwin, 1991.

Horne, Donald. *The Lucky Country*. Ringwood, VIC: Penguin, 1964.

Magner, Brigid. *Locating Australian Literary Memory*. London: Anthem Press, 2019.

Moore, Nicole. *The Censor's Library: Uncovering the Lost History of Australia's Banned Books*. St Lucia, QLD: University of Queensland Press, 2012.

Niall, Richard. *The Making of the Australian Literary Imagination*. St Lucia, QLD: University of Queensland Press, 2002.

O'Regan, Tom. *Australian National Cinema*. London: Routledge, 1996.

O'Regan, Tom. *Australian Television Culture*. Sydney: Allen & Unwin, 1993.

Pierce, Peter. *The Country of Lost Children: An Australian Anxiety*. Melbourne: Cambridge University Press, 1999.

Perera, Suvendrini. *Australia and the Insular Imagination: Beaches, Borders, Boats and Bodies*. New York: Palgrave Macmillan, 2009.

Phillips, A.A. *The Australian Tradition*. Melbourne: Longman Cheshire, 1958, reissue 1980.

Rickard, John. *Australia: A Cultural History*. London: Longman, 1988.

Serle, Geoffrey. *From the Deserts the Prophets Come: The Creative Spirit in Australia 1788–1972*. Melbourne: Heinemann, 1973, rev. ed. 1987.

Turner, Graham. *National Fictions: Literature, Film and the Construction of Australian Narrative*. Sydney: Allen & Unwin, 1986.

White, Richard. *Inventing Australia: Images and Identity 1688–1980*. Sydney: Allen & Unwin, 1981.

Literary Guides and Critical Overviews

Ashcroft, Bill, Lyn McCredden and Frances Devlin-Glass. *Intimate Horizons: The Postcolonial Sacred in Australian Literature*. Adelaide: ATF Press, 2000.

Bandyopadhyay, Deb N., Paul Brown and Christopher Conti, eds. *Landscape, Place and Culture: Linkages between Australia and India*. Newcastle-on-Tyne: Cambridge Scholars Press, 2011.

Birns, Nicholas and Rebecca McNeer, eds. *A Companion to Australian Literature since 1900*. Rochester, NY: Camden House, 2007.

Birns, Nicholas. *Contemporary Australian Literature: A World Not Yet Dead*. Sydney: Sydney University Press, 2015.

Bode, Katherine. *A World of Fiction: Digital Collections and the Future of Literary History*. Ann Arbor: University of Michigan Press, 2018.

Brewster, Anne. *Reading Aboriginal Women's Autobiography*. Sydney: Sydney University Press, 1996.

Carter, David. *Always Almost Modern: Australian Print Cultures and Modernity*. Melbourne: Australian Scholarly Publishing, 2013.

Dixon, Robert and Brigid Rooney. *Scenes of Reading: Is Australian Literature a World Literature?* Melbourne: Australian Scholarly Publishing, 2013.

Dunstan, David, Deb Narayan Bandyopadhyay and Shibnath Banerjee, eds. *Australian Studies*. Delhi: Worldview Publications, 2010.

Dutton, Geoffrey, ed. *The Literature of Australia*. Ringwood, VIC: Penguin Books, rev. ed. 1976.

Gildersleeve, Jessica, ed. *The Routledge Companion to Australian Literature*. London: Routledge, 2021.

Gunew, Sneja and Kateryna O. Longley, eds. *Striking Chords: Multicultural Literary Interpretations*. Sydney: Allen & Unwin, 1992.

Gunew, Sneja. *Framing Marginality: Multicultural Literary Studies*. Melbourne: Melbourne University Press, 1994.

Hadgraft, Cecil. *Australian Literature: A Critical Account to 1950*. London: Heinemann, 1960.

Healy, J.J. *Literature and the Aborigine in Australia, 1770–1975*. St Lucia, QLD: University of Queensland Press, 2nd ed., 1989.

Hergenhan, Laurie. *Unnatural Lives: Studies in Australian Fiction about the Convicts, from James Tucker to Patrick White*. St Lucia, QLD: University of Queensland Press, 1983.

Hope, Alec Derwent. *Native Companions: Essays and Comments on Australian Literature 1936–1966*. Sydney: Angus & Robertson, 1974.

Huggan, Graham. *Australian Literature: Postcolonialism, Racism, Transnationalism*. Oxford: Oxford University Press, 2007.

Kerr, David and R.K. Dhawan, eds. *Australians and Indian Literature*. New Delhi: Indian Society for Commonwealth Studies, 1991.

Lever, Susan. *Creating Australian Television Drama: A Screenwriting History*. Melbourne: Australian Scholarly Publishing, 2020.

Modjeska, Drusilla. *Exiles at Home: Australian Women Writers 1925–45*. North Ryde, NSW: Angus & Robertson, 1981.

Mudrooroo. *The Indigenous Literature of Australia: Milli Milli Wangka*. Melbourne: Hyland House, 1997.

O'Reilly, Nathanael, ed. *Postcolonial Issues in Australian Writing*. Amherst, NY: Cambria Press, 2010.

Palmer, Vance. *The Legend of the Nineties*. Melbourne: Melbourne University Press, 1954.

Pierce, Peter, ed. *The Oxford Literary Guide to Australia*. Melbourne: Oxford University Press, rev. ed. 1993.

Reid, Ian. *Fiction and the Great Depression: Australia and New Zealand*. Melbourne: Edward Arnold, 1979.

Sarwal, Amit and Reema Sarwal, eds. *Reading Down Under: Australian Literary Studies Reader*. New Delhi: SSS Publications, 2009.

Schaffer, Kay. *Women and the Bush: Forces of Desire in the Australian Cultural Tradition*. Cambridge: Cambridge University Press, 1988.

Sheridan, Susan. *Along the Faultlines: Sex, Race and Nation in Australian Women's Writing 1880s–1930s*. Sydney: Allen & Unwin, 1995.

Shoemaker, Adam. *Black Words, White Page: Aboriginal Literature 1929–1988*. St Lucia, QLD: University of Queensland Press, 1989.

Stephen, Anne. *Modern Times: The Untold Story of Modernism in Australia*. Melbourne: Melbourne University Press, 2008.

Sareen, Santosh, Sheel C. Nuna and Malati Mathur, eds. *Cultural Interfaces*. New Delhi: Indialog, 2004.

Sareen, Santosh, ed. *Australia and India Interconnections: Identity, Representation, Belonging*. New Delhi: Mantra, 2006.

Sareen, Santosh, ed. *Australia and India: Convergences and Divergences*. New Delhi: Mantra, 2010.

Trigg, Stephanie, ed. *Medievalism and the Gothic in Australian Culture*. Melbourne: Melbourne University Press, 2005.

Vanden Driesen, Cynthia, ed. *Austral-Asian Encounters: From Literature and Women's Studies to Politics and Tourism*. New Delhi: Prestige Publications, 2003.

Vanden Driesen, Cynthia and Ian vanden Driesen, eds. *Change, Conflict and Convergence: Austral-Asian Scenarios*. New Delhi: Orient Blackswan, 2011.

Vanden Driesen, Cynthia and Ralph Crane, eds. *Diaspora: The Australasian Experience*. New Delhi: Prestige, 2005.

Van Toorn, Penny. *Writing Never Arrives Naked: Early Aboriginal Cultures of Writing in Australia*. Canberra: Aboriginal Studies Press, 2006.

Webby, Elizabeth, ed. *The Cambridge Companion to Australian Literature*. Cambridge: Cambridge University Press, 2000.

Wilde, William H., Joy Hooton and Barry Andrews, eds. *The Oxford Companion to Australian Literature*. Melbourne: Oxford University Press, 1985.

Wilkes, G.A. *Australian Literature, A Conspectus*. Sydney: Angus & Robertson, 1969.

Literary Histories

Bennett, Bruce and Jennifer Strauss, eds. *The Oxford Literary History of Australia*. Melbourne: Oxford University Press, 1998.

Goodwin, Ken. *A History of Australian Literature*. London: Macmillan, 1986.

Green, H.M. *A History of Australian Literature, Pure and Applied*. 2 volumes. Sydney: Angus & Robertson, 1961.

Hergenhan, Laurie, et al., eds. *The Penguin New Literary History of Australia*. Ringwood, VIC: Penguin, 1988.

Johnston, Grahame. *Annals of Australian Literature*. Melbourne: Oxford University Press, 1970.

Kramer, Leonie, ed. *The Oxford History of Australian Literature*. Melbourne: Oxford University Press, 1981.

Fiction

Blackford, Russell and Van Ikin. *Strange Constellations: A History of Australian Science Fiction*. Westport, CT: Greenwood Press, 1999.

Clancy, Laurie. *A Reader's Guide to Australian Fiction*. Melbourne: Oxford University Press, 1992.

Dixon, Robert. *Writing the Colonial Adventure: Race, Gender and Nation in Anglo-Australian Popular Fiction 1875–1914*. Melbourne: Cambridge University Press, 1995.

Ferrier, Carole, ed. *Gender, Politics and Fiction: Twentieth-Century Australian Women's Novels*. St Lucia, QLD: University of Queensland Press, 1992.

Gelder, Ken and Paul Salzman. *The New Diversity*. Melbourne: McPhee Gribble, 1989.

Gelder, Ken and Paul Salzman. *After the Celebration: Australian Fiction 1989–2007*. Melbourne: Melbourne University Press, 2009.

Howells, Coral Ann, Paul Sharrad and Gerry Turcotte, eds. *The Novel in Australia, Canada, New Zealand, and the South Pacific since 1950*. Oxford: Oxford University Press, 2017.

Knight, Stephen. *Australian Crime Fiction: A 200-Year History*. Jefferson, NC: Macfarland, 2018.

Rooney, Brigid. *Suburban Space, the Novel and Australian Modernity*. London: Anthem Press, 2018.

Wilding, Michael. *Studies in Classic Australian Fiction*. Sydney: Sydney Association for Studies in Society and Culture, 1997.

Williamson, Geordie. *The Burning Library: Our Great Novelists, Lost and Found*. Melbourne: Text Publishing, 2012.

Yu, Ouyang. *Chinese in Australian Fiction, 1888–1988*. Amherst, NY: Cambria Press, 2008.

Drama

Carroll, Dennis. *Australian Contemporary Drama*. Sydney: Currency Press, 1995.

Fitzpatrick, Peter. *After 'The Doll': Australian Drama Since 1955*. Melbourne: Edward Arnold, 1979.

Fotheringham, Richard, ed. *Community Theatre in Australia*. North Ryde, NSW: Methuen, 1987.

Gilbert, Helen. *Sightlines: Race, Gender and Nation in Contemporary Australian Theatre*. Ann Arbor: University of Michigan Press, 1998.

Love, Harold, ed. *The Australian Stage: A Documentary History*. Sydney: New South Wales University Press, 1984.

McCallum, John. *Belonging: Australian Playwrighting in the 20th Century*. Sydney: Currency Press, 2009.

Radic, Leonard. *Contemporary Australian Drama*. Blackheath, NSW: Brandl & Schlesinger, 2006.

Rees, Leslie. *A History of Australian Drama*. 2 volumes. Sydney: Angus & Robertson, 1973, 1987.

Williams, Margaret. *Australia on the Popular Stage 1829–1929*. Melbourne: Oxford University Press, 1983.

Poetry

Buckley, Vincent. *Essays in Poetry, Mainly Australian*. Melbourne: Melbourne University Press, 1957.

Kane, Paul. *Australian Poetry: Romanticism and Negativity*. Cambridge: Cambridge University Press, 1996.

Kirkby, Joan. *The American Model: Influence and Independence in Australian Poetry*. Sydney: Hale & Iremonger, 1982.

Mead, Philip. *Networked Language: Culture and History in Australian Poetry*. Melbourne: Australian Scholarly Publishing, 2008.

McCredden, Lyn and Stephanie Trigg, eds. *The Space of Poetry: Australian Essays on Contemporary Poetics*. Melbourne: Melbourne University Literary and Cultural Studies, vol. 3, 1996.

Page, Geoff. *A Reader's Guide to Contemporary Australian Poetry*. St Lucia, QLD: University of Queensland Press, 1995.

Taylor, Andrew. *Reading Australian Poetry*. St Lucia, QLD: University of Queensland Press, 1987.

Wilde, William. *Australian Poets and Their Work: A Reader's Guide*. Melbourne: Oxford University Press, 1996.

Wright, Judith. *Preoccupations in Australian Poetry*. Melbourne: Oxford University Press, 1965.

Memoir and Autobiography

Bowers, Jack. *Strangers at Home: Place, Belonging and Australian Life Writing*. Amherst, NY: Cambria Press, 2016.

McCooey, David. *Artful Histories: Modern Australian Autobiography*. Cambridge: Cambridge University Press, 1996.

Whitlock, Gillian. *Autographs*. St Lucia, QLD: University of Queensland Press, 1996.

Children's and Young Adult Literature

Lees, Stella and Pam MacIntyre, eds. *The Oxford Companion to Australian Children's Literature*. Melbourne: Oxford University Press, 1993.

Niall, Brenda. *Australia Through the Looking-Glass: Children's Fiction 1830–1980*. Carlton, VIC: Melbourne University Press, 1984.

Saxby, H.M. *A History of Australian Children's Literature 1841–1941*. 2 volumes. Sydney: Wentworth Books, 1969, 1971.

Saxby, Maurice. *The Proof of the Puddin': Australian Children's Literature 1970–1990*. Gosford, NSW: Ashton Scholastic, 1993.

Anthologies

Gilbert, Kevin, ed. *Inside Black Australia*. Melbourne: Penguin, 1988.

Goodwin, Ken and Alan Lawson, eds. *The Macmillan Anthology of Australian Literature*. South Melbourne: Macmillan, 1990.

Jose, Nicholas, et al., eds. *The PEN Anthology of Australian Literature*. Sydney: Macquarie University/Allen & Unwin, 2009. (Also as: *The Literature of Australia*. New York: Norton, 2009.)

Comparative Timeline for Australian Literature

Author's note: Where it is not evident from the titles: P indicates a book of poetry; H, history or life writing; N, novel; S, short stories; D, drama; and Y, literature for young readers. Events from world history and literature are printed in square brackets.

c. 65,000 BCE
First evidence of human habitation in Australia.

c. 42,000 BCE
Mungo Lady and Man ritually interred (discovered in 1968 and 1974, respectively).

c. 18,000 BCE
[Lascaux cave paintings in France.]

c. 9,700 BCE
End of Ice Age; Australia separates from New Guinea, Indonesian islands.

c. 2,500 BCE
[Harappan civilisation.]

200 CE
[Ptolemy posits southern landmass.]

1522
[Magellan, Elcano circumnavigate the globe.]

1556
[Mughal emperor Akbar's reign begins. Second Battle of Panipat.]

1600
[East India Company founded.]

1605
Pedro de Quiros popularises legend of Great South Land.

1606
Luis Vaez de Torres sails past northern Australia; strait named after him.

1616
Dirk Hartog lands on western coast.

1642
Abel Tasman maps part of Tasmania; names it 'Van Diemen's Land'. Two years later, he maps part of northern Australian coast.

Comparative Timeline for Australian Literature

1688
William Dampier, first Englishman to reach Australia; makes unfavourable report of west coast land and Aboriginal people.

1703
A Voyage to New Holland in the Year 1699 published.

1757
[Clive wins Battle of Plassey.]

1770
James Cook lands in Botany Bay; maps the east coast northward; claims the country for Britain.

1776
[US declaration of independence from Britain.]

1788
Captain Arthur Phillip becomes governor of a troop of marines and 700 convicts. The 'First Fleet' settles around Sydney Cove, starting the colonisation of Australia.
La Perouse's French expedition visits Australia.

1789
[French Revolution.]
First play performed in Australia: George Farquhar's *The Recruiting Officer*.
Watkin Tench, *A Narrative of the Expedition to Botany Bay*.

1790
First official punitive expedition against Aboriginal people.

1796
First theatre opens in Australia.

1797
Merino sheep introduced into Australia.

1798
[Wordsworth & Coleridge, *Lyrical Ballads*.]

1799
Pemulwuy leads Aboriginal resistance to settlements around Parramatta and Hawkesbury (1799–1803).

1801
'Ticket of leave' system begins to turn convicts into free settlers. Matthew Flinders circumnavigates Australia. Baudin expedition.

1802
First book published in Australia: *New South Wales General Standing Orders*.

1803
Hobart town established.
First newspaper printed in Australia: *The Sydney Gazette*.

1804
200 Irish convicts rebel.

First locally published poem: 'The Vision of Melancholy'.

1805
Policy to encourage free settler migration.

1808
'Rum Rebellion' against Gov. Bligh by military and landowners.

1810
Gov. Macquarie: civic development, 1810–1821.
Poet laureate Michael Massey Robinson publishes odes in the *Sydney Gazette*.

1813
[Austen, *Pride and Prejudice*.]
Blaxland, Lawson and Wentworth cross the Blue Mountains, see inland plains.

1818
Thomas Wells, *Michael Howe, the Last and Worst of the Bushrangers of Van Diemen's Land*. N

1819
Barron Field, *First Fruits of Australian Poetry*.
The Memoirs of James Hardy Vaux.

1821
First agricultural shows.

1823
W.C. Wentworth wins Cambridge poetry prize, publishes 'Australia'.

1824
Convict settlement at Moreton Bay.
Masters and Servants Act.

1825
Norfolk Island reopens as convict settlement.

1826
First (subscription) library.
First book of verse by Australian-born author: Charles Tompson, *Wild Notes from the Lyre of a Native Minstrel*.

1828
Martial law declared against Aboriginal people of Van Diemen's Land.
Charles Sturt explores Murray River.

1829
Swan colony in Western Australia.
Henry Savery, *The Hermit in Van Diemen's Land*. N

1830
Port Arthur prison established in Van Diemen's Land.
Bushranging Act passed.

1831
First shipload of assisted free settlers.
First book novel published in Australia: Henry Savery, *Quintus Servinton*.

1834
[Balzac, *Le père Goriot*.]
Henry Melville, *The Bushrangers*. D

1835
Batman and Fawkner 'buy' land at Port Phillip Bay.
William Buckley found living with Aboriginal tribesmen.
George Augustus Robinson appointed 'Protector' of Aboriginal people in Van Diemen's Land.
John Dunmore Lang founds the Australian College, Sydney.
R.M. Martin, *History of Australia*.
First play book published in Australia: E.H. Thomas, *The Bandit of the Rhine*.

1836
South Australia founded as non-convict colony.
Thomas Mitchell explores, finds 'Australia Felix'.
Flinders Island Chronicle produced by Aboriginal people.

1837
First overland mail between Sydney and Port Phillip.

1838
German settlers arrive in SA.
Myall Creek massacre. White perpetrators hanged for it.
First novel published in Sydney: Anna Maria Bunn, *The Guardian: A Tale by an Australian*.

1839
Gov. Gipps declares equal rights under law for Aborigines.
Port Darwin named during Darwin's voyage on *The Beagle*.

1840
Transportation of convicts to NSW abolished.
Eyre explores from SA to WA.
First book of verse by a woman published in Australia: Fidelia Hill, *Poems and Recollections of the Past*.

1841
[Longfellow, *The Wreck of the Hesperus*.]
Caroline Chisolm supports female immigrants.
First children's book: Charlotte Barton, *A Mother's Offering to Her Children by a Lady Long Resident in New South Wales*.

1842
Australian Sugar Company founded.
David Burn, *Plays and Fugitive Pieces*.
Henry Parkes, *Stolen Moments*. P

1843
First land sales in Brisbane.
Start of economic depression.
S.P. Hill, *Tarquin the Proud*. D
Charles Rowcroft, *Tales of the Colonies*. N

1844
Sturt fails to find the Inland Sea.
Leichhardt travels from Sydney to Carpentaria.
Edward Geoghegan, *The Currency Lass*. D

1845
[Poe, *The Raven* (and stories).]
First major art exhibition (in Hobart).
Charles Harpur, *Thoughts: A Series of Sonnets*.
Tomas McCombie, *Arabin: Or, the Adventures of a Colonist in New South Wales*. N
James Tucker, *Ralph Rashleigh, or the Life of an Exile*. N
Mary Vidal, *Tales for the Bush*. S

1846
Leichhardt disappears.
First newspapers in Brisbane and Melbourne.
Alexander Harris, *Settlers and Convicts*. N
Charles Rowcroft, *The Bushranger of Van Diemen's Land*. N

1847
First opera composed and staged in Australia (in Melbourne): *Don John of Austria*.
Alexander Harris, *Settlers and Convicts*. N

1848
[Marx, *The Communist Manifesto*.]
Native police company founded.
Iron ore smelted in Mittagong.

1849
First gold found northwest of Melbourne.
Alexander Harris, *The Emigrant Family*. N

1850
Convicts arrive in Swan Colony.
University of Sydney founded.
Australia League formed to promote end of transportation, male suffrage and land reform.

1851
[Melville, *Moby Dick*.]
Victoria proclaimed as separate colony.
Gold found at Ballarat (VIC) and Bathurst (NSW).

1852
[Stowe, *Uncle Tom's Cabin*.]
George Roberston opens bookshop in Melbourne.
John Dunmore Lang, *Freedom and Independence for the Golden Lands of Australia*.

1853
First paddle steamers on Murray River.
Melbourne public library opens.
Charles Harpur, *The Bushrangers, a Play in Five Acts and Other Poems*.

1854
[Thoreau, *Walden*.]

Eureka Stockade insurrection by miners at Ballarat.
R.H. Horne, *Orion*. D
William Howitt, *A Boy's Adventures in the Wilds of Australia*. YN
Catherine Helen Spence, *Clara Morison*. N

1855
NSW and Victoria establish bicameral parliaments.
Restrictions on Chinese immigration.
John Lang, *The Forger's Wife*. N

1856
Male suffrage in SA.
Van Diemen's Land renamed Tasmania.
First May Day march in Melbourne celebrates eight-hour workday.
First critical work: Frederick Sinnett, 'The Fiction Fields of Australia'.

1857
[Flaubert, *Madame Bovary*.]
Caroline Atkinson, *Gertrude the Emigrant*.

1858
Population exceeds one million.
First Australian Rules football match in Melbourne.

1859
Queensland proclaimed separate colony.

Henry Kingsley, *The Recollections of Geoffrey Hamlyn*. N
Caroline Leakey, *The Broad Arrow*. N
Charles Whitehead, *The Spanish Marriage*. D

1860
Burke and Wills expedition supports myths of heroic failure.
Hunter River Coal Miners' Mutual Protective Association starts union culture.
John Robertson's land redistribution reduces squatter estates and creates small-holder 'cockies'.

1861
[Dickens, *Great Expectations*.]
Lambing Flat riots (attacks on Chinese by white miners).
First Melbourne Cup horse race.
First tour by English cricket team.

1862
John McDouall Stuart crosses continent.
Charles Harpur, *A Poet's Home*.
Henry Kendall, *Poems and Songs*.

1863
Northern Territory established under SA jurisdiction.
Ben Hall's bushranging gang at work.

1864
[Mallarmé, *Hérodiade*.]
William Walker, *Australian Literature*.

1865
Charles Harpur, *The Tower of the Dream*. P
C.H. Spence, *Mr Hogarth's Will*. N

1866
G.B. Barton, booklets on NSW writing for Paris Exhibition.
R.H. Horne, *The South Sea Sisters*. D

1867
Queensland gold rushes begin.
Adam Lindsay Gordon, *Sea Spray and Smoke Drift*. P

1868
Convict transportation ceases (last in WA).
Polynesian Labourers' Act controls 'blackbirding' in Queensland.
Christian Brothers (Irish Catholic teaching order) arrive in Melbourne.
Aboriginal cricket team tours England.
Charles Harpur dies.

1869
[Tolstoy, *War and Peace*.]
Free elementary schooling in Queensland.
Henry Kendall, *Leaves from Australian Forests*. P
Marcus Clarke, *Long Odds*. N
Richard Rowe, *The Boy in the Bush*. YN

1870
All British troops leave Australia.
Overland telegraph construction begins.
A.L. Gordon, *Bush Ballads and Galloping Rhymes*.
Marcus Clarke serialises *His Natural Life*. N

1871
Anthony Trollope visits Australia.
'Waif Wander' (Mary Fortune), *The Detective's Album*. N
James Brunton Stephens, *Convict Once*. P

1872
[Whitman, *Leaves of Grass*.]
Australian Natives' Association formed (for patriotic locally-born whites).
J.D. Lang, *Poems Sacred and Secular*.

1873
[Trollope, *Australia and New Zealand* and *Harry Heathcote of Gangoil*. N]
G.G. McCrae, *The Man in the Iron Mask*. P
John Boyle O'Reilly, *Songs from the Southern Seas*. P
Garnet Walch, *Australia Felix*. D

1874
George French Angas, *The Wreck of the Admella*. P
Catherine Martin, *The Explorers*. N

1875
Ada Cambridge, *The Manor House* and *Up the Murray*. N

1876
Irish prisoners escape to America on the *Catalpa*.
Invention of the stump-jump plough extends farming.
William Foster, *The Weirwolf*. D
J.B. Stephens, *A Hundred Pounds*. N

1878
Kelly gang becomes active.
Australian cricket team tours England.
George Rankin, *Windabyne*. N
'Ironbark', *Southerly Busters*. P

1879
[Fitzgerald, *Rubaiyat of Omar Khayyam*.]
[Ibsen, *A Doll's House*.]
Joseph Conrad visits Australia for first time.
First intercolonial trade union congress.
J.B. O'Reilly, *Moondyne*. N

1880
Ned Kelly hanged.
First telephone exchange (Melbourne).
Major drought till 1886.
First issue of *The Bulletin*.
Henry Kendall, *Songs from the Mountains*. P
Rosa Praed, *An Australian Heroine*. N

1881
[James, *The Portrait of a Lady*.]
Population reaches two million.
Women admitted to Melbourne and Sydney universities.
Marcus Clarke dies.
C.H. Spence, *Gathered In*. N

1882
Henry Kendall dies.
Marcus Clarke, *For the Term of His Natural Life*. N
Rolf Boldrewood serialises *Robbery Under Arms*. N

1883
Broken Hill Proprietary Mining company founded.
First regular trains between Sydney and Melbourne.
George Rusden, *History of Australia*.
Cambridge, *The Three Miss Kings* serialised in *Australasian*.

1885
[Zola, *Germinal*.]
[Twain, *The Adventures of Huckleberry Finn*.]
First Australian overseas military expedition (to Sudan).
WA gold rush.
Sydney's Archbishop Moran first Australian cardinal.
Mary Hannay Foott, *Where the Pelican Builds*. P

1886
Australian Antarctic Exploration committee formed.

Australian Association for the Advancement of Science formed.
Amalgamated Shearers' Union formed.
J.F. Archibald edits *The Bulletin* (till 1902).
Francis Adams, *Australian Essays*.
Fergus Hume, *The Mystery of a Hansom Cab*. N

1888
Miners' strikes.
Douglas Sladen publishes three anthologies of Australian verse in London.
Francis Adams, *Songs of the Armies of the Night*. P
Louisa Lawson starts *Dawn: A Journal for Australian Women*.

1889
First meeting of all premiers.
Henry Parkes's Tenterfield oration calls for national unity.
Ernest Giles, *Australia Twice Traversed*. H
Rosa Praed, *The Romance of the Station*. N
'Tasma' (Jessie Couvreur), *Uncle Piper of Piper's Hill*. N

1890
WA granted self-government.
Maritime strike.
Robert Louis Stevenson in Australia.
Rolf Boldrewood, *The Miner's Right*. N
Catherine Martin, *An Australian Girl*. N

1891
Rudyard Kipling in Australia.
Shearers' strike broken by troops.
Ada Cambridge, *The Three Miss Kings*. N
Henry Lawson, 'Freedom on the Wallaby'. P

1892
[Kipling, *Barrack Room Ballads*.]
Gold rushes around Kalgoorlie.
Francis Adams, *Australian Life*. S
'Price Warung', *Tales of the Convict System*. S
William Lane, *The Working Man's Paradise*. N

1893
Fourteen banks fail.
Lane takes colonists to Paraguay.
Simpson Newland, *Paving the Way*. H
Francis Adams, *The Australians*.

1894
SA women gain right to vote and stand for parliament.
Lawrence Hargrave flies in his box kites.
Louis Becke, *By Reef and Palm*. S
Guy Boothby, *In Strange Company*. N
Henry Lawson, *Short Stories in Prose and Verse*.
Ethel Turner, *Seven Little Australians*. YN

1895
Mark Twain in Australia.

Major drought till 1902.
'Waltzing Matilda' first sung
in Queensland.
Angus & Robertson begins
publishing, issues A.B. 'Banjo'
Paterson, *The Man from Snowy
River*. P
First comic tales by Steele Rudd in
the *Bulletin*.
Rosa Praed, *Australian Life*
sketches.

1896
First motion pictures shown
in Australia.
Bulletin 'Red Page' starts.
Henry Lawson, *While the Billy
Boils*. S
John Le Gay Brereton, *The Song of
Brotherhood*. P
K. Langloh Parker, *Australian
Legendary Tales*. S

1897
Barcroft Boake, *Where the Dead
Men Lie*. P
C.J. Brennan, *VXIII Poems*.
Mary Gaunt, *Kirkham's Find*. N
Louise Mack, *Teens*. YN

1898
First referendum on
federation fails.
Exhibition of Heidelberg school
and Sydney Society of Artists
in London.
New South Wales Bookstall
Company founded.
Victor Daley, *At Dawn and Dusk*. P

Will Ogilvie, *Fair Girls and Gray
Horses*. P
H.G. Turner & Alexander
Sutherland, *The Development of
Australian Literature*.

1899
Australian troops sent to Boer War.
Spencer & Gillen's first book on
central Australian anthropology.
Australian Literature Society
founded (Melbourne).
A.G. Stephens publishes
Bookfellow (till 1925).
Ernest Favenc, *My Only Murder*. S
Steele Rudd, *On Our Selection*. S
J.L. Brereton, *Landlopers*. N
Ethel Pedley, *Dot and the
Kangaroo*. YN

1900
British parliament approves
constitution for Commonwealth
of Australia.
Bubonic plague.
Governor brothers kill family and
elude capture.
Rolf Boldrewood, *The Babes in the
Bush*. N
Henry Lawson, *On the Track and
Over the Sliprails*. S

1901
First federal parliament
of Australia.
Immigration Restriction Act.
William Farrar produces wheat
strain suited to Australia.

Frederick Drake-Brockman explores Kimberley region.
Edward Dyson, *The Gold Stealers*. S
Miles Franklin, *My Beautiful Career*. N
Henry Lawson, *Joe Wilson and His Mates*. S
Louise Mack, *Dreams in Flower*. P

1902
[Conrad, *Heart of Darkness*.]
Federal Franchise Act gives vote to women.
Telegraph cables laid to South Africa and Canada.
Prime Minister Barton resigns; Alfred Deakin becomes PM.
Barbara Baynton, *Bush Studies*. S
T.G. Tucker, *The Cultivation of Literature in Australia*.

1903
[Chekhov, *The Cherry Orchard*.]
Bernard O'Dowd, *Dawnward?* P
Joseph Furphy, *Such Is Life*. N
Frank Wilmot, *Some Verses*.

1904
[O. Henry, *The Four Million*.]
Spencer & Gillen, *The Northern Tribes of Central Australia*.

1905
[Japan defeats Russia.]
Herbert Hoover founds mining company (now Conzinc Rio Tinto).
Mrs Aeneas Gunn, *The Little Black Princess*. YN
Paterson, *Old Bush Songs*. P

First critical monograph on an Australian writer: A.G. Stephens, *Victor Daley*.

1906
British New Guinea becomes territory of Australia.
Pacific Phosphate Company enables expansion of farming.
Surf life-saving first organised at Bondi.
First Australian orchestra: Melbourne Symphony.
Miles Franklin moves to US.
Edward Dyson, *Fact'ry 'Ands*. S
Bertram Stevens, *An Anthology of Australian Verse*.
First commercial narrative feature film: *The Story of the Kelly Gang*.

1907
[Synge, *The Playboy of the Western World*.]
Basic wage legislated in Australia.
WA completes 1116-mile rabbit-proof fence.
First issue of *Lone Hand* magazine.
Albert Edmunds, *The Squatter's Daughter*. D
Nathan Spielvogel, *The Cocky Farmer*. S
Walter Murdoch, *The Enemies of Literature* (essay).

1908
Commonwealth Literary Fund established.
Films of *Robbery Under Arms* and *For the Term of His Natural Life* screened.

First Australian wins at Davis Cup and Wimbledon.
William Blocksidge, *Songs o' the South*. P
Mrs Aeneas Gunn, *We of the Never Never*. H
Dorothea Mackellar, 'My Country'. P
Henry Handel Richardson, *Maurice Guest*. N
Paul Wenz, *Diary of a New Chum*. S

1909
Dulcie Deamer, *In the Beginning*. S
Hugh McCrae, *Satyrs and Sunlight*. P
Bertram Stevens (ed), *The Golden Treasury of Australian Verse*.

1910
First Labor government elected.
Catherine Helen Spence dies.
C.E.W. Bean, *On the Wool Track*. H
Mary Grant Bruce, *A Little Bush Maid*. YN
Mary Gilmore, *Marri'd and Other Verses*.
H.H. Richardson, *The Getting of Wisdom*. N

1911
[Russian Revolution.]
Australian Capital Territory established.
Mawson Antarctic expedition.
Louis Stone, *Jonah*. N

1912
[Tagore, *Gitanjali*.]
Commonwealth Bank established.
John Flynn begins mission to central Australia.

Bailey & Duggan, *On Our Selection* (stage version).
Louis Esson, *The Time Is Not Yet Ripe*. D
Bernard O'Dowd, *The Bush*. P

1913
First Australian postage stamp.
C.J. Dennis, *Backblock Ballads*. P
Norman Lindsay, *A Curate in Bohemia*. N

1914
[First World War begins.]
[Yeats, *Responsibilities*.]
Australia takes over German New Guinea. Troops sent to Egypt.
A.H. Adams, *Three Plays for the Australian Stage*.
C.J. Brennan, *Poems 1913*.
Nettie Palmer, *The South Wind*. P

1915
Allied landing at Gallipoli, April 25.
BHP opens steelworks at Newcastle.
C.J. Dennis, *Songs of a Sentimental Bloke*. P
Douglas Mawson, *The Home of the Blizzard*. H
Vance Palmer, *The World of Men*. S
K.S. Prichard, *The Pioneers*. N

1916
Australian troops in France.
Prime Minister 'Billy' Hughes fails to create conscription.
Suppression of coal miners' strike.
Returned Servicemen's League founded.

C.J. Dennis, *The Moods of Ginger Mick*. P

1917
Archbishop Mannix opposes conscription.
Women's Peace Army marches in Melbourne.
Anti-German feeling: towns renamed, some people interned.
'Capel Boake', *Painted Clay*. N
Leon Gellert, *Songs of a Campaign*. P
'Furnley Maurice', *To God, from the Weary Nations*. P
H.H. Richardson, *Australia Felix*. N

1918
[Armistice signed, 11 November.]
Sir John Monash first Australian to command Australian troops.
First direct wireless message, UK to Australia.
Walter Murdoch (ed), *The Oxford Book of Australian Poetry*.
May Gibbs, *Snugglepot and Cuddlepie*. YN
Norman Lindsay, *The Magic Pudding*. YN
C.J. Brennan, *A Chant of Doom*. P
Mary Gilmore, *The Passionate Heart*. P
'Trooper Gerardy', *The Road to Palestine*. P

1919
League of Nations formed; Australia signs as nation, not colony.
Spanish influenza epidemic.
Soldier settlement scheme for small farms.
Waterfront and mining strikes.
Ross and Keith Smith fly from UK to Darwin.
First issue of *Smith's Weekly*.
William Hay, *The Escape of the Notorious Sir William Deans*. N
John Shaw Neilson, *Heart of Spring*. P

1920
[Mansfield, *Bliss and Other Stories*.]
Communist Party of Australia founded.
Australian Country Party founded.
QANTAS begins operations.
Fight against prickly pear infestation.
Francis Adams, *The Australians*. N
Louis Esson, *Dead Timber*. D
Norman Lindsay, *Creative Effort* (essay).
Eustace Boylan, *The Heart of the School*. YN

1921
[Pirandello, *Six Characters in Search of an Author*.]
Edith Cowan first woman in parliament.
'Ginger Meggs' cartoon strip starts.
C.E.W. Bean, *The Story of Anzac*. H
John O'Brien, *Around the Boree Log*. P
Bernard O'Dowd, *Alma Venus!* P
K.S. Prichard, *Black Opal*. N

1922
[T.S. Eliot, *The Waste Land*.]
Empire Settlement Act assists migration of 300,000 British.

Queensland abolishes capital punishment.
Melbourne University Press founded.
State funeral for Henry Lawson.
Louis Esson, *The Battler*. D

1923
[D.H. Lawrence, *Kangaroo*.]
[Shaw, *Pygmalion*.]
[William Carlos Williams, *Spring and All*.]
White Guard militia founded to fight Bolshevism.
Vegemite invented.
First public radio stations in Australia.
Jack Lindsay & Kenneth Slessor, *Poetry in Australia*.
Catherine Martin, *The Incredible Journey*. N
John Shaw Neilson, *Ballad and Lyrical Poems*.
Norman Lindsay's *Vision* journal.

1924
Brown coal fuels first electricity plant in Victoria.
End of longest heatwave.
Mt Isa mines opened.
Molly Skinner & D.H. Lawrence, *The Boy in the Bush*. N
Nettie Palmer, *Modern Australian Literature* (essay).
Kenneth Slessor, *Thief of the Moon*. P

1925
[Dos Passos, *Manhattan Transfer*.]
British youth sponsored to migrate as farm workers.
Margaret Preston, 'The Indigenous Art of Australia' (essay).
Martin Boyd, *Love Gods*. N
Chester Cobb, *Mr Moffatt*. N
H.H. Richardson, *The Way Home*. N
Arthur Jose, *The Australian Encyclopedia*.

1926
Balfour Declaration confers equal standing on dominion states.
Creation of CSIRO for scientific research.
Hoyts Theatres builds 'picture palaces'.
Three-year drought.
Ada Cambridge dies.
Jack McLaren, *My Crowded Solitude*. H
K.S. Prichard, *Working Bullocks*. N
Kenneth Slessor, *Earth Visitors*. P

1927
[Woolf, *To the Lighthouse*.]
Parliament House opens in Canberra.
David Unaipon and others petition for separate Aboriginal state.
Australian Council of Trade Unions formed.
Oombulgurri massacre WA.
R.D. FitzGerald, *The Greater Apollo*. P
John Shaw Neilson, *New Poems*.
K.S. Prichard, *Brumby Innes*. D

1928
Coniston massacre (Queensland).
Royal Flying Doctor Service begins.
Don Bradman stars in English test tour in Australia.
First meeting of the Fellowship of Australian Writers.
First *Bulletin* prize for fiction shared by Prichard's *Coonardoo* and M. Barnard Eldershaw's *A House Is Built*.
Martin Boyd, *The Montforts*. N
Vance Palmer, *The Man Hamilton*. N
Betty Rowland, *The Touch of Silk*. D
Arthur Upfield, *The House of Cain*. N

1929
[New York Stock Exchange crash.]
[Hemingway, *A Farewell to Arms*.]
Great Depression starts in Australia.
Rail line to Alice Springs opens.
Joyce's *Ulysses* (1922) banned in Australia.
M. Barnard Eldershaw, *A House Is Built*. N
Edward Dyson, *The Golden Shanty*. S
Frederick Manning, *The Middle Parts of Fortune*. N
David Unaipon, *Legendary Tales of the Australian Aborigines*.

1930
[Faulkner, *As I Lay Dying*.]
Harold Lasseter dies, leaving behind a legend of a lost reef of gold.
Phar Lap wins the Melbourne Cup.
Doris Fitton founds the Independent Theatre Company in Sydney.
W.K. Hancock, *Australia*. H
H.M. Green, *An Outline of Australian Literature*.
Norman Lindsay, *Redheap*. N
Vance Palmer, *The Passage*. N
H.H. Richardson, *The Fortunes of Richard Mahony*.

1931
[O'Neill, *Mourning Becomes Electra*.]
Isaac Isaacs first Australian governor general.
General Motors Holden formed.
Frank Dalby Davison, *Man Shy*. N
Ion Idriess, *Lasseter's Last Ride*. H
Kenneth Slessor, 'Five Visions of Captain Cook'. P

1932
Unemployment in Australia at thirty per cent.
Australian Broadcasting Commission founded.
Opening of Sydney Harbour Bridge.
'Bodyline' bowling by English test cricketers.
Velia Ercole, *No Escape*. N
Leonard Mann, *Flesh in Armour*. N
Kenneth Slessor, *Cuckooz Contrey*. P

1933
[Hitler comes to power.]

[Lorca, *Bodas de Sangre*.]
F.T. Macartney, *Hard Light*. P
First issue of *Australian Woman's Weekly*.
Frank Clune, *Try Anything Once*. H
Frank Walford, *Twisted Clay*. N
A.B. Paterson, *The Animals that Noah Forgot*. YP
Dorothy Wall, *Blinky Bill*. YN

1934
Egon Kisch defies anti-communist ban and jumps from ship to give anti-fascist lectures.
Australian Travel Association publishes *Walkabout*.
Eleanor Dark, *Prelude to Christopher*. N
Mary Gilmore, *Old Days, Old Ways*. H
J.M. Harcourt, *Upsurge*. N
Brian Penton, *Landtakers*. N
Christina Stead, *Seven Poor Men of Sydney*. N
P.L. Travers, *Mary Poppins*. YN
Frank Wilmot, *Melbourne Odes*. P

1935
Cane toads introduced to control sugarcane pest; become pests.
Fellowship of Australian Writers calls for end to censorship.
Rex Ingamells, *Gumtops*. P
Leonard Mann, *Human Drift*. N
Kylie Tennant, *Tiburon*. N
Patrick White, *The Ploughman and Other Poems*.

1936
[Spanish Civil War.]

[Auden, *Look Stranger!*]
5,000 titles banned in Australia.
Clifford Odets play *Till the Day I Die* banned.
Dymphna Cusack, *Jungfrau*. N
Miles Franklin, *All That Swagger*. N
Jean Devanny, *Sugar Heaven*. N
Sydney Tomholt, *Bleak Dawn*. D
P.R. Stephensen, *Foundations of Culture in Australia* (essay).

1937
Japan invades north China; unions stop iron going to Japan.
Assimilation policy for Aboriginals.
Polio epidemic.
First 'Dad and Dave' radio show (based on Steele Rudd's stories).
Ernestine Hill, *The Great Australian Loneliness*. H
Kenneth Mackenzie, *The Young Desire It*. N
Helen Simpson, *Under Capricorn*. N

1938
[Germany invades Czechoslovakia and Austria.]
[Raja Rao, *Kanthapura*.]
Sesquicentenary of Australian colonisation; Aborigines Progressive Association declares 'Day of Mourning'.
Contemporary Art Society founded.
C.J. Dennis dies.
Aboriginal-run *Abo Call* publishes six issues.
Jindyworobak group founded.
Daisy Bates, *The Passing of the Aborigines*. H

A.P. Elkin, *The Australian Aborigines*.
Eleanor Dark, *Waterway*. N
H. Drake-Brockman, *Men Without Wives*. D
R.D. FitzGerald, *Moonlight Acre*. P
Xavier Herbert, *Capricornia*. N
Rex Ingamells, *Conditional Culture* (essay).
Ronald McCuaig, *Vaudeville*. P
John Shaw Neilson, *Beauty Imposes*. P

1939
[Steinbeck, *The Grapes of Wrath*.]
Britain and Australia declare war on Germany.
Internment of suspect foreigners and 'ethnic' Australians.
H.G. Wells's lecture tour in Australia.
Southerly founded.
Miles Franklin & Dymphna Cusack, *Pioneers on Parade*. D
Hugh McCrae, *Poems*.
Kenneth Slessor, *Five Bells*. P
Patrick White, *Happy Valley*. N

1940
[Quit India campaign.]
[France surrenders. Allied forces shipped out from Dunkirk.]
Britain sends European refugees to Australia on the *Dunera*.
Communist Party banned in Australia.
Commonwealth Literary Fund initiates lecture tours.
Douglas Stewart becomes editor at the *Bulletin*.
First issues of *Meanjin* and *Angry Penguins*.
Martin Boyd, *Nuns in Jeopardy*. N
F.D. Davison, *The Woman at the Mill*. S
Ian Mudie, *Corroboree to the Sun*. P
Christina Stead, *The Man Who Loved Children*. N
Douglas Stewart, *Elegy for an Airman*. P

1941
[Hitler invades Russia.]
[Brecht, *Mother Courage*.]
Japan starts Pacific War. Labor PM Curtin turns to America.
First issue of *Coast to Coast* story anthology.
Flexmore Hudson starts *Poetry* quarterly.
'Banjo' Paterson dies.
Eleanor Dark, *The Timeless Land*. N
Lesbia Harford, *Poems*.
Ernestine Hill, *My Love Must Wait*. N
Tom Inglis Moore, *Emu Parade*. P
Kylie Tennant, *The Battlers*. N
Douglas Stewart, *The Fire on the Snow*. PD

1942
[Singapore surrenders to Japanese forces. Japan bombs Darwin. Battle of Coral Sea won by US.]
Australian POWs in Changi; moved to Thai–Burma railroad.
Australia wins control of Kokoda Trail in New Guinea.
Australian ban on communists lifted.

John Shaw Neilson dies.
Gavin Casey, *It's Harder for Girls*. S
Dymphna Cusack, *Morning Sacrifice*. D
G.L. Dann, *Fountains Beyond*. D
Eve Langley, *The Pea Pickers*. N
Hal Porter, *Short Stories*.
Douglas Stewart, *Ned Kelly*. PD

1943
Enid Lyons and Dorothy Tangney first women in federal parliament.
Louis Esson dies.
Australian New Writing and *Barjai* appear.
Max Harris, *The Vegetative Eye*. P
William Hart-Smith, *Columbus Goes West*. P
Kylie Tennant, *Ride On Stranger*. N

1944
[Tennessee Williams, *The Glass Menagerie*.]
Japanese POWs break out from Cowra Camp.
Unemployment and sickness benefits legislated.
Liberal government formed by Robert Menzies.
Ern Malley poems faked. Max Harris charged with obscenity for publishing them.
Peter Cowan, *Drift*. S
Rosemary Dobson, *In a Convex Mirror*. P
Louis Esson et al., *Six One-Act Plays*.
'Brian James', *First Furrow*. S
Kenneth Slessor, *One Hundred Poems*.

Christina Stead, *For Love Alone*. N

1945
[Germany surrenders. US drops atomic bombs on Japan.]
'Doc' Evatt and Jessie Street help establish the UN.
Curtin dies, replaced by Ben Chifley as Labor prime minister.
Aboriginal stockmen strike in Pilbara.
Howard Florey wins Nobel for work on penicillin.
Australian Book Council founded.
John Blight, *The Old Pianist*. P
Colin Roderick, *The Australian Novel*.
Sidney Baker, *The Australian Language*.

1946
T.A.G. Hungerford and Hal Porter part of occupation forces in Japan.
Trans-Australia Airlines founded.
Three-year drought.
British-assisted immigration resumes.
Children's Book of the Year Award begins.
Henry Handel Richardson dies.
'Capel Boake', *The Twig Is Bent*. N
Martin Boyd, *Lucinda Brayford*. N
Miles Franklin, *My Career Goes Bung*. N
James McAuley, *Under Aldebaran*. P
Douglas Stewart, *The Dosser in Springtime*. P

Alan Marshall, *Tell Us About the Turkey, Jo.* S
Judith Wright, *The Moving Image.* P
H.M. Green, *Modern Australian Poetry.*
Leslie Rees, *Australian Radio Plays.*
F. Dalby Davison, *Dusty.* YN

1947
European immigration programme begins.
Traditional Markets Agreement controls book production and distribution.
Bob and Dolly Dyer start US-style radio quiz show *Pick a Box.*
T.G.H. Strehlow, *Aranda Tradition* (anthropology).
Jon Cleary, *You Can't See Round Corners.* N
M. Barnard Eldershaw, *Tomorrow and Tomorrow.* N
Patrick White, *The Ham Funeral.* D
John Morrison, *Sailors Belong Ships.* S

1948
[F.R. Leavis, *The Great Tradition.*]
Australian citizenship separates from British.
'Doc' Evatt becomes president of UN General Assembly.
Holden enters the market as the national car.
Ethel Anderson, *Indian Tales.* S
Nan Chauncey, *They Found a Cave.* YN
Eleanor Dark, *Storm of Time.* N
Rosemary Dobson, *The Ship of Ice.* P

Sumner Locke Elliott, *Rusty Bugles.* D
Ruth Park, *The Harp in the South.* N
Vance Palmer, *Golconda.* N
Francis Webb, *A Drum for Ben Boyd.* P
Patrick White, *The Aunt's Story.* N

1949
[Mao creates the People's Republic of China.]
[Arthur Miller, *Death of a Salesman.*]
Chifley inaugurates Snowy Mountains hydro scheme.
Robert Menzies becomes prime minister.
Papua New Guinea becomes UN trust territory under Australian control.
Sidney Nolan exhibits his 'Ned Kelly' paintings in Paris.
Gwen Meredith begins *Blue Hills* radio serial.
David Campbell, *Speak with the Sun.* P
R.D. FitzGerald, *Heemskerck Shoals.* P
Ruth Park, *Poor Man's Orange.* N
Roland Robinson, *Language of the Sand.* P
Judith Wright, *Woman to Man.* P
Alan Marshall, *How Beautiful Are Thy Feet.* N
Percival Searle, *Dictionary of Australian Biography.*

1950
[Korean War begins.]
[Neruda, *Canto General.*]

Colombo Plan brings Asian students.
Frank Hardy, *Power Without Glory*. N (Tried for libel next year.)
K.S. Prichard, *Winged Seeds*. N
Nevil Shute, *A Town Like Alice*. N
Ivan Southall, *Meet Simon Black*. YN
Dymphna Cusack, *Three Australian Three-Act Plays*.

1951
ANZUS defence pact signed with US.
Menzies fails to ban Communist Party.
Dymphna Cusack & Florence James, *Come In Spinner*. N
Rex Ingamells, *The Great South Land*. P
Kenneth Mackenzie, *Dead Men Rising*. N

1952
[Frank O'Hara, *A City Winter*.]
Australia joins SEATO.
Britain starts nuclear tests in Australia.
Australasian Book Society and *Realist Writer* founded.
Martin Boyd, *The Cardboard Crown*. N
Ralph de Boissière, *Crown Jewel*. N
R.D. FitzGerald, *Between Two Tides*. P
T.A.G. Hungerford, *The Ridge and the River*. N
Judah Waten, *Alien Son*. N
Francis Webb, *Leichhardt in Theatre*. P

1953
[Elizabeth crowned queen of UK and Commonwealth realms.]
[Beauvoir, *The Second Sex*.]
First volume of story series *The Tracks We Travel*.
Wilfred Burchett, *Their Monstrous War*. H
Eleanor Dark, *No Barrier*. N
Leslie Rees, *Towards an Australian Drama*.

1954
Royal visit to Australia.
First permanent Australian base in Antarctica.
Vladimir Petrov defects.
Australian Association for Cultural Freedom founded.
Australian Elizabethan Theatre Trust founded.
Overland and *Poetry Magazine* begin.
Miles Franklin dies.
Vincent Buckley, *The World's Flesh*. P
Oriel Gray, *The Torrents*. D
Vance Palmer, *The Legend of the Nineties*. H
Chris Wallace-Crabbe, *Light in Darkness*. P

1955
[Beckett, *Waiting for Godot*.]
Democratic Labor Party splits from Labor.
First university course in Australian Literature.

Ray Lawler, *Summer of the Seventeenth Doll*. D
Barry Humphries stages Edna Everage.
Rosemary Dobson, *Child with Cockatoo*. P
A.D. Hope, *The Wandering Islands*. P
Alan Marshall, *I Can Jump Puddles*. H
Darcy Niland, *The Shiralee*. N
Patrick White, *The Tree of Man*. N
Judith Wright, *The Two Fires*. P

1956
[Russia invades Hungary.]
[Suez crisis.]
[Baldwin, *Giovanni's Room*.]
Melbourne Olympics.
Television starts.
Australian troops in Malaya.
Quadrant and *Westerly* begin.
Brian James, *The Bunyip of Barney's Elbow*. S
James McAuley, *A Vision of Ceremony*. P
Vivian Smith, *The Other Meaning*. P
Randolph Stow, *The Haunted Land*. N
Judith Wright (ed), *A Book of Australian Verse*.

1957
[Kerouac, *On the Road*.]
[Frame, *Owls Do Cry*.]
First Miles Franklin Award for fiction. White's *Voss* first winner.
Hugh Atkinson, *The Pink and the Brown*. N

Richard Beynon, *The Shifting Heart*. D
'Nino Culotta', *They're a Weird Mob*. N
Elizabeth Harrower, *Down in the City*. N
Nevil Shute, *On the Beach*. N
Kenneth Slessor, *Poems*.
Morris West, *Children of the Sun*. H
Vincent Buckley, *Essays in Poetry, Mainly Australian*.

1958
[Zukofsky, *Five Statements for Poetry*.]
Liberal–Country Party coalition begins long time in power.
Major drought begins.
National Institute of Dramatic Art opens.
Children's Book Council founded.
Thea Astley, *Girl with a Monkey*. N
Nancy Cato, *All the Rivers Run*. N
Elizabeth Harrower, *The Long Prospect*. N
Christopher Koch, *The Boys in the Island*. N
Hal Porter, *A Handful of Pennies*. N
Randolph Stow, *To the Islands*. N
Russel Ward, *The Australian Legend*. H
A.A. Phillips, *The Australian Tradition*.

1959
[Lowell, *Life Studies*.]
Australia's population reaches ten million.
Vance Palmer dies.

R.D. FitzGerald, *The Wind at Your Door*. P
Oriel Gray, *Burst of Summer*. D
Dorothy Hewett, *Bobbin Up*. N
Peter Kenna, *The Slaughter on St Theresa's Day*. D
Chris Wallace-Crabbe, *The Music of Division*. P
Morris West, *The Devil's Advocate*. N

1960
[Ionesco, *The Rhinoceros*.]
National Library of Australia opens.
First Adelaide Festival of Arts.
Thea Astley, *A Descant for Gossips*. N
Nan Chauncey, *Tangara*. YN
A.D. Hope, *Poems*.
Evan Jones, *Inside the Whale*. P
Alan Seymour, *The One Day of the Year*. D
Douglas Stewart (ed), *Voyager Poems*.
Robin Boyd, *The Australian Ugliness*. H
Bernard Smith, *European Vision and the South Pacific*. H
Cecil Hadgraft, *Australian Literature*.

1961
[Britain begins moving away from colonies to European markets.]
[Neruda, *Selected Poems*.]
The contraceptive pill on sale. Start of gender roles changing.
Bruce Beaver, *Under the Bridge*. P
Vincent Buckley, *Masters in Israel*. P
Mena Calthorpe, *The Dyehouse*. N
L.H. Evers, *The Racketty Street Gang*. YN
Nene Gare, *The Fringe Dwellers*. N
H.M. Green, *History of Australian Literature*.
Hal Porter, *The Tilted Cross*. N
Peter Porter, *Once Bitten, Twice Bitten*. P
Thomas Shapcott, *Time on Fire*. P
Colin Thiele, *The Sun on the Stubble*. H
Patrick White, *Riders in the Chariot*. N

1962
[Cuban missile crisis.]
[Borges, *Labyrinths*.]
[Lessing, *The Golden Notebook*.]
Australian military advisers in Vietnam.
First chair in Australian Literature at Sydney University.
Australian issues of *Texas Quarterly* and *London Magazine*.
Makar poetry magazine begins.
Mary Gilmore dies.
Thea Astley, *The Well Dressed Explorer*. N
David Campbell, *Poems*.
Bruce Dawe, *No Fixed Address*. P
David Martin, *The Young Wife*. N
Hal Porter, *A Bachelor's Children*. S
Criena Rohan, *The Delinquents*. N
Ivan Southall, *Hill's End*. YN
Douglas Stewart, *Rutherford*. P
Patrick White, *The Season at Sarsaparilla*. D

1963
[John F. Kennedy assassinated.]
[Robbe-Grillet, *Pour un nouveau roman*.]
Australian Society of Authors founded.
Penguin Australia starts its own list.
Oz satirical magazine begins.
Australian Literary Studies and *Southern Review* begin.
Jessica Anderson, *An Ordinary Lunacy*. N
John Blight, *A Beachcomber's Diary*. P
Gwen Harwood, *Poems*. P
Shirley Hazzard, *Cliffs of Fall*. S
Sumner Locke Elliott, *Careful, He Might Hear You*. N
Hal Porter, *The Watcher on the Cast-Iron Balcony*. H
Eleanor Spence, *The Green Laurel*. YN
Randolph Stow, *Tourmaline*. N
Colin Thiele, *Storm Boy*. YN
Morris West, *The Shoes of the Fisherman*. N
Judith Wright, *Five Senses*. P
Grahame Johnston, *Australian Literary Criticism*.
Louise Rorabacher (ed), *Two Ways Meet* (migrant writing).

1964
[Fuentes, *The Death of Artemio Cruz*.]
Ballot to conscript national service soldiers begins.
The Beatles tour Australia.
Rupert Murdoch starts the *Australian* newspaper.
Poetry Australia starts.
Hesba Brinsmead, *Pastures of the Blue Crane*. YN
George Johnston, *My Brother Jack*. N
James McAuley, *Captain Quiros*. P
David Rowbotham, *All the Room*. P
Kath Walker, *We Are Going*. P
White, *The Burnt Ones*. S
Donald Horne, *The Lucky Country*. H
Geoffrey Dutton, *The Literature of Australia*.
C.D. Narasimhaiah (ed), *An Introduction to Australian Literature*.

1965
[Plath, *Ariel*.]
[Olson, *Human Universe and Other Essays*.]
Australian troops in Vietnam.
Sun Books founded.
Lady Chatterley's Lover and *Lolita* unbanned.
First issue of the *Journal of Commonwealth Literature*.
Mena Abdulla, *Time of the Peacock*. S
Peter Cowan, *The Empty Street*. S
Bruce Dawe, *A Need of Similar Name*. P
R.D. FitzGerald, *Forty Years Poems*.
Colin Johnson, *Wild Cat Falling*. N
Thomas Keneally, *The Fear*. N
Christopher Koch, *Across the Sea Wall*. N
Les Murray & Geoffrey Lehmann, *The Ilex Tree*. P

Ivan Southall, *Ash Road*. YN
Randolph Stow, *The Merry-Go-Round in the Sea*. N
Patrick White, *Four Plays*.

1966
[Pynchon, *The Crying of Lot 49*.]
[Capote, *In Cold Blood*.]
Prime Minister Menzies retires.
Harold Holt goes 'All the way with LBJ'.
Beginnings of mining boom.
Gurindji walk-off at Wave Hill station.
Japan becomes Australia's leading trade partner.
Decimal currency introduced.
Jane Street Theatre opens.
Vincent Buckley, *Arcady and Other Places*. P
Elizabeth Harrower, *The Watchtower*. N
A.D. Hope, *Collected Poems*.
Morris Lurie, *Rapaport*. N
Peter Mathers, *Trap*. N
Kath Walker, *The Dawn Is at Hand*. P
Patrick White, *The Solid Mandala*. N
Geoffrey Blainey, *The Tyranny of Distance*. H

1967
First Australian satellite launched from Woomera.
Last hanging in Australia.
Referendum gives citizenship and vote to Aboriginal people.
La Mama theatre founded.
Five Islands Press for poetry founded.

Bruce Beaver, *Open at Random*. P
Shirley Hazzard, *People in Glass Houses*. S
Jack Hibberd, *White with Wire Wheels*. D
Thomas Keneally, *Bring Larks and Heroes*. N
Joan Lindsay, *Picnic at Hanging Rock*. N
Roland Robinson, *Grendel*. P
Eric Rolls, *Sheaf Tosser*. P
Vivian Smith, *An Island South*. P
Chris Wallace-Crabbe, *The Rebel General*. P

1968
[Barthes, 'The Death of the Author'.]
Discovery of Mungo Lady pushes back known date of human occupation of Australia.
Australia Council for the Arts founded.
Sydney Theatre Company starts.
Alex Buzo, *Norm and Ahmed*. D
David Campbell, *Collected Poems*.
Kevin Gilbert, *The Cherry Pickers*. D
David Ireland, *The Chantic Bird*. N
Tom Keneally, *Three Cheers for the Paraclete*. N
Geoffrey Lehmann, *A Voyage of Lions*. P
R.A. Simpson, *After the Assassination*. P
Patricia Wrightson, *I Own the Racecourse!* YN

1969
Malaysian race riots spark migration to Australia.

Equal pay for women legislated.
Norman Lindsay dies.
K.S. Prichard dies.
Bruce Beaver, *Letters to Live Poets*. P
Alex Buzo, *Rooted*. D
Bruce Dawe, *Beyond the Subdivisions*. P
Jack Hibberd, *Dimboola*. D
A.D. Hope, *New Poems*.
George Johnston, *Clean Straw for Nothing*. N
Frank Moorhouse, *Futility and Other Animals*. S
Les Murray, *The Weatherboard Cathedral*. P
Francis Webb, *Collected Poems*.

1970
[García Márquez, *A Hundred Years of Solitude* (English tr).]
[Foucault, *The Order of Things* (English tr).]
[Vietnam moratorium marches.]
Voting age lowered to 18 in NSW and WA.
Australian Film Development Corporation founded.
Indecency trial of *Portnoy's Complaint*.
Germaine Greer, *The Female Eunuch*.
Poetry Magazine renamed *New Poetry*.
UQP starts literary list.
Robert Adamson, *Canticles on the Skin*. P
Michael Boddy & Bob Ellis, *The Legend of King O'Malley*. D
Jack Davis, *The First Born*. P
A.D. Hope, *Dunciad Minor*. P
David Malouf, *Bicycle*. P
Hal Porter, *Mr Butterfry*. S
John Romeril, *Chicago, Chicago*. D
Dal Stivens, *A Horse of Air*. N
David Williamson, *The Coming of Stork*. D
Patrick White, *The Vivisector*. N

1971
Jack Mundey starts 'green bans' on urban development.
Kenneth Slessor dies.
Currency Press founded.
Bruce Dawe, *Condolences of the Season*. P
J.S. Harry, *the deer under the skin*. P
Dorothy Hewett, *The Chapel Perilous*. D
David Ireland, *The Unknown Industrial Prisoner*. N
Tom Keneally, *A Dutiful Daughter*. N
James McAuley, *Collected Poems*.
Jim McNeill, *The Chocolate Frog*. D
David Williamson, *The Removalists* and *Don's Party*. D

1972
[Nixon visits China.]
Gough Whitlam elected Labor PM.
Australian troops withdrawn from Vietnam.
Aboriginal 'tent embassy' in Canberra.
Women's Electoral Lobby founded.
National Black Theatre founded.
Refractory Girl and *Tabloid Story* begin.

First performance of Prichard's
1927 *Brumby Innes*.
Michael Dransfield, *Drug Poems*.
Jack Hibberd, *A Stretch of the
Imagination*. D
Tom Keneally, *The Chant of Jimmie
Blacksmith*. N
Peter Mathers, *The Wort Papers*. N
Rhyll McMaster, *The Brineshrimp*. P
Frank Moorhouse, *The Americans,
Baby*. S
Les Murray, *Poems Against
Economics*.
Richard Tipping, *Soft Riots*. P
John Tranter, *Red Movie*. P
Michael Wilding, *Aspects of the
Dying Process*. SN

1973
[US implicated in overthrow of
Allende in Chile.]
[Britain joins EU.]
Sydney Opera House opens.
Whitlam visits China.
End of White Australia Policy
legislated.
Australian Film and Television
School established.
First National Playwrights'
Conference.
Patrick White wins Nobel Prize.
Literature Board set up under the
Australia Council.
National Book Council established.
Francis Webb dies.
Pino Bosi, *The Checkmate and
Other Stories*.
Rae Desmond Jones, *Orpheus with
a Tuba*. P

Barbara Hanrahan, *The Scent of
Eucalyptus*. HN
Peter Kenna, *A Hard God*. D
Patrick White, *The Eye of the
Storm*. N
Patricia Wrightson, *The Nargun
and the Stars*. YN

1974
'Advance Australia Fair' replaces
'God Save the Queen'.
Cyclone Tracey destroys Darwin.
Free tertiary education.
Public Lending Right pays authors
for library use.
Wild & Woolley publisher founded.
National Book Council and the *Age*
create prizes.
Patrick White Award established.
Alex Buzo, *Coralie Landsdowne
Says No*. D
Peter Carey, *The Fat Man in
History*. S
Peter Kocan, *Ceremony for the
Lost*. P
Jennifer Maiden, *Tactics*. P
Frank Moorhouse, *The Electrical
Experience*. S
Gerald Murnane, *Tamarisk Row*. N
Les Murray, *Lunch and Counter
Lunch*. P
John Romeril, *The Floating World*. D
Vicki Viidikas, *Wrappings*. S

1975
[Indonesia invades East Timor.]
Saigon falls; Vietnamese migrants
start arriving in Australia.
Papua New Guinea becomes
independent from Australia.

Australian honours replace British ones.
Governor general ousts Whitlam government.
Homosexuality decriminalised in South Australia.
Hecate: A Women's Interdisciplinary Journal begins.
McPhee Gribble publisher founded.
Jessica Anderson, *The Commandant*. N
Murray Bail, *Contemporary Portraits*. S
Ron Blair, *The Christian Brothers*. D
Bruce Beaver, *Odes and Days*. P
Xavier Herbert, *Poor Fellow, My Country*. N
A.D. Hope, *A Late Picking*. P
Kate Jennings, *Come to Me My Melancholy Baby*. P
David Malouf, *Johnno*. N
Bob Merritt, *The Cake Man*. D
Dorothy Porter, *Little Hoodlum*. P
John Tranter, *The Alphabet Murders*. P
B. Wongar, *The Trackers*. N
Kate Jennings (ed), *Mother, I'm Rooted*.
Anne Summers, *Damned Whores and God's Police*.

1976
[Spivak's English translation of Derrida's *Of Grammatology*.]
Pastor Doug Nicholls becomes first Aboriginal governor (SA).
End of Traditional Markets Agreement.
Fremantle Arts Centre Press founded.
Playbox Theatre founded.
Scribe Publications established.
Vincent Buckley, *The Golden Builders*. P
Gerry Bostock, *Here Comes the Nigger*. D
Alex Buzo, *Martello Towers*. D
Joanne Burns, *Adrenalin Flicknife*. P
Robert Drewe, *The Savage Crows*. N
John Forbes, *Tropical Skiing*. P
David Ireland, *The Glass Canoe*. N
Elizabeth Jolley, *The Five Acre Virgin*. S
Gerald Murnane, *A Lifetime on Clouds*. N
Les Murray, *The Vernacular Republic*. P
Mark O'Connor, *Reef Poems*.
Steve Spears, *The Elocution of Benjamin Franklin*. D
Patrick White, *A Fringe of Leaves*. N
Judith Wright, *Fourth Quarter*. P

1977
[Showalter, *A Literature of Their Own*.]
Civil rights attacked in Queensland.
Kerry Packer starts World Series cricket.
SBS founded for multicultural broadcasting.
Association for the Study of Australian Literature founded.
Australian Literary Studies begins.
Hale & Iremonger publishing established.
R.D. FitzGerald, *Product: Later Verses*.

Kevin Hart, *Nebuchadnezzar*. P
Helen Garner, *Monkey Grip*. N
Barbara Hanrahan, *The Albatross Muff*. N
Vasso Kalamaras, *Other Earth*. S
Colleen McCullough, *The Thorn Birds*. N
Louis Nowra, *Inner Voices*. D
Ruth Park, *Swords, Crowns and Rings*. N
Roger Pulvers, *Yamashita*. D
Eleanor Spence, *A Candle for Saint Anthony*. YN
Brian Kiernan (ed), *The Most Beautiful Lies*. S
Inprint short story magazine starts.

1978
[Said, *Orientalism*.]
First wave of 'boat people' seeking asylum.
First Gay and Lesbian Mardi Gras parade.
Mattoid poetry magazine starts.
Australian Book Review restarts.
Jessica Anderson, *Tirra Lirra by the River*. N
Alex Buzo, *Makassar Reef*. D
Monica Clare, *Karobran*. N
Bruce Dawe, *Sometimes Gladness*. P
Kevin Gilbert, *People Are Legends*. P
C.J. Koch, *The Year of Living Dangerously*. N
Geoffrey Lehmann, *Ross's Poems*.
David Malouf, *An Imaginary Life*. N
Les Murray, *Ethnic Radio*. P
Louis Nowra, *Visions*. D
'π.o.', *Panash*. P

John Tranter, *Crying in Early Infancy*. P
Patrick White, *Big Toys*. D
B. Wongar, *The Track to Bralgu*. S

1979
[Seamus Heaney, *Field Work*.]
First NSW Premier's Literary Awards.
Island magazine begins.
Glenda Adams, *The Hottest Night of the Century*. S
Thea Astley, *Hunting the Wild Pineapple*. S
Gabrielle Carey & Kathy Lette, *Puberty Blues*. H
Peter Carey, *War Crimes*. S
Jack Davis, *Kullark*. D
Dorothy Hewett, *The Man from Mukinupin*. D
David Ireland, *A Woman of the Future*. N
Randolph Stow, *Visitants*. N
Chris Wallace-Crabbe, *The Emotions Are Not Skilled Workers*. P
Patrick White, *The Twyborn Affair*. N
David Williamson, *Travelling North*. D
John Tranter (ed), *The New Australian Poetry*.

1980
[Anti-Apartheid protests.]
Noonkanbah protest at mining threat to sacred sites.
Era of publishing mergers.

First Vogel Literary Award for first fiction.
Murray Bail, *Homesickness*. N
Pam Brown, *Country and Eastern*. P
Peter Corris, *The Dying Trade*. N
Beverley Farmer, *Alone*. N
Albert Facey, *A Fortunate Life*. H
Helen Garner, *Honour & Other People's Children*. S
Shirley Hazzard, *The Transit of Venus*. N
Clive James, *Unreliable Memoirs*.
Elizabeth Jolley, *Palomino*. N
Les Murray, *The Boys Who Stole the Funeral*. PN
Ruth Park, *Playing Beatie Bow*. YN

1981
[Rushdie, *Midnight's Children*.]
First edition of *The Macquarie Dictionary* published.
Scripsi magazine starts.
The Oxford History of Australian Literature published.
Peter Carey, *Bliss*. N
Blanche D'Alpuget, *Turtle Beach*. N
A.B. Facey, *A Fortunate Life*. H
Gwen Harwood, *The Lion's Bride*. P
Angelo Loukakis, *For the Patriarch*. S
Eric Rolls, *A Million Wild Acres*. H
Archie Weller, *Day of the Dog*. N
Patrick White, *Flaws in the Glass: A Self Portrait*. H
Drusilla Modjeska, *Exiles at Home: Australian Women Writers, 1925–1945*.
Henry Reynolds, *The Other Side of the Frontier*. H

1982
Aboriginal people at Hermannsburg gain freehold title.
National Gallery of Australia opens.
Australian Short Stories series begins.
Australasian Drama Studies begins.
Booker Prize for Tom Keneally's *Schindler's Ark*.
Thea Astley, *An Item from the Late News*. N
Jack Davis, *The Dreamers*. D
Lionel Fogarty, *YoogumYoogum*. P
Peter Goldsworthy, *Readings from Ecclesiastes*. P
Jannette Turner Hospital, *The Ivory Swing*. N
Victor Kelleher, *The Master of the Grove*. YN
Tess Lyssiotis, *I'll Go to Australia and Wear a Hat*. D
Olga Masters, *The Home Girls*. S
Gerald Murnane, *The Plains*. N
Les Murray, *The Vernacular Republic*. P
Gerard Windsor, *The Harlots Enter First*. S
Fay Zwicky, *Kaddish*. P

1983
Bob Hawke becomes PM. Creates 'accord' for labour relations.
Australia wins America's Cup.
Economic boom and scandals.
First internet communications.
Australian Journal of Cultural Studies begins.
Vincent Buckley, *Cutting Green Hay*. H
Brian Castro, *Birds of Passage*. N

Beverley Farmer, *Milk*. S
David Foster, *Plumbum*. N
Mem Fox, *Possum Magic*. YN
Colin Johnson, *Doctor Wooreddy's Prescription for Enduring the End of the World*. N
Vasso Kalamaras, *The Bread Trap*. D
Antigone Kefala, *The Island*. N
Robin Klein, *People Might Hear You*. YN
Les Murray, *The People's Otherworld*. P
Stephen Sewell, *The Blind Giant Is Dancing*. D
Dimitris Tsaloumas, *The Observatory*. P
Patrick White, *Signal Driver*. D

1984
Decade of internationalising trade.
Outrider founded for multicultural writing.
Hal Porter and Xavier Herbert die.
Pam Brown, *Selected Poems*.
Rosa Cappiello, *Oh Lucky Country*. N
Helen Garner, *The Children's Bach*. S
Robert Gray, *The Skylight*. P
Kate Grenville, *Bearded Ladies*. S
Eva Johnson, *Tjinderella*. D
Elizabeth Jolley, *Milk and Honey*. N
Daniel Keene, *Cho Cho San*. D
Antigone Kefala, *The Island*. N
Amanda Lohrey, *The Morality of Gentlemen*. N
Tess Lyssiotis, *Hotel Bonegilla*. D
David Malouf, *Harland's Half Acre*. N
Olga Masters, *Loving Daughters*. N
Gig Ryan, *Manners of an Astronaut*. P

Randolph Stow, *The Suburbs of Hell*. N
Tim Winton, *Shallows*. N

1985
[France sinks *Greenpeace Warrior* in NZ.]
[Don DeLillo *White Noise*.]
First Spoleto Festival in Melbourne.
First Victorian Premier's Literary Awards.
Eleanor Dark dies.
Douglas Stewart dies.
Adam Aitken, *Letter to Marco Polo*. P
Janis Balodis, *Too Young for Ghosts*. D
Marion Campbell, *Lines of Flight*. N
Peter Carey, *Illywhacker*. N
Jack Davis, *No Sugar*. D
Ee Tiang Hong, *Tranquerah*. P
Helen Garner, *Postcards from Surfers*. S
Kate Grenville, *Lilian's Story*. N
Kate Llewellyn, *Trader Kate and the Elephants*. P
Ernest Macintyre, *Let's Give Them Curry*. D
David Malouf, *Antipodes*. S
Olga Masters, *A Long Time Dying*. S
Jan McKemmish, *A Gap in the Records*. N
Louis Nowra, *The Golden Age*. D
Peter Skrzynecki (ed), *Joseph's Coat: An Anthology of Multicultural Writing*.
Judith Wright, *Phantom Dwelling*. P

1986
Australian courts are delinked from UK.

American Association for Australian Literary Studies founded.
Diane Fahey, *Voices from the Honeycomb*. P
Patricia Cornelius, *Lily and May*. D
Michael Gow, *Away*. D
Robert Gray, *Selected Poems*.
Elizabeth Jolley, *The Well*. N
Gillian Rubinstein, *Space Demons*. YN
Suzanne Spunner, *Running Up a Dress*. D
Alan Wearne, *The Nightmarkets*. P
Patrick White, *The Memoirs of Many in One*. N
Tim Winton, *That Eye, the Sky*. N
Susan Hampton & Kate Llewellyn (eds), *The Penguin Book of Australian Women Poets*.

1987
[US stock market crashes.]
[Deleuze & Guattari, *A Thousand Plateaus*.]
First Black playwrights conference.
Fitzgerald Inquiry into Queensland corruption.
'Black Deaths in Custody' Royal Commission.
Antipodes (US Australian literary journal) begins.
Manning Clark completes six-volume history.
R.D. FitzGerald dies.
Thea Astley, *It's Raining in Mango*. SN
Bruce Beaver, *Headlands*. P
Judith Beveridge, *The Domesticity of Giraffes*. P
Alma De Groen, *The Rivers of China*. D
Laurie Duggan, *The Ash Range*. P
Dorothy Hewett, *Alice in Wormland*. P
Tom Keneally, *The Playmaker*. N
Brian Matthews, *Louisa*. H
Sally Morgan, *My Place*. N
George Turner, *The Sea and Summer*. N
David Williamson, *Emerald City*. D
Eric Willmot, *Pemulwuy*. N
Paul Carter, *The Road to Botany Bay*. H
Robert Hughes, *The Fatal Shore*. H

1988
Queen Elizabeth opens new Parliament House.
Burnum Burnum claims UK for Aboriginal peoples.
World Expo in Brisbane.
Bicentennial celebrations and protests.
Imparja TV established.
Kylie Tennant dies.
Peter Carey wins Booker for *Oscar and Lucinda*.
The Australian National Dictionary published.
The Penguin New Literary History of Australia published.
Jack Davis, *Barungin* (D) and *John Pat and Other Poems*.
Marele Day, *The Life and Crimes of Harry Lavender*. N
Diane Fahey, *Metamorphoses*. P
John Forbes, *The Stunned Mullet and Other Poems*.

Kate Grenville, *Joan Makes History*. S
Rodney Hall, *Captivity Captive*. N
Gwen Harwood, *Bone Scan*. P
Janette Turner Hospital, *Charades*. N
Eva Johnson, *Murras*. D
Ruby Langford, *Don't Take Your Love to Town*. H
Mudrooroo, *Dalwurra, the Black Bittern*. P
Bruce Pascoe, *Fox*. N
Kevin Gilbert (ed), *Inside Black Australia*. P

1989
[Fall of Berlin Wall.]
[Ashcroft, Griffiths & Tiffin, *The Empire Writes Back*.]
Tiananmen Square massacre prompts acceptance of Chinese migrants.
Restructure of higher education with new fees.
David Unaipon Award for new Aboriginal writers.
Robert Adamson, *The Clean Dark*.
Bryce Courtenay, *The Power of One*. N
Robert Drewe, *The Bay of Contented Men*. S
Nick Enright, *Daylight Saving*. D
Mary Fallon, *Working Hot*. N
Tom Flood, *Oceana Fine*.
John Forbes, *Thin Ice*. P
Peter Goldsworthy, *Maestro*. N
Geoff Goodfellow, *Bow Tie and Tails*. P
Kerry Greenwood, *Cocaine Blues*. N

Elizabeth Jolley, *My Father's Moon*. N
John Kinsella, *Night Parrots*. P
Jill Ker Conway, *The Road from Corain*. H
Kate Llewellyn, *Honey: Selected Poems*.
Alex Miller, *The Tivington Nott*. N
Bill Neidjie, *A Story About Feeling*. PS
'π.o.', *Fitzroy Poems*.
Dorothy Porter, *Driving Too Fast*. P
Philip Salom, *Barbecue of the Primitives*. P
Ania Walwicz, *Boat*. P
Sue Woolfe, *Painted Woman*. N
Ken Gelder & Paul Salzman, *The New Diversity: Australian Fiction 1970–1988*.
Adam Shoemaker, *Black Words, White Page*.

1990
[A.S. Byatt, *Possession*.]
Australian military in first Gulf War.
Deregulation of airline industry.
First woman premier (WA).
Joan Sutherland's farewell performance in Sydney Opera House.
Melbourne declared world's 'most livable city'.
Text Publishing founded.
National Festival of Australian Theatre begins.
David Brooks, *Sheep and the Diva*. S
Isobel Carmody, *The Farseekers*. YN
Jimmy Chi, *Bran Nue Day*. D
Gary Crew, *Strange Objects*, YN
Barry Dickins, *Strange English*. D

Graeme Dixon, *Holocaust Island*. P
Marion Halligan, *Spider Cup*. N
Alex Harding, *Blood and Honour*. D
Janette Turner Hospital, *Isobars*. S
Tess Lyssiotis, *The Forty Lounge Café*. D
Jennifer Maiden, *Play with Knives*. N
David Malouf, *The Great World*. N
Drusilla Modjeska, *Poppy*. H
Mudrooroo, *Writing from the Fringe*.
Gerald Murnane, *Velvet Waters*. S
Mark O'Connor, *Firestick Farming*. P
Hannie Rayson, *Hotel Sorrento*. D
Wendy Richardson, *Lights Out, Nellie Martin*. D
Gig Ryan, *Excavation*. P
Chris Wallace-Crabb, *For Crying Out Loud*. P
Sam Watson, *The Kadaitcha Sung*. N

1991
Paul Keating becomes prime minister.
Australian Republican Movement begins.
Asbestos products banned.
Peter Carey, *The Tax Inspector*. N
Brian Castro, *Double Wolf*. N
Alma De Groen, *The Girl Who Saw Everything*. D
Rosemary Dobson, *Collected Poems*.
Yasmine Gooneratne, *A Change of Skies*. N
Di Morrissey, *Heart of the Dreaming*. N
Mudrooroo, *Masters of the Ghost Dreaming*. N

Ron Pretty, *Bald Hill with Gliders*. P
Randolph Stow, *Visitants*. N
Katherine Thompson, *Diving for Pearls*. D
Joy Williams, *Blackberry's Child*. P
David Williamson, *Money and Friends*. D
Tim Winton, *Cloudstreet*. N

1992
High Court admits Mabo land rights claim.
Keating delivers 'Redfern Speech'.
Ken Bolton, *Selected Poems*.
Greg Egan, *Quarantine*. N
Lionel Fogarty, *Kudjela/Ngutji*. P
Alan Gould, *Formerlight: Selected Poems*.
Michael Gurr, *Sex Diary of an Infidel*. D
Dorothy Hewett, *Collected Plays*.
Janette Turner Hospital, *The Last Magician*. N
Gail Jones, *House of Breathing*. S
Jill Jones, *The Mask and Jagged Star*. P
Antigone Kefala, *New and Selected Poems*.
Melina Marchetta, *Looking for Alibrandi*. YN
Andrew McGahan, *Praise*. N
Alex Miller, *The Ancestor Game*. N
Dorothy Porter, *Akhenaten*. P
Louis Nowra, *Così*. D
Beth Yahp, *The Crocodile Fury*. N

1993
Singer Galarrwuy Yunupingu first Aboriginal voted Australian of the Year.

Greens party enters politics.
Native Title Act passed.
Kath Walker/Oodgeroo dies.
Christopher Cyrill, *The Ganges and Its Tributaries*. N
Peter Goldsworthy, *Little Deaths*. S
David Malouf, *Remembering Babylon*. N
John Marsden, *Tomorrow When the War Began*. YN
Philip McLaren, *Sweet Water, Stolen Land*. N
Joanna Murray-Smith, *Love Child*. D
Louis Nowra, *Radiance*. D
Emily Rodda, *Rowan of Rin*. YN

1994
[Nelson Mandela becomes leader of post-Apartheid South Africa.]
The Wollemi pine fossil tree found alive.
Peter Boyle, *Coming Home from the World*. P
John Muk Muk Burke, *Bridge of Triangles*. N
'Helen Demidenko', *The Hand that Signed the Paper*. N
Richard Flanagan, *Death of a River Guide*. N
Kevin Gilbert, *Black from the Edge*. P
Adib Khan, *Seasonal Adjustments*. N
Simone Lazaroo, *The World Waiting to Be Made*. N
Tobsha Learner, *The Gun in History*. D
Rhyll McMaster, *Flying the Coop*. P
Dorothy Porter, *The Monkey's Mask*. PN

Sneja Gunew, *Framing Marginality: Multicultural Literary Studies*.

1995
Mary McKillop becomes Australia's first Catholic saint.
General privatisation of government services; Telecom becomes Telstra.
Gwen Harwood dies.
Helen Garner, *The First Stone*. H
Nick Enright, *Blackrock*. D
J.S. Harry, *Selected Poems*.
Linda Jaivin, *Eat Me*. N
Rae Desmond Jones, *Selected Poems*.
John Kinsella, *The Silo*. P
Philip McLaren, *Scream Black Murder*. N
Peter Minter, *Rhythm in a Dorsal Fin*. P
Eileen Moreton, *The Callused Stick of Wanting*. P
Joanna Murray-Smith, *Honour*. D
Garth Nix, *Sabriel*. YN
Christos Tsiolkas, *Loaded*. N
David Williamson, *Dead White Males*. D
Ouyang Yu, *Moon Over Melbourne*. P

1996
John Howard leads a decade of Liberal–National government.
Gunman kills tourists at Port Arthur; prompts gun control laws.
Malouf wins IMPAC Dublin award for *Remembering Babylon*.
Les Murray wins T.S. Eliot Prize for *Subhuman Redneck Poems*.

First issue of *HEAT* magazine.
Thea Astley, *The Multiple Effects of Rain Shadow*. N
Lisa Bellear, *Dreaming in Urban Areas*. P
Joanne Burns, *penelope's knees*. P
David Foster, *The Glade within the Grove*. N
Julie Janson, *Black Mary*. D
Jenny Kemp, *The Black Sequin Dress*. D
Adib Khan, *Solitude of Illusions*. N
Tobsha Learner, *Quiver: A Book of Erotic Tales*. S
Mailman & Enoch, *The Seven Stages of Grieving*. D
Doris Pilkington Garimara, *Follow the Rabbit-Proof Fence*. H
Kerry Reed-Gilbert, *Black Woman, Black Life*. P
Sue Woolfe, *Leaning Towards Infinity*. N

1997
[Roy, *The God of Small Things*.]
BHP closes Newcastle steelworks.
Pauline Hanson founds One Nation party.
Australia signs Kyoto environment protocol.
Bringing Them Home report on the Stolen Generation released; Reconciliation movement begins.
Cordite Poetry Review begins.
Peter Carey, *Jack Maggs*. N
Timothy Conigrave, *Like Stars in My Hands*. D
Richard Flanagan, *The Sound of One Hand Clapping*. N
Geoffrey Lehmann, *Collected Poems*.
Melissa Lucashenko, *Steam Pigs*. N
Leah Purcell & Scott Rankin, *Box the Pony*. D
Alexis Wright, *Plains of Promise*. N

1998
Waterfront conflict. General attack on unions.
John Forbes dies.
Geoffrey Dutton dies.
Murray Bail, *Eucalyptus*. N
Jennifer Compton, *The Big Picture*. D
Bin Duy, *The Monkey Mother*. D
Marion Halligan, *The Golden Dress*. N
John Forbes, *Damaged Glamour*. P
Jane Harrison, *Stolen*. D
Anita Heiss, *Token Koori*. P
Daniel Keene, *Untitled Monologue and other plays*.
Anthony Lawrence, *New and Selected Poems*.
Les Murray, *Fredy Neptune*. P
Matthew Reilly, *Ice Station*. N
Gig Ryan, *Pure and Applied*. P
Eva Sallis, *Hiam*. N
Archie Weller, *Land of the Golden Clouds*. N
Oxford Literary History of Australia published.

1999
Referendum rejects Australian republic.
Australian troops with UN in East Timor.

CSIRO develops wireless LAN technology.
Morris West dies.
Thea Astley, *Drylands*. N
Merlinda Bobis, *The White Turtle*. S
Michelle de Kretser, *The Rose Grower*. N
Kate Grenville, *The Idea of Perfection*. N
John Muk Muk Burke, *Night Song and Other Poems*.
Suneeta Peres da Costa, *Homework*. N
Dong Le Quy, *Market of Lives*. D
Kim Scott, *Benang: From the Heart*. N

2000
Sydney Olympics; boom in international tourism.
Black Inc. publishing founded.
A.D. Hope, Judith Wright, Jack Davis die.
Peter Carey wins Booker Prize again for *The True History of the Kelly Gang*.
Liam Davison, *Collected Stories*.
Wesley Enoch, *Black Medea*. D
Michael Farrell, *Living at the Z*. P
Anita Heiss, *Dhuuluu Yala: To Talk Straight*.
Nicholas Jose, *The Red Thread*. N
Simone Lazaroo, *The Australian Fiancé*. N
Chandani Lokugé, *If the Moon Smiled*. N
David Malouf, *Dream Stuff*. S
Tom Petsinis, *The Death of Pan*. D
Hoa Pham, *Vixen*. N

Hannie Rayson, *Life After George*. D
Shaun Tan, *The Lost Thing*. YN
Hsu-Ming Teo, *Love and Vertigo*. N
Sam Wagan Watson, *Of Muse, Meandering and Midnight*. P
Gerard Windsor, *The Mansions of Bedlam*. S

2001
Twin Towers attack provokes 'war on terror' restrictions and anti-Muslim feeling. Australia sends troops to Afghanistan.
Howard prevents *Tampa* landing with rescued 'boat people'.
Robert Adamson, *Mulberry Leaves*. P
Andrew Bovell, *Holy Day*. D
Steven Carroll, *The Art of the Engine Driver*. N
Vivienne Cleven, *Bitin' Back*. N
Richard Flanagan, *Gould's Book of Fish*. N
John Forbes, *Collected Poems*.
Anita Heiss, *Who Am I? The Diary of Mary Talence, Sydney 1937*. YN
Bronwyn Lea, *Flight Animals*. P
Andy Quan, *Calendar Boy*. S
Gig Ryan, *Heroic Money*. P
Sam Wagan Watson, *Hotel Bone*. P
Alan Wearne, *The Lovemakers*. P
Tim Winton, *Dirt Music*. N
Arnold Zable, *Café Scheherazade*. N

2002
Ten-year 'el niño' drought. Bushfires. Riots in refugee detention camps. Bombing of Bali tourist spots kills Australians.

Keith Windshuttle questions research on colonial violence against Aboriginal peoples, prompts 'history wars'.
Dorothy Hewett dies.
Ben Ellis, *Falling Petals*. D
Gail Jones, *Black Mirror*. N
Sylvia Lawson, *How Simone de Beauvoir Died in Australia*. S
Anthony Lawrence, *Skinned by Light*. P
Alex Miller, *Journey to the Stone Country*. N
Dorothy Porter, *Wild Surmise*. P
Ouyang Yu, *Eastern Slope Chronicle*. N

2003
Major bushfires.
Australian troops sent to Iraq despite protests.
Australia secures gas supply contract with China.
Debate over ethics of live cattle export.
J.M. Coetzee wins Nobel Prize.
Inez Branay, *Neem Dreams*. N
Clem Christesen, editor of *Meanjin*, dies.
Judith Beveridge, *Wolf Notes*. P
Peter Carey, *My Life as a Fake*. N
Brendan Cowell, *Rabbit*. D
Michelle de Kretser, *The Hamilton Case*. N
Shirley Hazzard, *The Great Fire*. N
Clive James, *The Book of My Enemy*. P
Adib Khan, *Homecoming*. N
Chandani Lokugé, *Turtle Nest*. N

2004
Sydney riots this year and last over police hounding of Black youth.
Nation-wide rallies opposing employer-centred reforms to industrial relations.
Beginnings of long tussle over water management in Murray–Darling Basin.
China by now biggest trading partner based on iron ore exports.
Thea Astley and Bruce Beaver die.
Ron Elisha, *Blood Libel* and *Honour Killing*. D
Peter Goldsworthy, *Collected Stories*.
Gail Jones, *Sixty Lights*. N
Andrew McGahan, *The White Earth*. N
Romaine Moreton, *Post Me to the Prime Minister*. P
Tim Winton, *The Turning*. S

2005
Competition over space on Cronulla beach (Sydney) sparks race riot between 'Aussies' and 'Lebs'.
Bruce Beaver, *The Long Game*. P
J.M. Coetzee, *Slow Man*. N
Patricia Cornelius, *Love*. D
Brendan Cowell, *Ruben Guthrie*. D
Michel Faber, *The Fahrenheit Twins*. S
Alan Gould, *The Past Completes Me*. P
Jill Jones, *Broken/Open*. P
Daniel Keene, *The Nightwatchman*. D

John Kinsella, *The New Arcadia*. P
Jennifer Maiden, *Friendly Fire*. P
David McCooey, *Blister Pack*. P
Jaya Savige, *Latecomers*. P
Christos Tsiolkas, *Dead Europe*. N
Marcus Zusak, *The Book Thief*. N

2006
Ali Alizadeh, *eyes in time of war*. P
Tony Birch, *Shadowboxing*. S
Michelle Cahill, *The Accidental Cage*. P
Michael Farrell, *BREAK ME OUCH*. P
Kate Grenville, *The Secret River*. N
Gail Jones, *Dreams of Speaking*. N
Cate Kennedy, *Dark Roots*. S
David Malouf, *Every Move You Make*. S
Alice Pung, *Unpolished Gem*. H
Shaun Tan, *The Arrival*. YN
Tara June Winch, *Swallow the Air*. N
Alexis Wright, *Carpentaria*. N

2007
Kevin Rudd elected prime minister.
Bernie Banton wins damages against Hardy asbestos company for work-acquired lung disease.
Judith Bishop, *Event*. P
Peter Boyle, *Reading Borges*. P
Joanne Burns, *an illustrated history of dairies*. P
Steven Carroll, *The Time We Have Taken*. N
Michelle de Kretser, *The Lost Dog*. N
Anita Heiss, *I'm Not Racist, But....* P
Heiss, *Not Meeting Mr Right*. N
Gail Jones, *Sorry*. N

Adib Khan, *Spiral Road*. N
David Malouf, *Typewriter Music*. P
Alex Miller, *Landscape of Farewell*. N
David Milroy, *King Hit*. D

2008
[Global Financial Crisis.]
[Aravind Adiga, *The White Tiger*.]
Quentin Bryce becomes first female governor general.
P.M. Rudd delivers apology to Stolen Generation.
Australian troops withdrawn from Iraq.
Macquarie PEN Anthology of Aboriginal Literature published.
John Clanchy, *Her Father's Daughter*. S
Richard Flanagan, *Wanting*. N
Helen Garner, *The Spare Room*. N
Elizabeth Hodgson, *Skin Painting*. P
Sarah Holland-Batt, *Aria*. P
Tom Holloway, *Don't Say the Words*. D
Nam Le, *The Boat*. S
Shaun Tan, *Tales from Outer Suburbia*. S
Christos Tsiolkas, *The Slap*. N
Alan Wearne, *The Australian Popular Songbook*. P
Tim Winton, *Breath*. N
Ouyang Yu, *The Kingsbury Tales*. P
Andrew Bovell, *When the Rain Stops Falling*.

2009
Black Saturday fires around Melbourne destroy 2,000 homes.
Trove database of newspapers starts.

The Macquarie PEN Anthology of Australian Literature published.
Peter Carey, *Parrot and Olivier in America*. N
Tom Cho, *Look Who's Morphing*. S
Jennifer Maiden, *Pirate Rain*. P
David Malouf, *Ransom*. N
Alex Miller, *Lovesong*. N
Marie Munkara, *Every Secret Thing*. N
Peter Temple, *Truth*. N
Of Sadhus and Spinners story collection traces links to India.

2010
Julia Gillard becomes first woman prime minister.
'Boat people' drown near Christmas Island, prompting new deterrents on 'people smugglers'.
Ruth Park and Randolph Stow die.
Bonny Cassidy, *Said to Be Standing*. P
Sulari Gentill, *A Few Right Thinking Men*. N
Amanda Lohrey, *Reading Madame Bovary*. S
Daniel Keene, *Life Without Me*. D
Jennifer Maiden, *Intimate Geography*. P
Gretchen Shirm, *Having Cried Wolf*. S
Kim Scott, *That Deadman Dance*. N
John Tranter, *Starlight: 150 Poems*. P
Ouyang Yu, *The English Class*. N

2011
Syrian civil war and growth of ISIS creates tensions in Australia.

Michelle Cahill, *Visvarupa*. P
Diane Fahey, *The Wing Collection*. P
Marion Halligan, *Shooting the Fox*. S
Janette Turner Hospital, *Forecast: Turbulence*. S
Gail Jones, *Five Bells*. N
Jeanine Leane, *Purple Threads*. S
Alex Miller, *Autumn Laing*. N
Tim Richards, *Thought Crimes*. S

2012
Gillard restarts the 'Pacific Solution': island detention for 'boat people'.
Merlinda Bobis, *Fish-Hair Woman*. N
Peter Carey, *The Chemistry of Tears*. N
Ali Cobby Eckermann, *Ruby Moonlight*. P
Raimondo Cortese, *Buried City*. D
Nick Earls, *Welcome to Normal*. S
Michelle de Kretser, *Questions of Travel*. N
Ambelin Kwaymullina, *The Interrogation of Ashala Wolf*. YN
Rhyll McMaster, *Late Night Shopping*. P
Jennifer Mills, *The Rest is Weight*. S
Gerald Murnane, *A History of Books*. N
Ryan O'Neill, *The Weight of a Human Heart*. S
Geordie Williams, *The Burning Library*.

2013
Tony Abbott leads conservative return to government.

Stella Prize for Australian women's writing founded.
Ali Alizadeh, *Transactions*. S
Vanessa Badham, *The Bull, the Moon and the Coronet of Stars*. D
Georgia Blain, *The Secret Lives of Men*. S
J.M. Coetzee, *The Childhood of Jesus*. N
Rae Desmond Jones, *It Comes from All Directions*. P
Hannah Kent, *Burial Rites*. N
Melissa Lucashenko, *Mullumbimby*. N
Alex Miller, *Coal Creek*. N
Maria Takolander, *The Double and Other Stories*.
Chris Wallace-Crabbe, *The Foundations of Joy*. P
Tim Winton, *Eyrie*. N
Alexis Wright, *The Swan Book*. N
Turn to transnational literary networks.

2014
Iranian migrant takes hostages in Sydney café.
Richard Flanagan wins Booker Prize for *The Narrow Road to the Deep North* (2013).
Maxine Beneba Clarke, *Foreign Soil*. S
Ceridwen Dovey, *Only the Animals*. S
Michael Gow, *Once in Royal David's City*. D
Sophie Laguna, *The Eye of the Sheep*. Y/N
Liane Moriarty, *Big Little Lies*, N
Christos Tsiolkas, *Merciless Gods*. S
Ellen van Neerven, *Heat and Light*. N
Charlotte Wood, *The Natural Way of Things*. N

2015
Malcolm Turnbull replaces Tony Abbott.
Power moves to small parties.
Tegan Bennett Daylight, *Six Bedrooms*. S
Merlinda Bobis, *Locust Girl*. N
James Bradley, *Clade*. N
Isobelle Carmody, *The Red Queen*. YN
Angus Cerini, *The Bleeding Tree*. D
Ali Cobby Eckermann, *Inside My Mother*. P
Elizabeth Harrower, *A Few Days in the Country*. S
Kevin Hart, *Wild Track: New and Selected Poems*.
Subhash Jaireth, *Moments*. S
Gail Jones, *A Guide to Berlin*. N
Nakkiah Lui, *Kill the Messenger*. D
Susan Midalia, *Feet to the Stars*. S
Suzie Miller, *Caress/Ache*. D
Charlotte Wood, *The Natural Way of Things*. N

2016
Era of 'fly in, fly out' mine workers.
House prices move beyond reach of young families.
Peter Boyle, *Ghostspeaking*. P
Michelle Cahill, *Letter to Pessoa*. S
Lionel Fogarty, *Harvest Lingo*. P

Roanna Gonsalves, *The Permanent Resident*. S
Jane Harper, *The Dry*. N
John Kinsella, *Graphology Poems 1995–2015*.
Susan McCreery, *Loopholes: Microfiction*. S
Paddy O'Reilly, *It Happened Off the Leash*. S
Alana Valentine, *Letters to Lindy* and *Ladies' Day*. D
Ellen van Neerven, *Comfort Food*. P
Sam Wagan Watson, *Monsters Ink*. P
Josephine Wilson, *Extinctions*. N

2017
National Aboriginal conference approves 'Uluru Statement' demanding permanent voice to parliament.
Plebiscite approves gay marriage.
Royal Commissions investigate abuses in banking, aged care and disability care.
Tony Birch, *Common People*. S
Peter Carey, *A Long Way from Home*. N
Michelle de Kretser, *The Life to Come*. N
Shastra Deo, *The Agonist*. P
Stephen Orr, *Datsunland*. S
Hoa Pham, *Lady of the Realm*. S
Alex Skovron, *The Man Who Took to His Bed*. S
Amy Witting, *Selected Stories*.

2018
Scott Morrison becomes prime minister.
National unease over state of universities, climate change and reliance on China trade.
Michael Mohammed Ahmad, *The Lebs*. N
Judith Beveridge, *Sun Poems: New and Selected*.
Ken Bolton, *Starting at Basheer's*. P
Gary Disher, *Kill Shot*. N
Robert Drewe, *The True Colours of the Sea*. S
Gail Jones, *The Death of Noah Glass*. N
Anthony Lawrence, *101 Poems*.
Jeanine Leane, *Walk Back Over*. P
Melissa Lucashenko, *Too Much Lip*. N
A.S. Patric, *The Butcherbird Stories*.

2019
[Covid-19 pandemic.]
White extremist from Australia guns down worshippers in New Zealand mosques.
Major bushfires and floods along east coast of Australia.
Mudrooroo and Les Murray die.
Debra Adelaide, *Zebra and Other Stories*.
Michael Farrell, *Ashbery Mode*. P
Joshua Lobb, *The Flight of Birds*. S
Susan McCreery, *This Person Is Not That Person*. S
Gerald Murnane, *A Season on Earth*. N
Louis Nowra, *Collected Stories*.
Charmaine Papertalk-Green, *Nganajungu Yagu*. P

Christos Tsiolkas, *Damascus*. N
David Williamson, *Collected Plays*.
Tara June Winch, *The Yield*. N

2020
General Motors closes Holden plant, underlining loss of manufacturing in Australia.
China bans imports of Australian wine, barley, seafood.
Bruce Dawe dies.
Jordie Albiston, *The Atomic Weight and Radius of Love*. P
Richard Flanagan, *The Living Sea of Waking Dreams*. N
Dennis Glover, *Factory 19*. N
Jill Jones, *A History of What I'll Become*. P
Amanda Lohrey, *The Labyrinth*. N
Laura McKay, *The Animals in That Country*. N
Jaya Savige, *Change Machine*. P
Mandy Sayer, *Crime and Other Pastimes*. S
Elizabeth Tan, *Smart Ovens for Lonely People*. S
Ouyang Yu, *Terminally Poetic*. P
Arnold Zable, *The Watermill*. S

Index

Abdullah, Mena 248
Aboriginal history xiii, 2, 5, 7, 49, 52, 77, 126, 152–154, 185, 195–199, 239, 244, 269
    1967 referendum 126
    Bennelong 2, 5, 7
    Black deaths in custody 153, 239, 269
    Burney, Linda 244
    Day of Mourning 77
    disease 2
    Freedom Ride 126
    Gurindji Wave Hill walk-off 126
    Lake Mungo 126
    land rights 152–153, 185, 232
    Mabo, Eddie 195
    massacres 52
    Native Title Act 196
    Nicholls, Pastor Doug 152
    reconciliation march 198
    Redfern Speech 196
    Stolen Generation/sorry 77, 196–197, 199, 210–211, 239, 263
    Tent Embassy 185
    Uluru statement 244
    Wyatt, Ken 244
Aboriginal people, writing about 48, 54, 60, 74, 79, 94, 131, 133–134, 151, 156, 165, 172, 203, 207–208, 212, 215, 234, 251

Aboriginal writing xv–xvi, 5, 121, 144, 150, 156, 170, 173–174, 185, 191, 193, 200, 215–217, 220, 231–232, 238–239, 241, 253–254, 257, 263–264, 268–270
Adams, A.H. 54, 70–71, 73
Adams, Francis 34, 40, 44
Adamson, Robert 139, 143, 173, 178, 225
Adelaide, Debra 256
Ahmad, Michael Mohammed 256
Aitken, Adam 230–231
Albiston, Jordie 263
Alizadeh, Ali 230
Allen, Pamela 241
Anderson, Ethel 134, 248
Anderson, Jessica 113, 134, 157–158, 171
Angas, George French 44
Araluen, Evelyn 264
Astley, Thea 110–111, 114, 132–133, 167–168, 203–204, 221
Atkinson, Hugh 248
Atkinson, Louisa 26
autobiographies *see* **life writing**

Badham, Van 266–267
Bail, Murray 134, 136, 214
ballads 20, 38–44, 142, 176, 178
Balodis, Janis 191, 235
Baranay, Inez 248

Barton, Charlotte 11
Barton, G.B. 23
Baynton, Barbara 64–65
Beach, Eric 175
Beaver, Bruce 119–120, 139, 141, 173, 177, 225
Becke, Louis 34
Bellear, Lisa 231
Beneba Clarke, Maxine 257
Bennett Daylight, Tegan 258
Beveridge, Judith 225, 259–260
Beynon, Richard 122
Birch, Tony 257, 264
Bird, Carmel 171, 223
Bishop, Judith 262
Blain, Georgia 256
Blair, Ron 146
Blight, John 120
Boake, Barcroft 40
Boake, Capel 63–64
Bobis, Merlinda 171, 255–256
Boddy, Michael and Bob Ellis 144
'Boldrewood, Rolf' 31–32
Bolton, Ken 261
Boothby, Guy 33–34
Bosi, Pino 138
Bostock, Gerry 150, 185
Bovell, Andrew 236–237, 265
Boyd, Martin 63, 101
Boylan, Eustace 96
Boyle, Peter 224
Bozic, Streten 172
Bradley, James 222, 254
Brand, Mona 144
Brennan, Christopher J. 38, 44, 66, 69–70
Brereton, John LeGay 44
Briggs, Tony 239

Brinsmead, H.F. 151
Broderick, Damien 222
Brooks, David 223
Brooks, Geraldine 220
Brophy, Kevin 171
Brown, Pam 173, 175, 179–180, 227
Bruce, Mary Grant 75, 96
Buckley, Vincent 119, 184
Buckmaster, Charles 143, 173
Bunn, Anna Maria 10
Burke, John Muk Muk 231
Burns, Joanne 175, 227, 260,
bushrangers xix, 4, 10–12, 15, 21, 31–32, 45–46, 142, 198, 206, 213, 239
Buzo, Alex 145

Cahill, Michelle 257, 262
Cambridge, Ada 27–28, 44
Campbell, David 81, 91–92, 138, 180
Campbell, Marion 169
Cappiello, Rosa 156
Carey, Peter xix, 93, 128, 134–137, 165–166, 205–206, 219, 249–250
Carmody, Isobelle 240
Carmody, Kev 232
Carroll, Steven 171, 214–215
'Carter Brown' 113
Carter, David and Roger Osborne 247
Casey, Gavin 85
Cassidy, Bonny 263
Castro, Brian 162
censorship 80–81, 84, 93–94, 100, 173
Cerini, Angus 268
Chauncy, Nan 124

Cheetham, Deborah 239
Chi, Jimmy 239
children's and young adult literature 46–48, 74–75, 95–96, 124, 150–151, 193–194, 201, 209, 239–241
Cho, Tom 256
Claire, Jennifer 190
Clancy, John 171, 222
Clare, Monica 170
Clarke, Doreen 190
Clarke, Marcus 30–31
Cleary, Jon 102, 113
Cleven, Vivienne 217
Clift, Charmian 81, 171
Clune, Frank 79
Cobb, Chester 63
Cobby Eckerman, Ali 264
Coburn, Anthony 122
Coetzee, J.M. 219
Compton, Jennifer 144, 190, 234
Condon, Matthew 223
Conigrave, Timothy 234
convicts xii–xiii, 1, 10, 12, 21, 25–26, 31–32, 34–35, 44, 83, 91, 134, 157, 211, 263, 267
Conway, Jill Ker 241
Cornelius, Patricia 236, 265–266
Corris, Peter 172
Cortese, Raimondo 265
Couani, Anna 175, 182
Courtenay, Bryce 201, 223
Coutts Armour, R. and John G. Brandon 96
Couvreur, Jessie 29
Cowan, Peter 86, 114
Cowell, Brendan 238
Crew, Gary 240

crime genre 33–35, 64, 87, 113, 168, 172, 203–204, 211–212, 220, 226, 259, 261
Croggon, Alison 269
Cross, Zora 173
'Culotta, Nino' 101
cultural context xii–xiii, 20, 28–34, 37, 51, 62, 76–77, 82, 100, 102, 122, 125, 135, 152, 159, 162, 179, 208, 235–236, 244
  anti-intellectual xiii
  class 28–34, 77, 82, 97, 108, 152, 157, 162, 208, 214, 235–236, 241
  counter-culture rebellion 100, 125, 135, 159, 173, 179
  cultural cringe 102
  egalitarian/social welfare 100
  larrikinism 62, 122
  luck and raw talent 20
  mateship xiv, 37, 51, 76, 123, 244
  mistrust of authority xii
  secularism xii
  suburbia 82, 97, 108, 152, 157, 180, 214, 241
Cusack, Dymphna 60, 79, 81, 86, 95, 121
Cuthbertson, James Lister 38
Cyrill, Christopher 217

Daley, Victor 43, 115
D'Alpuget, Blanche 162
Dalton, Trent 253
Dann, George Landen 94
Dark, Eleanor xix, 83–85
Darville, Helen 202
Davis, Jack xix, 144, 174, 185, 191, 239

Davison, Frank Dalby 86, 96, 114
Davison, Liam 222
Dawe, Bruce 120–121, 139–140
Day, Marele 172
de Boissière, Ralph 100, 108
De Groen, Alma 187–188
de Kretser, Michelle 211, 252
Dennis, C.J. 71, 122
Deo, Shastra 262
Devanny, Jean 100
Dickins, Barry 171
Disher, Gary 171, 220, 240, 259
Dixon, Graeme 231
Dixon, Robert and Brigid
    Rooney 247
Dobson, Rosemary 88–90, 92,
    115, 173
Dovey, Ceridwen 258
Dowling, Terry 222
Drake-Brockman, Henrietta 85, 94,
    114
Dransfield, Michael 139, 143, 173
Drewe, Robert 156, 206, 221, 256
Duggan, Laurie 173, 177
Dunlop, Eliza Hamilton 14
Durack, Mary and Elizabeth 96
Dutton, Geoffrey 81, 103
Dyson, Edward 65

Earls, Nick 223
economy 17, 19, 52–53, 76, 97–98,
    126, 152–154, 156, 169,
    195–197, 205, 243
    corruption/collapses 19, 153–154,
        195, 205, 243
    decimal currency 126
    depression 52–53, 76
    deregulation 154, 156, 195–197

eighties boom 153, 212
gold rushes 17
post-war boom 97–98
'Edmunds, Albert' 73
education 6, 98–99, 102, 118, 129,
    156, 168, 173, 184, 201
    Australian literature, teaching/
        universities xviii, 6, 99, 102,
        118, 129, 168, 173, 184
    creative writing, teaching 129,
        156, 184, 201
    schooling 6, 98
Egan, Greg 222, 254
'Eldershaw, M. Barnard' 83–84, 114
Elisha, Ron 236–237
Elliot, Sumner Locke 81, 95, 101
Ellis, Ben 238
Enoch, Wesley 239
Enright, Nick 236
environment xi–xiii, xvi, 1, 10, 14,
    21, 26, 39, 47–48, 61, 91, 93,
    167, 181, 184, 244–245, 251,
    254, 258
Esson, Louis 66, 73–74
Evans, George Essex 38
Evers, L.H. 150
exploration xiv–xvi, 3–6, 8–9, 18,
    21, 32, 49, 50, 54, 88–89, 105,
    116–117, 166, 183, 191
    Burke and Wills 21, 32
    Cook, Captain James 6, 89
    Dampier, William 6
    Eyre, Edward John 5, 9, 89, 117
    Flinders, Captain Matthew xv, 3
    Leichhardt, Ludwig 5, 9, 89, 105,
        116–117, 191
    Mawson, Douglas 50, 54
    Mitchell, Thomas 5, 8

Oxley, John 5, 8
Stuart, John McDouall 18
Sturt, Charles 5, 8, 117
voyager poems 89

Faber, Michel 222
Facey, A.B. 193
Fahey, Diane 228, 263
Fallon, Kathleen Mary 205, 258
Farmer, Beverley 170–171
farming 2–3, 8, 16, 20, 30, 35, 49, 50, 52, 66, 73, 83, 152, 162, 224, 246
  cockies 16, 20, 35, 66
  irrigation 49
  Macarthur, John and Elizabeth 2
  Ruse, James 2
  sheep 2
  squatters 3, 16, 20, 52, 73, 83, 162
  wheat 2, 50
Farquhar, George 15
Farrell, Michael 229, 261
Favenc, Ernest 35
feminism 28, 30, 77, 87, 99, 113, 127, 134, 140, 147, 155, 157, 161, 171, 181, 188, 190, 192, 205, 208–209, 227–228, 242
Field, Barron 13
film 53, 80, 97, 129, 152, 154, 201, 226
Fitton, Doris 74, 95
FitzGerald, R.D. 66, 88–92, 115, 138
Flanagan, Richard 211–212, 250–251
Flood, Tom 168–169
Flower, Pat 113, 121
Fogarty, Lionel 186
Foott, Mary Hannay 44
Forbes, John 173, 176, 226–227

Forster, William 45
Fortune, Mary 35
Foster, David 205
Fox, Mem 193
Frank the Poet 13
Franklin, Miles 55–57, 80, 82, 95, 172
French, Jackie 241
Furphy, Joseph 57–58

Garner, Helen 155, 159–160, 171, 242
Gask, Arthur 87
Gaunt, Mary 30
gay and lesbian themes 86, 150, 152, 165, 190, 205, 223, 229, 234, 243
Geason, Susan 220
Gellert, Leon 66, 70
Geoghegan, Edward 15, 144
Gibbs, May 75
Gilbert, Kevin 150, 156, 173–174, 185–186
Giles, Zeny 171
Gilmore, Mary 38, 68–69, 115, 138, 173
'Ginger Meggs' 53
Gleitzman, Morris 240
Glover, Dennis 269
Goldsworthy, Kerryn 134
Goldsworthy, Peter 202–203
Gonsalves, Roanna 257
Goodfellow, Geoff 178
Gooneratne, Yasmine 218
Gordon, Adam Lindsay 38–39
gothic 39–40, 65, 85, 212, 215, 222
Gough, Julie 264
Gould, Alan 227

Gow, Michael 187, 234, 266
Grant, Jamie 182, 230
Grattan, C. Hartley 54, 80
Gray, Oriel 95, 121–122
Gray, Robert 139, 181
Green, H.M. 80, 87, 102
Greenwood, Kerry 220
Greer, Germaine 127
Grenville, Kate xix, 171, 214, 251, 265
Griffiths, Andy 240
grunge 212, 220
Gunew, Sneja 155
Gunn, Mrs Aeneas 55, 74
Gurr, Michael 234
Gutya, Burraga 231
Gwynne, Phillip 241

Hall, Rodney 138, 139, 251
Halligan, Marion 204, 222
Hammial, Philip 173
Hampton, Susan 171–173
Hanrahan, Barbara 160
Harcourt, J.M. 81
Harding, Alex 234
Hardy, Frank 86, 100, 106–107, 131, 171
Harford, Lesbia 173
Harper, Jane 259
Harpur, Charles 14, 38, 45, 115
Harrex, Syd 184
Harris, Max 93, 103
Harris, Rory 182
Harrison, Jane 239
Harrower, Elizabeth 112–113, 134
Harry, J.S. 139, 179
Hart, Kevin 182, 227
Hart-Smith, William 89

Harwood, Gwen 140, 173, 180
Haskell, Dennis 184
Hasluck, Nicholas 77
Hazzard, Shirley 101, 137–138, 160–161
Heiss, Anita 200, 217, 231, 241
Hemensley, Kris 173
Herbert, Xavier 82, 188
Heseltine, Harry 134
Hewett, Dorothy 86, 100, 107, 144, 147–148, 180–181, 188–189
Hibberd, Jack 123, 145–146
Hill, Ernestine 79
Hill, Fidelia 14
Hill, S.P. 15
historians
  Blainey, Geoffrey xiv, 128
  C.E.W. Bean 55
  Clark, Manning 102, 128
  Hancock, W.K. 80
  Reynolds, Henry 199–200
  Serle, Percival 101
  Ward, Russel 101
  Windschuttle, Keith 200
history xi–xii, xvi, xviii–xix, 1
  as a theme 166, 168, 172, 251
  colonial xi, xii, 1–74, 126, 188
  history wars 199–200
  lack of history xviii
  multiple histories xvi
  revisions of xix, 171
  see also **politics** *and* **wars**
hoaxes 93, 172, 202, 206, 212
  B. Wongar 172
  Ern Malley 93, 104, 118, 138, 206
  'Helen Demidenko' 202
Hodgson, Elizabeth 263
Holland-Batt, Sarah 259

Holloway, Tom 268
Holt, Yvette 263
Hope, A.D. 115–118, 184
Horne, Donald 98
Horne, Richard Henry / Hengist 'Orion' 45
Hospital, Janette Turner 219–221, 258
Howitt, William 46
Huggins, Jackie 193
Hume, Fergus 33
Humphries, Barry 100, 101, 148
Hungerford, T.A.G. 78

Idriess, Ion 79
Ingamells, Rex 79, 87, 89, 124
international relations
    Chile 126
    China 127, 201, 207, 245–246
    Colombo Plan 98
    India xi, 246
    Japan 78, 126, 147, 186, 195, 210, 229, 237
    New Guinea 49, 50, 78, 127, 188
    UK 125
    USA 99, 125, 138, 173, 186, 206, 229, 246, 247, 249
Ireland, David 123, 129–131, 169, 171

Jaireth, Subhash 257
Jaivin, Linda 205
James, Brian 114
James, Clive 101, 242
Janson, Julie 239
Jindyworobaks 79, 85, 87–88
Johnson, Colin *see* Mudrooroo
Johnson, Eva 174, 185, 191, 238

Johnston, George 108
Johnston, Martin 173
Jolley, Elizabeth 134, 144, 158–159, 171, 204
Jones, Gail 209–211, 251–252
Jones, Jill 228–229, 260
Jones, Rae Desmond 173, 178
Jose, Nicholas 200, 205, 231, 247
journals *see* **magazines**

Kalamaras, Vasso 138, 182, 191
Kay, Pippa 258
Keene, Daniel 237–238, 266
Kefala, Antigone 182–183
Kelleher, Victor 193
Kelly, Ned 21, 31–32, 53, 89, 101, 198, 206
Kemp, Jenny 237
Kendall, Henry 38–39, 115
Keneally, Thomas 78, 133–134, 144, 154, 245, 251
Kenna, Peter 122, 146
Kennedy, Cate 223
Kent, Hannah 259
Khan, Adib 217
Kiernan, Brian 136
Kingsley, Henry 22
Kinsella, John 183–184, 258, 260, 264
Kipling, Rudyard 22
Klein, Robin 193
Kocan, Peter 143
Koch, Christopher J. 109, 162, 248
Koh, Julie 258
Kwaymullina, Ambelin 270

Laguna, Sofie 252
Lanagan, Margo 240

Lane, William 18, 24
Lang, John 25, 33, 248
Lang, John Dunmore 6, 24, 44
Langford, Ruby 171, 193
Langley, Eve 107
language xii, xvii, 6, 8, 25, 83, 156, 174, 185, 188, 215–216, 222, 235, 253
Lawler, Ray 122
Lawrence, Anthony 182, 229, 261
Lawrence, D.H. 54, 77
Lawson, Henry 35–37, 38, 41, 85
Lawson, Louisa 24, 36, 191–192
Lazaroo, Simone 219
Le, Nam 256
Lea, Bronwyn 230
Leakey, Caroline 14, 26
Leane, Jeanine 257, 264
Learner, Tobsha 223, 237
Lehmann, Geoffrey 139, 182
life writing 160, 171, 177, 180–181, 183, 191–193, 219, 234, 241–242, 249, 258
Lilley, Kate 184
Lindsay, Norman 54, 62, 75
literary support infrastructure
   Adelaide Festival of the Arts 102, 152
   Arts Council 128, 139
   Association for the Study of Australian Literature 155
   Australian Society of Authors 101
   Children's Book Council 102
   Commonwealth Literary Fund 54, 80
   digitised archives 246
   Federation of Australian Writers 68, 79–80, 101
   festivals 156
   National Book Council 80
Llewellyn, Kate 173, 181
Lobb, Joshua 258
Lohrey, Amanda 255
Lokugé, Chandani 218
Lord, Gabrielle 172
Lucashenko, Melissa 253
Lui, Nakkiah 268–269
Lurie, Morris 134, 136
Lyssa, Alison 190
Lyssiotis, Tess 235

Macintyre, Ernest 235
Mack, Louise 47, 66–67
Mackellar, Dorothea 66
magazines 19, 23, 36, 53, 62, 77, 79, 80, 86, 99–100, 102, 127–129, 139, 155, 171, 174, 201, 221, 224, 247, 256, 261
   Australian Book Review 102
   Australian Letters 102
   Australian Literary Studies 102, 103
   Australian Poetry 102
   Boxkite 174
   Bulletin, The 19, 23, 35–36, 62, 247
   HEAT 174, 221, 224
   Inprint 171
   Island 155, 255
   Jacket 224
   Kill Your Darlings 221
   Lone Hand, The 53
   Makar 128, 139
   Meanjin 80
   New Poetry 139
   Outrider 155

Overland 102
Quadrant 102
Salt 174, 184
Scripsi 155, 224
Smith's Weekly 53
Southerly 80
Southern Review 129
Tabloid Story 128
Text 201
Westerly 86, 102
Maiden, Jennifer 173, 177, 226, 260, 263
Mailman, Deborah 239
Malouf, David 131–132, 139, 163–164, 212–214, 221
Manning, Frederick 63
Mansell, Chris 175, 182
Marchetta, Melina 240
Marsden, John 240–241
Marshall, Alan 85–86, 172
Martin, Catherine 32–33
Martin, David 86, 108, 151
Masson, Sophie 240
Masters, Olga 158
Mathers, Peter 168
Matthews, Brian 191–192
Maza, Bob 150, 239
McAuley, James 81, 89, 115, 118–119, 184
McCombie, Thomas 10, 15
McCooey, David 263
McCrae, Hugh 38, 66, 68
McCreery, Susan 257
McCullough, Colleen 138, 223
McDonald, Roger 139
McGahan, Andrew 212
McKemmish, Jan 169, 172
McKinty, Adrian 259

McLaren, Jack 54
McLaren, Phillip 220
McMaster, Rhyll 139, 224
McNeil, Jim 149
McTiernan, Dervla 259
Mead, Philip 184
Mears, Gillian 171
Melville, Henry 15
Meredith, Gwen 94, 121
Merritt, Robert 150
Midalia, Susan 258
middlebrow literature 157, 200–201, 214
migrant writing *see* **multicultural writing**
migration xi, 18, 28, 49, 51–52, 63, 66, 81, 98, 101, 122, 127, 141, 152, 160–162, 198–199, 211, 214, 217–218, 235, 241, 254, 257
  assimilation xiv
  Chinese 18, 162
  Cronulla riots 199
  expatriates 63, 101, 141, 160–161, 220, 223
  Germans 51, 66, 124
  Hanson, Pauline 196
  refugees 198, 218
  White Australia Policy 18, 49, 152
Milgate, Rodney 144
Miller, Alex 207–208, 248–249
Miller, Suzie 268
Mills, Jennifer 258
Milroy, David 239
mining 17, 19, 49, 52, 58, 65, 98, 100, 103, 169, 196–197, 216, 232, 235, 253
Minter, Peter 200, 231

modernism 63, 69–70, 72, 76, 79, 84, 86, 93, 103, 209
Modjeska, Drusilla 156, 192
Moorhead, Finola 220
Moorhouse, Frank 114, 134–136, 175, 221
Morgan, Sally xix, 193
Moriarty, Liane 223
Morrison, John 85, 86
Morrissey, Di 223
Morton, Kate 259
Mudie, Ian 87
Mudrooroo 113, 169–170, 185, 200, 215
multicultural writing xvii, 54, 74, 107–108, 138, 156, 162, 170, 182–183, 190, 218–219, 230, 235, 240, 248, 256–257, 262
    Chinese 162, 218, 230
    Greek 138, 170, 182–183, 190, 235
    Italian 138, 156, 240
    Middle Eastern 230, 256
    South Asian 217, 218, 248, 262
    Southeast Asian 218, 219, 230, 257
    Vietnamese 235, 256
Mulvaney, Kate 265
Munkara, Marie 217
Murdoch, Walter 54, 66, 85
Murnane, Gerald 162–163, 201, 248, 258
Murray, Les 139, 141–143, 225
Murray-Smith, Joanna 233
Musa, Omar 256

nature *see* **environment**
Neilson, John Shaw 66, 71–72, 102, 115, 181

Nguyen, Huong and Phi Hai 235
Nix, Garth 240
Nowra, Louis 188, 234–235, 258–259

Oakley, Barry 136, 146
'O'Brien, John' 71
O'Connor, Mark 183
O'Dowd, Bernard 66–68
Ogilvie, Will 40
O'Neill, Ryan 258
Oodgeroo Noonuccal 121, 126, 144, 173–174, 180, 185
O'Reilly, Dowell 85
Ottley, Reginald 151
Ouyang Yu 230, 261
Oxford History of Australian Literature 156, 200
Oxford Literary History of Australia 200

painting 23, 76, 79, 101, 107, 164, 207, 209, 249, 252
Palmer, Nettie 54, 59
Palmer, Vance 19, 59, 66–67, 74, 86, 100–101, 121
Papertalk-Green, Charmaine 174, 263–264
Park, Ruth 79, 96, 107–108, 121, 193
Parker, K. Langloh 48
Pascoe, Bruce 171
Paterson, A.B. 'Banjo' 22–23, 38, 40–43
Patric, A.S. 258
Patrikareas, Theodore 190–191
Pedley, Ethel 47–48
PEN Anthology of Aboriginal Literature 200
PEN Anthology of Australian Literature 247

Penguin Book of Australian Women Poets 173
Penguin New Literary History of Australia 156
Penton, Brian 82–83
Peres da Costa, Suneeta 218
Petsinis, Tom 258
Phillips, Arthur A. 101–102, 114
'Pi O' / 'π.o.' / Peter Oustabasidis 175, 182
Plunkett, Felicity 230
politicians
    Abbott, Tony 243
    Bjelke-Petersen, Joh 152–154
    Chifley, Ben 77
    Curtin, John 77
    Deakin, Alfred 49
    Dunstan, Don 152
    Evatt, H.V. 'Doc' 78
    Gillard, Julia 243, 260
    Hawke, Bob 153–154, 195, 197
    Howard, John 196–198
    Hughes, W. 'Billy' 51
    Keating, Paul 154, 195–196
    Menzies, Robert 77, 97, 126
    Morrison, Scott 243
    Parkes, Henry 13, 17, 19
    Rudd, Kevin 199, 201, 243
    Turnbull, Malcolm 243
    Whitlam, Gough 127–129, 149, 154, 158, 190, 250
politics 1–4, 17–18, 37, 49, 52, 60, 76–78, 81, 93, 97–100, 125–128, 153–154, 187, 196–199, 237, 244
    citizenship 78
    Cold War 100, 125
    communism 52, 60, 76–77, 81, 99, 187
    Dismissal 128
    eight-hour day 17
    ending transportation 4
    Eureka Stockade 17
    Federation 49
    First Fleet 1
    Greens 195
    Isaacs, Sir Isaac 76
    labor 18
    liberal 97
    Macquarie, Governor Lachlan 3
    nuclear testing 97, 153
    One Nation 196
    parliament 49, 52, 154
    Petrov defection 99
    Phillip, Governor Arthur 2
    Port Arthur 197
    republic 195
    Rum Rebellion 3
    state parliaments 17–18
    Tampa scandal 198
    terror, war on 198–199, 244
    unions 17, 37, 52, 99, 127, 187, 197, 237
Porter, Dorothy 182, 226
Porter, Hal 78, 114–115, 134
Porter, Peter 101, 140–141, 180
Praed, Rosa 28
Pretty, Ron 184
Prichard, Katharine Susannah 59–61, 74, 79, 85, 100, 103
prison writing 143, 149, 169, 185, 215
prizes
    Booker Prize 154, 166, 207
    David Unaipon Award 217, 231, 254, 263
    Kenneth Slessor Prize (poetry) 264

Mary Gilmore Award (poetry)
228, 263
Miles Franklin Award 101,
104, 110, 134, 157, 161,
202–203, 207, 212, 216,
220, 255
Nobel Prize 129, 219
Premier's Literary Awards 155
Thomas Shapcott Poetry Prize
261, 262
Vogel Literary Award 155,
161, 212
publishing xvii, 5, 22–23, 35, 53,
80, 85, 101, 103, 114–115,
128, 155, 172, 174, 184, 201,
221, 224
Affirm 222
Angus & Robertson 22–23, 80,
114–115, 128, 174
Australasian Book Society 83, 85
Black Inc. 172, 221
Brandl & Schlesinger 200
Currency Press 129
Five Islands Press 139, 155, 174,
184, 224
Fremantle Arts Centre Press
128, 174
Ginninderra 222
Giramondo 200, 224, 248, 258
globalising 201
Hale & Iremonger 174
McPhee Gribble 128, 155
mergers 155
Paper Bark Press 174
Penguin 222
Public Lending Right 129
Puncher & Wattman 224
Salt 184
Scribe 201

Spineless Wonders 222
Sun Books 103
Sybylla Press 155
Text 248
Traditional Markets Agreement 80
University of Queensland Press
128, 174, 221, 224
Vagabond Press 224
Wakefield Press 174
Wild & Woolley 128
Pulvers, Roger 188
Pung, Alice 258
Purcell, Leah 239, 269

Quan, Andy 223
Quy, Duong Le 235

Radic, Thérèse 235
Randall, Bob 232
Rayson, Hannie 233–234, 237
realism 53, 57–58, 60, 100, 105, 146,
162, 186, 191
Reed-Gilbert, Kerry 231
Reilly, Matthew 223
religion 24, 29, 71, 133–134, 142,
146, 166, 181, 245
Richardson, Henry Handel xix,
58–59, 119
Richardson, Wendy 235
Riddell, Elizabeth 120
Roach, Archie 232
Roberts, Nigel 173
Robinson, Michael Massey 13
Robinson, Rowland 180
Rodda, Emily 240
Rodriguez, Judith 139, 173
Roland, Betty 74, 95
Rolls, Eric 81, 156
romance 20–32, 67, 217, 222, 259

Romeril, John 146–147, 234
Rose, Peter 230
Roughsey, Dick 194
Rowcroft, Charles 10
Rowe, Richard 46
Rowlands, Graham 175, 182
Rubinstein, Gillian 193
'Rudd, Steele' 35, 73, 94
Ryan, Gig 175, 228

Sallis, Eva 218
Sant, Andrew 182
Saunders, Brenda 264
Savery, Henry 10
Savige, Jaya 261
Sayer, Mandy 223, 258
science fiction 222, 254, 270
Scott, John A. 173
Scott, Kim xix, 215–216
Sejavka, Sam 235
Sewell, Stephen 187, 234
Sexton Blake series 96
Seymour, Alan 122
Shapcott, Thomas 138, 180
Shirm, Gretchen 258
short story 34–37, 64–65,
    85–86, 114–115, 134–138,
    158–159, 162–163, 171–172,
    203–205, 208–209, 221–223,
    248–249, 254–258
Shute, Nevil 81, 99
Simpson, Helen 66, 87
Sinnett, Frederick 23
Skinner, Mollie 248
Skovron, Alex 230, 257
Skrzynecki, Peter 139, 155
Slessor, Kenneth 66, 71–73, 81,
    89–90, 229, 251

Smith, Martin 150
Smith, Vivian 184
Southall, Ivan 124
Spears, Steve J. 146
Spence, Catherine Helen 24–25, 134
Spence, Eleanor 124, 193
Spielvogel, Nathan 65–66
sport 23, 53, 76, 79, 97, 141, 153,
    198, 217, 267
    America's Cup 153
    Bradman, Don 53, 79
    Darcy, Les 79
    football 217, 267
    Olympic Games 97, 198
    Phar Lap 79, 141
    Wimbledon 53
Spunner, Suzanne 190
Stead, Christina 84–85, 134
Stephens, James Brunton 43–44
Stephensen, P.R. 'Inky' 80
Stevens, Bertram 38
Stewart, Douglas 89, 91, 114–115
Stivens, Dal 86, 114, 168–169
Stone, Louis 62–63
Stow, Randolph 109–110
Strachan, Tony 188
Strauss, Jennifer 184, 200
Summers, Anne 127
Sussex, Lucy 222

Ta, Binh Duy 235
Takolander, Maria 230, 258
Talbot, Norman 184
Tan, Elizabeth 258
Tan, Shaun 241
'Tasma' *see* Couvreur
Taylor, Alf 231
Taylor, Andrew 139, 184

Temple, Peter 220
Tench, Watkin 7
Tennant, Kylie 60, 79, 82, 86–87, 121
Teo, Hsu-Ming 218
theatre companies 46, 73–74, 94, 102, 144, 146–147, 150, 152, 186, 190, 237, 267–268
    Australian Elizabethan Theatre Trust 102
    Australian Performing Group 147
    Belvoir Street 186
    Doppio Teatro 190
    Hole in the Wall 186
    Home Cooking 190
    Independent Theatre Company 74
    J.C. Williamson 46, 73
    Jane Street Theatre 144
    La Mama theatre 146, 237
    Melbourne Theatre Company 237
    Melbourne Workers' Theatre 237
    Milk Crate Theatre 268
    National Black Theatre 150
    National Institute of Dramatic Art 102, 267
    New Theatre League 94
    Nimrod 146
    Old Tote 102, 144
    Playbox 186, 237
    Pram Factory, The 146
    Red Shed, The 186
    Sidetrack Theatre 186
    South Australian Theatre Company 152
    Stables, The 146
    Sydney Theatre Company 144, 267
    Women's Theatre Group 147

Thiele, Colin 124
Thomas, E.H. 15
Thomas, Jared 217
Thompson, Katherine 235
Timms, E.V. 64, 96
Tipping, Richard 139, 178
Tomholt, Sydney 94
Tompson, Charles 13
Tranter, John 139, 172–176, 229
Travers, P.L. 96
Treasure, Rachael 222
Trollope, Anthony xvii, 22
'Trooper Gerardy' 70
Tsaloumas, Dimitris 182
Tsiolkas, Christos 220–221
Tucker, James 11
Turner, Ethel 46–47
Turner, George 254
Twain, Mark xvii, 22, 136

Unaipon, David 52, 66
Upfield, Arthur 64

Valentine, Alana 267–268
van Neerven, Ellen 254, 264
Viidikas, Vicki 139, 143, 173

Wagan Watson, Sam 231–232, 263
Walch, Garnet 45
Walford, Frank 87
Walker, Kath *see* Oodgeroo
Walker, Robert 185
Wall, Dorothy 96
Wallace-Crabbe, Christopher 139, 184–185
Walwicz, Ania 173, 175, 182

wars and military actions
  Boer War 19
  First World War 50, 69–70, 73, 134, 154, 164
    Anzac 50
    Bean, C.E.W. 55
    conscription 50
    Gallipoli 50
    League of Nations 51
    Monash, Sir John 50
  Iraq 195
  Korea 99
  Malaya 99
  Second World War 78, 81, 92, 108, 110, 188, 213, 223, 237, 250
  Sudan 19
  Vietnam 99, 125, 149, 189, 217
'Warung, Price' 34–35
Waten, Judah 86, 107
Watson, Maureen 185
Watson, Sam 215
Wearne, Alan 139, 173, 176
Webb, Francis 9, 89, 116–117, 225
Weller, Archie 170, 174, 215, 223, 231
Wenz, Paul 54–55
West, Morris 101, 121
Wheatley, Nadia 240
White, Patrick 9, 81, 87, 101–106, 123, 129, 134, 164–165, 190
Whitehead, Charles 45

Wilding, Michael 134–135
Wilkes, G.A. 102
Williams, Joy (Janaka Wiradjuri) 174, 231
Williamson, David 144, 148–149, 189–190, 232–233
Williamson, Geordie 247
Willmot, Eric xix, 170
Wilmot, Frank 67
Wilson, Josephine 254
Winch, Tara June 216–217, 253–254
Windsor, Gerard 222
Winton, Tim 155, 161–162, 171, 208–209, 252
Witting, Amy 171
Womersley, Chris 258
Wongar, B. *see* Bozic
Wood, Charlotte 255
Woolfe, Sue 205
Wright, Alexis 200, 216, 254
Wright, Judith 90–94, 102, 138, 173, 180
Wrightson, Patricia 151, 193–194

Yahp, Beth 218, 258
young adult literature *see* **children's and young adult literature**

Zable, Arnold 258
Zusak, Markus 223
Zwicky, Fay 184